A CONCISE HISTORY OF
CANADIAN PAINTING

DENNIS REID

Toronto
OXFORD UNIVERSITY PRESS
1973

PUBLICATION OF THIS BOOK WAS ASSISTED BY THE CANADA COUNCIL

THE SUPPORT OF THE DIRECTOR
AND OF THE STAFF
OF THE NATIONAL GALLERY OF CANADA
IS ALSO GRATEFULLY ACKNOWLEDGED

ISBN 0-19-540207-3 (clothbound)

ISBN 0-19-540206-5 (paperbound)

23456–87654

Printed in Canada by
YORK LITHO LIMITED

Contents

Colour Plates

Abbreviations

AAM Art Association of Montreal; became the MMFA 1939

AEAC Agnes Etherington Art Centre, Queen's University, Kingston

AGH Art Gallery of Hamilton

AGO Art Gallery of Ontario, Toronto

AGT Art Gallery of Toronto; became the AGO 1965

BAG Beaverbrook Art Gallery, Fredericton, N.B.

CAS The Contemporary Arts Society, Montreal

CGP The Canadian Group of Painters

HH Hart House, University of Toronto

MCC The McCord Museum, McGill University, Montreal

MCM The McMichael Canadian Collection, Kleinburg, Ont.

MAC Musée d'art contemporain, Montréal

MMFA Montreal Museum of Fine Arts

MQ Musée du Québec, Québec

NGC The National Gallery of Canada, Ottawa

NMAG Norman Mackenzie Art Gallery, University of Saskatchewan, Regina

OSA Ontario Society of Arts

PAC Public Archives of Canada, Ottawa

RCA Royal Canadian Academy of Arts

RMCL The Robert McLaughlin Gallery, Oshawa

ROM The Royal Ontario Museum, Toronto

VAG The Vancouver Art Gallery

WAG The Winnipeg Art Gallery

Preface

This guide to looking at the work of Canadian painters was written in the belief that of all the arts in Canada, painting is the one that most directly presents the Canadian experience. Painters in Canada have consistently reflected the moulding sensibility of the age: a history of their activities inevitably describes the essence of our cultural evolution. And painting is probably the only one of our cultural activities of which the productions of the 'two nations' can be examined virtually as a whole. There are notable, perhaps even historically essential, interactions between English- and French-speaking painters. Hamel, Borduas, and Molinari, for example, are significant figures in any study of the painting of their English-speaking compatriots, of whom Brymner, Morrice, and Lyman (to choose only three names) are important to an understanding of French-Canadian art.

The recorded history of Canadian painting reflects the major developments in Europe, and more recently the United States, which have largely defined the art as it is now recognized internationally. However, painting in Canada is still 'Canadian', and its history demonstrates an internal continuity from the seventeenth century to the present day.

We still know very little about the activities of even our earliest painters, and the first few chapters of this book reflect that lack of knowledge. After Confederation, however, details begin to accumulate and the story of an inspiring series of co-operations unfolds. Artists' societies, of which there has been a proliferation, and even more conspiratorial—if less formal— associations have been found necessary by our artists to project their vision onto the public consciousness. The remarkable dialectic perpetuated by successive generations—each championing a position opposite to that of its predecessor on the question of whether Canadian painters should seek their measure against an international (i.e. mid-Atlantic) standard or in purely indigenous values—gives the history of our painting its unique shape. As a historian I have attempted to present the two views objectively in the firm belief that all our best painters have managed to find common ground in their genuine desire to confront the Canadian sensibility through the medium of their art.

I think of this book as a 'guide' because it is both a narrative history and a handbook. The first few chapters are derived from the work of J. Russell Harper, although I have attempted to impose an order on material that in his monumental *Painting in Canada: A History* (University of Toronto Press, 1966), because of its inclusiveness, had to be slightly diffuse. From Chapter 6 on I have relied principally on my own research. Those who are familiar with the literature, however, will frequently recognize my espousal of interpretations first presented by others. I have often discussed paintings that are not reproduced, wishing to encourage the reader to seek them out either in the collections that house them (the NGC, AGO, MCM, HH, AEAC have all published amply illustrated catalogues of their Canadian collections) or in other books on Canadian art.

Because of space limitations arising from the desire to keep the price down, a bibliography could not be included. *Canadian Art Today* (1970) edited by William Townsend for Studio International of London includes a good general bibliography. William Withrow's *Contemporary Canadian Painting* (McClelland and Stewart, Toronto, 1972) contains reading-lists on some modern painters. My own *Bibliography of the Group of Seven* (The National Gallery of Canada, 1971) is another reference. *Early Painters and Engravers in Canada* (University of Toronto Press, 1970) by J. Russell Harper, a biographical dictionary including all Canadian painters born before 1867, has a thorough bibliography. That volume and his *Painting in Canada* are the two firm legs upon which Canadian art history now stands. I offer this work of mine as a small acknowledgement of the respect I feel for Mr Harper.

NOTE: An asterisk preceding a picture title indicates a black-and-white illustration; a dagger indicates a colour reproduction.

I

Painting in
New France
1665-1760

The 'Father of New France', Samuel de Champlain, was an amateur painter but was far from being the father of its painting too. What little has remained of his work (sixty-two documentary watercolours in the Brown University Library, Providence, R.I.) is charming but uninspiring: a near-contemporary described some of his paintings in the church of Notre-Dame-de-la-Recouvrance, destroyed by fire in 1640, merely as 'quelques pauvres images du travail'. Champlain died in 1635 and for the next three decades New France remained little more than an exploitable resource; its leading town, Québec, was a fur-trade depot. It was only in 1663, when a decision was made to invest in New France the institutions of a province—governor, intendant, and sovereign council —that French civilization really began to take root. In that year Bishop Laval founded the Grand Séminaire* and the first artist left France to settle in Québec. Louis xiv poured nearly a quarter of a million *livres* a year into the colony for the rest of the decade, immigration was encouraged, and under the industrious and far-sighted intendant, Jean Talon, New France was transformed. Religion was at its centre, as it had been for the previous thirty years. The Jesuit martyrdoms that had taken place in Huronia in 1648-9 still represented to Frenchmen the noblest ideal of European involvement in the new world, and the intense Counter-Reformation missionizing zeal, which had so marked the earliest decades of French involvement in America, continued. Our first artist —in fact every artist who was to work here in the seventeenth century —was a cleric.

ABBÉ HUGUES POMMIER (1637-86), who was born southwest of Paris in

*The second-oldest institution of higher learning in North America, it became the Université Laval in 1852.

the region of Vendôme, arrived in Québec in June 1664 and taught in the Séminaire for five years. He was apparently called upon from time to time to exercise the skills of a painter. The great pioneer scholar of the art of New France, Gérard Morisset, has attributed to him an oil copy of a 1664 engraving of *Le Martyre des Pères Jésuites chez les Hurons* (Hôtel-Dieu, Québec), but there is no supporting evidence and no reason to believe the work was even painted in the colony. A strangely languorous portrait, *La Mère Marie-Catherine de Saint-Augustin* (Hôtel-Dieu, Québec), can be attributed to the abbé with somewhat more authority. The Hôtel-Dieu arranged to have a portrait-of-record painted of the dearly loved nun, who died in May 1668, in the first hours after death. As far as we know Pommier was then the only painter in the city. Unfortunately the portrait seems to have been later altered to disguise the fact that its subject was not living. The only other work that can be securely attributed to Pommier also now exists in a form that is removed from the original. It is a portrait of one of the most famous women of New France—a nun (and an absorbing letter-writer) who alternated as Superior of the Ursuline Convent in Québec from 1639 until her death in 1672. *La Mère Marie de l'Incarnation* (Monastère des Ursulines, Québec) was painted shortly after she died. Pommier seems again to have been the only possible author, but what we have now is a copy sent to France some time before the original was destroyed by fire in 1686. Pommier returned to France in 1678. Although we have no real evidence of his ability as an artist, we can perhaps take seriously the remark of an early commentator that in Québec no one appreciated his paintings, and that 'il espéra qu'en France son talent seroit mieux connu'. We have no information that it was. This uncertainty concerning Pommier's activities unfortunately extends to our knowledge of the whole period of New France.

In the Monastère des Ursulines at Québec there is a canvas grandly titled †*La France apportant la foi aux Indiens de la Nouvelle-France* that is a mysterious and beautiful symbol of the place of art in seventeenth-century New France, and indeed in the whole of the French colonial period. It also reflects our general ignorance concerning those other ancient pieces of painted canvas, adrift from their sources and enshrouded in centuries of legend, among which we have chosen to place it. Of the few paintings we believe were part of the culture of seventeenth- and eighteenth-century Canada that have survived the many destructive fires, only a small number were certainly painted here. And most of these relics are in such poor condition that they seldom give evidence of their original appearance. *La France apportant la foi* is at

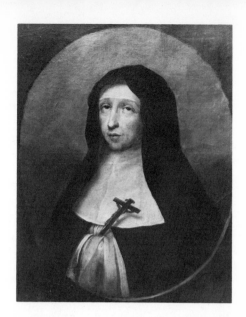

Attributed to L'Abbé Hugues
Pommier. *La Mère Marie-
Catherine de Saint-Augustin*,
1668. Canvas, 28½ x 23½.
Hôtel-Dieu, Québec.

least in sound condition. In it a humble native on the banks of the St
Lawrence River, his naked body cloaked with the lilies of France,
kneels in respectful awe before a regal female, the figure of France.
She in turn instructs him in the Christian faith, and to assist this task
she displays a painting that depicts the Trinity surrounded by the Holy
Family. As if to stress that the painting is but an image of the holy
realm, she points to the heavens where we can see, seated in comfortable
glory, the Holy Family itself. To the left of the Indian, among the trees,
are two rude chapels, and to the right of the figure of France lies the
sturdy ship that brought her across the ocean to New France. We do
not know the painting's author, when or where it was painted, or for
what specific purpose it was made. It is usually attributed to Frère Luc,
the only artist to work in New France who is securely connected to the
mainstream of French painting. It has been suggested that the figure of
France is a likeness of Anne of Austria, wife of Louis XIII and mother
of Louis XIV, who exercised the prerogatives of the crown in her son's
place from 1643 to 1660—precisely the time when the zealous missionizing efforts the painting symbolically represents were in fullest
force. In style it is typical of provincial work of the second half of the
seventeenth century—a somewhat naive and extremely restrained
variation on the grand symbolic masterpieces of Rubens or Poussin. It
is a large picture for early Canada—over seven feet square—and has
been a valued possession of the Ursulines in Québec at least since about
1820 when it appeared in an inventory, and possibly for the century
and a half before. It represents simply and directly the noblest inten-

tions of the first Europeans in settling the St Lawrence valley and as directly proclaims the central role that French culture, and particularly painting, would play in the realization of those intentions.

There was probably more painting done in Canada for the Indians in these early years than for the whites. As *La France apportant la foi* shows us, the communicating value of pictures was well recognized. Of the numerous priests who took prints to the Indian missions, or who drew or painted, two Jesuits in particular have been remembered. The most accomplished was probably PÈRE JEAN PIERRON (1631-1700). Born in Lorraine, he was a painter before entering the Jesuit order in 1650 and continued to practise his art until his departure for Québec in April 1667. Three weeks after arriving he was in the Iroquois missions, in what is now upstate New York, where he remained—except for a trip to Québec in 1668 and brief postings to the Beaupré coast—until 1674. He passed that winter in Acadia, and the next year he travelled in disguise through the Protestant territories of New England, Maryland, and Virginia. After three more years with the Iroquois he returned to France where he died, at Pont-à-Mousson, in February 1700. He was a successful missionary, according to Marie de l'Incarnation, because the Iroquois were impressed with his paintings. None has survived, but she has left quite a detailed description of two. One, an 'Enfer', showed demons so horrible that 'on ne peut les voir sans frémir'. A 'Paradis' showed angels bearing 'les âmes de ceux qui meurent après avoir reçu le saint Baptême'. He was so talented that 'il fait ce qu'il veut au moyen de ses peintures'.

PÈRE CLAUDE CHAUCHETIÈRE (1645-1709) arrived in New France in 1677, just before the departure of Pierron, and spent the rest of his life there. Born in Poitiers, he had joined the Jesuits at Bordeaux in 1663. He was assigned to the Hurons at Québec upon arrival, and then two years later was posted to the Iroquois mission at Sault-Saint-Louis (Caughnawaga). We know he made drawings there to illustrate holy teachings that he bound in book form so that his Iroquois charges could carry them into the field. He also accompanied his reports with drawings, some of which were engraved as illustrations for his *Narration annuelle de la Mission du Sault* of 1686. And the great event of Chauchetière's life took place at Caughnawaga, where he was privileged to know the Mohawk convert and mystic Kateri Tekakwitha. A year after her death in 1680 she appeared to him in a vision, asking that he paint her so that her image might be distributed among the faithful. He ignored the request, so the story goes, and two years later she appeared again. This time he complied and wrote a brief biography as well. A delicate, naive, full-length portrait now in the Caughnawaga Mission church has been associated with this legend. If Chauchetière's work underlies it, though, his hand has been obscured by later 'improvements'.

The importance of the missions diminished rapidly after 1663 and interest consequently focused on the growing white settlements. By 1670 Québec was clearly in need of a skilled painter who could decorate the new churches in the manner to which Frenchmen were accustomed. Unfortunately the tiny community was unable to support talent of that order for any length of time, so an accomplished artist was brought in for a period of concentrated work. FRÈRE LUC (1614-85) has since become the star round which the lesser constellations of early Canadian painting revolve. To what extent he deserves this exalted position is open to debate. His reputation has perhaps been inflated by the fact that he is the subject of Gérard Morisset's only monographic work on a painter. However, virtually every accomplished seventeenth-century picture in the province has at one time been attributed to him, which demonstrates that his fifteen months in this country left a very great impression indeed.

Born in Amiens, Claude François (his secular name) showed an early interest in drawing and painting and in 1632 was placed in the studio of one of the most prominent of the Court painters, Simon Vouet. After three years with Vouet, François moved to Rome to continue his studies; he returned to Paris probably in 1639. Vouet then introduced him to the superintendent of the king's buildings who placed him in the team that was completing the decoration of the Galerie du Bord de l'Eau in the Louvre. (Nicolas Poussin headed this team for eighteen months in 1640-1.) Claude François left his work in 1642, by which time he had received the title of 'king's painter'. After ten years of study, partly under two of the greatest painters of the day, it can be assumed that he would have been prepared for a distinguished career as a painter in the 'grand manner' of Classical Baroque. Instead, at the death of his mother in 1644, he forsook the life of a court painter and joined the Recollet order. It was not an unusual decision during the Counter-Reformation, when piety was expected of most educated men and women and celibacy and self-mortification were common even among the laity. We know of only one work painted prior to 1645, an *Assomption* after a painting by Bassano that was copied in Rome in 1635 (Eglise de Longueau, France).

François made his profession in 1645, taking the name Frère Luc, after the patron saint of painters. He then worked for twenty-five years as a painting teacher in the Recollet establishment on the rue Saint-

Martin in Paris. (His only student of note was the historian Roger de Piles.) Then, in the spring of 1670, he was one of six Recollets chosen to travel to Québec to re-establish the order and restore the monastery that had been abandoned after the capture of the city by English privateers in 1629. They landed in Québec on August 18. Frère Luc, who had had some architectural experience, drew the plans for the new chapel, sketched out the retable to be constructed behind the main altar, and painted the *Assomption* that adorns it. The cornerstone was laid by the Intendant Jean Talon on June 22, 1671, and the first mass was celebrated by Bishop Laval that October. It still stands today, virtually intact, as the chapel of the Hôpital-Général. Frère Luc also designed the wing of the procurator's office of the Séminaire, which was built in 1677-8.

A number of Frère Luc's paintings were mentioned by early commentators. These include some other pictures he painted for the Recollet Chapel that were removed to another location in 1693 and there destroyed by fire a century later. A *Sainte-Famille* painted for Notre-Dame-de-Québec was destroyed in the English siege of 1759. An *Assomption* and an *Adoration des Mages*, painted for the Jesuits, are also lost. There are early records or traditions that attribute to Frère Luc paintings for the churches at l'Ange-Gardien, Château-Richer, Beaupré, Sainte-Famille on the Ile d'Orléans, and for the Hôtel-Dieu in Québec. It seems an impossible production for a stay in Canada that was a little over a year; doubtless many imported French pictures were ascribed to such a prominent visitor. The only surviving work that we are certain he completed in Québec is the grand altarpiece painted for his order's headquarters. The **Assomption*, signed and dated 1671, is a robust example of the French Classical Baroque, though a little shallow in depth and too heavy in modelling. The soft, sensitive colouring in the flesh and sky is thoroughly typical of its period, and the dramatic red and blue robes of the Virgin and the orange drape of one of the angels are of that intense, whitened colour so familiar from the luminous draperies of Poussin. The composition is conventional. Rather stiff, even awkward in the light of the artist's contemporaries in France, in Québec in 1671 it must have appeared a very vision of beauty and of inspired religious emotion.

Frère Luc returned to France immediately after the Recollet Chapel was sanctified in October 1671 and the following year was installed in the monastery at Sézanne in Champagne where he taught and continued to paint. In 1675 he returned to Paris where once again he became interested in Canada, actively recruiting for its religious houses and even sending pictures. He painted an *Ex-voto à la Vierge Marie* (Eglise de

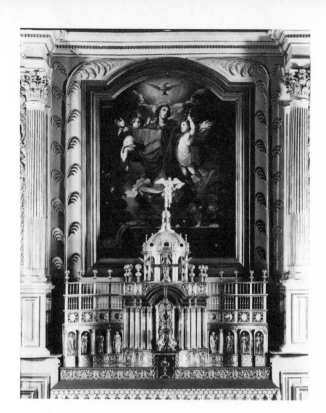

Frère Luc.
L'Assomption, 1671.
Canvas, 81 x 62.
Hôpital-Général,
Québec.

Saint-Philippe, Trois Rivières) about then for the Recollets in Trois-Rivières; it was saved from a fire in 1908 and seems to have been quite heavily restored. A pair of canvases, *Saint Joachim et la Vierge Enfant* (signed and dated 1676) and *La Vierge et l'Enfant Jésus,* were sent by Laval in 1678 to Sainte-Anne-de-Beaupré, where they remain still. Not as ambitious as the earlier *Assomption,* and more severely austere, they show the same swollen modelling, the same predilection for the heightened reds, blues, oranges and yellows of Poussin, and the same slightly awkward stiffness. However, like the *Assomption* they are sincerely motivated expressions of profound religious belief. To some they may verge on the sentimental.

Morisset has given a great many more pictures to Frère Luc, and all of these attributions will some day have to be examined on their individual merits. Five paintings might be mentioned for their interesting subject matter. There are two portraits: *Jean Talon* (Hôtel-Dieu, Québec) and *Monseigneur de Laval* (Séminaire de Québec). A *Sainte-Famille à la Huronne* (Monastère des Ursulines, Québec) arouses our interest because of the presence in the group of a Huron girl. (One suspects, however, that it was much repainted in the nineteenth century.)

The striking *Une Hospitalière soignant Notre Seigneur dans la personne d'une malade* (Hôtel-Dieu, Québec) is very reminiscent of Philippe de Champaigne and its classical feeling has little to do with the more robust Baroque style of Frère Luc's work. Then there is *La France apportant la foi aux Indiens de la Nouvelle-France*. It *could* be a propaganda work of about 1675, reflecting renewed interest in Canada, because in style it is closest to his later work. But there is no earlier evidence of its provenance than the inventory of about 1820.

We know of only one person in Québec who might have been creatively inspired by the brief presence there of Frère Luc. ABBÉ JEAN GUYON (1659-87) can lay claim to the distinction of being Canada's first native-born painter. Born at Château-Richer near Québec (his father was an habitant), he entered the Séminaire about 1670 and began to paint —encouraged, we can assume, and perhaps even instructed, by Frère Luc. He took minor orders late in 1677 and the following summer set off for France to continue his philosophical and theological studies. While there he also took further instruction in painting. Returning to Québec in August 1682, he was ordained on November 21, 1683, appointed canon, a year later, and then left for Paris as secretary to Bishop Laval. He died there in January 1687.

Guyon's services as a trained painter were available to his native city, then, for only twenty-seven months, less than twice the time spent there by Frère Luc. The only works ascribed to him with any certainty are a group of botanical studies in water colour, once in the Séminaire and now presumably lost. Morisset has also attributed a fine early portrait, that of *La Mère Jeanne-Françoise Juchereau dite de Saint-Ignace* (Hôtel-Dieu, Québec), which he has consequently dated to 1684. We will probably never know if Canada's first painter was in fact capable of the sensitive competence revealed in that canvas.

By the last quarter of the century, modest talent with pencil or brush was not uncommon in Québec, even among the laity. A number of cartographers and engineers have left charming examples of their skill. JEAN-BAPTISTE FRANQUELIN (c.1651-1718) was probably the most accomplished. He arrived in Québec first in 1672 and returned a number of times. Some of his beautiful maps were the first to incorporate the discoveries of Jolliet, La Salle, and Cadillac and were often corroborated by the explorers themselves. Another cartographer, ROBERT DE VILLENEUVE (c.1645-after 1692), was in Québec from 1685 to 1692. Although in no way so well trained or so active as the English topographers who worked in the region a century later, he doubtless entertained and delighted his friends with his sketches of familiar landmarks. A native Quebecker,

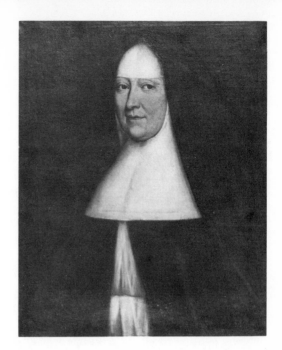

Attributed to L'Abbé Jean Guyon. *La Mère Jeanne-Françoise Juchereau dite de Saint-Ignace*, c.1685. Canvas, 28 x 23. Hôtel-Dieu, Québec.

CHARLES BÉCARD DE GRANVILLE (1675-1703), who first went to sea as a French marine and then returned to his birthplace to work as a cartographer and engineer, has left a delicate view of his city that was engraved as a map cartouche in 1699.

The belief that civilization consisted to some extent in the cultivation of creative talents, coupled with the desire to develop a self-sufficiency even in the ability of the colony to decorate its own churches, led to the establishment of Canada's first school of arts and crafts towards the end of the seventeenth century. Talon had expressed an interest in such a school shortly after his arrival in 1665, and a decade later some attempt was made to recruit instructors. From these efforts ultimately developed in 1684 the Ecole des Arts et Métiers de Saint-Joachim, situated on a model farm about thirty miles east of Québec near Sainte-Anne-de-Beaupré. It was conceived as an extension of the Petit Séminaire (a secondary school founded in 1668 to prepare students for the Grand Séminaire) and instruction was available in Greek, Latin, theology, mathematics, and drawing—as in Québec—but it uniquely gave training in agriculture and a memorandum of 1685 lists among its other offerings woodworking, sculpture, painting, and gilding for the ornamentation of churches, and masonry and carpentry. By 1705 the school was little more than an agricultural college, there being by then enough craftsmen in the towns that the apprenticeship system precluded the need for institutional training. It had closed by 1715.

In the area of the arts, most activity at Saint-Joachim was centred on the training of competent sculptors and woodworkers to finish the interiors of the many new churches being constructed in the growing communities. But painting did receive some attention between 1690 and 1705 when the artist JACQUES LEBLOND DE LATOUR (1671-1715) was instructing. Born in Bordeaux, where his father was an important local painter, Leblond was raised in a cultured environment—a younger brother later became an engineer and city planner in New Orleans— and was trained as a painter and architect. Probably recruited in France, he arrived in Québec in May 1690, aged twenty, and almost immediately began teaching at Saint-Joachim. He was also a competent sculptor and apparently directed his students in the decoration of the chapel of the Séminaire in Québec from 1693 to 1696. (This chapel was destroyed by fire in 1701.) He probably also directed work on a number of church interiors, which doubtless would have included some of his paintings. None has been substantially identified. Morisset attributes two portraits to his hand but presents no documents to support his contention that Leblond painted either the *Monseigneur de Laval* (l'Archevêché, Québec) or the likeness of his successor, *Monseigneur de Saint-Vallier* (Hôpital-Général, Québec). Leblond took the habit in 1696, was ordained in 1706 and was that year appointed to the parish of Baie-Saint-Paul where he later died.

Rudimentary art instruction was also available in Montreal at the end of the century. PIERRE LE BER (1669-1707), issue of two of the wealthiest families in the city and a pious and generous man, joined in 1688 to assist François Charon de la Barre, another wealthy Montrealer, to found an alms-house. The Le Ber family contributed a farm towards the support of the venture and Pierre designed a three-storey stone building to house the institution, inaugurated in 1694. In 1700 it was awarded letters patent designating it as a formal religious community—the only male community ever founded in Canada—and its members soon became known popularly as les Frères Charon. Pierre Le Ber joined the community and there instructed orphans and other indigents in the art of painting. It seems that he was a painter of some seriousness, for the inventory drawn up at his death includes a studio full of paints, brushes, canvas, and other supplies one associates with a professional. We know very little about him. Because he apparently never left the country, it has been suggested that he studied painting in Québec. He is known to have erected a chapel to Sainte-Anne outside of Montreal in 1697 and to have decorated it with his own paintings. Nothing remains of it today. The Hôpital-Général in Montreal took over the Charon institution when

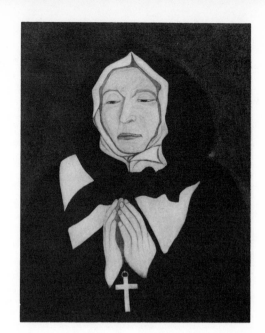

Pierre Le Ber. *Marguerite Bourgeoys*, 1700. Canvas, 24½ x 19½. Congrégation de Notre-Dame, Montreal.

it failed in 1747 and it has been assumed that some of the pictures pre-served in the Hôpital are by Le Ber. No real research has been brought to the examination of this assumption. Le Ber's sister Jeanne was in her day a famous benefactor and recluse of the Congrégation de Notre-Dame in Montreal and Morisset has attributed certain pictures there to her brother. But only one seems to be supported by documentation: a severe, primitive portrait of the founder of the congregation, *Marguerite Bourgeoys* (Les Soeurs de la Congrégation de Notre-Dame), painted immediately after her death in January 1700 and preserved in the con-vent since then; though 'preserved' is perhaps too generous a word. Recently, during cleaning, the portrait thought to be by Le Ber turned out to be the *second* over-painting; neither it nor the painting im-mediately beneath in any way resembled the stark, powerful image of a strong-willed woman revealed by their removal. The compelling design, the raw, immediate force of this one remarkable work of Le Ber's—certainly the single most moving image to survive from the French period —must lead us to designate him the great talent of his age.

There is some evidence that more than one accomplished primitive painter like Le Ber was working in Montreal around the turn of the century. A large anonymous canvas depicting *Une Salle de l'Hôtel-Dieu, Montréal* and still hanging in that institution, although much repainted, has strong, simplified forms, emphatic design, and a stark realism that can still move the viewer. The way the artist has articulated space with his rendering of the long row of canopied beds, and his

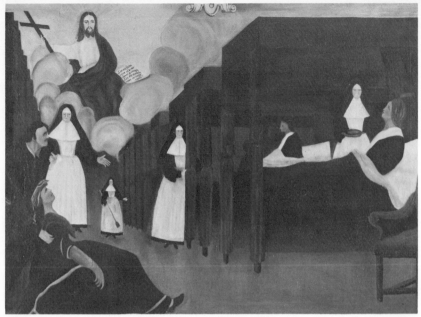

Anonymous. *Une Salle de l'Hôtel-Dieu, Montréal,* c.1700. Canvas, 35½ x 50. Hôtel-Dieu, Montreal.

effective introduction of incidental details—particularly the distraught man supporting his sick wife in the left foreground—suggest a natural creative ability approaching Le Ber's.

We begin to notice signs of a richer cultural life in the eighteenth century resulting from an expanding community. The population of New France was growing steadily. In 1698 there were 13,815 whites in the colony (Québec had just under 2,000, Montreal 1,200), 16,500 in 1706, 21,000 in 1720, and 42,500 by 1740. In 1705 the first 'local' man was appointed governor. The Marquis de Vaudreuil was not a native Canadian but he had been in the country for eighteen years, had risen through the ranks of the local administration, and had married a Canadian woman. Thirty years of peace (1713-43) also helped to stimulate vigorous expansion and prosperity and the development of virtual self-sufficiency in the colony. Early in the eighteenth century, as has been remarked by one historian, 'Québec could boast of more and finer public buildings than could any other colonial capital north of Mexico City.'

This trend was revealed as well in the number of paintings acquired and displayed by the churches (the church in as remote a place as Detroit had no less than sixteen in 1711) and even by private individuals. A man named Cugnet seems even to have been a collector of sorts. An inventory drawn up at his death in 1742 lists twenty-eight pictures; they were mainly religious, but there were also three mythological scenes, five landscapes, two royal portraits, five family portraits, and three still-lifes. Finer homes were now expected to contain one or two devotional pictures, perhaps a portrait of the king or of a member of one's family; there is even a record of a group portrait. Paradoxically this increasing interest in painting did not seem to lead to an increase in the number or quality of painters. Almost to the contrary. Morisset has explained this by drawing our attention to the great number of French pictures then being imported—paintings were one of the principal luxury importations before the Conquest. Almost exclusively church or private devotional pictures, and all by lesser artists, they nonetheless represented the backbone of the local market in paintings.

Painters continued to work in the colony and for the first time some were non-clerics. JEAN BERGER (1682-after 1710) was one of the first of these secular artists and certainly the most colourful. Born near Lyons, he arrived in Québec in 1700 as a marine. He somehow became involved with a group from Wells, Maine, who had been carried to Québec as prisoners of the Abenakis. Berger was jailed in Montreal with some of them for a brief period, charged with counterfeiting card-money. A year or so later in Québec he married one of the women of this same group, a certain Rachel Storer. Then in 1707 he set himself up in Montreal as a painter. He was deported two years later for having written an insulting song on the subject of justice in New France while he was in jail on an assault charge. He probably lived the rest of his life with his wife in the English colonies to the south. The only documented work by this interesting character is an altar frontal painted for a church on the Ile d'Orléans in 1706 and now lost. Jules Bazin suggests the attribution of two portraits now in the McCord Museum: those of the Hertel brothers of Trois-Rivières. They both served as officers in the colonial army but neither left New France, so their portraits must have been painted here about 1710. Harper attributes one more picture, *Chevalier Jean-Louis de La Corne*, to the author of the Hertel portraits. He does not support their being given to Berger, however.

Morisset believes that the Hertel portraits belong to another secular painter who worked in New France early in the eighteenth century, MICHEL DESSAILLIANT DE RICHETERRE (active 1701-23). We know nothing of his early life. He is first recorded in Montreal in 1701 selling a portrait of a prominent local figure, *Mme de Repentigny*, that has never been found. He was in Detroit in 1706 to paint a large retable for the Sieur de Cadillac; in Montreal in 1707; and went back to Québec where he was recorded a number of times before 1723.

Dessailliant is now best known as the supposed author of a number of early Ex-votos. These painted offerings meant to record gratitude for miraculous salvation began to appear in a popular naive form early in the eighteenth century. While often very crude (their efficacy was in no way dependent upon their aesthetic force), they are also vivid and moving depictions of ordinary people caught in crisis. One of the most stirring of those attributed to Dessailliant, the *Ex-voto de Monsieur Edouin* (Sainte-Anne-de-Beaupré) of 1712, is over five feet high and vigorously conceived. While on a trip from Plaisance, Nfld., to Québec in 1709, Captain Edouin's ship was caught in a crushing storm, which it survived only because Sainte-Anne interceded in answer to the prayers of a priest on board. The picture was commissioned three years later as a thankoffering.

The most spectacular of the pictures ascribed to Michel Dessailliant, however, is the **Ex-voto de l'Ange-gardien* (Hôtel-Dieu, Québec) of about 1707. Based on a French Baroque engraving, it owes the dramatically successful pose of the angel to that source. But its real quality lies in the evocative exaggeration of the angel's figure, its huge legs taking up almost two-thirds of the body's bulk. A little girl stands beside the forward-thrusted leg, seeming frail in comparison with that vigorous limb. Her fingers touching in prayer, she turns her head as the giant angel gently rests its hand on her shoulder. The girl's face—supposedly a portrait of the child whose placement under the protection of the angel the picture celebrates—is one of the most sensitively modelled to survive from the period.

A signed *Marie Madeleine repentante* (Cap-de-la-Madeleine) of 1720 and its pendant, a *Madone tenant son enfant,* are the only known paintings by JEAN JACQUIER DIT LEBLOND (1688-after 1724), a Belgian who arrived in Canada about 1712 and married in Montreal in 1715. An undistinguished artist on the evidence of these two pictures, Jacquier was also a sculptor and, it appears, an importer-dealer in works of art. One suspects that such a thorough business approach to the market for art was widespread in New France during the early eighteenth century.

Only two painters of some merit are known from the last decades of the French era. One, PÈRE FRANÇOIS (Jean-Melchior Brekenmacher), re-introduces the artist-priest of the sort that held exclusive sway during the previous century. Probably German-born, he was ordained in Québec in 1713 and was first mentioned as an artist in 1735, the date of a payment for a 'grand tableau de Sainte-Anne' he painted for the church at Varennes. Morisset attributes a number of other works to Père François, the most interesting of which is the portrait of **Le Père Emmanuel Crespel* (MQ) of about 1756. The open, almost ingenuous

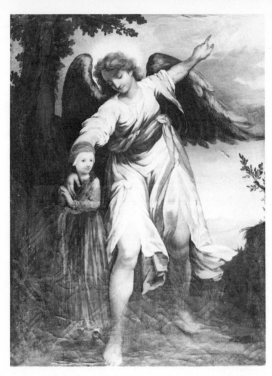

Attributed to Michel
Dessailliant de Richeterre.
Ex-voto de l'Ange-gardien,
c.1707. Canvas, 46½ x 33.
Hôtel-Dieu, Québec.

face of the Recollet is convincingly modelled. The simple gesture of his
right hand, thoughtfully positioned in relation to the face and other
hand to draw the viewer's eyes around the composition in an endless
circle of delightful exploration, denotes an artist of considerable training and ability. PAUL MALEPART DE BEAUCOURT (1700-56), who was born
in Paris, arrived in New France as a soldier in 1720 and was stationed
there for the next twenty years, principally at Laprairie near Montreal.
He left the army in 1741 and then rather surprisingly established
himself in Québec as a painter. Two works signed by him (1746) have
been recently lost, but on the basis of stylistic analysis Morisset has
made of Beaucourt the principal Ex-voto painter of the second half of
the eighteenth century. There is, however, considerable variation in
technique and ability in those unsigned works to which his name has
been attached. The well-known *Ex-voto des trois naufragés de Lévis*
(Sainte-Anne-de-Beaupré) of 1754, though charming, is extremely naive
and even crude in its handling of detail. The *Ex-voto de Notre-Dame
de Liesse* (Rivière-Ouelle) of about 1745, on the other hand, is sophisticated in its treatment of faces, more imaginative in composition, and
in every detail shows a considerable knowledge of the art of painting.
These two works could not be from the same hand. A third painting, the
spectacular *Ex-voto de l'Aimable Marthe* (Notre-Dame-des-Victoires,

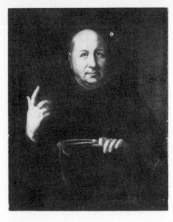

Attributed to Père François. *Le Père Emmanuel Crespel*, c.1756. Canvas, 31¾ x 25½. MQ.

Québec) of 1747, reveals yet another distinct talent. Sensitive in colour, exciting in its breadth of conception, and realistic in its depiction of the foundering ship, it is impossible to reconcile with any of the other canvases we identify with Beaucourt.

Until more research is applied to it, painting in New France from the beginning to the end must remain a body of isolated artifacts tentatively associated with a few elusive artists.

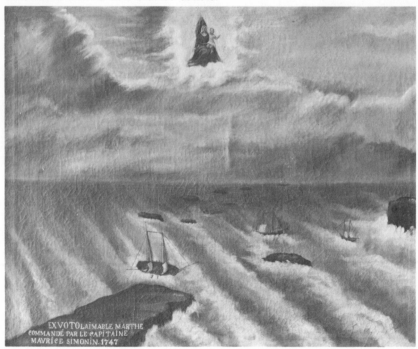

Attributed to Paul Malepart de Beaucourt. *Ex-voto de l'Aimable Marthe*, 1747. Canvas, 25 x 32½. MQ.

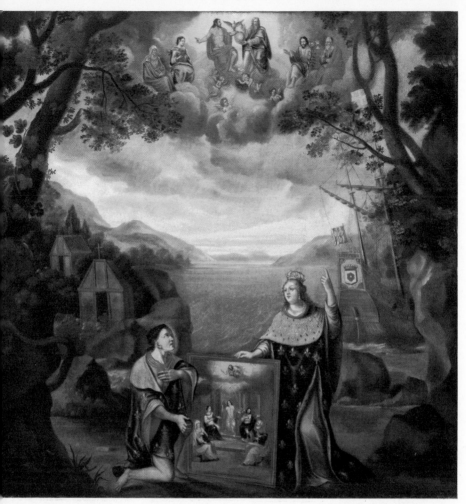

—Attributed to Frère Luc. *La France apportant la foi aux Indiens de la Nouvelle-France*, 1675. Canvas 86 x 86. Monastère des Ursulines, Québec.

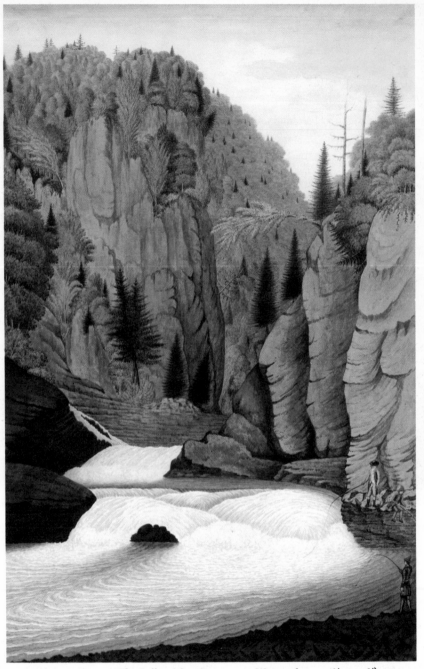

II—Thomas Davies. *The Falls of Ste Anne, 1790.* Watercolour, 20¼ x 13½. NGC.

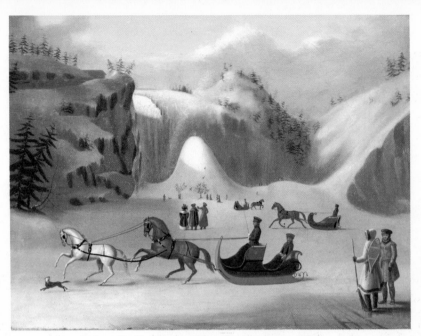

III—Robert Todd. *The Ice Cone, Montmorency Falls,* c.1845.
Canvas, 13½ x 18. NGC.

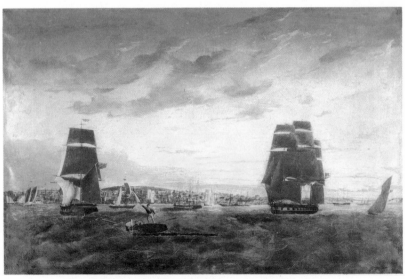

IV—John O'Brien, *Halifax Harbour,* c.1850. Canvas, 19½ x 30.
Halifax Board of Trade.

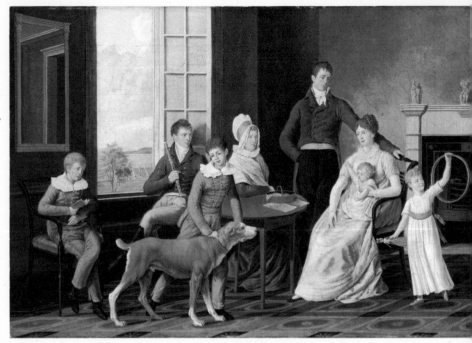

v—William Berczy. *The Woolsey Family*, 1808. Canvas, 25¾ x 34½. NGC.

2

Painting in
British North America
1760-1860

Halifax was established as a British military colony in 1749, Québec was taken in 1759, and Montreal surrendered to British troops in 1760. With the Treaty of Paris in 1763 Canada was ceded to Britain. Some English-speaking civilians soon began to settle adjacent to the garrisons, working in the civil service, as merchants or in the lucrative fur trade, and their numbers increased greatly in the early 1780s with the influx of political refugees from the United States. These immigrants forced a change in British policy. Prior to their arrival in Canada, the maintenance of the garrisons was the overriding reason for the British presence. After the newcomers settled, new towns gradually appeared that were in large part independent of the military, and Montreal and Québec began to lose the look of occupied cities. In 1791 a constitutional government was established in the administrative areas of Upper and Lower Canada, with one capital at Newark (Niagara-on-the-Lake)—which was moved to York (Toronto) in 1796—and another in Lower Canada, at Québec.

The imperial garrison at Québec was the second oldest in Canada and existed into the 1870s, but it was the most isolated from the vital life of its host city. It was, after all, a British army of occupation in a city of French culture, and French was the language of most of the towns-folk. With its sizeable group of high-ranking officers—often accompanied by family—the garrison was itself a community of sophisticated culture. It figures prominently in the 'first Canadian novel', Frances Brooke's *The History of Emily Montague* (1769), and it even brought its own accomplished artists.

These were officers whose training—usually at the Royal Military Academy at Woolwich—included instruction in the taking of topographical views. Objective, precise depictions of landscape, such views were of obvious military use before the days of the camera. Drawings by HERVEY SMYTH (1734-1811), aide-de-camp to General Wolfe, were engraved and published in London in 1760 as *Six Views of the Most Remarkable Places of the Gulf and River St Lawrence*. The most famous of these views shows the unsuccessful attack (on July 31, 1759) made by Wolfe at Montmorency Falls. There is also an engraving of a Smyth drawing of the landing at Wolfe's Cove before the Battle of the Plains of Abraham in September, but this was not included in the St Lawrence series. RICHARD SHORT (active 1759-61), a purser on HMS *Prince of Orange*, made sketches of Halifax and Québec in 1759 that were later engraved in London and sold as two sets. There are seven views of Halifax and twelve of Québec, which Short visited with the conquering British forces. The Québec views are mostly of prominent buildings and show the damage resulting from the bombardment. Both handsome and accurate, they are among the finest Canadian prints from the eighteenth century and would have found a ready market in England, where such scenes of foreign places were in demand.

The topographical views of military officers were, in fact, simply one manifestation of the romantic inclination of English gentlemen of the later eighteenth century to delight in the splendours of natural scenery or in anything they found in their travels that was charmingly primitive, quaint, or exotic—in a word, picturesque. Every young Englishman taking his grand tour was either proficient with pencil or brush or accompanied by his personal artist. Sustained largely by the enthusiasm of amateurs and refined and heightened by numerous dissertations on the correct limits of the taste (Uvedale Price's *An Essay on the Picturesque* (1794) is one of the better-known manuals describing the rich rewards of such a developed sensibility), the English craze for the picturesque by the beginning of the nineteenth century had spread to most of Europe.

Although the production of the English topographers is mainly of historical value, a few of them produced work that reveals a truly creative response to the Canadian scene. The most talented of these authentic artists was THOMAS DAVIES (c.1737-1812). He was an officer in the Royal Regiment of Artillery who ultimately rose to the rank of lieutenant-general. Though his four visits to Canada were brief—and usually violent—he always found time to produce sketches. He first saw Canada in 1757 when he was posted to Halifax and took part in the capture of Louisbourg and the burning of the French settlements on the St John River. Then in 1759 he served on Lake Champlain and took part in the capture of Montreal. One of his drawings, now in the Public

Archives of Canada, shows General Amherst's flotilla running the rapids of the St Lawrence. He did two charming watercolour views of Montreal: one from St Helen's Island in 1762 and the other from the mountain, painted in 1812, the year of his death and long after he left Canada. He often made watercolours from sketches produced years earlier. Davies saw Halifax again a number of times during the American Revolution when he was engaged in campaigns around Boston and New York. In 1786 he returned to Canada when he was posted to Québec for four years of peace. Although he was always an accomplished draughtsman, the watercolours from this last Canadian tour are surpassingly beautiful. Their colour is vibrant—most are set in full autumn—and their line is alive. Detail is multiplied in rhythmic patterns that swell into forms that seem to breathe, to be organic. And, as in †The Falls of St Anne (NGC) of 1790, virtually every picture shows civilized men enjoying themselves amidst splendid natural scenery. Those four years must have been among the happiest of his life.

Six views of North American waterfalls by Davies were engraved about 1768 and thirty years later other watercolours were reproduced in a travel book. These were the only examples of Davies' work known to Canadians before 1953, when the great bulk of the watercolours we treasure so highly today were first released from one of the great English private libraries, that of the Earl of Derby.

Another outstanding view-painter, GEORGE HERIOT (1766-1844), had a long residence in the garrison community of Québec. In fact he was probably Canada's first resident English-speaking artist. His earliest Canadian paintings, such as his Ruins of the Intendant's Palace, Québec (ROM) of 1795, could have been painted anywhere there were Englishmen. The ruins were the result of British bombardment some thirty-five years before, but Heriot seems to have imagined himself inside some ruined castle. Soon, however, he began to accept the picturesque values of the Canadian scene on their own terms. By about 1800, when he painted *West View of Château-Richer (NGC), he was paying attention to topographical exactitude while still suggesting the romantic reveries that such a scene evoked. This is a good example of his large 'finished' watercolours. Heriot had great facility in the medium and could handle space with ease.

Born in Scotland into a middle-class family, he entered the University of Edinburgh but left about 1786 before graduating. He then enrolled in the Royal Military Academy, Woolwich, and there learned watercolour painting from the famous Paul Sandby. Upon graduation he entered the colonial service—he probably could not afford to buy a

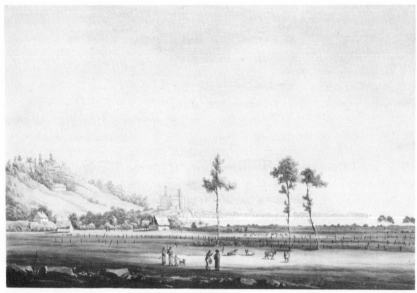

George Heriot. *West View of Château-Richer*, c.1800. Watercolour, 8½ x 12¾.
NGC.

commission, as was then the custom—and was posted to the West
Indies. In 1791 he was transferred to Québec as a civil servant attached
to the army paymaster's office, and nine years later was appointed
deputy postmaster-general for British North America. He retained this
post until 1816 when, in conflict with his superior, he was asked to
resign and returned to England. It is not known how he then earned a
living, but he published a travel book and continued to sketch around
Europe for the rest of his life.

Heriot's job in Québec was peculiarly suited to his avocation. He
had to visit and inspect all the post offices from Halifax to the Detroit
River, and always carried a sketch book. (The McCord Museum in
Montreal has some 600 of his small wash sketches.) Upon his return
to Québec he would work these up into finished watercolours. Some
were later reproduced as aquatint illustrations in his *Travels Through
the Canadas* (2 vols, London, 1807). A classic Canadian contribution to
the picturesque travel book, it was popular enough to appear in a
pirated edition in 1809 and was reissued in the United States in 1813.
It is even today a satisfying book, crammed with interesting details of
life in Canada and including a dictionary of the Algonkian language.
Earlier, in 1804, Heriot had published *A History of Canada from Its
First Discovery* and some poetry.

While he travelled frequently, Heriot appears also to have enjoyed Québec society. There are numerous large watercolours, often delicately washed, of Montmorency Falls and other of the garrison community's favourite pleasure haunts around Québec. Though he lived in Québec for twenty-five years, it is not likely that Heriot made a contribution to any continuing tradition. The bulk of his work would have been taken back to England by returning British officers.

The garrison itself had some artists, but their influence did not penetrate much beyond the officers' mess or fashionable English homes. The best-known garrison artist is JAMES COCKBURN (1778-1847), who arrived in Québec about 1826. Like Heriot, Cockburn loved to travel. Unlike Heriot, he probably did so at his own expense. When we see how much he travelled in Upper and Lower Canada and along the Atlantic seaboard, we realize that it was passion rather than a desire for amusing recreation that drove him. He too had a considerable reputation as an illustrator and author of picturesque travel books—while maintaining a rising army career that culminated in the rank of major-general. In fact he published much more than Heriot. Before his Québec posting he had published at least six books of European tours. After his arrival in Canada he published Québec and its Environs (1831), illustrated with his own views, and two years later he brought out a folio of prints of Niagara and Québec. Writing to a niece in 1831, Lady Aylmer, the governor's wife, described Cockburn's amazing energy. 'He continues (at his present age)', she wrote, 'to be indefatigable and his passion for the beauties of nature can only be gratified by his unceasing perseverance in delineating them.' As he was well into middle age when he arrived in Québec and, as Spendlove suggests, had probably given up more strenuous amusements in favour of sketching, this was probably his daily recreation for most of the time he spent there.

As a painter Cockburn is uneven compared to Heriot. His working sketches are mere notations, stiff and awkward, with little aesthetic appeal. His larger watercolours, on the other hand, are often surprisingly accomplished. His Passenger Pigeon Net, St Anne's Lower Canada (PAC) of 1829 is strikingly composed and deftly executed. Most satisfying of all, perhaps, are the many watercolours of urban scenes, primarily of Québec and Montreal. Exact in the depiction of architectural monuments, yet open and airy in colour and lively with human anecdote, paintings like his *Corpus Christi Procession, Québec (MQ) of 1830, are clearly the work of a dedicated artist. They have rightly become national treasures. Cockburn was in fact considered to be an 'artist' by his contemporaries, and before leaving Québec in 1836 he exhibited two pictures

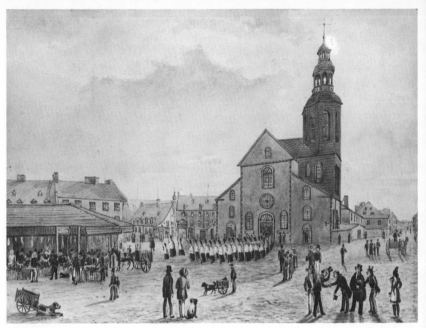

James Cockburn. *Corpus Christi Procession, Québec,* 1830. Watercolour, 10½ x 14½. MQ.

with the National Academy in New York. There was no such public place to exhibit in Québec.

ROBERT TODD (1809-65), who emigrated from England to Québec in 1834, is the only English-speaking 'professional' artist of interest to work in Québec prior to Krieghoff's arrival in 1853. Todd advertised himself as a 'house, carriage and ornamental painter', painting coats-of-arms and such for the garrison and gentry, and his production of pictures, as presently known, appears to have been secondary to this occupation as an ornamental painter. Todd's most famous painting is †*The Ice Cone, Montmorency Falls* (NGC) of about 1845. It has been suggested that this beautiful scene was painted as a portrait of the dashing team of horses in the foreground, but two other Todd paintings of Montmorency in winter have recently come to light in which various sleighs, dogs, snowshoers, and other holiday-makers disport themselves on the frozen river. These pictures would likely have been painted as souvenirs of one of Québec's most famous sights. The scarcity of known paintings by Todd could be explained by the fact that his work was taken away by visitors.

One can assume that the naive quality of his paintings precluded Todd's being treated seriously as an artist in Québec and that he himself thought of them as being related to the 'ornamental' work that he advertised. He left Québec about 1854. It is not known whether he had exhausted the demand for his line of work or whether the competition of Cornelius Krieghoff (see p. 62 ff.) forced him out. Todd settled in Toronto and remained there—complaining in 1861 that 'Toronto is too new and too poor to support an ornamental artist'—until his death. The civilian population of Québec who spoke English was relatively small and it failed to support professional artists during the early years, although it enjoyed the work of the French-speaking painters of the city. It is around Joseph Légaré and Antoine Plamondon (see the next chapter) that the city's art scene really developed.

Halifax was founded in 1749 as a planned colonial town and military post to offset the French fort at Louisbourg. Its garrison grew steadily after the seige of Louisbourg in 1758 and then during the American Revolution; after 1783, 13,000 political refugees arrived from New England. Most moved on to New Brunswick and elsewhere, but enough stayed that by 1794 and the arrival of Edward—the son of George III (and later the father of Queen Victoria)—Halifax was a bustling town of 7,000. Prince Edward, burdened with debts from student days, had been sent by his father to command the garrison. Finding an ugly makeshift town that had seen too many thousands pass through, he immediately began to indulge his favourite habit of spending money by rebuilding the fortifications and military buildings and putting up a villa for himself and a number of striking public buildings. With his beautiful mistress Mme Saint-Laurent he also entertained lavishly. Society was never again so brilliant in Halifax and further improvements over the next six years made the whole town shine. The impetus of this moment sustained the cultural pretensions of the community for decades.

With the departure of the Prince—now the Duke of Kent—in 1800, construction stopped on all military works and the city went into a depression. 'But', as Thomas Raddall writes in his history of Halifax, 'the golden crust of Halifax, the circle of well-salaried officials and the war-enriched merchants and speculators still managed to do themselves well.' It was from this segment of society that the membership of the first Canadian art club was drawn: the Halifax Chess, Pencil and Brush Club. Founded about 1787, it persisted until about 1817. Richard Bulkeley, the secretary of the province, was president, and its sole purpose was the promotion of drawing and watercolour painting (as well as chess) as polite pursuits. It was also this privileged society that encouraged the settlement of Halifax's first resident professional artist.

Halifax was on the northern periphery of an English provincial culture that had developed along the Atlantic seaboard. Over the past century or more the English colonies to the south had created a cultural environment that was in most ways similar to the milieu that existed in provincial centres in England. Once a certain level of affluence had been reached, American merchants and landowners sought, like the British gentry, to demonstrate their stature by commissioning portraits reflecting their pride in themselves and their understanding of the values of cultivated society. The prominent citizens of Halifax, many of whom were American by birth and upbringing, felt this same need and commissioned portraits from American painters, even the famous John Singleton Copley. The time inevitably came when Halifax was ready to welcome a portraitist of its own.

In May 1808 ROBERT FIELD (c. 1769-1819) set up a studio in a bookshop on King Street. Born in Gloucestershire, he had studied painting at the Royal Academy School in London. He immigrated to the United States in 1794 and worked as a portraitist in Baltimore, Washington, and Boston. Approaching war with Britain attracted him to Halifax: in 1808 it had a population, with the garrison, that was almost half that of Boston. Field obviously had the social connections then essential to a portraitist; the year of his arrival, 1808, he painted both the lieutenant-governor, Sir George Prevost, and Sir John Wentworth, the New Hampshire Loyalist who had been the previous lieutenant-governor. The latter portrait was the first of a series of three-quarter lengths completed for the Rockingham Club, whose membership was drawn exclusively from the 'better' classes of Halifax. With their patronage Field was kept busy for eight years.

Most of Field's Halifax portraits in oil seem to have been painted before 1814, by which time he had probably satisfied virtually everyone who was willing and able to pay. However, he continued to find a steady demand for miniature portraits painted on ivory. His local fame as a portraitist and the relative inexpensiveness of miniatures meant that he was required to produce these almost until the day he left Halifax. Probably late in the summer of 1816 he departed for Kingston, Jamaica, a town built—like Halifax—around a British garrison. A newspaper notice announcing his impending departure suggests that he may have intended to return to Halifax, but premature death in Jamaica from yellow fever put an end to his plans.

From pictures like *Lieutenant Provo William Parry Wallis* (NGC) of about 1813 it is apparent that Field relished formal dress with its rich adornments, the subtleties of flesh tints, and the sensuousness or beauty in a face; surface qualities such as these gave him an opportunity to highlight his paintings with sparkling, sophisticated detail. This painter of lively and attractive likenesses has been compared to the famous

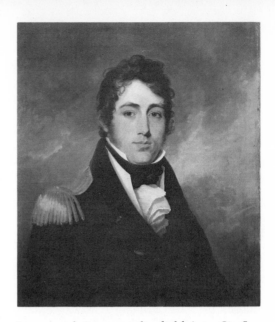

Robert Field. *Lieutenant Provo William Parry Wallis*, c.1813. Canvas, 30 x 25. NGC.

American portraitist Gilbert Stuart and (more outlandishly) to Sir Joshua Reynolds. But in that company he was merely a talented journeyman.

Yet Field remains the best painter Halifax has ever enjoyed. One who might have challenged him was lost to the city. Harry Piers in his *Artists in Nova Scotia* (1914) has called GILBERT STUART NEWTON (1794-1835)—the nephew of the American painter—'unquestionably the greatest artist Nova Scotia has ever produced'. The truth of the matter is that Newton was *conceived* in Halifax and spent the first nine years of his life there. But when his father died in 1803 his mother returned to Boston—her husband had been a Loyalist—and young Gilbert was raised there to be a painter by his namesake uncle. He never returned to Halifax.

A number of itinerant painters passed through Halifax during the first half of the century. One, a certain W. H. JONES (active 1829-30) from Boston and Philadelphia, conducted fashionable classes on the Parade at Dalhousie College during 1829 and 1830. The highlight of his visit was what was probably Halifax's first art exhibition, sponsored and organized in large part by members of the garrison. It was held in Jones's rooms at Dalhousie from May 10 to 29, 1830, and the bulk of the works on display were by Jones's students: ladies and gentlemen of both garrison and town, with the balance most decidedly weighted towards the garrison. The exhibit was augmented with drawings by the lieutenant-governor, Sir Peregrine Maitland (and with war booty in the possession of the chief justice!).

Two years after this exhibition a Mechanics' Institute was founded in Halifax where drawing classes and lectures on art were held.* Local amateurs met in the Institute's reading room and hung their works on its walls. In 1848, eighteen years after the Dalhousie exhibition, a committee of the Mechanics' Institute organized Halifax's second exhibition. However, the change in the base of art patronage that this promised was never fully accomplished, though a greater involvement of the middle class in artistic matters did help to bring another portraitist into prominence.

WILLIAM VALENTINE (1798-1849) was born in England and immigrated to Halifax in 1818. He is said to have had a 'passion' for painting throughout his whole life. Arriving two years after Field's departure, the self-taught Valentine was the antithesis of that fashionable painter. Valentine was a Methodist, which made him very *un*fashionable, and although by 1821 he had opened a drawing school, he still had to paint houses to make a living. He was on the founding committee of the Mechanics' Institute and painted portraits of two of its presidents, which he donated to the Institute. He also drew virtually all of his commissions from the middle-class merchants and professionals who supported the Institute; there is only one military man among his known sitters and he is depicted in civilian clothes. The fashions and values of the society whose tone was set by the garrison did not loom very large in Valentine's life.

Around August 1836 Valentine visited London, staying about eight months. He apparently took no formal instruction there but copied portraits by the famous Academicians that he later gave to the Mechanics' Institute. This experience improved his technique markedly, and the period from his return to Halifax in 1837 to about 1845 was his most prolific and accomplished. Seeking to satisfy his clients' needs for inexpensive yet accurate portraits, Valentine introduced the daguerreotype** to Halifax in 1844. He died only five years later. Valentine is difficult to evaluate. There has been very little effort to discover the extent of his production (there has never been a comprehensive exhibi-

---

*The first Mechanics' Institute was founded in England in 1823 by public-spirited middle-class professionals to promote self-education among the working classes through evening courses, lectures, literary readings, and art exhibitions. They were found in Canada in some numbers by 1835 and from that time a broader, more popular basis for the support of art appeared possible.

**A photographic process invented in Paris in 1839 by Louis Jacques Mandé Daguerre.

tion of his painting). The excuse is often made that a studio fire shortly before his death destroyed a large amount of his work. But this could not have included the many commissioned portraits, the bulk of his output. From the evidence of the few that have been available for examination—including the *Reverend William Black* (Mrs H. Connor, Halifax) of 1827 and a *Self-Portrait* (Provincial Archives, Halifax) of about 1840—we would expect to find that Valentine's portraiture was generally relaxed and informal, revealing the human warmth of the sitter and, in the later work, rich and warm in tone itself.

The activities around the Mechanics' Institute suggest that the years just before and after Valentine's death might represent a high point of artistic production and civilian patronage in Halifax. Adding considerably to this moment, with marine paintings like †*Halifax Harbour* (Halifax Board of Trade) of 1850, was JOHN O'BRIEN (1832-91). He, with Valentine, was closest to being a native artist of stature as Halifax was to see in the nineteenth century. Born on shipboard out of Cork, Ireland, his youthful attempts at painting later caught the attention of some Haligonians who arranged for him to study in London, Paris, and probably Rome. He returned to Halifax and during the middle years of the century painted ships with considerable flair. Heavy drinking apparently destroyed his health and affected his abilities: the later paintings are dull and awkward. Again, however, only very few of his canvases have been seen together at one time and no evaluation has been attempted.

Painters of ability failed to build upon these beginnings and a 'scene' for painting never did develop in Halifax. The brave attempts of O'Brien, Valentine, and the Mechanics' Institute, with their 1848 exhibition, went for nothing. The third art exhibition held in Halifax, in 1863, defaulted to the garrison once again when three army captains arranged it in the armoury of the volunteers' drillroom. Even today Halifax salutes the ghosts of the garrison: its public gallery is housed deep in a powder magazine in the heart of the Citadel.

There were imperial troops in Montreal in the first decades of the century, and gala social events certainly had the required military air of the period, but the leading English families—whose fortunes were derived mainly from the fur trade and most of whom were in fact Scottish—identified themselves with the community at large, not just with the British presence. Montreal was the largest, fastest-growing city in Canada. In 1800 its population was about the same as that of Halifax: 9,000. But by 1840 it was 40,465—more than twice that of Halifax. Montreal had the earliest Mechanics' Institute in Canada, founded in

1828, and also the first YMCA in North America, which opened in 1851. Although the role of the garrison was very small in the developing art traditions of the city, the lure of the picturesque landscape appears to have been as strong there as elsewhere.

One of our earliest native topographers, JOSEPH BOUCHETTE (1774-1841), was born in Montreal. His father, Jean Baptiste Bouchette, was commander of British naval forces on Lake Ontario, and young Joseph first served with the navy and then obtained a job with his uncle, Samuel Holland, surveyor-general of Canada. In 1796 he studied painting with François Baillairgé of Québec but continued as a survey-engineer and in 1817 replaced his uncle as surveyor-general. He published topographical books on Canada in 1815 and 1832, illustrated in part by his own sketches; a lithograph of Montreal was published in 1831. Three sons also shared his love of painting: one in the army, the other two as civilians. One succeeded his father as surveyor-general and the other, a lawyer, joined the Rebellion of 1837 and was transported to Bermuda, although he later returned under the general amnesty.

Bouchette's views, such as *Kilbourn's Mill, Stanstead, Quebec* (MCC) of 1827, are clear and straightforward, yet sensitive and subtle in colour and composition. They differ from the work of British-trained artists like Heriot and Cockburn primarily in their subject matter. Where the visiting artist was attracted to great natural wonders like Montmorency Falls, or to city scenes, Bouchette singled out the farms and small communities that were opening up to the east and south of Montreal. These he depicted with attention to observed detail, yet with a sweep and scale that lend great weight of importance to them.

A community the size of Montreal offered opportunities for portraitists that were matched nowhere else in Canada, and the city benefited from a number of accomplished portrait painters at the turn of the century. Most were French-speaking and will be discussed in the next chapter, but one in particular, WILLIAM BERCZY (1744-1813), seems to have enjoyed a large part of the patronage of the English merchants and garrison officers. Berczy was born in Saxony. He worked in Europe as a painter, architect, and writer, was part of the German artistic colony in Italy, and exhibited at the Royal Academy in London. He came to Canada as overseer of a group of German settlers who were destined for upstate New York. Bad faith on the part of the land company that employed him led Berczy to throw in his lot with his immigrants, who finally settled near the new capital of Upper Canada. Arriving in York in 1794, Berczy was active thereabouts in real-estate speculation until 1805. He designed and had constructed some of the earliest buildings

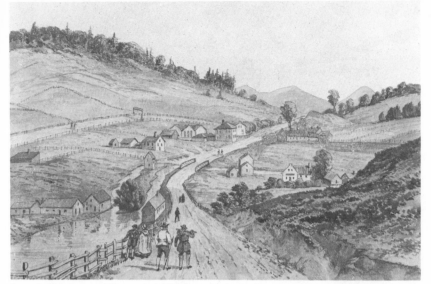

Joseph Bouchette. *Kilbourn's Mill, Stanstead, Quebec*, 1827. Watercolour, 10¼ x 16. MC C

and became known as a gentleman-painter. Business difficulties with political overtones led to a number of trips to Montreal and Québec. Finally, about 1805, his ventures in York became hopelessly involved and he gave up and moved to Montreal. There he decided to live from his skill as a painter and rented lodgings and studio space from a friend, the painter Louis Dulongpré.

Berczy had visited Joseph Brant, Loyalist chief of the Mohawks, in 1794 and had painted his portrait in watercolour (Séminaire de Québec). Later he painted an exquisite small full-length portrait in oils *(NGC) in the classical style then current in Europe. Berczy's fame spread quickly in Montreal and he received numerous portrait commissions, executed church decorations, and did some architectural work. By late 1808, when John Woolsey invited him to Québec to paint his family, he must have been the most fashionable painter of the day. He was also the best, and †*The Woolsey Family* (NGC) is one of the few exceptional Canadian paintings of the first half of the century. The complex inter-relationship of the figures, the masterly treatment of the patterned floor covering, the purely pleasurable attention to the landscape seen through the open window, to the door-jamb and ceiling detail reflected in the mirror to the left, all go far beyond anything accomplished in the country before, or for some time after. It is one of the masterpieces of Canadian art.

Berczy travelled a lot in the promotion of various schemes, and it

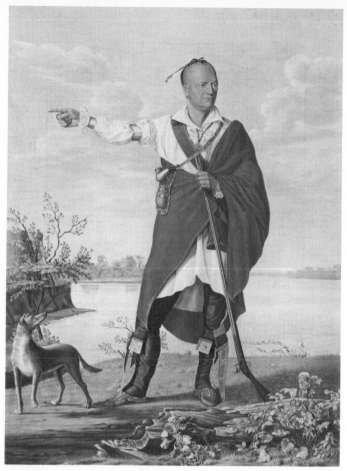

William Berczy. *Joseph Brant*, c.1805. Canvas, 24 x 18. NGC.

was on such a trip to Boston in 1813 that he died. His two sons, wife, and daughter-in-law also painted, and the thorough examination of his painting that needs to be carried out will have to deal with some complicated attributions and collaborations.

While portrait needs for the next fifty years were met by French-speaking artists mainly resident in Québec and by itinerant Americans, including William Dunlap, the famous painter and historian of Philadelphia, the picturesque view-painting tradition was kept alive by a train of professionals, culminating in two who decided to stay in Montreal, ROBERT A. SPROULE (1799-1845) and James Duncan. Both were born in Ireland and both arrived in Montreal in the mid-to-late-1820s. Sproule lived there until about 1840, painting miniatures on ivory and landscape views. He is primarily known for six prints of Montreal published in 1830, and four of Québec that appeared in 1832.

JAMES DUNCAN (1806-81), the more accomplished of the two, arrived in Canada in 1825, settled in Montreal in 1827, and lived there until his death. He ran a design-printing house and also taught drawing in a number of Montreal-area schools and young ladies' academies. According to a contemporary advertisement, Duncan once planned to collaborate with Krieghoff on a panorama of Canada. But he is today best known for the scenes of Montreal that he painted in such numbers. *Montreal from St Helen's Island* (MCC) of about 1850 is one of the best, with its rich detail and easy, rhythmical recession into distant space.

There is surprisingly little known about Duncan's painting activities in Montreal, in spite of the fact that he was a relatively prominent figure for fifty-four years. Spendlove has expressed the opinion that 'no artist has been more neglected by Canadians . . . although he was probably for some years the best water-colourist in Canada.' He suggests that this 'conspiracy of silence' has been due to the fact that Duncan ran a commercial printing house, and as a consequence has been slighted as a painter. His best-known works, however, are often commercially

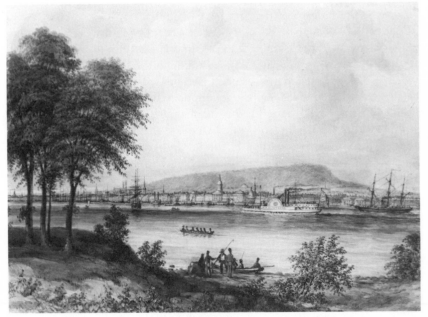

James Duncan. *Montreal from St Helen's Island*, c.1850. Watercolour, 17 x 24½.
MCC

anecdotal, like his view of *The Gavazzi Riot, Montreal* (Séminaire de Québec) of 1853. Duncan often sketched such newsworthy events for the *Illustrated London News*. He seems to have been a painter caught in the shift of history. He arrived too late to pursue a career solely as a view painter in Montreal, yet he was not equipped to satisfy the increasing demands for more self-conscious 'art'. The fact that so many of his pictures exist in numerous versions suggests that he was working under the pressure of a demanding market. But did he consider them pot-boilers, or did they represent to him significant variations on a theme? The same questions are raised by the work of Krieghoff and await the same long-overdue research for an answer.

Out of the considerable artistic activity in Montreal during the first half of the nineteenth century grew the first sustained professional art society in Canada: the Montreal Society of Artists, founded in 1847. At least it *appears* to have been a professional society, for we know little about this early organization except that it existed, and that artists such as Duncan were members. In 1860 the Art Association of Montreal was founded by a group of collectors and some members of the Montreal Society of Artists to develop a collection and a regular exhibition program. In 1939 its name was changed to The Montreal Museum of Fine Arts. It is the oldest art museum in the country.

The pattern of artistic development in Toronto follows somewhat that in Montreal, although things were slower starting in muddy York. Founded in 1793 as the capital of an uninhabited Upper Canada, it had in 1830 a population of only 2,860. Artistic patronage fell to an educated establishment, leaders of government who achieved positions of privilege and power around the lieutenant-governor and shared the same cultural aspirations, of which Upper Canada College—founded in 1829 by Lieutenant-Governor Sir John Colborne—was one manifestation. It was modelled on an English public school (what we call a private school) and drawing and watercolour painting were part of the curriculum from the beginning. An English architect and civil engineer named JOHN G. HOWARD (1803-90) arrived in York in 1832 and assumed the position of drawing master at the college the next year. In 1834, the year York was incorporated as the city of Toronto, Howard organized the Society of Artists and Amateurs of Toronto. It was to be a permanent exhibiting society and thus pre-dates the idea of the Montreal Society of Artists by some thirteen years. Captain R. H. Bonnycastle (1791-1847) of the Royal Engineers was president, and the lieutenant-governor and Archdeacon John Strachan were the patrons. The society appears, however, not to have outlasted its first exhibition staged the year of its founding. The list of exhibitors suggests one reason for its short life: there were really no professionals then in Toronto and thus no real focus for such an association. Of the exhibitors we can identify today, two—Charles Daly (1808-64) and Howard—were teachers who continued to live in Toronto. The only others who could be called professionals were S. B. Waugh and G. S. Gilbert, both Yankee itinerants; John Linnen, a Scottish itinerant; and S. O. Tazewell, a lithographer. All left Toronto within a year of the exhibition. There was one exhibitor, however, who did subsequently contribute to the development of painting in the city. This was Paul Kane (see p. 53 ff.), who was then twenty-four years old. He was at that time preparing to begin his career as a professional, but in two years he would leave for the United States.

A Mechanics' Institute had been founded in 1832 where drawing lessons were given, and itinerant portrait painters continued to pass through. Most were American, and Nelson Cooke (1817-92), one of the more talented, was patronized by Toronto's élite. But they had to wait for over a decade before enjoying the services of a resident portraitist of ability.

Although GEORGE THEODORE BERTHON (1806-92) may have visited Toronto first in 1837, he didn't finally settle in the city until about 1844, and all his famous portraits date from after then. He was born in Vienne, France. His father, who had studied in the studio of the famous Jacques-Louis David, was a portrait painter attached to the court of Napoleon I. In 1827 young Berthon immigrated to England, where he worked as French-language and drawing tutor to Sir Robert Peel's daughters. While there he absorbed that sweetly romantic style of English portraiture made famous by Franz Winterhalter. Soon after his arrival in Toronto, Berthon received commissions from government leaders. A painting of Chief Justice Sir John Beverley Robinson of about 1845 led to a series of portraits of the members of the Law Society of Upper Canada, which are still hanging in the offices of the Society at Osgoode Hall.

Berthon's portraits often display a smooth perfection—found in its extreme in *The Three Robinson Sisters* (AGO) of 1846—and an obtrusive smugness that are disagreeable, but these qualities are sometimes overcome, as in *Mrs Wm Boulton as a Bride* (AGO) of 1847. Though the artist's obsessive attention to the detail of the intricate laces and rich silks of the bridal dress threatens to turn the sitter into a fetishistic doll, the young woman's determined expression and assured stance counteract this tendency and a curiously satisfying state of tension is produced.

Berthon is another of the key figures of early art in Canada of whom

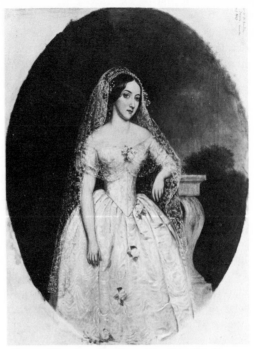

George Theodore Berthon. *Mrs Wm Boulton as a Bride*, 1847. Canvas, 23¼ x 17½. AGO.

we know very little. That Toronto was able to support a fashionable portraitist by the mid-forties, however, points to a rapid acceleration of interest in painting, and another attempt was made to found a society, in 1847, with John Howard again the prime mover. The Toronto Society of Arts was limited to professional artists, and the organizers went far afield to invite serious contributors. Nelson Cooke from upstate New York, John Linnen also of New York, and S. B. Waugh then of Philadelphia—all itinerants included in the 1834 exhibition—were again represented. Cornelius Krieghoff, recently moved to Montreal after possibly having spent a brief time in Toronto, also exhibited. Paul Kane showed some of his first Indian pictures. Berthon and Hoppner Meyer (1832-62) both displayed portraits. It was an impressive exhibition for Toronto, and it seems that two more were held in 1848. Kane held a one-man exhibition later in 1848, marking a new stage in the public appreciation of painting that would lead ultimately to the Ontario Society of Artists and the perpetuation of serious painting in Toronto to our day.

3

French-speaking Artists
in Montreal 1785-1830
and Québec 1820-1860

We have seen that during the French régime the Church was virtually the sole patron of painting in Canada. After the Conquest a growing moneyed class in Québec and Montreal, both French and English, responding to the stability of peace after decades of war, began to show a new interest in painting. Portraiture became almost a fad in the 1780s and 1790s and a number of French-speaking artists rose to the occasion. Particularly in Montreal, it would seem, what can almost be identified as a local school of portraiture developed. A large number of portraits from the two or three decades both before and after the turn of the century have survived, though many are in a sorry state of preservation. Virtually all are half-length, or even just head-and-shoulders, and almost none are signed. They have as a group been called 'primitive' or 'naive', although they display characteristics often found in developed provincial schools of painting. They are generally shallow in modelling, decoratively embellished, and follow one or two simple portrait compositions. The clothes of the period, particularly the elaborately gathered headdresses of the women, were well suited to such a schematized, decorative handling. Very little critical study has been brought to bear on this important body of material and most of the pictures extant have been attributed to the more familiar painters. Most attributions are thus suspect. There are some paintings, such as the beautiful *Mrs Charles Morrison* (NGC), that might be the work of itinerant Americans. It does appear, however, that three portraitists distinguished themselves in Montreal during the last two decades of the eighteenth century.

The most prolific was probably LOUIS DULONGPRÉ (1754-1843), a Frenchman who settled in Montreal in the mid 1780s and who is supposed to have painted over 3,000 portraits before retiring from the scene after 1815. Considering the attributed paintings, his work seems

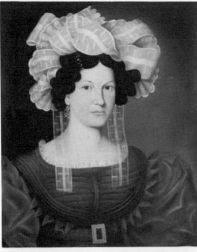

Anonymous. *Mrs Charles Morrison*, c.1825. Canvas, 26 x 22¼. NGC.

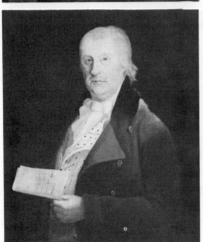

Louis Dulongpré. *James McGill*, 1806. Canvas, 33¼ x 26¾. MQ.

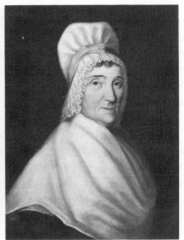

Attributed to Louis-Chrétien de Heer. *Mme Gabriel Cotté*, c.1805. Canvas, 25 x 19¾. The Detroit Institute of Arts.

extremely uneven in quality. His best portraits, however, such as *James McGill* (MQ) of 1806, are strong, almost severe likenesses, yet decorative and—even in the depiction of male clothing—lively. Simple clothing has been exploited particularly well in the portrait of *Mme Gabriel Cotté* (Detroit Institute of Arts) attributed to another of these Montreal portraitists, LOUIS-CHRÉTIEN DE HEER (c.1750-c.1808). He was born in Alsace and worked in Montreal from about 1783. He opened a studio in Québec in 1787, was back in Montreal in 1789, and seems to have worked in both cities until his death about 1808.

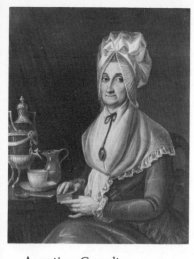

François Beaucourt. *Mme Trottier dite Desrivières*, 1793. Canvas, 31½ x 25¼. MQ.

A native Canadian, FRANCOIS BEAUCOURT (1740-94), was the best of this group of Montreal portraitists, though he worked in Canada for only the last eight years of his life. Born in Laprairie, outside of Montreal, he was sent to France shortly after the Conquest by his father, the painter Paul Malepart de Beaucourt. He studied painting in Bordeaux, married his teacher's daughter there in 1773, and spent a number of years travelling around Europe; he even visited Russia. He returned to Canada in 1786, the year he painted his famous *Portrait of a Black Slave* (MCC). He travelled throughout the settled regions, working on Church commissions, and finally in 1792 settled down in Montreal and put an advertisement in the *Gazette* proclaiming a long list of skills, which included portraits and interior decoration. By then—as we can see in his *Mme Trottier dite Desrivières* (MQ) of 1793—he had picked up many of the wonderful decorative qualities of the contemporary portraiture of his province. Unfortunately he died the next year.

Québec had its portraitists too, but there was then really only one of interest, and he is more important as an architect and a sculptor. FRANÇOIS BAILLAIRGÉ (1759-1830) was a brilliant, many-talented man. From an artistic Québec family—his father was also a sculptor and architect—Baillairgé was sent to the Académie Royale in Paris in 1778. He studied there for three years under Jean-Baptiste Stouf and Jean-Jacques Lagrenée, and then set himself up in a Québec studio as an architect, sculptor, and painter. The contemporary French taste for a severe, classical, profile treatment of the human face is evident in a drawing of one of his brothers in the Séminaire de Québec. But when it came to commissioned portraits, Baillairgé too could paint in the best local manner. His *Mme Ranvoyzé* (private collection) of about 1800 is wonderfully colourful and decorative.

When examining French-speaking artists in Lower Canada during the nineteenth century, then, we must remember the rich precedent set by these earlier portraitists. This is most evident in the case of JEAN-BAPISTE ROY-AUDY (1778-c.1848). Born at Charlesbourg, Roy-Audy received all of his training in his home province. He studied for a short while with François Baillairgé and worked first as a carver and gilder, but by 1818 he was describing himself as a painter. Most of his early work was for the Church.

Roy-Audy travelled quite widely following Church commissions; he worked in Rochester, N.Y., from 1834 to 1837, and in Toronto in 1838. As with the painters of the generation before, the extent of his work is unclear to us at present. Only a few signed paintings have been found, and the dissimilarity of works attributed to him has led to confusion and doubt. From his *Portrait de l'Archiprêtre P. Fréchette* (NGC) of 1826, however, we can see that he continued in that wonderful tradition of portraiture we have been able to isolate at the end of the previous century. If anything he lavished even more sensitive care than did his predecessors on the repeating forms of hair and head, and has even been able to present the simple clothing of a priest as a decorative delight. Roy-Audy represents the end of what had become a strong native tradition by bringing the style of portraiture that flourished in the late eighteenth century to a culmination early in the nineteenth.

One reason for the flowering of a local school of portraiture just before and after the turn of the century may have been Canada's enforced separation from current French cultural forces caused by the French Revolution and the Napoleonic Wars. Between 1817 and 1820, however, a French priest, Louis-Joseph Desjardins, sold in Québec almost two hundred European pictures of the sixteenth, seventeenth, and eighteenth centuries, which his brother, also a priest, had purchased in France from a speculator who had earlier bought them from aristocrats fleeing the Revolution. Many have since been lost in fires, but it appears that most were copies or the work of minor painters (though at least one major altarpiece by Philippe de Champaigne still exists). These works took on great symbolic significance in Canada as representing a legacy of French visual culture. Also, these landscapes, still lifes, religious and historical pictures represented a range in painting that Canadian artists had never to that time considered. Many of these pictures were bought by one remarkable man, JOSEPH LÉGARÉ (1795-1855), and were later exhibited in his private museum, the first art gallery in Canada.

Légaré was born in Québec and apparently harboured a great love

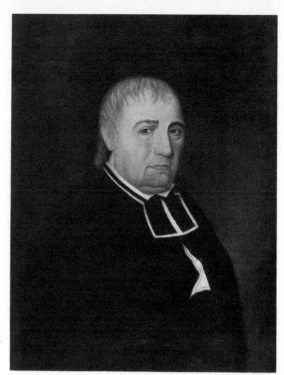

Jean-Baptiste Roy-Audy.
*Portrait de L'Archiprêtre P.
Fréchette*, 1826. Canvas,
26¼ x 20¼. NGC.

for painting even in his early youth. When he bought the first Desjardins pictures in March 1817 he immediately set himself up in a studio and proceeded to restore and clean them. He was then only twenty-two, and as far as we know this was his only artistic training. Commissions began to arrive for copies of the pictures, and for the next few years copying was his main activity and principal source of income. He continued to build his collection—adding a large group of prints as well as more pictures—and opened it to the public in 1838 and again in 1852. After his death in 1855 a large part of it was acquired by the Université Laval, and this forms the core of their present holdings.

As might be expected of someone whose skills were the result of years of copying old European pictures, much of Légaré's original work has the look of old, darkened European painting. Such is his *Paysage au monument Wolfe* (MQ) of about 1840, with its romantic blasted trees, crumbling ruins, nobly classical Indian, and dark tonality. But perhaps we should see this more positively as an attempt, as it doubtless was, to introduce a new set of premises into the art of painting in Canada—a small awareness of the value of some 350 years of accumulated visual history. As early as 1828 the Montreal Society for the Encouragement of Science and Art recognized this fact in awarding

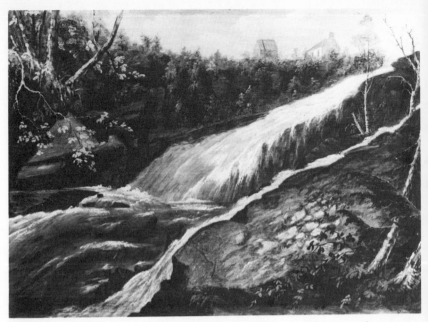

Joseph Légaré. *Cascades de la Rivière Saint-Charles*, c.1840. Canvas, 22½ x 33. MQ.

Légaré their medal, the citation of which described him as Canada's first 'historical painter': that is, a painter of noble themes from the past. Only portraits and religious pictures had been painted before. Of course Légaré painted these too. His religious pictures, however, like all those painted in Canada, were copies, and many of his portraits were copies too. There was a portrait of Lord Elgin, and one of Queen Victoria after Thomas Sully, which he raffled off. Another large portrait, copied from a print of George Ramsay's *George III*, was sold to the legislative council of Lower Canada.

But we now recognize that Légaré's most original contribution was in the field of landscape. He is certainly one of the earliest Canadians to paint oil pictures of landscape, which he did purely for pleasure. Some of these are obviously related to wild romantic scenes of the Salvatore Rosa variety; there were a number of pictures attributed to this famous seventeenth-century Italian in the Desjardins collection. And other of his landscapes have been related to specific works from among the Desjardins pictures. But Légaré also painted the Canadian landscape directly and frankly, as in his *Cascades de la Rivière Saint-Charles* (MQ) of about 1840. There is here no attempt to press the experience into a European mould. His most remarkable works, however, are those that were painted in response to community crises of vast proportions. As early as the 1830s he depicted the horrors of the cholera plagues that

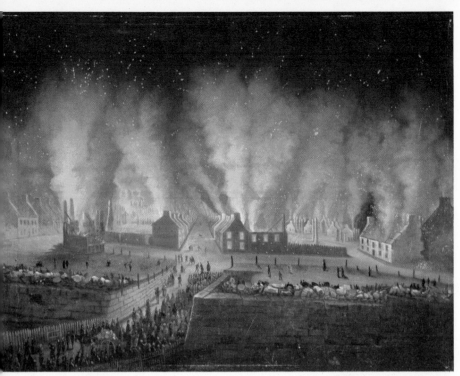

vi—Joseph Légaré. *L'Incendie du quartier Saint-Roch*, 1845. Canvas, 32 x 43½. MQ.

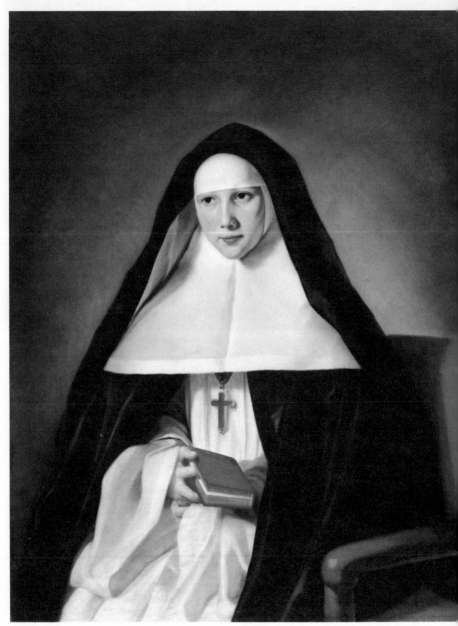

VII—Antoine Plamondon. *Soeur Saint-Alphonse*, 1841. Canvas, 36 x 28½. NGC.

swept through Canada, killing thousands. In 1844 a rock slide at Cap-aux-Diamants in the city of Québec impressed him so greatly with its horror that he recorded it on canvas. And the next year a terrible fire in the Québec suburb of Saint-Roch, which destroyed 730 houses and took more than 100 lives, was depicted both at its height in †*L'Incendie du quartier Saint-Roch* (MQ), and in its hell-like, smouldering aftermath in *Les Ruines après l'incendie du Faubourg Saint-Roch* (private collection).

None of Légaré's apprentices appear to have followed on his innovations in urban landscape. His most famous student, in fact, marked out his successful career in the field of portraiture. ANTOINE SÉBASTIAN PLAMONDON (1802-95) was born at Ancienne-Lorette, near Québec, and at the age of seventeen was apprenticed to Joseph Légaré and set to work restoring and copying the Desjardins pictures. By 1825 he had absorbed all that Légaré and his pictures could teach and so set up his own studio. The next year his work came to the attention of the vicar-general of Québec and money was found to send him to Paris. (It had been forty-eight years since the last French-Canadian, François Baillairgé, had gone to France to study!) Plamondon enrolled with Paulin Guérin, a minor classical portraitist who had painted one of the Desjardins brothers.

In Paris, Plamondon soon achieved the refined austerity of the classical style. He stayed in the French capital for four years, until the Louis-Philippe uprisings of 1830 when he returned to Québec. He opened a studio, advertising himself as an 'élève de l'Ecole française', and portrait commissions began to appear almost immediately. Sitters like Thomas Paud, who was painted in 1831 (MMFA), were delighted with the severe classical treatment they received at the hands of the young portraitist. By the mid 1830s Plamondon was firmly established in Québec. He was in fact succeeding so well that he began to consider Québec his personal precinct and guarded his 'rights' jealously. Any itinerant painter who dared set up shop was viciously attacked in the newspapers. Some actually fled in the face of his abuse.

Plamondon reached his prime about 1841. In that year he painted a series of young nuns of the Hôpital-Général, all daughters of prominent Québec merchant families. They are among the most beautiful and moving portraits ever painted in Canada. Each is distinguished by wonderfully balanced colour, simplicity of composition, delicate but full modelling, and a remarkable sense of psychological penetration—as in †*Soeur Saint-Alphonse* (NGC). Attention to the texture of the clothing and to the space within which the carefully modelled forms are placed conveys aspects of character only hinted at in the intelligent yet impassive face.

Throughout this period Plamondon was able to fill religious commissions, and even painted scenes of everyday life. But most of these genre scenes, including the memorable *La Chasse aux tourtes* (AGO), date from after 1850 when he gave up his Québec practice and retired to the country at Neuville. There he lived as a gentleman-farmer and painted largely for personal pleasure. One of his last works is an *Autoportrait* (Séminaire de Québec), painted at the age of eighty. He lived for another thirteen years!

Plamondon firmly established the dominance of Québec over Montreal in the painting sphere—at least among French-speaking artists. And there was certainly no other painter in Canada who could approach him in his best years, from about 1835 to 1845. Even if they had felt adequate to the challenge, few painters would have faced his jealous wrath. It is a wonder, then, that THÉOPHILE HAMEL (1817-70) was able to work at his side for some ten years. Hamel was also born in the Québec region, in the suburb of Sainte-Foy, and was apprenticed to Plamondon at the age of seventeen. An *Autoportrait* in the Séminaire de Québec was painted some three years later, probably about the same time as an *Autoportrait* by another apprentice of Plamondon, Francis Matte (1809-39), now in the Detroit Institute of Arts. These may have been their 'master' pieces—proofs of their skill and advertisements of their standing as independent painters. Although Hamel's has a quality of gentleness not usually found in Plamondon, its classical composure marks the influence of the older painter.

In 1843 Plamondon persuaded Hamel to go to Europe to further his studies. With a few copying commissions to help pay the way he left for London, went on to Naples, and arrived in Rome in the spring of 1844. He enrolled in the Accademia di San Luca and worked there for a while before moving on to Florence, Bologna, and Venice. In 1845 a public subscription was raised in Québec to allow him to stay another year, and when the money arrived he headed north. He visited Belgium and France and finally in 1846 returned home. Another *Autoportrait* (MQ), with warm colours and softly modelled forms, was painted immediately upon his return. He was now an accomplished, up-to-date Romantic and quickly became very popular. This situation may have hastened Plamondon's retirement, but for whatever reason Hamel had the field to himself after 1850. Orders flowed in. He was commissioned by the parliament of the United Canadas to paint the present and all of the past Speakers of both the legislative council and the assembly.

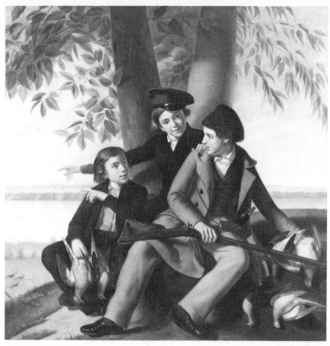

Antoine Plamondon. *La Chasse aux tourtes*, 1853. Canvas, 72½ x 72. AGO.

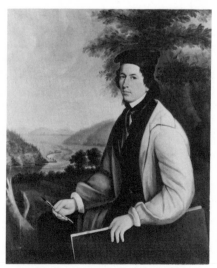

Théophile Hamel. *Autoportrait*, c.1837. Canvas, 48 x 40. Séminaire de Québec.

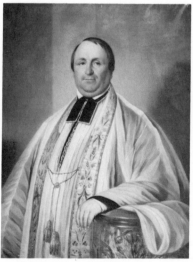

Théophile Hamel. *L'Abbé Edouard Faucher*, 1855. Canvas, 42 x 32. Eglise de Saint-Louis, Lotbinière.

He travelled to Montreal, Ottawa, Kingston, Toronto, and Hamilton fulfilling the commission and probably finding more work at every stop. Like all Québec artists, he did church work as well, although his religious pictures appear to be particularly uninspired.

Hamel's best period seems to have been about ten or twelve years after Plamondon's—that is, about 1852-4. A portrait of *L'Abbé Edouard Faucher* (Eglise de Saint-Louis, Lotbinière) of 1855, still in the church it was painted for, comes closest to challenging Plamondon. The same attention to texture and substance and the expressionless yet engaging face brings us uncomfortably close to the sitter's character. Nuns and priests seem to have been the most accessible of all sitters to these painters.

Hamel had an active career until close to his death in 1870. But by 1860 his work was in decline. A portrait of *Sir Allan MacNab*, painted in 1862 and now hanging in the Senate of Canada, is probably closer to the look and personality of the man than we would think. But there is also a sense of hollow monumentality, an almost comical overscaling.

With Hamel ended a continuous tradition in Québec stretching back some sixty years, handed on from the Desjardins collection, through Légaré and Plamondon. Hamel himself had students, but photography had begun to challenge portraiture and the old traditions no longer commanded a following. The works of Hamel's best-known students—his nephew Eugène Hamel (1845-1932), and Napoléon Bourassa (1827-1916)—achieve a sugary perfection that is strangely morbid. Although a long-overdue study of the church painting of late-nineteenth-century Québec might reveal aspects of their work that are unknown to us, to the extent of our present knowledge they are of little interest.

4

Paul Kane
and
Cornelius Krieghoff
1845-1865

Although PAUL KANE (1810-71) claimed to have been born in York, he actually arrived in the small capital of Upper Canada at about the age of nine. He was born in County Cork, Ireland, and crossed the ocean with his family, his father setting up in York as a 'wine and spirits merchant' on the corner of present-day Yonge and Adelaide Streets. Kane was apprenticed as a 'decorative painter' to W.S. Conger, who ran a furniture factory on Front Street. Around 1830 he approached Thomas Drury (active 1825-33), the drawing master at Upper Canada College, for a critique and Drury took Kane as a pupil. Kane was by then established on King Street as a coach, sign, and house painter. Although there was no possibility at that time of an artist's supporting himself in Toronto other than by teaching or by working as a house painter or decorator, there was a small art scene. Its clearest manifestation was the Society of Artists and Amateurs, and in the newspaper notices of the 1834 exhibition Kane was singled out for praise. As we have seen (p. 41), there were itinerant artists in Toronto in 1834. Two of them, Americans, were friends of Kane. Both S.B. Waugh and James Bowman doubtless opened Kane's eyes to the possibilities of a career as a painter.

Later in 1834 Kane moved to Cobourg (east of Toronto on the north shore of Lake Ontario), then a prosperous, growing community. Whether he went there to follow his old employer, Conger, who had moved to Cobourg in 1829, or to pursue portrait commissions is not clear. He didn't work for Conger but possibly for a man named Clench, who also made furniture. (Years later Kane married Clench's daughter Harriet.) Kane spent almost two years in Cobourg and there got his start as a portraitist. His work of this period is difficult to identify. He apparently completed at least a dozen portraits, though none is signed.

Kane had kept in touch with Waugh and Bowman. In 1836 he left

Cobourg for Detroit from which the three of them had planned to leave together for Rome. Bowman, however, had just married, and Waugh set out for Italy alone—Kane had decided to rent a studio in Detroit. He advertised for portrait commissions and worked there for more than a year before moving on to St Louis, then down the Mississippi to New Orleans, where he arrived late in 1838. A few more commissions got him to Mobile, Ala, where he again rented a studio. In the two-or-so years Kane spent in Mobile he achieved sufficient reputation to be featured in the local newspaper. Finally he saved enough money for his trip to Europe. On June 18, 1841 he sailed from New Orleans.

After a sea voyage of almost three months he arrived in Marseilles. He left immediately for Genoa and then for Rome, which was at that time the world centre of art study. (Hamel arrived two years after the Torontonian.) The winter was spent copying Old Masters. Murillo, Andrea del Sarto, and Raphael appear to have been Kane's favourites. He copied portraits primarily and was most concerned to increase his skill in the use of colour.

In March 1842, with a young artist from Edinburgh, Kane visited Naples and then headed north, hiking throughout northern Italy until the autumn, still copying Old Masters. These canvases were shipped to London and then the two young men crossed into Switzerland and made their way to Paris. On October 20 they sailed from Calais and were soon in London. As Russell Harper has pointed out, Kane's sojourn in London was to be the great turning-point in his career. He had worked almost exclusively as a portraitist and all of his studies in Europe seem to have been aimed at improving his ability in that field. In London, however, his discovery of the work of the American artist George Catlin caused his interests to shift dramatically and irrevocably.

Between 1830 and 1836 Catlin had painted among some forty-eight different Indian tribes as far west as the foot-hills of the Rockies. He may at first have considered the Indians simply as exotic or picturesque subject-matter, but he soon grew to understand their culture and society and became distressed at their plight. During his travels on the frontier he recognized that he was witnessing the initial stages of the Indians' destruction. Catlin was not alone in this concern, but in this romantic era the response was one of reflective pathos rather than outrage. Even Catlin accepted the inevitability of the disappearance of Indian culture, and perhaps of the Indian race. For him the most important need was to make a visual record and he dedicated his life to that end. It was this record, displayed in a gallery in London's Piccadilly, that inspired Paul Kane.

Letters to Kane from his English friends suggest that when he left London in the spring of 1843 he was determined to return to Toronto and set out from there to record a gallery of Canadian Indians that would surpass the record of Catlin. In fact he went back to Mobile and worked there for two more years. But finally, in the spring of 1845, after nine years' absence, he did return to Toronto. Now thirty-five years old, he was ready to proceed with his great plan. On June 17, 1845 he set out on a sketching tour among the Indians, visiting first the Saugeen reservation on Lake Huron, then travelling through to Georgian Bay, northern Lake Michigan, and going south into Wisconsin. His one artistic aim was to depict the true appearance of the Ojibwa and their environment and he was determined to paint as many portraits as possible. The portraits he sketched in oil and pencil, as well as his drawings of houses, villages, rituals, ceremonial and other tools, impress us even today as being direct, informative, and visually pleasing.

Before returning home Kane called at Sault Ste Marie, where Lake Huron joins Lake Superior, and there met John Ballenden, the local Hudson's Bay Company factor, to whom Kane described his ambitious plans. Ballenden wrote to Sir George Simpson, governor of the Hudson's Bay Company, asking him to assist Kane. Simpson was the virtual ruler of all of the land we call Manitoba, Saskatchewan, Alberta, British Columbia, Washington, and Oregon, and of the vast region to the north. All fur-trading forts were owned and administered by the Company and any traveller proceeding west of Sault Ste Marie was dependent upon the Company's hospitality. It was essential that Kane receive Simpson's support.

Kane returned to Toronto late in the fall of 1845 and followed up Ballenden's letter with one of his own. He then rented a studio and began to paint his first Indian canvases. *Indian Encampment on Lake Huron* (AGO) was probably painted during the winter of 1845-6. It does not retain the fresh clarity of the sketches, but from the carefully composed composition, the richly orchestrated sky, the variety of anecdotal detail and overall sense of refined harmony and rational order, we recognize the values Kane had ·absorbed in European salons and museums. His sketches for him were mere notes; he intended that his reputation as an artist—as the proponent of clear, thought-out visual experiences—should stand on these larger canvases.

Early in 1846 Kane still had received no reply from Simpson. In March he decided to call on Sir George in Montreal and on the strength of that visit was able to arrange to travel to the Lakehead with him. The party left Toronto on May 9. Everything proceeded smoothly until at

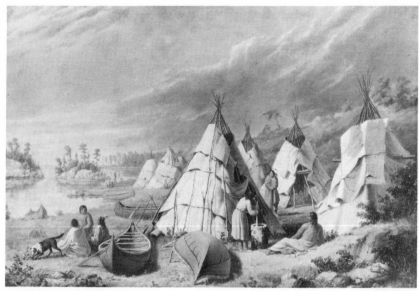

Paul Kane. *Indian Encampment on Lake Huron*, 1845-6. Canvas, 19 x 29. AGO.

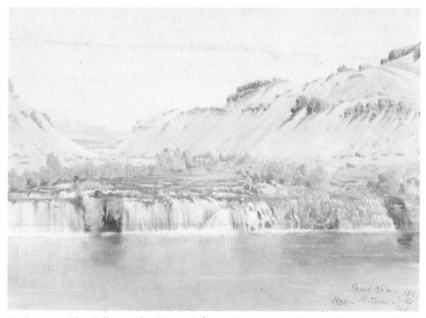

Paul Kane. *The Falls on the Upper Pelouse River*, 1847. Paper, 8⅛ x 13⅜. Stark Foundation, Orange, Texas.

one overnight stop Kane was accidentally left behind. He hired a row-boat and some men and set out in full chase. When he overcame Simpson's party at Rainy River, Simpson was so impressed with Kane's determination that he supplied him with a letter giving him the right to travel with the fur brigades and free hospitality at all Company posts. Kane now began an unprecedented artistic adventure. He travelled with Simpson as far as Fort Garry. While there he was first confronted by one of his favourite subjects, the disappearing buffalo, which he sketched even while taking part in one of the last great buffalo hunts. He described the scene as 'one of intense excitement; the huge bulls thundering over the plain in headlong confusion, whilst the fearless hunters rode recklessly in their midst, keeping up an incessant fire at but a few yards' distance from their victims.' He was thrown from his horse and 'was completely stunned, but soon recovered my recollection'! On July 5 he left Lower Fort Garry in a sloop with a brigade of traders and proceeded up Lake Winnipeg. Taking the Saskatchewan River route, they headed west and arrived in Fort Edmonton towards the end of September. On October 6, in spite of the threat of an early winter, the traders struck out to cross the Rockies, Kane with them. After great suffering from snow and cold, they reached Fort Vancouver on the Lower Columbia River on December 8.

The winter was passed in the immediate area of the fort, but in February Kane began to explore the country that was about to be ceded to the United States. He travelled far and wide throughout the Oregon Territory and northwest to the coast, sketching such natural wonders as *The Falls on the Upper Pelouse River* (Stark Foundation). After about eight months on the coast he headed back east on July 1, 1847. Delayed frequently in the Rockies, he again found himself deep in snow and sub-zero weather, but he reached Fort Edmonton early in December. He spent the winter there, happily involved in the social activities of the holiday season. When the weather allowed, he ventured out on excursions. One of his favourite companions was a Métis guide named François Lucie, whom he sketched (Stark Foundation). He left the fort in April and on the first of October reached Sault Ste Marie, two-and-half years after he had visited that post on his way west. There he caught a Great Lakes steamer and returned to Toronto in some comfort. He reached home on October 13, 1848.

News quickly spread of his travels. Interest was so great that it was suggested to Kane that he hold an exhibition of his sketches in the old City Hall on Front Street, then being used as a market. Kane agreed, and the exhibition, one of the first public one-man shows held in

Canada, was opened on November 9, 1848. There was a catalogue in which 240 sketches in oil and watercolour were listed, as well as various Indian artifacts collected by Kane. The newspaper reports unanimously praised him, recognizing the qualities of objectivity and factuality that Kane himself valued. They acknowledged Catlin as a predecessor but considered the Canadian to be superior. In their view Catlin was too romantic.

Sir George Simpson was greatly impressed with the success of the Toronto showing and offered to sponsor an exhibition in Montreal. Kane declined; he wanted to get on with the canvases he planned to work up from the sketches. Then, in the spring of 1849, he accepted the invitation of a young aristocratic British adventurer who offered him £200 to accompany himself and two others on a journey to the west coast; after a series of misadventures, however, Kane was back in Toronto by mid-September. (As far as is known he did no sketching at all on this trip.) He set himself up in his King Street studio and by 1851 had completed some of the grand cycle of one hundred canvases that were to constitute a panorama of Indian life from the Great Lakes to the Pacific. Eight were exhibited that fall at the Upper Canada Provincial Exhibition in Brockville. Kane attended the opening and was treated as a celebrity. The reviews were lengthy and laudatory.

The canvases painted after the summer of 1849 show no change in style from those of 1845-6. Beginning as usual from one of his beautiful, sparkling sketches—which he still considered to be the raw material of his art, a record of the immediate experience—he proceeded to construct a large showpiece canvas. He took pains to introduce qualities of reflection and taste, conceiving of his work as being part of a long tradition of European painting. The landscapes—like his *White Mud Portage* (NGC)—are carefully composed and thoughtfully modelled to be harmonious and pleasing to the eye. (One of the reviewers of the 1851 exhibition in Brockville thought Kane's compositions were 'a little similar to some of Poussin's.) †*The Man That Always Rides* (ROM), for which there is no known sketch, is a work of the imagination, in which the dramatic landscape is a fitting stage-set for the elegantly caparisoned white horse and its equally elegant rider—a natural aristocrat of the prairie. Kane would have seen such a romantic equestrian pose in European pictures. Even the individual portraits are in this same tradition of European romanticism. Intense, emotional colour in both costume and flaming sky bring highly charged associations of violence to *Mah-Min or 'The Feather'* (MMFA) that did not exist in the original sketch. Nor is the brutality we see in Mah-Min's face borne out by

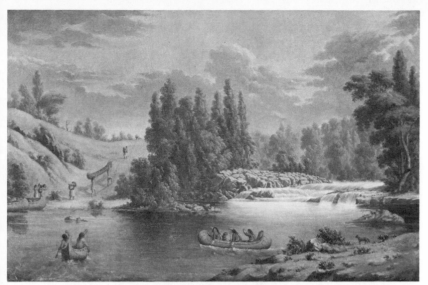

Paul Kane. *White Mud Portage*, 1856. Canvas, 17½ x 28½. NGC.

Kane's description of meeting the Assiniboine chief, who 'permitted me to take his likeness, and after I had finished it, and it was shown to the others, who all recognized and admired it, he said to me, "You are a greater chief than I am, and I present you with this collar of grizzly bear's claws, which I have worn for twenty-three summers, and which I hope you will wear as a token of my friendship." This collar I have, of course, brought home with me.'

Kane applied for government assistance while completing his canvases. The appeal dragged on, gradually gaining support, until in August 1851 the provincial government decided that, rather than award a grant, it would purchase twelve canvases for £500. These would be replicas painted by Kane of existing works in his cycle of a hundred. Content with the guarantee of that income, Kane returned to his work—and put off delivery to the government for almost five years. The government threatened to sue and in the spring of 1856 Kane delivered the twelve canvases. Eleven of them—one was destroyed in a fire—are now in the National Gallery. The full cycle of a hundred appears to have been finished late in 1855. Amazingly enough Kane found a buyer in Toronto—the wealthy George Allan, a collector of sorts who had befriended Kane at the time of his 1848 show. Allan paid $20,000 for the hundred canvases and displayed them in his house until his death in 1901, when they were purchased by Sir Edmund Osler; in 1912 they were donated to the Royal Ontario Museum. So, some fifty-five years after they were completed, they finally ended up on permanent public display as a group, as Kane had wished.

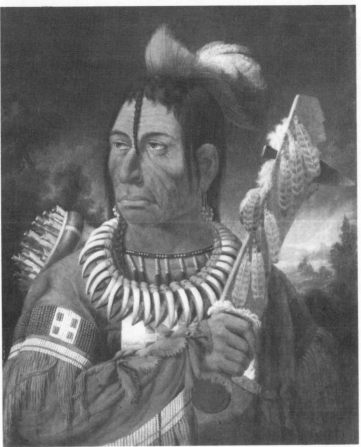

Paul Kane. *Mah-Min or 'The Feather'*, c.1856. Canvas, 30 x 25. MMFA.

These hundred canvases, completed over about a six-year period, were the culmination of Kane's life work. He did little else afterwards. In 1853, at the age of forty-four, he had married his old sweetheart, Harriet Clench of Cobourg. They built a house on Wellesley Street in Toronto and proceeded to raise children. Kane's travels were over.

Only one more work of art can safely be dated to the period following the completion of Kane's canvas cycle in 1855. This is a lithograph of *The Death of Big Snake*, published in Toronto in 1856, the first large coloured lithograph produced in Canada. Kane did not witness the incident depicted—Big Snake in fact died in 1858—but he expressed it as an episode of violent nobility, played out on a stage that existed only in the romantic reveries of the artist.

This print was probably made to help advertise the second part of Kane's Indian program, the publication of an illustrated book of his travels and experiences among the Indians. From the time he completed his canvases early in 1856 until the book's publication in 1859, all of his energies appear to have been expended on this one project. The first evidence of his literary efforts appeared in March 1855 when he read a paper to the Canadian Institute on the Chinook Indians; this later appeared virtually unchanged as a chapter in his book.

In 1858 Kane went to London to find a publisher. He consulted Simpson before leaving and in London had the assistance of his Toronto patron, George Allan, who was there on business. After some delay he found a British publisher and in 1859 his *Wanderings of an Artist Among the Indians of North America* appeared, illustrated with thirteen wood engravings of his sketches and eight chromo-lithographs after the Allan canvases. Dedicated to George Allan,* the book was an immediate success and attracted considerable critical attention, including a lengthy and enthusiastic review in the prestigious *Revue des deux mondes* of Paris. The English edition sold out quickly and three foreign-language editions appeared in quick succession: in French (1861), in German (1862), and in Danish (1863). Its popularity has never seriously waned. Its interesting anecdotes, exciting incidents, and vivid descriptions of the life of Indians, Métis, white traders, and missionaries just before mid-century unfold in a measured narrative of compelling authenticity. It is a Canadian classic. A 1925 edition was reprinted in 1968; that was recently superseded by a lavishly illustrated scholarly edition (1971), with a biographical introduction and notes by Russell Harper.

Kane had plans for a further publication, a selection of prints with explanatory text, but this never appeared. Partial blindness, first noticed in 1859, increased over the years and he withdrew from public life. After the publication of his book he stopped exhibiting and apparently stopped painting as well. He gave up his studio in the early 1860s. During his last years he was a familiar if somewhat distant figure in Toronto. In the warm weather he visited Toronto Island every day and doubtless dreamed of his two-and-a-half years of adventure in the West. He died on February 20, 1871, a legend from the past in his own time.

*Simpson was deeply offended that his support had not been acknowledged. This apparently led to a complete falling-out and may have had something to do with the curtailment of Kane's travels in later life. In 1861 he considered a trip to Labrador but made it clear in a letter that he no longer had Sir George Simpson's necessary support for such a venture.

There is no record that Paul Kane ever knew CORNELIUS KRIEGHOFF (1815-72), although the rumour that they once met in Toronto was passed on by Marius Barbeau in his biography of Krieghoff (1934). It is true that both painters exhibited with the Toronto Society of Arts in 1847, but Kane's five works were submitted by an agent, for he was then on the Pacific Coast, and we have no reason to believe that Krieghoff, who was then living in Longueuil, accompanied his three canvases.

Little is known of Krieghoff's early life, although it has been established that he was born in Amsterdam of a German father and a Dutch mother. He is supposed to have spent most of his childhood in Dusseldorf and to have lived for two years near Schweinfurt, Bavaria. He was trained as a painter and possibly as a musician. About 1833 he left home to wander about Europe, living a bohemian existence on the returns from his painting and music. He arrived in New York City early in 1837 with his brother Ernest. Barbeau says it was likely there that he met Louise Gautier *dite* Saint-Germain, a young girl from Longueuil, a small town across the St Lawrence River from Montreal. His brother soon joined the United States Navy and Cornelius, on July 5, 1837, enlisted in the U.S. Army. Possibly he worked as a documentary artist, although he gave his occupation as 'clerk' upon enlisting.

For the next three years he was in Florida fighting in the Seminole Wars, but by May 1840 we find him at the other end of the country—in Burlington, Vermont. There he was discharged. But he re-enlisted as a topographical artist and then, mysteriously, deserted later the same day! Whether Louise Gautier had anything to do with this strange behaviour is not known, but about ten days later she gave birth to a boy they named Henry. (This first child lived little more than a year, but the parents' grief at his death would have been somewhat softened by the birth of a daughter, Emily, probably that same year.) Burlington is about seventy miles from Longueuil. Given its proximity, Krieghoff and Louise could simply have crossed the border. (Louise did in fact cross into Canada, alone, to have her son baptized.) But Barbeau suggests that, since they hadn't formalized their marriage—they seem never to have done so—they may not have wanted to settle near Louise's parents so soon. One story has it that Cornelius set up a studio in Rochester, N.Y., and there worked up canvases based on his Seminole sketches for the U.S. Government. That would seem very unlikely, given his service record. A more plausible story is that his brother Ernest, who had also deserted, made his way on foot to Buffalo and there met Cornelius. They both would have stayed there briefly before crossing the border and going on the hundred miles or so to Toronto. Ernest set up in the cabinet-making business and Cornelius presumably found a studio. This would have been about 1840-1.

The Krieghoffs eventually did move to Longueuil to live with Louise's parents, but there is no record of when they arrived. Henry Jackson, the grandfather of A.Y. Jackson of the Group of Seven, was a neighbour and friend of Louise's family and it is known that he bought three canvases from Krieghoff, probably in 1847. There are few works that can be dated convincingly before then, though from the evidence of the one known Jackson picture we can be sure that he had been painting for some time. It is the highly successful *The Ice Bridge at Longueuil (NGC). Doubtless drawn from life, it is nonetheless closely related to genre painting then very popular in the United States and Europe, which in turn was based on the works of Dutch seventeenth-century minor masters that Krieghoff would also have known at first hand.

The *Ice Bridge* and similar works of this period must have caused a considerable stir among artists in the Montreal region. There were no other painters then working there who were able to paint in oils with Krieghoff's precision of detail, to say nothing of achieving as well his breadth of sky and snowy ground. The exact rendering of the distinctive sleighs and clothing of the local habitants must have excited Krieghoff's Canadian admirers. He was almost immediately accepted as a man of ability by his painter colleagues and in 1847 was invited to join with some of them to form the Montreal Society of Artists. The Montreal group included the portraitist William Sawyer (1820-89), James Duncan, and Martin Somerville (active 1839-56), who from 1847 to 1850 taught painting with Krieghoff at the Misses Plimsoll's School. Somerville's specialty was the small souvenir genre scene of an old Indian woman selling moccasins or baskets in the snow. Variations on these were very popular with tourists and soldiers and Krieghoff soon caught on and turned out these 'pot-boilers' by the hundreds himself.

Krieghoff, Louise, and their daughter moved across the river to Montreal in 1849. In that year he painted a *Winter Landscape* (NGC), one of his most ambitious canvases—it is more than four feet wide. He wasn't able to sell it until four years later in Québec, however, as Montreal was then arid ground for a painter. This was a difficult period in Krieghoff's career, but he tried the usual ways to make money from his art. Besides teaching, he and Duncan planned a 'panorama of Canada' for commercial viewing (this was a popular entertainment of the time); under the patronage of Lord Elgin, the governor-general, he published a set of prints. His works were eminently saleable and he seems to have sold many small paintings as souvenirs. But the larger,

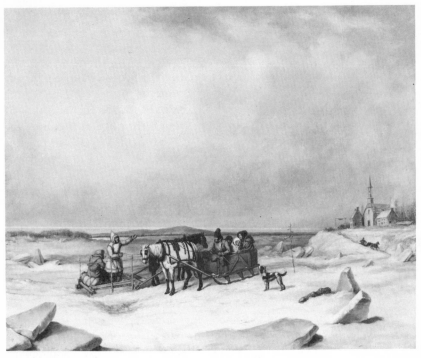

Cornelius Krieghoff. *The Ice Bridge at Longueuil*, 1847. Canvas, 23 x 29. NGC.

more ambitious canvases that would support him both creatively and financially could not be sold. Montreal businessmen were not yet ready to collect art. Finally, in 1851, Krieghoff almost stopped painting.

In this discouraging situation it is a wonder that he stayed in Canada. He did have a Canadian wife, however, and presumably arrest for desertion was awaiting him in the United States. Shortly after arriving in Longueuil Krieghoff had met an auctioneer from Québec City named John Budden, who bought a few pictures. Early in 1853 they met again and Budden made Krieghoff a proposition. If he would move to Québec, where he was certain there was a market for Krieghoff's work, Budden would act as his agent. Krieghoff accepted the offer and he, Louise, and Emily relocated there. They even moved in with Budden.

Québec, which is a good deal further north than Montreal, is well into the Laurentians; the land is more hilly and rugged and the autumn colour more intense and pervasive. A surprising number of new themes came off Krieghoff's easel in the summer and fall of 1853 and the spring of 1854. In the obligatory *Montmorency Falls in Winter* (MMFA) and his first pure landscapes he responded to his new surroundings with direct-

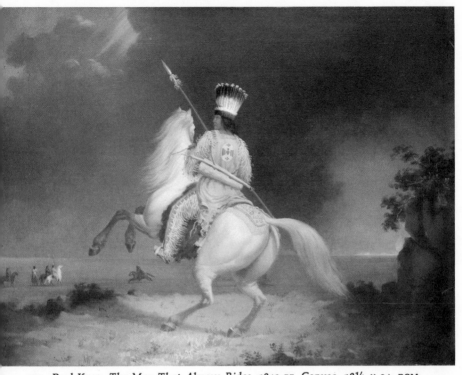

VIII—Paul Kane. *The Man That Always Rides*, 1849-55. Canvas, 18¼ x 24. ROM.

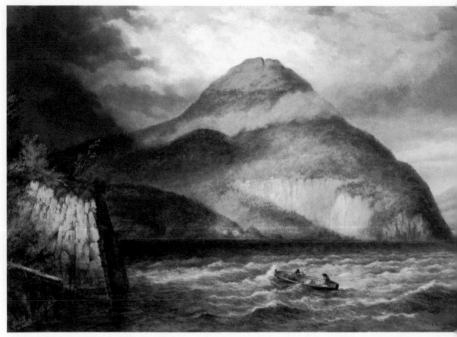

IX—Cornelius Krieghoff. *Owl's Head, Lake Memphremagog,* 1859. Canvas, 17¼ x 24. NGC.

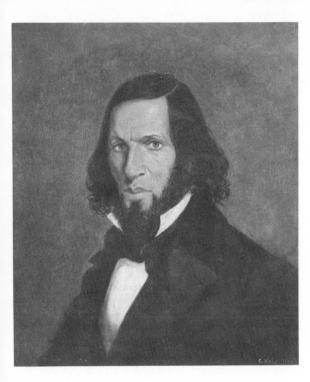

Cornelius Krieghoff.
Self-portrait, 1855.
Canvas, 11½ x 10.
NGC.

ness and freshness. He still painted the habitant scenes that had attracted John Budden to him. But now he increased the amount of observed local detail and generally enriched the anecdotal qualities. Indian subjects became more common. There should not be any confusion with the intention behind Kane's work, however. Krieghoff was not involved in any systematic program. He simply sought out picturesque genre subjects with local flavour. Canadian peasants and Canadian aborigines equally well fulfilled the requirement.

Krieghoff's clientele in Québec was drawn almost exclusively from the English-speaking governing classes and the garrison. Some businessmen, like John Budden and James Gibb, were his closest friends and supporters. They all admired his scenes of Indian hunters and rollicking habitants and encouraged him to paint richer and richer images of the simple but jolly life they imagined the local folk led. The French-speaking bourgeousie, however, did not buy his pictures.

Barbeau suggests a basic difference in the cultural aspirations of the two races. He claims that francophone Quebeckers insisted on the classical hierarchy in the arts in which genre scenes were the 'lowest' form of painting. There was doubtless something in this, but there must equally have been embarrassment for educated Quebeckers in Krieghoff's patronizing view of the jolly habitant as the typical native of the province. Be that as it may, Barbeau seems convinced that it was French-speaking friends in Québec who talked Krieghoff into returning to Europe. They believed that he needed a refresher course in the noble aims of the art of painting. He and Louise left for London in the spring of 1854. It is not known how long they stayed—probably between six months and a year. They were definitely back by the summer of 1855.

From London they went to Paris, where Krieghoff copied in the Louvre, and then on to Germany. They spent most of their time at Dusseldorf, which then was enjoying a great reputation as the seat of a vigorous school of grand-scale landscape and genre painting. Krieghoff painted copies of Old Masters to sell in Canada and very soon after his return—while still on the boat, Barbeau contends—he painted the *Self-portrait* that is now in the National Gallery. Fresh from Europe, he would have wanted to demonstrate his assured grasp of the current modes, and in this painting he has presented himself as a dark, brooding figure, the very image of the romantic artist. Barbeau sees the first of Krieghoff's elaborate canvases to depict the Jolifou Inn—*After the Ball, chez Jolifou* (private collection) of 1856—as a renewed commitment to the native scene and a rejection of Continental 'airs'. However, this type of 'stage-set' genre scene with many figures had been developed at Dusseldorf and was currently popular across Europe and in the United States.

This period (1856–c.1862) was Krieghoff's most fruitful, and the bulk of his finest snow scenes dates from it. The years before 1862 also saw a further exploration of the theme of autumn; he responded warmly, with rich, intense colour. During the late fifties and early sixties he travelled extensively around the province—as far west as the Ottawa River, south to the Eastern Townships, and north up the Saint-Maurice River to Shawinigan Falls. The year 1859 was a creative peak in his career. His †*Owl's Head, Lake Memphremagog* (NGC) and *Coming Storm at the Portage* (BAG) both date from that year. Both are dramatic, rich in detail, thoughtfully composed, and unified in mood and emotional thrust. Technically superb, they are also works of art of considerable force. Krieghoff continued to turn out souvenir 'pot-boilers' for sale to tourists and the garrison throughout these years, but this necessity seems not to have impinged on his creativity.

In 1860 he produced a painting that was the culmination of one of his most popular themes: the all-night revel at the country inn. *Merry-

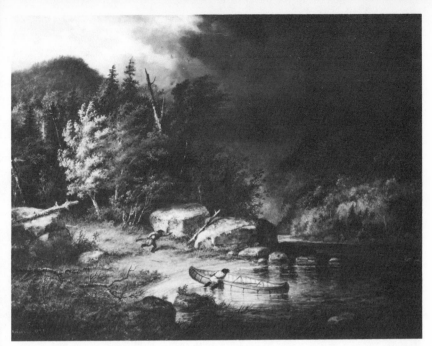

Cornelius Krieghoff. *Coming Storm at the Portage*, 1859. Canvas, 13 x 18. BAG.

making (BAG) is not only one of his largest works—four feet wide—but is one of his most pleasing. He lavished great attention on all the tiny figures—there are more in this work than in any other—and yet through a masterly use of arrangement, colour, and atmosphere he retained a unified whole. One of his masterpieces, it comes close to marking the end of his period of creativity.

It is not clear why his work went into a decline. He was only forty-five in 1860, yet by 1862 he had almost stopped painting. One reason might be that Louise left him during the later fifties. He remarried, how-ever. Perhaps more to the point is the departure of his daughter Emily, to whom he was devoted. She left home in 1862 to marry Lieutenant Hamilton Burnett of the 17th Regiment. A young officer of the garrison was the dream of every Canadian girl at the time and the fact that she married so well was a comment on the circles she and her father fre-quented. Burnett died within two years of the marriage and Emily is rumoured to have taken as her second husband a Russian count and to have moved with him to Chicago.

When the Society of Canadian Artists was founded in Montreal in 1867 Krieghoff gave it his support but did not involve himself in its affairs. Later in that year he left Canada to join Emily and her husband in Chicago. He returned only once, in 1870, when he visited Montreal

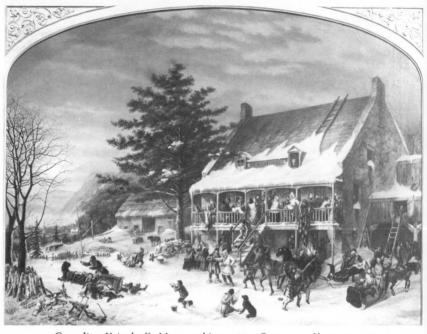

Cornelius Krieghoff. *Merrymaking*, 1860. Canvas, 34½ x 48. BAG.

and Québec. Budden was still in Québec and he encouraged Krieghoff to paint once more. The artist did return to his easel and, given the circumstances, with surprising success. Three large, beautiful paintings are known from 1871, including the accomplished *The Blacksmith Shop* (AGO). But it was a swan song. The garrison was gone, the art scene in Québec was by then almost non-existent, and Krieghoff, though only fifty-six, was tired. He returned to his daughter in Chicago and died there the next year.

5

English Immigrant Artists
in Canada West
1850-1870

In Paul Kane's Toronto there was little awareness of artistic continuity
—a minor though unfortunate consequence of the unstable social fabric
resulting from massive settlement between 1820 and the 1850s.* By the
middle of the century, however, most of the arable portions of the province were settled, and out of the relative stability of the next decade
there evolved what has been called a 'healthy local rural culture' that
sought mainly to satisfy the physical and spiritual needs of the comfortable, independent farmer. The majority of the province's population
was then rural, and the large stone and brick houses built by the more
prosperous between about 1850 and 1875 still dot the countryside, monuments to a life that was isolated yet vital, simple yet fulfilling. It was
largely in this rural environment that immigrant artists settled when
they came to Canada West in the fifties. Despite Berthon, Kane, and the
Society of Arts, there was really nothing in Toronto to attract them.
This lack of significant artistic institutions in the urban centres reflected
a truly decentralized, or at least a precentralized, cultural milieu. For
nearly twenty years the most significant evidence of artistic activity in
the province was the work being done by various English painters who
were scattered from the Ottawa River to Lake Huron.

The one thing that did give these English immigrants some sense of
artistic community was the annual Upper Canada Provincial Exhibition,
founded in 1846. Exhibitions, then as now, were the principal means
artists had of communicating with other artists and the general public.
A painter who did not exhibit might almost not have existed. Like
everything in Ontario at the time, the Provincial Exhibition was decen-

*Ontario's population increased ten times: from 95,000 in 1814 (when it was called
Upper Canada) to 952,000 in 1851 (when it was called Canada West).

tralized. Little more than a glorified fall fair devoted primarily to agricultural products and a large stock show, it was rotated annually among the various larger communities of the province. At the first exhibition, held in Toronto, paintings were shown in the hobby and craft department. It was not until 1852 that a category was introduced for professional painters (as late as 1856 false teeth were still being included in the 'art' division), but whether it was held in Toronto, Cobourg, Hamilton, or any of the other host communities, this fair was the regular meeting-place of all the province's artists. When in the late sixties and early seventies Toronto began to dominate the province economically and an art scene developed, they exhibited their work regularly there. But they were then soon superseded by a vigorous new group of painters who lived in the capital (see chapter 6).

Much like the picturesque or topographical painting of the earlier years, the watercolours of the immigrant artists—they painted mainly in that medium—were primarily landscapes, meant to be kept in portfolios, or if framed to be displayed in country parlours. A few of these painters came to terms creatively with their new home, and the painting of W. G. R. Hind, Daniel Fowler, and Robert Whale, for instance, belongs to the history of Canadian not British art. However, William Cresswell, Thomas Mower Martin, Marmaduke Matthews, James Griffiths, and others remained transplanted Englishmen who worked in a style that was a popular variation on the great English tradition of watercolour landscape painting. For years they painted mainly to sustain a memory and in the hope of somehow recreating the England of their youth in the wilderness.

WILLIAM CRESSWELL (1822-88) was born in Devonshire and, like many of these immigrant painters, was trained professionally in London. In 1855, at the age of thirty-three, he immigrated to Canada, settling near Seaforth, a small town in the west of Ontario near Lake Huron. An income from England allowed him to set himself up as a modest country squire, passing his time with fishing, painting, and managing his farm. *Landscape with Sheep* (AGO) of 1878 is typical of his work in both oil and watercolour. A pastoral landscape that could have been painted almost anywhere, it adequately suited the taste of the immigrant settlers he had chosen to live among.

THOMAS MOWER MARTIN (1838-1934) was born in London, Eng., where he became interested in an art career at an early age and briefly studied watercolour painting, though he was largely self-taught. He immigrated to Canada with his wife in 1862, first attempting to homestead in Muskoka. The farm failed and the Martins moved to another at York

Mills, near Toronto, in 1863. Later he opened a studio in Toronto to which he commuted daily and where, about 1880, he painted *Summer Time* (NGC). Martin lived for ninety-six years and tried to keep up with painting fashion through most of his life. *Summer Time* is an attempt at a monumental wilderness theme and is thus current with the concerns of more vital painters—John Fraser, Lucius O'Brien, and Frederick Verner—who were then working in Toronto. But it is contrived and over-elaborate. Martin constantly strove to satisfy the art-buying public —he visited the west coast some ten times after 1886 seeking spectacular scenes and a less sophisticated market—but his work was then considered out-of-date in the east.

MARMADUKE MATTHEWS (1837-1913) came to Toronto in 1860. Born in Barcheston, Warwickshire, he studied under T. M. Richardson at Oxford. In 1873 he settled on a small farm on the outskirts of the city (just north-west of Bathurst and Davenport Road). His detailed watercolour landscapes have a brittle quality, much like those of Martin. He also visited the Rockies and the coast a number of times after 1888 and some of his western pictures—like *Hermit Range, Rocky Mountains* (AGO) of about 1888—have a sweep that almost compensates for the obsessive detail. Matthews made his most interesting contribution to the art scene in 1891 when he developed his farm as a co-operative artists' community called Wychwood Park; many prominent painters built there, including George Reid. It is still maintained as a private co-operative housing estate in the heart of the metropolis.

JAMES GRIFFITHS (1814-96) was probably born in Newcastle and immigrated to London, Ont., in 1854. Though a painter of china in England, he worked as a civil servant in London while painting in his spare time watercolours of still-lifes and flowers, exhibiting in the Provincial Exhibitions, later with the Ontario Society of Artists, and even with the Royal Canadian Academy of Arts. His pictures—*Flowers* (NGC) is a typical example—are in their detailed attention to every petal and leaf clearly dependent upon his earlier experience as a china painter. This did not detract from their merit in the eyes of his Canadian patrons. The decorative vitality of his work in fact assured him an enthusiastic response whenever he exhibited.

Some of these English immigrants, either through circumstance or creative ability, produced works that grew directly out of a more intense involvement in their new homeland. WILLIAM ARMSTRONG (1822-1914) was born in Dublin but in 1838 was sent to England to apprentice as a railway construction engineer. He immigrated to Canada in 1851, and because he hoped to continue to work as an engineer he chose to settle

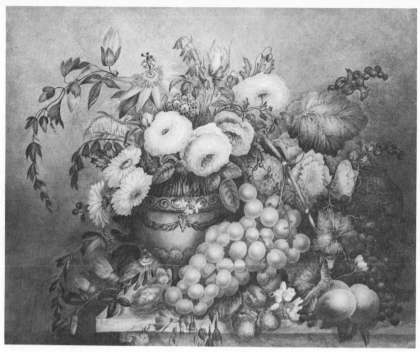

James Griffiths. *Flowers*, c.1865. Watercolour, 11 x 14. NGC.

in Toronto. Painting was for him a serious hobby and over the next sixty years he attracted a sizeable following. He soon came to know Paul Kane's work and in 1861 painted the sensitive *Portrait of an Indian Woman* (NGC), which was first owned by the famous railroad builder Sir Casimir Gzowski. But it was his watercolours—like *The Arrival of the Prince of Wales at Toronto* (NGC) of 1860—that were so greatly admired. His illustrations of current events and of the confrontation of the heroic railway engineers with the wilderness, which he observed along the north shore of Lake Superior, and his numerous loving depictions of sporting boats on the Great Lakes, were greatly enjoyed in his own time and delight us today as records of early Canada. They are modest works of art, however. He was an earnest craftsman with an essentially documentary aim.

WILLIAM G. R. HIND (1833-89) is in a different class. He was one of those private, intensely personal artists that Canada has been blessed with from time to time—a man *of* his time but largely overlooked by his contemporaries. Only when an exhibition of his work was organized by Russell Harper in 1967 did we become aware of Hind's accomplishment. We are still trying to put the pieces of his life together.

Hind was born in Nottingham and studied art in London and on the

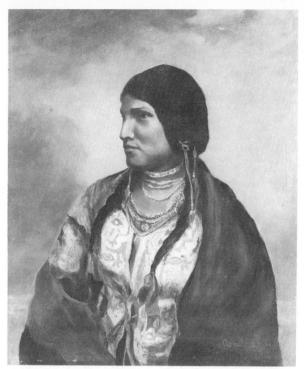

William Armstrong. *Portrait of an Indian Woman,*
1861. Board, 12 x 10¼. NGC.

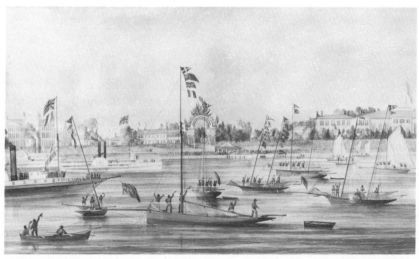

William Armstrong. *The Arrival of the Prince of Wales at Toronto,* 1860. Watercolour, 13¼ x 22¾. NGC.

Continent. His brother, Henry Youle Hind, immigrated to Toronto in 1846, working out of that city as a geologist and explorer. William followed his brother to Toronto in 1852 and taught drawing there for four or five years. He returned to England, but was back in Toronto by 1861.

When Paul Kane wanted to visit Labrador in 1861 he probably intended to accompany Henry Youle Hind, who that year made a trip of exploration. Hind instead took his brother William as the official artist. The Labrador watercolours and drawings—a number of which were reproduced as chromo-lithographs and woodcuts to illustrate the official expedition report—go far beyond their documentary function. All are remarkable works of art. Harper has pointed out Pre-Raphaelite elements in Hind's work, and we can see in †*The Game of Bones* (MMFA) the simple, strong composition, the great attention to detail, and the rich colour of the then-popular English style. Hind so involved himself in the excitement of the moment that the intense concentration of the gambling Indians appears to permeate the whole picture.

The party returned to Toronto in the fall of 1861. The restless artist had enjoyed his taste of rugged travel and the following spring went off again, this time with a party of gold-seekers, the famous 'Overlanders of '62', who intended to cross the continent to the Cariboo gold fields of British Columbia. Like Kane—who had covered much the same route sixteen years earlier—Hind kept a close pictorial record of the incidents of the journey. The party arrived at Lillooet in the Cariboo just as snow began to fall, and Hind remained only long enough to sketch scenes of the gold rush—of miners on the Fraser, panning for gold, lounging in a bar—that are as exotic in their way and yet as deeply felt as those sketched in Labrador. He arrived in Victoria in mid-October and immediately left for San Francisco where he spent the winter. Back in Victoria in the spring of 1863, he set up a studio and proceeded to accept commissions and to work up his prairie and Cariboo sketches into finished watercolours and even oils. A *Self-portrait* (MC C) painted then shows him to be a man radiating a profound sense of his being.

Hind left Victoria after only two years. His brother had moved to Windsor, N.S., and William joined him there, working for various Maritime railways (possibly as a draughtsman). About 1880 he settled down in Sussex, N.B., and died there nine years later. He was buried in Windsor and promptly forgotten.

Hind and DANIEL FOWLER (1810-94) were the finest watercolourists among the English immigrants. Unlike Hind, Fowler exhibited regularly

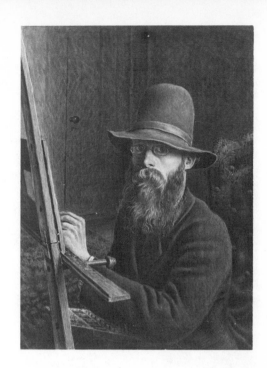

W.G.R. Hind. *Self-portrait*,
c.1863. Watercolour, 12 x 9.
MCC.

at the Provincial Exhibition after 1862 and was known and respected
by his peers and by the younger generation. Born in Kent, he trained
as an artist with the London watercolourist J. D. Harding, travelled and
painted on the Continent, and worked in London as a professional from
1834 to 1842. Suffering from consumption, he immigrated to Upper
Canada in 1843 in search of a healthier climate. He found a farm on
Amherst Island in Lake Ontario just off Kingston and became a farmer.
He didn't paint for fifteen years. In the winter of 1857-8 he visited
England and when he returned to Amherst Island he set up a small
studio in the back of his house and began to paint again, exhibiting at
the Provincial Exhibition in the amateur class that same year. From 1862
until the end of his life he exhibited professionally at every opportunity
—never, however, leaving his home for longer than a short trip to go
to an exhibition or to visit artist friends. He was devoted to his Canadian
farm where he had found a way of life suited to his temperament.

Fowler painted only in watercolour and by the early seventies had
achieved a forceful, mature style of his own, working within a limited
subject range of still-lifes and landscapes. *The Wheelbarrow* (AGO) of
1871 is intimate and intense, with a clear sense that a picture must be
'alive' at every point. By the 1880s his handling had become more open,
looser, but he was able to make of the whole picture surface a single
integrated image. His †Fallen Birch (NGC) of 1886 crackles with creative

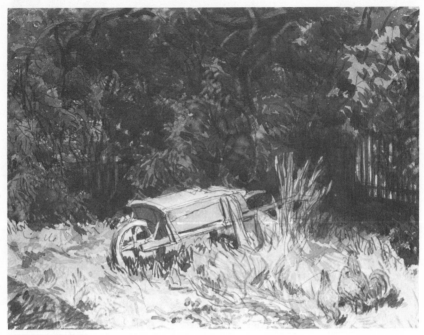

Daniel Fowler. *The Wheelbarrow*, 1871. Watercolour, 9¼ x 13¼. AGO.

energy. Working alone on Amherst Island, he had reached the point where he could touch existence itself in a single watercolour. Fowler had become what we might venture to call a great artist.

Not as good a painter, yet as interesting for his development in Canada, is ROBERT WHALE (1805-87). Born in Cornwall, he studied painting in England and worked there as a professional before immigrating to Canada in 1852. He lived first at Burford, a small town near Brantford, and then moved to Brantford in 1864. Unlike Fowler, Whale arrived with the full intention of continuing in his profession and began exhibiting at the Provincial Exhibitions immediately. Because he painted for a living, his work has all the earmarks of the journeyman; in this, and in his willingness to paint anything, he was like the Yankee itinerants who had worked in the province during the previous three decades and who still made fleeting visits to the more populous rural districts. Every year he and his sons, who were also painters, would cart crates of oil paintings to the Provincial Exhibition, always submitting the maximum number of pictures allowed in each of the categories. They relied on the prize money, for there was almost no market for art. Whale intended to benefit from such a market as did exist, however, and

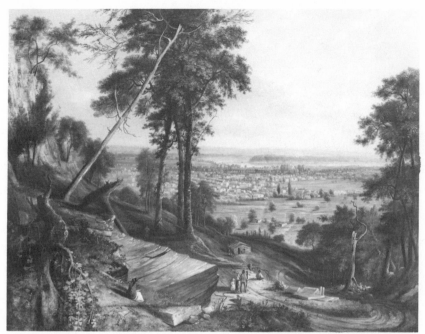

Robert Whale. *General View of Hamilton*, 1853. Canvas, 35¾ x 47½. NGC.

so painted portraits, landscapes, and in later years a panorama of the Indian Mutiny that he exhibited as an attraction throughout Ontario. One of his first Canadian pictures—he worked almost exclusively in oils—is the *General View of Hamilton* (NGC) of 1853. Likely painted for some wealthy city-father, it is in the tradition of the distant city-view that reaches back more than a hundred years to Richard Wilson in England. With its imaginative vantage point, sensitive light, and impressive breadth, it reflects a creative ambition that surpasses the merely commercial. Whale also responded to the growing interest in wilderness themes and in what was thought to be a picturesque dying race, the Indian, while trying as well to satisfy the nostalgia felt by many immigrants for an older, more settled landscape. In one canvas an Indian and a canoe seem to be sitting on the edge of an English country estate. The landscape is idyllic, remembered from so long ago that it exists only in the shared imagination of artist and audience.

Whale returned to England after the death of his wife in 1871 and stayed for four years while his son completed his schooling. He then returned to Brantford and semi-retirement, living with his daughter until his death ten years later. Always responsive to the market, his

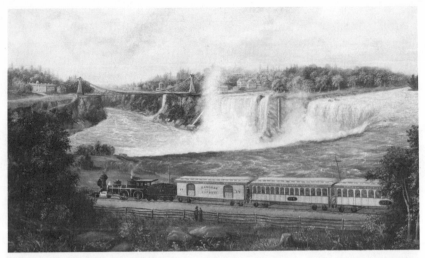

Robert Whale. *The Canada Southern Railway at Niagara,* c.1875. Canvas, 23 x 40. NGC.

painting changed as his clients' tastes were moulded by the experience of life on the burgeoning continent and were stimulated by the dynamic popular culture developing in the United States. When railways became the symbol of everything progressive in North America, Whale painted a group of 'portraits' of trains. They are thoroughly North American— they could not have been painted in England. *The Canada Southern Railway at Niagara* (NGC) dates from about 1875. Over the years Niagara Falls had become a symbol of the dynamic energy of the continent. Placing the train in front of the Falls is an obvious but effective device to link those two symbols of progress and untapped energy in praise of future potential. Now less nostalgic about what was left behind, Whale and his patrons were able to become swept up in hope for the future. But that basic driving force of North American society found more forceful interpreters in the successors to these English immigrant painters of the fifties.

6

Landscape Painters
in Montreal and Toronto
1860-1890

Although in mid-century Ontario the English immigrants constituted a significant phenomenon, Montreal nonetheless superseded Québec as the principal centre of art activity in Canada during the later 1860s. Here painters worked and exhibited who were attempting to respond to the Canadian landscape in all of its splendour, in a way that reflected the eagerness then felt by politicians and entrepreneurs to encompass the vast land and to tap its mighty resources. The English painters in Ontario were essentially pastoral, even domestic, in their outlook. It was left to three German artists—Otto Jacobi, William Raphael, and Adolphe Vogt—to set a new direction.

OTTO JACOBI (1812-1901), the best of these German artists who worked in Montreal during the sixties, was born in Prussia, studied in Dusseldorf at the famous academy, and also taught there. Later he was court painter to the Grand Duke of Nassau for almost twenty years. Paintings like *The Splugen Pass* (MMFA) of 1855 sold widely in England and the United States. He was visiting New York in 1860 when he was invited to paint Shawinigan Falls as a present for the Prince of Wales—who made a state visit to the Canadas in that year—and Jacobi decided to settle in Montreal. Throughout his life in Canada he turned out monumental canvases like his *Falls of Ste Anne, Quebec* (AGO) of 1865. Carefully composed in the Dusseldorf fashion, with the crashing white water naturally framed within its own rock boundaries, it is a stirring image of sublime majesty. Its colour is clear and luminous, its scale is grand, and the heroic landscape is charged with a sense of importance that transcends the depicted scene. Jacobi stayed in Montreal about ten years and then moved to Philadelphia. In 1876 he was invited to join the Ontario Society of Artists in Toronto and moved there two years later. Over the next fifteen years he worked in these three cities. Upon the

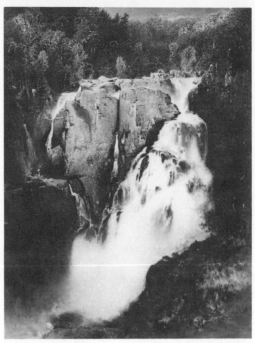

Otto Jacobi. *Falls of Ste Anne, Quebec,* 1865.
Canvas, 30 x 23. AGO.

death of his wife he joined a son in the Dakota Territory, where he
died in 1901 in the town of Jarva.

WILLIAM RAPHAEL (1833-1914) was born in Prussia into a Jewish-
German family. He studied in Berlin and in 1856 immigrated to New
York City, where he worked as a portraitist. He moved to Canada the
next year, seeking commissions in Québec and Montreal, where he
settled, although continuing to work for short times in other parts of
the province. His famous *Immigrants at Montreal* (NGC) was painted
in 1866. As a genre scene it is more complex than Krieghoff would have
painted. The careful light effects evident in the treatment of the figures
and buildings and the bold symmetry—as in the profile of the woman,
hands on hips, left of centre—are derived from that German Romantic
painting of the early nineteenth century that is now best known from
the work of Caspar David Friedrich. The luminous clarity and studied
composure of Raphael's canvas can be seen reflected in later Canadian
works.

ADOLPHE VOGT (1842-71) was born in Germany but at the age of twelve
he immigrated to Philadelphia where he immediately began to take painting lessons from other German immigrants. In 1861 he left for Munich
and Zurich for further study. He was in Montreal in 1865, but set out

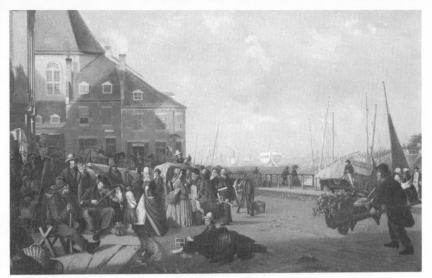

William Raphael. *Immigrants at Montreal*, 1866. Canvas, 26½ x 43. NGC.

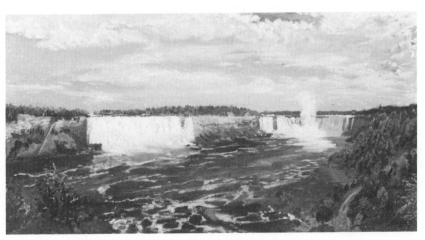

Adolphe Vogt. *Niagara Falls*, 1869. Canvas, 20 x 39. NGC.

for Paris the next year. He was back in Montreal by September 1867. His beautiful *Niagara Falls* (NGC), painted in 1869, introduced a new breadth of treatment, a sense of scale and a depth of meaning to Canadian landscape art. Vogt moved to New York in September 1870 and died there of smallpox the next year.

There were many reasons why these artists were attracted to Montreal. The businessmen who largely controlled the city had become wealthy and sophisticated enough to found the Art Association of

Montreal in 1860 for the purpose of holding exhibitions, building a collection, and generally promoting the arts. The decline of Hamel and Krieghoff by 1865 meant that Québec no longer had important artists. In fact there was a general decline in intellectual and artistic life among French-speaking Catholics in the 1860s, brought about by Bishop Bourget's attempts to suppress the Institut Canadien—a society that had been founded in 1844 as a forum for advanced liberal views—and by reactionary opposition to the parti rouge, which had been formed in 1848 by members of the Institut. The creative field was virtually left open to the new arrivals. The photographic firm of William Notman, which regularly hired skilled artists to colour photos and paint backgrounds, acted as a focus for the intense new activity that developed. And the Society of Canadian Artists, founded in Montreal in 1867 by a group of professional painters (Jacobi, Raphael, and Vogt were all charter members), reflected the potential they then believed the city held as a centre for the arts.

ALLAN EDSON (1846-88) was a talented native Canadian who developed in this Montreal milieu. Born at Stanbridge in the Eastern Townships of American parents, he arrived in Montreal in 1861 to work in a wholesale house. He first took painting lessons from the black American artist Robert Duncanson (1817-72), who earlier had been raised in Montreal. Then in 1864, using his own savings and with the help of a Stanbridge banker, he was able to go to England where he studied for two years. He returned to Montreal in 1867 in time to become a charter member of the Society of Canadian Artists. His work of this period shows a careful attention to detail, probably reflecting the influence of Pre-Raphaelite taste that he had absorbed in England. Yet there is a concern for atmosphere and a clarity and assertion of foreground elements that suggest the style of Duncanson, his first teacher, of Otto Jacobi, and to a lesser degree of Raphael and Vogt. *Mount Orford and the Owl's Head from Lake Memphremagog* (NGC) of 1870 first impresses the viewer with its atmosphere of lyrical quietude achieved by Edson's subtle use of tones; then it can be seen that every object has been picked out, almost defined, by a ring of intensely reflected light. Edson was a painter of great individuality and imagination. His vision is perhaps not as expansive as that of the other Montreal painters, but it is more penetrating, more concerned with secret moments of quiet in nature. His *Trout Stream in the Forest* (NGC) of about 1880, with its mounds of soft green moss and brightly splashing brook running between the rocks, partakes of this same stillness. Edson lived in Montreal until about 1880, when he went to Paris for three years. He returned to

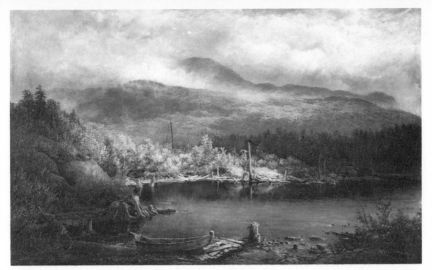

Allan Edson. *Mount Orford and the Owl's Head from Lake Memphremagog*, 1870. Canvas, 36 x 60. NGC.

Montreal, but settled in Glen Sutton in the Eastern Townships in 1886. He died there at the height of his powers, aged only forty-two.

The president of the Society of Canadian Artists was an Englishman, John Bell-Smith (1810-83), who had arrived in Montreal in 1866. Though he was a mediocre portraitist, he had been secretary-treasurer of the Institute of Fine Arts, Portland Gallery, in London, and so had administrative skills to offer. His son, FREDERIC MARLETT BELL-SMITH (1846-1923), was also a member of the Society. He was born in London and was twenty when he arrived in Montreal. He had studied painting with his father and also at the South Kensington Art School. Nonetheless he worked primarily as a photographer: in Montreal until 1871, in Hamilton until 1874, and then in Toronto until 1879. He later turned to art teaching, notably as Director of Fine Arts at Alma College, St Thomas, Ont. Throughout this whole period after 1871 he also worked as an illustrator for *The Canadian Illustrated News* and other publishers. The influence of both photography and the hard line of newspaper illustration is evident in the stiff, contrived watercolours he painted before he visited Paris in 1891. This French experience enabled him to achieve a looser, more expressive handling of colour and atmosphere in his later oils.

HENRY SANDHAM (1842-1910), another member of the Society who was well known in his time, was born in Montreal. He worked at Notman's, and many of his paintings are exact renditions of composite photographs manufactured there. In his oils he showed a concern for light and colour that was doubtless learned from his German colleagues (he took lessons from Jacobi), as in his *Beacon Light, Saint John* (NGC) of 1879. But there is a dogged literalness about his Canadian work that screams of the photograph. Sandham was sent to open a branch of the Notman firm in Saint John in 1879 and moved to Boston in the early eighties. He eventually ended up in London, Eng., where he died.

The Society of Canadian Artists held its last exhibition in 1872. By 1873, with the first exhibition of the Ontario Society of Artists, the centre of art activity in Canada had moved to Toronto. Egerton Ryerson had established in Ontario an elaborate, and largely admirable, provincial educational system. It included the Canadian Educational Museum, which opened in 1857 in the Toronto Normal School. A large collection of plaster casts, oil copies, and prints of the great masterpieces of European visual culture, it was the only public display of paintings in the whole province and it attracted every young person with an interest in art.

By the late sixties and early seventies a surprising number of young people from rural Ontario had discovered such an interest, and the centralization of provincial services accelerated with the influx of these people into the cities—primarily Toronto. A cultural environment consequently developed in the capital that enabled it to sustain an art scene in which traditions were established that have supported an active climate for art to this day. These forces were focused in the later 1860s mainly by one man.

JOHN A. FRASER (1838-98) was born in London, Eng., where he studied at the Royal Academy School. Upon graduation he worked as a portrait painter. His father, a tailor, was a prominent member of the left-wing Chartist movement, and probably because of his political views was forced to leave England about 1856. He took his family to the Eastern Townships of Quebec, where his son continued to paint and soon had a reputation as a prodigy. About 1860 John moved to Montreal and was hired by William Notman to tint photographs. Some seven years later he was one of the major figures in the establishment of the Society of Canadian Artists, and his departure from Montreal later in 1867 portended the Society's ultimate demise.

He was sent to Ottawa by Notman to set up an office, and later the same year to Toronto. The Toronto branch was a partnership: Notman-Fraser. Fraser hired, on a casual basis, most of the active artists in Toronto. Tinting photographs was lucrative and only slightly demeaning, to be worked at when sales of paintings were slow. The gallery he built for the Notman-Fraser studio was also available to the painters associated with the firm. Fraser was aggressive and self-confident, and people liked him tremendously or hated him. All found him necessary, however. He was responsible for organizing the Ontario Society of Artists, of which he was first vice-president (the president was an honorarily appointed layman), and its first exhibition was held in the Notman-Fraser galleries.

Most writers have stressed Fraser's role in the art politics of his day rather than his development as an artist. As with most of our early artists, all but a handful of his paintings have been lost to sight, and so we cannot talk with real authority of his ability. But from the evidence of *A Shot in the Dawn* (NGC) of 1873—exhibited in the first OSA exhibition—we can see that he had considerable skill. The magnificent colour of a morning sky has become in his hands an expression of the sublime majesty of nature. As in the work of Raphael and of Fraser's other German friends from Montreal, light is important in establishing figures in space.

In 1874 Fraser came into conflict with another prominent member of the OSA, LUCIUS R. O'BRIEN (1832-99). One suspects that distinctions of class underlay the disagreement. Fraser was aggressively lower middle-class and liberal. O'Brien, who aspired to the upper classes, was conservative and gentlemanly and his art reflected this sense of decorum. He was born in Shanty Bay, a small community on the northwest arm of Lake Simcoe founded by his father, Colonel Edward O'Brien, a half-pay officer retired from the British army. Lucius graduated from Upper

John Fraser. *A Shot in the Dawn*. 1873. Canvas, 16 x 30. NGC.

Canada College in 1848 and is supposed to have immediately entered an architect's office. In November 1854, however, he was given the responsibility of running one of the family businesses, situated in Orillia, just northeast of Shanty Bay. He was still in Orillia in January 1859 when he was elected reeve of the township. In April of that year he married a local woman. He travelled extensively in the immediate area north of Lake Simcoe throughout these early years and in January-February 1869 visited England and the south of France. He appears to have moved to Toronto shortly thereafter.

O'Brien painted as an amateur from at least 1852 but it was only in 1872, with the foundation of the OSA, that he decided to turn to painting as a profession. The result of his disagreement with Fraser in 1874 was that Fraser and some supporters resigned from the OSA. O'Brien replaced him as vice-president, a position he held until 1880 when he became the first president of the Royal Canadian Academy. Various writers have suggested that O'Brien's social aspirations ideally suited him in his role as president of the RCA. He was required to work closely with Lord Dufferin, the governor-general, and with Dufferin's successor the Marquis of Lorne and his wife, the Princess Louise, daughter of Queen Victoria. (Fraser would not have been suitable for such an intimate relationship with royalty!) O'Brien steered the RCA through its difficult first ten years with tact and discretion.

As a late beginner in the profession of painting—he was forty-one in 1873—O'Brien quickly achieved great presence in his work. This is evident in his famous *Sunrise on the Saguenay* (NGC)—painted in 1880, exhibited in the first RCA exhibition, and that same year deposited in the new National Gallery of Canada as the first academy diploma piece. In its depiction of sublime grandeur in nature, in its subtle coloration and atmosphere and use of light to infuse the scene with a spiritual force, it embodies a view of the Canadian landscape O'Brien clearly shared with Fraser and the German painters of Montreal. It also represents most closely in Canada a style of painting—now known as 'luminism'—that had become very popular in the United States through the work of Fitz Hugh Lane, Martin Johnson Heade, and John F. Kensett, among others. These American painters achieved a crisp but poetic landscape vision that reflected a moody quietude arising from a developed sense of pervasive order. Much research is required before the relationship of the Canadians to these painters can be clarified, for there are several possibilities. Fraser exhibited in New York and Philadelphia throughout his career and travelled south both as a representative of the Notman firm, and, we must assume, to look at pictures. O'Brien also travelled

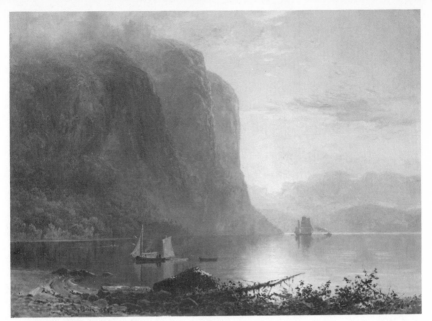

Lucius O'Brien. *Sunrise on the Saguenay*, 1880. Canvas, 34½ x 49½. NGC.

in the United States. But what complicates a simple reading of this as a direct American influence on the Canadian painters is that we can show that the Canadian 'luminist' style developed, at least in part, from the influence of those three German painters working in Montreal in the 1860s. (Interestingly enough, it also developed in the United States partly through contact with nineteenth-century German painting.) Raphael, Vogt, and Jacobi all lived in the USA at various points in their careers, however, and American artists visited Canada; some, like Robert Duncanson, even lived here. There are also British painters we could call 'luminists'.

One place the research will have to begin is with the work of the American painter Albert Bierstadt (1830-1902). Born in Germany, he was brought to the United States as an infant. He returned to Dusseldorf to study, but back in the United States he became one of the major exponents of the 'heroic' side of the luminist style of painting. He was a friend of Lord Dufferin and later of the Marquis of Lorne and Princess Louise; he visited them in Ottawa and Québec in the late seventies and early eighties. Paintings he did then were later exhibited in the Canadian section of the Colonial and Indian Exhibition in London in 1886. O'Brien met him and would have been familiar with his work. Lorne even donated one of Bierstadt's paintings to the Art Association of Montreal.

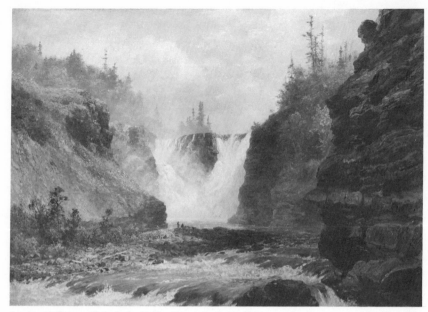

Lucius O'Brien. *Kakabeka Falls, Kaministikwia River*, 1882. Canvas, 32½ x 48. NGC.

O'Brien's *Kakabeka Falls, Kaministikwia River* (NGC) of 1882 was certainly created with some awareness of Bierstadt's work, but it is nevertheless a profound and personal response to the magnificence of the scene and to the glory of the painter's art. O'Brien continued to develop as a painter, his vision broadening to encompass the vast breadth of the nation that was, during these decades, growing literally from sea to sea. As president of the RCA he probably felt a responsibility to represent the variety of the country, and as art editor of the monumental two-volume *Picturesque Canada*, published in 1882, he travelled over much of it supervising his artists and making sketches for many of the illustrations himself. He first visited the Rockies in 1882 with his missionary brother, one of the first painters of his generation to do so, and went out west twice more. In 1888 he painted his lush †*A British Columbian Forest* (NGC). Factual in its depiction,* it is still pungent with the rich, fecund growth of the rain-forest. For Canadians of the time it was a fascinating new Eden-like image of their country.

John Fraser continued to paint imaginatively as well, although he was now effectively excluded from any organizational role in the Toronto

---

*There is a famous Notman photograph of the same massive tree, likely taken at the same time, though from a closer point of view.

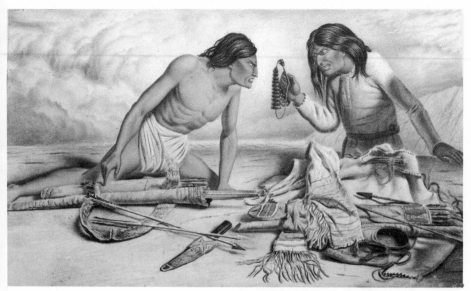

x—W.G.R. Hind. *The Game of Bones*, 1861. Watercolour, 10 x 16¾. MMFA.

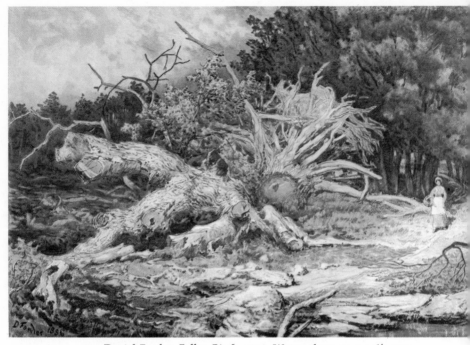

XI—Daniel Fowler. *Fallen Birch*, 1886. Watercolour, 19 x 27½. NGC.

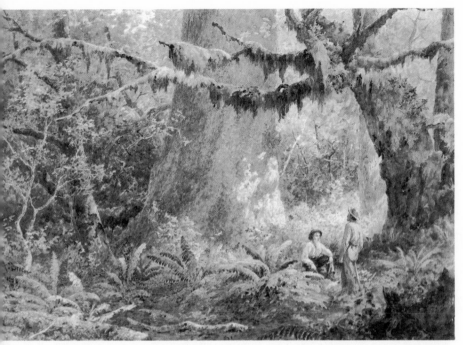

XII—Lucius O'Brien. *A British Columbian Forest*, 1888. Watercolour, 21¼ x 30. NGC.

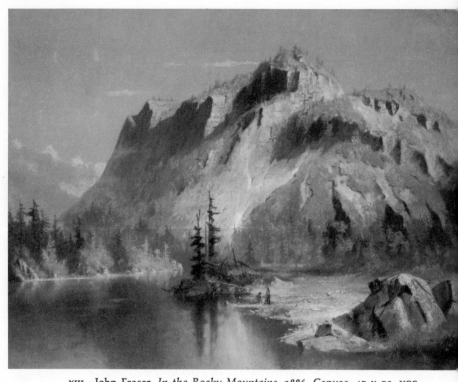

XIII—John Fraser. *In the Rocky Mountains*, 1886. Canvas, 45 x 50. NGC.

art scene after his resignation from the osa. About 1883 he left Toronto for Chicago and eventually went to New York. He maintained his Canadian connections, however, and when, in 1886, Sir William Van Horne of the Canadian Pacific Railway offered free passes to the Rockies for artists, Fraser was one of many who took up the offer. †*In the Rocky Mountains* (NGC) of 1886 was first owned by Gordon Brown of the Toronto *Globe*. With its wonderfully luminous colour, it is one of the finest pictures by the artists who chose to express the quality of the sublime in the Canadian landscape during the late sixties, seventies, and eighties.

This style of painting found yet another exponent in a Toronto-based painter who has in recent years received but brief attention from writers: FREDERICK ARTHUR VERNER (1836-1928). Born in Sheridan, Ont., he admired Paul Kane when he was a youth and decided to become a painter. With that intention he left for England in 1856 but soon joined the British army. In 1860-1 he fought in the British Legion with Garibaldi's troops in the liberation of Italy. In 1862 he returned to Toronto where he befriended Kane in his retirement. Following the ideas of the older artist, he travelled in the west recording the Indians and by 1870 was painting large horizontal oils. Only ostensibly based on Indian subjects, they were primarily concerned to express a sense of quietude, of magnificent peace. By 1873 he was the most popular artist working in Toronto. If we compare his *Indian Encampment at Sunset* (WAG) of that year with Fraser's *A Shot in the Dawn*—particularly the sky—we

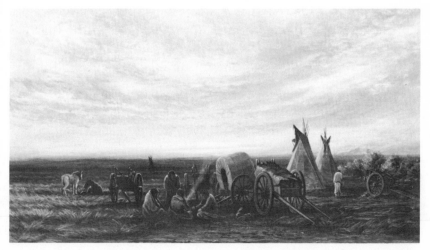

F.A. Verner. *Indian Encampment at Sunset*, 1873. Canvas, 20¼ x 36. WAG.

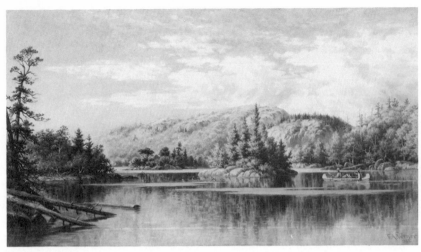

F.A. Verner. *The Upper Ottawa*, 1882. Canvas, 32½ x 59¾. NGC.

see that Verner shared the other artist's understanding of the qualities of light and colour and the force of sublime natural effects. By the eighties he had totally assimilated these concerns into his particular vision of landscape. Like Fraser and O'Brien—his contemporaries in Toronto—he was moved by the profound sweep of the Canadian sky. *The Upper Ottawa* (NGC) of 1882, full of the crystal light of a northern lake, is breathtaking in its stillness and clarity. It is a large painting, almost five feet wide.

Fraser, as we have seen, left Toronto about 1883. O'Brien painted until his death in 1899; but after 1890, when he retired from the presidency of the RCA, he attempted no ambitious works. Verner, perhaps sensing the passing of a generation, moved to London, Eng., about 1890. These three painters were among the first to make a concerted attempt to comprehend the Canadian experience in terms of the land itself. But they were replaced by a vigorous younger group of artists who looked outside of Canada, to Paris, for the necessary equipment and approach to express their sense of themselves as Canadian artists.

7

The 'French' Period
in Canadian Art
1880-1915

During the French colonial period, painting in Canada was naturally derived from the mother country. After the British Conquest of 1760 this influence began to diminish, although some artistic connections persisted. But with the French Revolution in 1789, even such cultural ties as the occasional training of an artist in France were broken, and if Antoine-Sébastian Plamondon briefly re-established the French-Canadian artistic allegiance, his pupil Théophile Hamel chose instead to follow the international current and studied in Rome and Florence. For the next thirty years other French Canadians followed his example. The strong landscape school that developed during this time in Montreal and Toronto drew on English, German, and American attitudes. French painting, for Canadians, held little or no interest.

By 1875, however, young art students in Canada again began to look to Paris and by 1890 virtually every artist of note under the age of thirty aspired to study in the French capital. At that time French painting had come to be considered the most accomplished in the world. Paris was the art capital, much as New York is today, and everyone looked to Paris for standards of quality and signs of trends. Painting was taken very seriously there: it had not only a broad and passionate public following but government support that was matched nowhere else. Another attraction was the large and inexpensive art-education system that had developed. The government-supported Ecole des Beaux-Arts was initially the most popular school, but as more and more students flocked to the capital, an informal system of private 'academies' developed. Here, for a relatively small fee, a student was supplied with plaster casts, live models, and criticism twice weekly by a renowned French painter. These academies proliferated, and by 1890 the largest and most famous, Julian's, had an enrolment of between 1,000 and 1,500 students, spread over ten large studios. There was no prescribed course of study and no official graduation. You judged your progress from the remarks made during criticism periods and, when a certain standard had been reached, by submitting works to the official Salon.

The Salon was yet another attraction Paris held out to young artists. Established by the state in 1673 as an annual showplace of current French painting, its reputation diminished in the nineteenth century because the selection process tended to support established artists to the exclusion of more experimental ones. It finally grew to be so controversial that in 1881 the running of the Salon was given to the new Société des artistes français; this resulted in a larger, more open exhibition that attracted more and more foreigners who worked in the French manner. While the Salon continued to establish standards of quality for the general public, it gradually became less significant to the more experimental French painters; during the last two decades of the century it became an object of derision to avant-garde figures like Gauguin and Van Gogh. These radical innovators ultimately triumphed in the struggle for critical and public approval, however, and as a consequence the great academic masters of the last years of the century have been relegated to the basements of our museums.

But in the eighties and nineties the names of Gérôme, Meissonier, Cabanel, and Bouguereau held a powerful attraction for young Canadian artists. All four painted in a highly finished naturalistic style that had enormous popular appeal. Their incredibly detailed, yet often large canvases functioned much as epic historical films do today: they were built upon extensive documentary knowledge—of animal and human anatomy, of the subtle graduations of colour and light—and imparted some psychological or emotional 'message'. They were often rich in what film makers call 'production values'. The academic system was set up in order to train the student systematically in the skills he would need to marshall all the necessary elements to 'construct' a vast heroic image—again much as a movie director does today. (The Toronto painter George Reid, after study in Paris, actually constructed studio 'sets' of hay-lofts, country kitchens, and the like in which to pose his models.) The basis of this academic system was a thorough training in the depiction of the human figure. The kind of large finished sketch that resulted—called an 'academy' and completed probably millions of times by hundreds of thousands of students—was usually a monochromatic exercise in tone rather than a naturalistic colour rendering and was meant to develop an intimate knowledge of the form and structure of the human body, and of art.

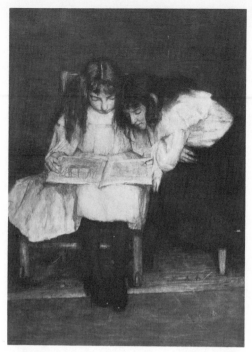

William Brymner. *Two Girls Reading*, 1898.
Canvas, 40½ x 29¼. NGC.

American artists responded to this approach two decades before Canadians. It is natural, then, that the first Canadian-born painter to study in Paris in the late nineteenth century first studied in the United States. WYATT EATON (1849-96) really was an American painter. Though born in the Eastern Townships (of American parents), he moved to New York City at the age of eighteen and never lived in Canada again. He first studied art in New York but in 1872 went to Paris and enrolled in the Ecole des Beaux-Arts under the famous Jean-Léon Gérôme. He later came to admire the work of Jean-François Millet, the great painter of peasant subjects who died the year before Eaton returned to the United States. Eaton's mature style, as in *The Harvest Field* (MMFA) of 1884, combines Millet's subject matter with the high finish and precise composition of Gérôme.

WILLIAM BRYMNER (1855-1925) was the first Canadian to study in Paris who later had a wide influence in Canada. His father was the first Dominion Archivist, and young William was able to study architecture with the government architect in Ottawa. In 1876 he was sent to Paris but soon gave up architecture for painting and enrolled in the Académie Julian, where he was instructed by William Bouguereau and Tony

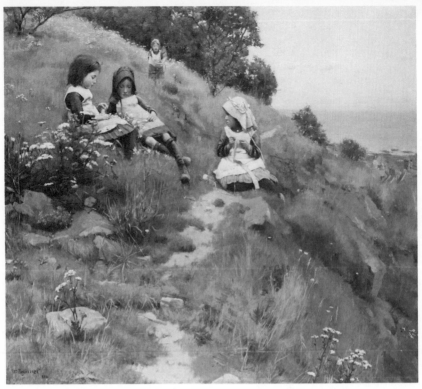

William Brymner. *A Wreath of Flowers*, 1884. Canvas, 47¼ x 55. NGC.

Robert-Fleury, famous exponents of 'grand manner' naturalism. At the Salon he was particularly attracted to the work of Ernest Meissonier, whose highly detailed illustrative paintings were immensely popular with the French public. Although Brymner apparently never attempted a large historical subject, he did specialize in domestic figure scenes until after the turn of the century. In the best of these the drawing and the application of paint are loose and broad. The *Two Girls Reading* (NGC) of 1898 also displays a careful treatment of light and his understanding of the force of a simple emphatic composition—effects he had learned in France.

Brymner stayed in Paris for nine years before settling in Montreal in 1885. The year before leaving he completed his masterpiece, *A Wreath of Flowers* (NGC), as proof of having mastered the rich detail and subtle tones that were then favoured in Paris. The year after his return to Montreal he was accepted as a member of the Royal Canadian Academy and deposited this picture in the National Gallery as his diploma piece. It was doubtless seen as work of an advanced order, but it did not cause a shock, for the French style had by then become almost familiar. While

Brymner was still in France, the trickle of Canadian students to Paris had become a flow.

ROBERT HARRIS (1849-1919) of Charlottetown, P.E.I., arrived in Paris a year after Brymner. He received his first training in Boston and by the end of 1876, at the age of twenty-seven, had reached London with enough money to enrol in the Slade School, which was then run by a Frenchman, Alphonse Legros. Three months later, encouraged by old schoolmates from Boston and no doubt by his contact with Legros, he decided to go to Paris. In the fall of 1877 he enrolled in the studio of Léon Bonnat, who was then considered to be one of the great painters of biblical and historical subjects.

Pranks, arguments, even fighting went on almost continuously in the studios, except for two afternoons a week when the master made his criticisms. Nonetheless most of the students—from all over the world— were serious in their work. Harris felt he was making great progress. After a year, when he believed he had attained a high standard of quality, he returned to Canada. Realizing that Toronto in 1879 was the principal art centre in Canada, he settled there and immediately became the object of attention with works like *The Chorister* (NGC) of 1880. George Reid, who was then a young student, remembered that Harris's arrival caused 'great excitement' in Toronto. He was asked to teach drawing at the art school and, according to Reid, 'almost at once introduced the French way of working, thereby considerably changing the teaching methods in the school.'

Harris stayed in Toronto only until the late spring of 1881 but he made a mark. He succeeded Lucius O'Brien as vice-president of the Ontario Society of Artists and encouraged young painters to look to Paris. He himself returned there in November 1881, joining an American sketch club and re-enrolling with Bonnat. He also sent a picture to the Salon of 1882, which to his great surprise was hung! And he enrolled at the Académie Julian under Jean-Paul Laurens and Alexandre Cabanel. This practice of studying with a number of masters appears to have been common with more experienced foreign students. It meant that their lives revolved almost totally around study, the activities of fellow students, and the annual Salon, and that they acquired even greater facility of technique and learned to produce even more dramatic 'effects' in their paintings. Like most foreigners, Harris also took the opportunity to travel. In September 1882 he left for Italy where he self-consciously steeped himself in the values of the European cultural past. Early in 1883 he was back in Canada.

As the Canadian artist most familiar with current techniques of monumental history painting, Harris was asked by the federal government to accept the most important official commission ever to be offered in Canada: the large group composition, *The Fathers of Confederation*. Harris approached the project in correct academic fashion. He collected reams of data on the people to be portrayed, prepared monochromatic gouache studies of various possible compositions, and finally prepared an oil sketch and a full-size charcoal cartoon before proceeding with the actual painting. The whole process took him two years. His finished picture was destroyed in the great Parliament fire during the First World War and all we have now are the cartoon and the preparatory sketches. The vigour and richness of the oil sketch (reproduced) and the monumental quality of the cartoon suggest that the painting was more successful than the static, lifeless group we are accustomed to seeing in contemporary engravings and more recent copies. This commission launched Harris as one of Canada's most fashionable portraitists. His **Sir Hugh Allan* (NGC) of 1885 seems to epitomize the self-confident spirit that was then welding Canada into a concrete reality. Its painstaking naturalism and substantial 'presence' are in the French style, yet it has great individuality. But Harris received the warmest response from the younger artists of the day with such genre subjects as the *Meeting of the School Trustees* (NGC) of 1885, and his deeply felt and sensitively expressed picture (1886) of his wife at a harmonium, called *†Harmony* (NGC). The ease with which he captured the beauty of the moment—placing figure and instrument in a convincing space and enveloping all in an atmosphere of tranquillity—is still moving today.

PAUL PEEL (1860-92), with his 'slick' technique and sentimental subjects, is the Canadian who comes closest to embodying in his art all that is popularly meant by the term 'academic' painting. Born in London, Ont., he was a precocious student and began studying at the Pennsylvania Academy in Philadelphia in 1877 when he was only seventeen. He worked under the Academy's famous teacher, the great Thomas Eakins, who, having studied in Paris, was causing a stir with his innovations. By 1880 Peel was studying with Gérôme at the Beaux-Arts and later with Lefebvre at Julian's. Both were masters of the slick brush, and as early as 1881—when he painted *The Spinner* (MMFA)—Peel had brought his handling of their style to a professional level. He had learned to paint with breadth as well, and a picture like **Devotion* (NGC) of 1881 impresses us with its light and space and natural ease of modelling—good solid academic virtues.

Although Peel married a Danish art student and settled in Europe, he continued to exhibit work in Canada and was therefore well known to

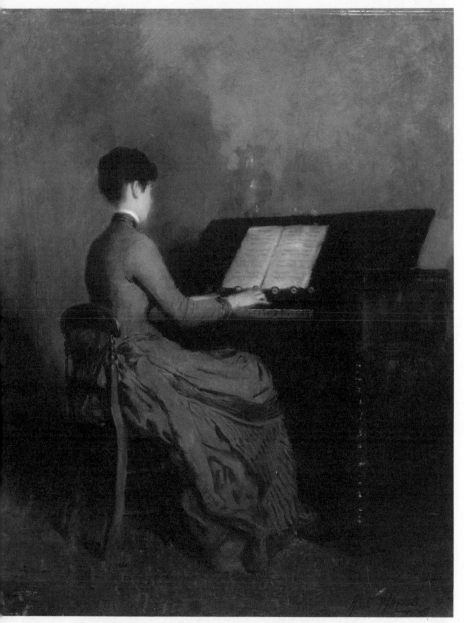

XIV—Robert Harris. *Harmony*, 1886. Board, 12 x 9¾. NGC.

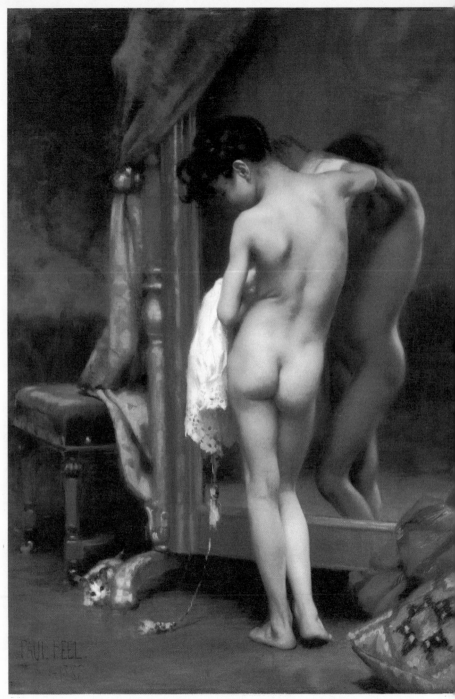

xv—Paul Peel. *A Venetian Bather*, 1889. Canvas, 61½ x 44½. NGC.

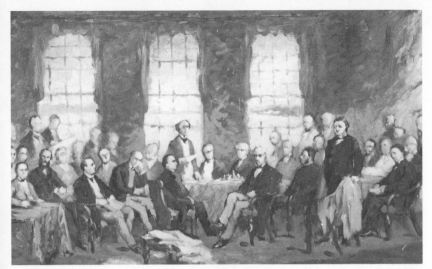

Robert Harris. *The Fathers of Confederation (Study)*, 1883. Canvas, 13 x 22½. Confederation Art Gallery, Charlottetown.

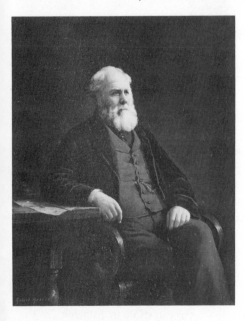

Robert Harris. *Sir Hugh Allan*, 1885. Canvas, 51 x 42. NGC.

the younger painters. In 1890, in fact, he held a one-man show and auction sale in Toronto where he exhibited his striking †*A Venetian Bather* (NGC), painted the year before in Paris. It was probably the first nude to be publicly exhibited in Toronto. The innocence of the young subject in her exotic setting allowed viewers who normally would be outraged at the display of such seductive flesh to luxuriate in the

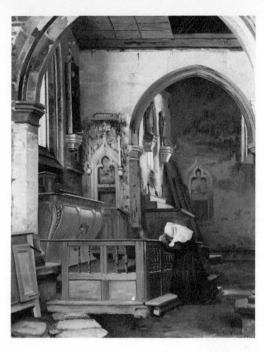

Paul Peel. *Devotion*, 1881.
Canvas, 35¾ x 27½ NGC.

delicious curves and soft glow; to savour pleasure for its own sake.
That same year his *After the Bath* (AGO) won a bronze medal at the
Salon. Probably today his most famous picture, it was found to be immensely appealing then too, and Sarah Bernhardt was among the collectors who vied to buy it off the Salon wall. It went to the Hungarian
state collection. Peel was rapidly becoming the first Canadian artist to
attract an international reputation. He unfortunately died in Paris only
two years later at the age of thirty-one.

Another painter who became so involved in the Paris art scene that
he never returned home was WILLIAM BLAIR BRUCE (1859-1906) of Hamilton. He studied with Bouguereau at Julian's from 1881, and, like Peel,
married a Scandinavian—a Swede. He lived longer than Peel, and probably as a consequence attempted more ambitious canvases than the
London painter. His huge paintings of glistening nudes—*La Joie des
néréides* (NGC) is nine feet square—were never exhibited in Canada
during his lifetime, however. Bruce had a reputation in Sweden by the
end of the century and his home on the Island of Gotland is now a
small museum housing works left by his sculptress wife and himself.

About 1889-90 a second wave of Canadians began to arrive in Paris
—most, it would appear, inspired by Robert Harris if they were from
Toronto or by William Brymner if they were from Montreal. The only
one to persist in the strict academic style of monumental figure painting

so prominent among the earlier Canadians was GEORGE REID (1860-1947). Indeed, he seemed to believe most in the academic precepts. Peel and Bruce discovered that there was a comfortable living to be made in the lucrative export market that existed for fashionable French painting— for which they had to stay close to Paris—but Reid never had any doubt that he would return home to apply newly acquired techniques to the examination of Canadian subjects and for the edification of a Canadian audience.

Reid was born on a farm near Wingham, in western Ontario. His father considered his youthful ambition to be an artist unmanly, but as the boy persisted he was apprenticed at the age of fifteen to a local architect. He enjoyed this experience enough to practise architecture later in a gentlemanly fashion, but he still burned to be a painter. So in 1878, at eighteen, he moved to Toronto and enrolled in the Ontario School of Art. The few paintings there were the first he had set eyes upon, except for some he had seen on a brief visit to the home of William Cresswell, who lived near Wingham.

Reid witnessed the great excitement in the fall of 1879 caused by the arrival in Toronto of the first artist with an up-to-date French training, Robert Harris. To his delight Harris took over one of his classes and proceeded to teach the French method of picture making; but with one key omission.

Nude models were not then posed in Toronto. Reid had read an article about the Pennsylvania Academy of Fine Arts and its radical teacher, Thomas Eakins, and left for Philadelphia as soon as he could. Accepted by Eakins, he received an intensive training in anatomy, life drawing, and pictorial structure. He was with Eakins from the fall of 1882 until the spring of 1885 and was among his last students at the Academy. In conflict with the reactionary forces in that institution for some time, the famous painter was finally forced to resign in 1886 for daring to remove the loin-cloth from a male model in the women's life class!

After graduation Reid married a fellow student from the Pennsylvania Academy and honeymooned on the continent, staying for ten days in the French capital; he could not yet afford to study there. In later years he remembered that this short trip, which fortunately coincided with the Salon, reaffirmed him in his belief that it was French painting that presented the greatest possibilities to the modern artist. Not everyone would have agreed. In fact when John Hodgsen, Royal Academician, was asked to comment on the Canadian participation at the 1886 Colonial and Indian Exhibition, his one strong note of disapproval was for the extent of French influence evident in the Canadian paintings—the

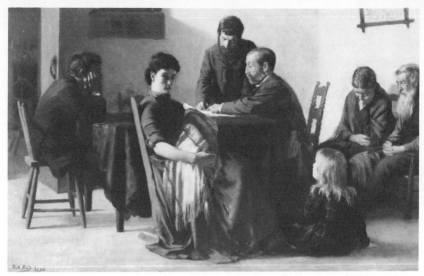

George Reid. *Mortgaging the Homestead*, 1890. Canvas, 50½ x 83½. NGC.

new tendency to produce broad effects and dramatically balanced tones. No one listened, of course, least of all the painters. Robert Harris commented that 'most of the old English Academicians' ideas of art rise to the level of a sort of Christmas card, and they are down on what they consider "Frenchy"!' Reid simply worked the harder to raise money to return to France and in the summer of 1888 he and his wife made it. They were met by Paul Peel, who found them a studio in the Latin Quarter. Their neighbour was Eugène Grasset, the famous French poster artist.

By the spring of 1889 Reid and his wife were fully involved in student rounds. Julian's seemed full of Canadians. Peel had signed up again. Brymner was there that spring, along with Maurice Cullen and Joseph Saint-Charles—also from Montreal—and Curtis Williamson from Toronto. Reid distinguished himself beyond all of them by tying for first place in figure competition. That same year he had a painting accepted at the Salon, and when he returned home in November it was in the full belief that he was an accomplished exponent of the most advanced painting of his day. His first painting in Toronto marshalled all of his talents to a theme from his childhood: *Mortgaging the Homestead*. It was deposited in the National Gallery when he was elected a full member of the Royal Canadian Academy the next spring.

Reid continued to send pictures to the Salon and to the Pennsylvania Academy, a good proportion of which were accepted; some were even sold. His usual working procedure involved the building of a 'set'—a hay-loft for his *Forbidden Fruit* (AGH) of 1889—and when his picture

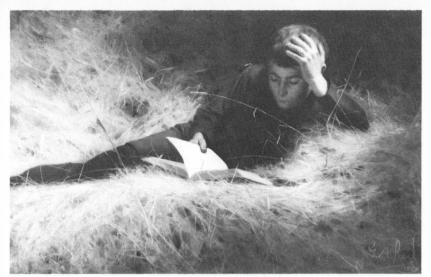

George Reid. *Forbidden Fruit*, 1889. Canvas, 30½ x 48. AGH.

was completed this set was cleared away and a private studio viewing was held for the Toronto art-public. Then the picture was sent off for exhibition. His paintings were large—*Mortgaging the Homestead* is seven feet wide—so one canvas could dominate a room crowded with people. And his studio would have been crowded, for Reid's work caught on immediately when he returned to Toronto. His striking light-and-shade effects, the dramatic placement of figures, and particularly the strong native sentiment in Reid's large 'show-pieces', appealed to the growing public interest in art. Reid sold steadily and for good prices. When the Ontario School of Art, his alma mater, was reorganized during the summer of 1890 as the Central Ontario School of Art and Design, he was hired as painting instructor.

His ambition went far beyond this conventional success, however. When he had been in Paris a program to decorate the Hôtel de Ville was announced and this sparked in Reid a lifelong ambition to do mural work. All the great academicians were heroic muralists. Their art was unashamedly 'public' in its subject and treatment and they sought exalted public situations for its display. With high hopes Reid approached Toronto City Council with an ambitious decorative scheme for the newly completed City Hall. His proposal was rejected for lack of funds. Reid persisted, struggling with various committees, until finally in desperation in 1897 he offered to begin the scheme at his own expense. Council of course agreed, and two years later Reid's free contribution to the decoration of the Toronto City Hall was installed in the entrance hall. Meanwhile he had received a number of domestic mural commissions—so many, in fact, that by the turn of the century he had largely stopped making large genre pictures.

Reid visited Paris again in 1896 and for the first time looked at the Impressionists. He had been developing an interest in landscape painting and the work of Monet encouraged him to eliminate detail, to break open his brushstrokes to let in light, and to key up his colour. Such 'impressionist' canvases as his *Vacant Lots* (NGC) of 1915 delighted his public after the turn of the century almost as much as had his earlier genre scenes. But as the years progressed and Reid grew older his landscapes grew darker, more traditional in composition, and much less interesting.

Reid probably would have found more sympathetic patronage for his mural schemes in Québec than he ever did in Toronto. CHARLES HUOT (1855-1930), who was born in Québec, and first studied there to be a teacher, enrolled in the Ecole des Beaux-Arts in Paris under Cabanel in 1878. Returning to Canada in 1886 he was then able to begin a career as a muralist that occupied him for the next forty years! His large historical murals were usually dull repetitions of tired formulae—*Le Premier parlement de Québec*, completed for the Québec Salle de l'Assemblée Législative in 1913, is his most famous—but his smaller studies have always been sought by collectors. *La Bataille des Plaines d'Abraham* (Maurice and Andrée Corbeil, Montreal) of 1900 is an exhilerating virtuoso performance. Such heroic themes obviously excited his creativity, but it was a long series of Church commissions that assured him his livelihood.

French-Canadian painters had traditionally sought patronage and direction from the Church and, as a curious mixture of educational experimentation and practical economics, the practice persisted in at least one instance in 1890. Abbé Chabert, an instructor at the Ecole des Arts et Manufactures in Montreal, devised a scheme whereby some of his old students would be sent to Paris for special studies at the Ecole des Beaux-Arts. Their training would involve the particular preparation of studies for a religious mural, for on their return to Montreal they were to execute a mural program in the Sacre-Coeur Chapel at Notre-Dame. The curé of Notre-Dame would, in return for this promised service, pay their sea passage. Believing this to be a relatively inexpensive way of obtaining a decorated chapel, the curé agreed to the arrangement. Two of Chabert's graduates who had only recently returned from two years in Paris—LUDGER LAROSE (1868-1915) and JOSEPH FRANCHÈRE (1866-1921) —were the first to leave in December 1890. Both soon completed their required work at the Beaux-Arts. Franchère then returned home and

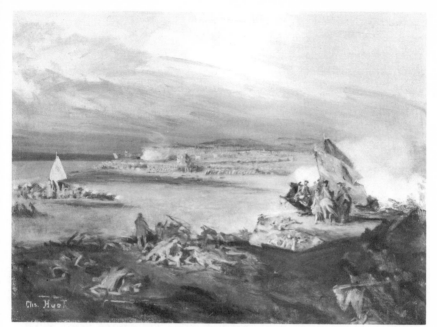

Charles Huot. *La Bataille des Plaines d'Abraham*, 1900. Canvas, 16 x 22½. Maurice and Andrée Corbeil, Montreal.

Larose went on to Rome to copy Old Masters. JOSEPH SAINT-CHARLES (1868-1956), CHARLES GILL (1871-1918), and HENRI BEAU (1863-1949) were also involved over the next two years. Their murals are in the chapel of Notre-Dame still; but they are minor embellishments to that magnificent cathedral (the largest church in North America when it was built).

All of these Chabert students continued to work as portraitists and church decorators (except for Charles Gill, who became a noted poet), but none was ever to achieve the fame of a young religious decorator from Arthabaska.

MARC-AURÈLE DE FOY SUZOR-COTÉ (1869-1937) had gone to Paris in 1889 to train as a singer, but in 1892 he contracted a serious throat infection that abscessed, and subsequent surgery destroyed any possibility of a singing career. He thereupon enrolled in the Ecole des Beaux-Arts under Bonnat and Elie Delaunay. A quick student, he progressed to the point of inclusion in the Salon of 1894. Upon graduation two years later he returned home briefly, but was soon back in Paris. In 1898 he enrolled at Julian's under Constant and Lefebvre. He also attended the Colarossi Academy, began to exhibit regularly in the Salon, and became the centre of a small French-Canadian group that met regularly at the Café Fleurus. Suzor-Coté had taken an early interest in landscape, but academic traditions remained very strong for him and as late as 1902 he painted an historical composition, *La Mort de Montcalm* (MQ). By this time he had begun to assimilate other influences, however, and in his *La Jeunesse en plein soleil* (NGC) of 1913 he shows his acceptance of the high-keyed colour and patterned brushwork he had found in Impressionism. Much like George Reid, Suzor-Coté became more conservative as he aged, and his work from before the First World War is the most adventurous he was ever to paint.

The academies of Paris, which exerted such an overwhelming effect on virtually every young Canadian artist during the eighties and nineties, inevitably lost their relevance. After the turn of the century very few painters—if any—from Toronto found their way to Julian's or the Colarossi. In Montreal, where there was both a culture based on the French tongue and William Brymner, the case was slightly different.

Brymner taught at the Art Association of Montreal from 1886 until 1921 and as a consequence Paris continued to exert a pull on young Montrealers that was unknown to most other Canadians. A. Y. Jackson, for instance, went there to study in 1907 and enrolled at Julian's under Laurens. But, like James Wilson Morrice, another Montrealer who had entered Julian's seventeen years earlier, Jackson did not stay long. After six months he quit the studio to travel for two years, visiting all of the painters' spots around France and painting assiduously. He even exhibited in the Salon. But he knew, as he writes in his autobiography, that it 'catered to foreigners, handing out bushels of medals each year'. It clearly was not the Salon that attracted him, nor the academies. It was, as he discovered after returning to Montreal, the artistic climate— the great numbers of painters, the artistic quarrels, the excitement of experimentation. As soon as he could save enough, he was back again for another year and a half.

8

Homer Watson
and
Ozias Leduc
1880-1930

Two of the very few young Canadian painters of the last two decades of the nineteenth century who did not eagerly rush off to Paris are among our greatest artists of the years around the turn of the century. Both Homer Watson and Ozias Leduc were born in tiny rural communities and both chose to continue living there. Both were largely self-taught and visited Europe only in their maturity.

HOMER WATSON (1855-1936) was born at Doon, Ont., now a suburb of Kitchener. His father, who owned a mill there and was an educated man with a small library, died when Homer was six, removing any pressure that might have developed for the boy to go into the family trade. By the age of fifteen, Watson had already revealed a consuming interest in art—fed exclusively, it would seem, by the illustrated magazines of the day. Like Horatio Walker and George Reid, he is another of the fruits of that rich rural culture found in Ontario after mid-century. And, like others of his generation, he found the germinating home inadequate to his aspirations and was drawn to the provincial capital.

Watson first visited Toronto in 1872 and called on T. Mower Martin, who gave him a little encouragement when he saw his drawings. Two years later, when he had turned nineteen, Watson received a small inheritance from his grandfather and moved to Toronto.

'I did not know enough to have Paris or Rome in mind,' he once wrote. 'I felt Toronto had all I needed and my first look at a collection of pictures was when I visited the Normal School to see the collection of old masters there.' This was the group of oil copies assembled by Egerton Ryerson almost twenty years before—the only public art gallery in Ontario. One of the few other galleries was the commercial premises of Notman-Fraser, and young Watson soon gravitated to that touchstone of art activity. There he met Henry Sandham, Lucius O'Brien, and

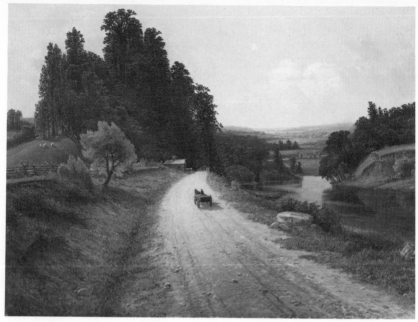

Homer Watson. *The Stone Road*, 1881. Canvas, 36 x 51¼. NGC.

of course John Fraser himself. He stayed in Toronto a little more than a year, working around Notman-Fraser's, sketching in the Normal School museum, and apparently receiving lessons from Fraser. It was probably Fraser who encouraged him to look further afield and in 1876 he left for New York City.

In New York, Watson visited the American landscape painter George Inness. He apparently called on Inness a number of times, and in emulation of the famous painter—then at the height of his career—he sketched along the Susquehanna and Hudson Rivers and in the Adirondacks on a leisurely journey home. Watson had decided firmly to become an artist. He set up a small studio in Doon and divided his time between there and Toronto, where he shared a studio with another painter.

His first real canvases began to appear. One of the earliest is a strange, romantic vision, *The Death of Elaine* (AGO), painted in 1877, probably at Doon, although possibly in New York. Illustrating the Tennyson poem *The Idylls of the King*, it is accomplished in treatment for a beginner; it has been suggested that it reveals a knowledge of current European, most likely French, art. (The Philadelphia centennial exhibition of 1876 included the first large group of French paintings seen in America and Watson could easily have visited it from New York.) *The Death of Elaine* is a 'sport', however. Watson was a landscape painter, and although he periodically turned to literary themes, all of his important pictures are landscapes. His earliest—such as *Landscape with River* (AGO) of 1878 and *Coming Storm in the Adirondacks* (MMFA) of 1879—are based on his American trip and in fact follow the style of late Hudson River School painting he would have seen in New York. Dry and contrived to our eyes, they probably represented the very appearance of art to Watson; that they depicted American scenes would only have added to their 'authenticity'.

Watson caught on quickly in Toronto. He first exhibited professionally—with the Ontario Society of Artists—in 1878, and was elected a full member the next year. In 1880, at the age of twenty-five, he was included in the first exhibition of the Royal Canadian Academy. Much to his surprise, his *The Pioneer Mill* (Windsor Castle Collection) was bought from the exhibition by Princess Louise. And what was even more newsworthy, it was bought for Queen Victoria! The story appeared in all the newspapers and Watson almost overnight became one of Canada's more famous painters. Although Lucius O'Brien was also honoured with a purchase, he was the president of the RCA, and a mature artist of forty-eight.

The purchase confirmed Watson's direction as an artist and it also allowed him to marry. He and his wife bought a house in Doon and settled in. He engaged a Toronto dealer and for the next seven years lived a quiet yet productive life, painting around Doon and leaving all business to his agent. These years resulted in Watson's strongest and in many respects his most Canadian canvases. With the aim of depicting his immediate environment, he spent years wandering, looking, thinking, and sketching. Intense experiences gave rise to large canvases such as *The Stone Road* (NGC) of 1881. Because Watson was finding his own way virtually isolated from other painters, such a work has its obvious faults. Yet it has tremendous strength. The curve of the road introduces just enough tension to keep the picture taut—frozen, as in a dream, with every iron-hard detail assuming great significance.

In May 1882 Oscar Wilde, the famous Irish writer and tastemaker, visited Toronto on a North American tour and there saw Watson's work. Believing he had unexpectedly found an artist of rare talent, he exclaimed 'The Canadian Constable!'. Watson, of course, had never seen a painting of Constable's; any similarity had doubtless grown out of a shared concern with the intense, intimate expression of familiar landscape. The remark, which made an impression on Watson, was reinforced when Wilde later wrote commissioning a work and offering support if Watson ever visited England. The painter's head remained unturned, however. Montreal collectors were beginning to buy, and a modest but steady income allowed Watson to keep working in his beloved Doon.

Watson's art was developing out of a driving need to comprehend the meaning of the familiar. His pictures were complex in their detail and had the slightly disjointed clarity of a dream vision. They were strong and individual in suggesting the strangeness of the particular when it is examined as a concept as well as a phenomenon. Many would have found them a bit naive.

When his work in the Colonial and Indian Exhibition held in London in 1886 was well received, Watson resolved to see what England offered. Before leaving Canada he wrote a friend in March 1887, 'Am painting like blazes. Have finished up that white road and dark sky affair and it is my best so far.' The picture—†*Before the Storm* (Mrs G. H. Strickland, Windsor)—was one of the best he was ever to paint, and suggests the route he might have followed if he had stayed in Canada. In clarity and quality it is, paradoxically, the closest he was to come to Constable.

Watson and his wife spent three years in England. He delivered the commissioned picture to Wilde, who introduced him to Whistler. He became interested in etching, and deciding that a print of *The Pioneer Mill* would sell well in Canada, he arranged with the Marquis of Lorne to see it again. He was flattered to find it hanging in the reception room at Windsor Castle. Lorne also helped him by recommending his work to the prestigious Goupil Gallery, and Watson was able to make some sales and to arrange to have pictures shown there regularly.

His art was irrevocably changed. *A Ravine Farm* (NGC) of 1889, painted near the end of his English sojourn, shows that he had been led away from his intense concern with content, with the detailed depiction of the vision he carried of his home environment. His new concern was with style as an end in itself: effect, breadth of handling, unified treatment, sweeping movement. *A Ravine Farm* is no longer particular, it has no magic of place. Though probably better painting, it is poorer art.

He returned to Doon. 'After some years of restless wandering in quest of adequate media of expression in art, a desire took possession of me to live again where I knew great quiet would blend itself luxuriously with the schemes I was developing for my painting. It came to me that among the nooks and scenes of this village nestling among the hills, I should find ample material to fix in some degree the infinite beauties that emanate from the mystery of sky and land. . . . True, the place was a village, and as such would, to a certain extent, hem me in, but in such an atmosphere, undisturbed by the clamour of man's con-

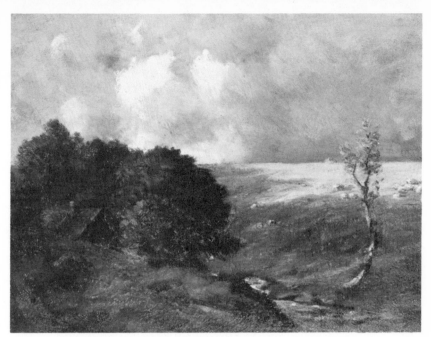

Homer Watson. *A Ravine Farm*, 1889. Canvas, 27¾ x 38¾. NGC.

tention, I could scarcely help being in accord with nature's spirit.' Although such reasoning was undoubtedly the basis for his decision to return, over the next thirty years the issue of *where* to live never left him. He often went back to London at the prompting of his English dealers and friends and maintained steady sales there, but he always returned to Doon to paint.

He was never to recapture the intensity of his involvement in the landscape of his home, although he struggled with his new style and finally achieved a degree of expression that was certainly above the ordinary. His *Log-cutting in the Woods* (MMFA) of 1893 won the first prize at the Art Association of Montreal Spring Show that year and was immediately bought by Lord Strathcona. Various prominent Montreal collectors vied for his works, and James Ross in particular almost guaranteed him support. Watson's stylish treatment of French Barbizon themes (see p. 118) appealed greatly to these collectors who were at the same time buying real Barbizon pictures. Perhaps feeling that this work suggested some compromise, he tried to reassert a commitment to his roots through a cycle of epic canvases depicting the pioneer beginnings of Waterloo County. But he succeeded in evoking only an idealized nostalgia. The paint handling is often very beautiful, but there is not the biting truth, the immediacy of experience of his pre-1887 canvases.

In 1899 Watson achieved the culmination of his international reputation with a successful one-man show in London, followed by another in New York. Returning to Doon, he painted the work he later considered to be his masterpiece: *The Flood Gate* (NGC). Certainly it is the finest painting in his mature manner. He deliberately chose a Constable subject, as though finally he felt equal to challenge the painter whose name had dogged him throughout his career. Watson now strove for breadth of treatment—one big idea rather than the accumulation of a group of small effects. No longer concerned with the detailed rendering of leaf, stone, and cloud, he gives a sweep to the whole: sky, trees, water, and brute animals all move in unison. Only man leans against the combined forces of nature.

The Flood Gate was shown at the Glasgow Institute to such acclaim that he was tempted once more to live in Britain. As Muriel Miller, his biographer, has commented: 'He decided against it finally, for he felt stultified in England and knew that the Canadian landscape had never failed to inspire him.' Watson's career continued into the twentieth century and he became first president of the Canadian Art Club. Work of this period is often monumental and is painted in a strange reddish-brown monochrome.

His wife died in 1918 and the loss shattered him. No longer able to paint, he wandered about aimlessly. One night she appeared to him, descending the stairs. The dream was so clear that he was not certain he was asleep. The experience changed his life. He adopted a notational style of painting he called 'impressionism' and returned to the artistic scene, accepting the presidency of the Royal Canadian Academy. After about 1922, however, deafness forced him almost to withdraw from public life. He had become a spiritualist and a friend of the Prime Minister (also a spiritualist), William Lyon Mackenzie King. King bought pictures from the artist and wrote to him about the trials of leadership.

In his later pictures Watson became enchanted with the problem of capturing light qualities. He has been unjustly accused of attempting to copy the Group of Seven, who had eclipsed him in the public eye. He in fact simply pursued to a logical conclusion his tendency to generalize forms and broaden his handling. In 1929 Watson visited the Rockies and the strongest of his last pictures are strange visions of mountain splendour. He died at Doon, aged eighty-one, a bankrupt, forgotten man. For most of his life he had struggled with the problem that has often plagued creative artists in Canada: whether to stay.

Although the career of OZIAS LEDUC (1864-1955) parallels Watson's in

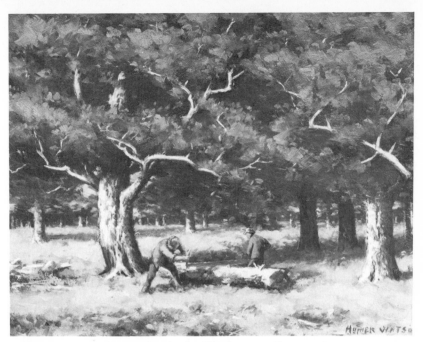

Homer Watson. *Log-cutting in the Woods*, 1894. Canvas, 18 x 24. MMFA.

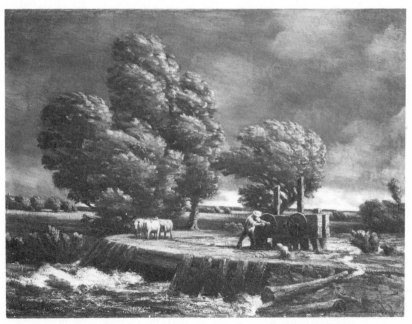

Homer Watson. *The Flood Gate*, 1900. Canvas, 32½ x 46¾. NGC.

many respects, it does not reflect this dilemma raised by foreign acclaim. Leduc enjoyed the appreciative attention of a few admirers during his life, but it was only after his death that a retrospective exhibition revealed the beauty of his work to even a national audience. This neglect was due both to Leduc's retiring mode of life and to the fact that he derived his livelihood from the traditional work of church decoration. His easel painting was almost exclusively for personal pleasure and that of a few friends.

Leduc was born at Saint-Hilaire, a small town nestled at the foot of a strange, steep-sided mountain east of Montreal. When he first began to paint there were no colours available except the serviceable paints used by his father, the village carpenter. Legend has it that he crushed stones to make pigments and that the resulting earth colours determined the range he was to prefer as a mature artist. None of these first works remains. They doubtless returned to dust.

Leduc's simple human qualities have been so generally praised that his life has taken on a saint-like quality. He does appear to have been an extraordinary man. He lived his whole adult life with his wife in a little house in the middle of a magnificent well-cared-for apple orchard on the slopes of Mont Saint-Hilaire. After he had decided to dedicate his life to painting and poetry, he built onto the house with his own hands a small stone library and a studio. He was the happiest of men and, according to those who knew him, the wisest.

Leduc worked very slowly, but he lived for ninety years and so accomplished much. His rare modesty, free of ambition and vanity, and his relative seclusion at Saint-Hilaire meant he had little involvement with other artists. Nevertheless he was for many years a member of municipal council, a church-warden, the founder and vice-president of the commission to arrange the decoration of his parish church of Saint-Hilaire, and a founding member and director of the regional historical society of Saint-Hyacinthe. He even wrote a history of Saint-Hilaire. His social priorities were thus very clear: his loyalties and concerns were exclusively centred on his immediate community—a community of proximity alone.

Leduc's artistic concerns reflected this intense sense of local community as well as the traditional Québec union of art and religion. He began working as an independent church decorator about 1890 and derived his livelihood from this occupation until his retirement, completing programs in twenty-seven cathedrals, churches, and chapels: a total of one hundred and fifty large paintings with interconnecting ornamentation. Church decoration fell into such disrepute in the later

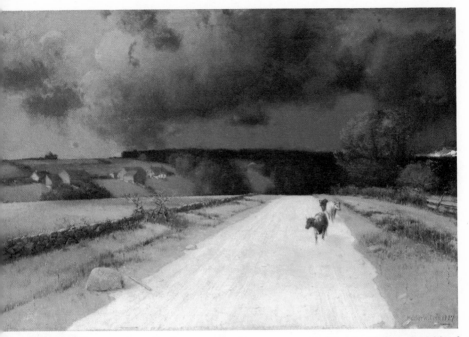

xvi—Homer Watson. *Before the Storm*, 1887. Canvas, 25 x 36. Mrs G. Hudson Strickland, Windsor, Ont.

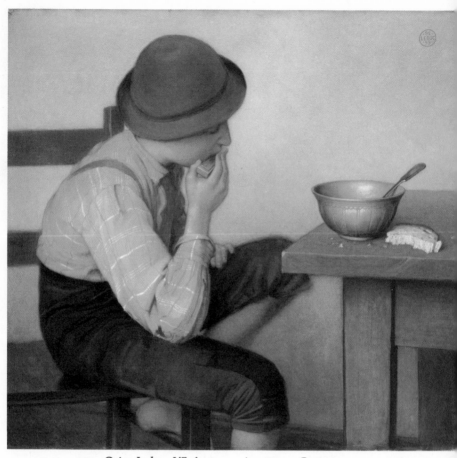

xvii—Ozias Leduc. *L'Enfant au pain*, 1892-9. Canvas, 20 x 22. NGC.

nineteenth century (much of that which survives in Québec is the work of hacks) that we have ignored this central aspect of Leduc's art: the activity on which he spent most of his time and energy remains virtually to be discovered. Jean-René Ostiguy has given some hints about what we might find. On the evidence of Leduc's canvases in the cupola of the Eglise du Saint-Enfant-Jésus in Montreal (c. 1916), and of his murals in the chapel of the Bishop's palace in Sherbrooke (1922-33)—his masterpiece, according to Ostiguy—Leduc appears to have single-handedly brought integrity back to the craft of church decoration.

He received his first training about 1880 with Luigi Cappello, one of the many foreign muralists to be employed by Québec churches in the late nineteenth century. Then in 1883 he assisted a friend of Charles Huot, the Jack-of-all-trades Adolphe Rho (1835-1905), on a decorative program at Yamachiche, just west of Trois-Rivières. His earliest known easel painting dates from four.years later. Painted when he was only twenty-three, *Les Trois Pommes* (Mme P.-E. Borduas, Belœil) is astonishingly accomplished. The apples seem to glow in the perfection of their natural geometry. Gilles Corbeil has remarked on how Leduc 'seems at every moment to have been conscious of some moral responsibility for the way he treated his canvases and handled his brush and his colours.' Such early still-lifes—they make up the bulk of his work from before 1900—are close in certain respects to the trompe l'œil painting then so popular in the United States. But Leduc never allowed his work to become formulary. He was not making these paintings to sell. He painted for private pleasure only in a slow search for meaning, for understanding. Consequently an impersonal, generalizing solution never entered his work. No two give the same 'feeling'. Their intense reality, their presence, becomes hallucinatory—truly mystical and religious. Like Watson's Canadian paintings between 1880 and 1886, they grew to satisfy personal needs, not to reflect an accepted idea of what 'art' should look like.

Leduc's remarkable †L'Enfant au pain (NGC), painted over a period of seven years (1892-9), reveals this same reverence for the simple appearances of life, this same intense reality. The precise colour and texture of shirt, bowl, and polished wood have been so obsessively pursued that the resulting images transcend the material. The silent musician plays in another world, at first so much like ours as to startle, but finally so ideal in its frozen moment that it represents a state of acute awareness towards which we can only aspire.

Two years before L'Enfant au pain was completed, Leduc took his one trip abroad—with Suzor-Coté. This brief visit to Paris seems not to have

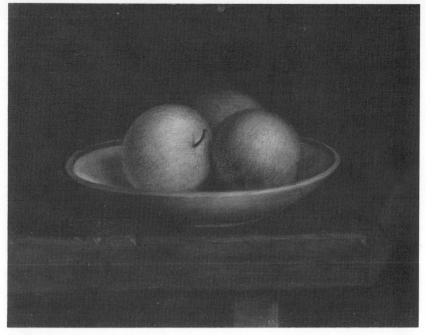

Ozias Leduc. *Les Trois Pommes*, 1887. Canvas, 9 x 12. Mme P.-E. Borduas, Belœil, Que.

markedly changed his art. His charmingly titled *Mon portrait* (NGC), painted two years later in 1899, is moody and atmospheric like some of his earlier still-lifes; a personality is formed from light out of the darkness. The current of the mainstream did not distract Leduc, unlike Watson. He accepted only what was consistent with his vision and would reinforce his art.

Leduc's retiring nature should not be stressed too much. He often picnicked with young poets from Montreal in his orchard on summer afternoons, and he illustrated a number of books as a result of these friendships. He also exhibited regularly in the AAM Spring Show, and with the RCA and OSA from 1891 until about 1920. By the turn of the century he had a small but loyal following. Perceptive artists outside his circle appreciated his work when they were able to see it. In a letter to a friend, A.Y. Jackson singled out Leduc's *Pommes vertes* as the best painting in the 1915 Spring Show, and the National Gallery bought it later that year.

This modest public attention culminated in 1916 when Leduc was invited to hold a one-man show at the new Bibliothèque Saint-Sulpice in Montreal. It was the only such exhibition he was ever to have; he apparently felt no motivation to court public favour. He was then fifty-

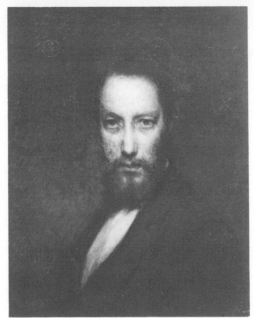

Ozias Leduc. *Mon portrait*, 1899. Board,
13 x 10¾. NGC.

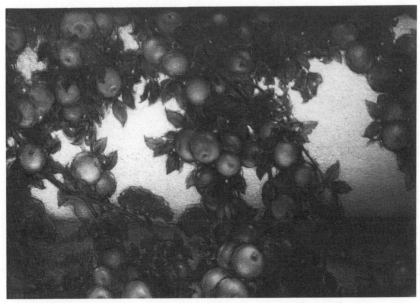

Ozias Leduc. *Pommes vertes*, 1914-15. Canvas, 24½ x 36½. NGC.

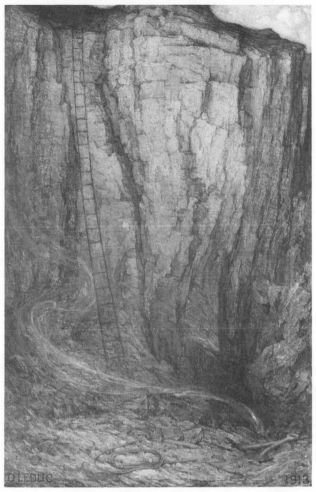

Ozias Leduc. *Fin du jour*, 1913. Canvas, 20 x 13¼. MMFA.

two. Two or three years before he had turned from still-life painting to landscape, and over the next eight years a series of strange, almost abstract visions of glowing light appeared. All are set on Mont Saint-Hilaire, the brooding geological accident that dominates the region around his home. All suggest symbolic meanings. Notice, in *Fin du jour* (MMFA), the rope-ladder hanging against the rock-face to the left and the wisp of smoke curling across the foreground. This work's alternate title—*Les Portes de fer*—only adds to the air of mystery. Jean-René Ostiguy has remarked that Leduc 'saw nature in the light of his dreams', and friends in Montreal, recognizing this 'other-worldly' quality of his vision, encouraged him to read symbolist authors like Huysmans and art historians like Emile Mâle, who in his books interpreted the symbolic meanings in the art of the great Christian eras. From 1916 Leduc's good friend, the priest Olivier Maurault, discussed with him the relevance of such symbolist painters as the Frenchman René Ménard and doubtless helped him to obtain magazines illustrating their work. It was Maurault as well, it appears, who directed him to the important symbolist theories of Maurice Denis, and much of Leduc's late and best church work—from about 1920 through to the mid-thirties—should be studied with the French religious painters' ideas and paintings in mind.

Leduc stopped exhibiting in 1920, even though most of his important church commissions were yet to appear, but he did continue to paint canvases. Many are portraits of friends, like *Le Père Breteux* (private collection) of about 1937. His work was now completely personal and totally free of public expectations or pressures. His latest paintings—like *Paysage de neige* (private collection) of 1939-40—show, like the later works of Homer Watson, a looser, more open quality and an absolute obsession with light. They are consistent with the vision he had pursued for almost sixty years.

Although both Watson and Leduc valued continuity, and sought it in the only way possible, by nurturing their roots, Ozias Leduc, who carried that concern to the point of virtual isolation, was paradoxically the one to make a real bridge to the future. Homer Watson had been passed over by the time he had died; no one followed in his footsteps. Leduc died in full awareness of the adulation of friends and of having fostered one of the great geniuses and leaders of the new art, Paul-Emile Borduas (see chapters 13 and 14). Borduas, who was born at Saint-Hilaire and often worked with Leduc as a church decorator from about 1920 through to 1932, has explained the debt he owed his master. Leduc showed him 'the way from the spiritual and pictorial atmosphere of the Renaissance to the power of illusion which leads into the future. Leduc's whole life shines with this magic illusion.'

9

The Canadian Art Club

1907-1915

While the Parisian academies continued to attract thousands of foreign art students throughout the nineties and into the twentieth century, and while the paintings produced as a result of this training continued in their thousands to please the vast public, the academic approach to painting suffered increasingly severe criticism from the more innovative painters. Academic painters were found to be guilty of cold objectivity, lifeless drawing, and overly reserved colouring. Their huge 'machines' were declared to be dull, superficial, often sentimental, and totally lacking any evidence of sensitive emotional commitment. In Paris such complaints had been heard for many years, but by the mid-seventies forceful alternatives to the slick narrative painting of the Salon had been found. The Impressionists began to attract foreign adherents after their first exhibition in 1874, and other alternatives also existed for students from across the Atlantic. During the 1870s a 'school' of Dutch artists collected in The Hague. Like the Impressionists, they were influenced by a group of painters that included Corot, Théodore Rousseau, and Millet who had lived around the hamlet of Barbizon in the forest of Fontainebleau. Working in direct response to nature, these Barbizon painters had brought a moving naturalism to landscape painting, elevating it to a position of public esteem. (The academicians had thought it greatly inferior as a subject to noble themes from the past.) Unlike the Impressionists—who saw everything in terms of light (colour=refracted light) and who strove to record their sensations objectively—the Hague School consciously expressed their feelings, their mood, in 'atmospheric', almost monochromatic paintings that stressed richness of tone. Observers referred to this as 'subjective' painting.

Yet another alternative, and one particularly attractive to the Anglo-American colony in Paris, was that represented by the work of James

McNeill Whistler, the American painter who by the time of his famous libel suit against the English critic Ruskin in 1878 was widely known for his refined studies of mood. A group was attracted to Whistler that was vigorously opposed to the academic values of the Salon. In 1898 it formed the International Society of Sculptors, Painters and 'Gravers, with Whistler as president. By the turn of the century the personal, expressive approach they advanced had superseded the academic style in the very academies themselves.

Canadians who studied in Europe—and they continued to do so in large numbers—began to reflect a tentative 'modernism'. The first evidence of changing concerns appeared in the whiter colours, looser brushwork, and studied attention to the effects of reflected light in the work of people like Brymner and Reid. But these vaguely 'impressionistic' touches were superficial, and the first shift away from academic naturalism in Canada was largely due to the influence of the Dutch painters of the late nineteenth century—notably the Hague School. By the late nineties, and particularly in Toronto, the young painter seeking serious instruction thought of looking for it—at least in part—in Holland. This preference was shared and probably stimulated by a number of prominent collectors in Montreal and Toronto who, acquiring the American taste for French Barbizon pictures rather late, soon discovered the similarly pastoral paintings of the Hague School. The lugubrious nature of the Dutch work also probably appealed to the Anglo-Saxon temperament more readily than did the heady sensuality of recent French painting. But for whatever reasons, large amounts of money were spent on these now almost-forgotten painters, and magnificent collections were assembled. Consequently the first art books ever published in Canada were *Landscape Painting and Modern Dutch Artists* (1906) and *The Subjective View of Landscape Painting* (1914)—a study of the work of Johannes Weissenbruch—both written by E.B. Greenshields, a prominent Montreal collector.

This taste began to be reflected in the exhibited work of at least two of the younger Toronto painters during the nineties, and most influentially in the paintings of the wealthy and independent young EDMUND MORRIS (1871-1913). Born in Perth, Ont., he attended his first art classes in Toronto. He soon moved on to the Art Students League in New York, where he studied with Kenyon Cox and William Merritt Chase, and then to Paris for the usual stint with Laurens and Constant at Julian's, and with Gérôme at the Ecole. Significantly he spent his summers painting in Holland. In 1896 he was back in Toronto and the next year exhibited his *Gathering Poppies, Holland* (AGO) in the RCA and then the

OSA. It was then bought by the famous local collector Byron (later Sir Edmund) Walker.

Morris's taste for Dutch subjects was tempered, however, by the fact that his father had been lieutenant-governor of Manitoba and the Northwest Territories, and the painter early developed a keen interest in the Indian people. In 1906 he accompanied a treaty commission to the James Bay region, and the following year he completed for the provincial government a large series of Indian portraits that are now in the ROM. He also sketched in the West. His *Indian Encampment on Prairie* (AGO) of about 1910, depicting a cluster of four teepees on a low horizon, is notable for the rich and subtle modulations of the immense sky: with its dark Dutch tonalities and its avoidance of any Kane-like documentation, it must have seemed strangely modern. Its interlocking range of moody earth-tones, from blue-black through to red, is unusually successful in evoking the binding forces of nature. Morris's typical works, however, were painted in the area of Québec City, where he worked with James Morrice, Brymner, and, more frequently, Horatio Walker. Dark, sonorous canvases like *The St Lawrence Near Québec* (NGC) of about 1912 seem to presage his tragic end. He drowned there in August 1913 while visiting Walker, aged only forty-two.

CURTIS WILLIAMSON (1867-1944), who was also born in a small Ontario town, Brampton, is the other young painter who introduced Dutch subjects and technique to Toronto before the turn of the century. Like Morris he first studied art in Toronto—with J.W.L. Forster (1850-1938) —but in 1889 he went directly to Julian's in Paris. After only a year he left the Academy and for the next two-and-a-half years worked mainly near the village of Barbizon. There he fraternized with a group of painters that included the two Philadelphians, Edward Redfield and Robert Henri, and the naturalist and illustrator, Ernest Thompson Seton (1860-1946). He returned to Toronto in 1892.

It is likely that Williamson had also visited the Low Countries, for immediately upon his return he painted his most famous early picture, *Klaasje* (NGC). A large portrait study of a red-cheeked Dutch woman, it emulates the rich tone and colour of Rembrandt and the gusto of Hals. In 1894 Williamson was back in Europe again, and for the next ten years he travelled mainly in the Low Countries, painting dark peasant interiors lit by single golden windows or a few glowing embers in a black grill.

In 1904, done with European travel, he returned to Toronto. During the summer of 1907 he visited Newfoundland, and back in his studio the following spring he painted the beautifully luminous and atmos-

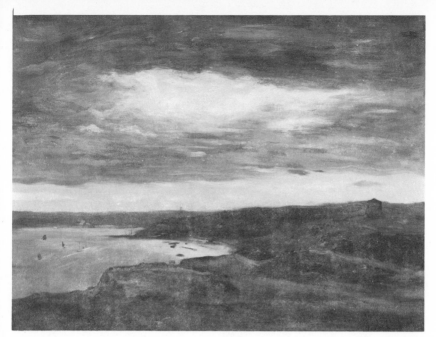

Edmund Morris. *The St Lawrence near Québec*, c. 1910. Canvas, 29¾ x 40. NGC.

pheric *Fish Sheds, Newfoundland* (NGC). More than four feet tall and free of anecdote or sentimentality, it was an ambitious, startling picture in its time. With such works as this, and his striking, uncompromising full-length portraits—like *Archibald Browne* (private collection, Kingston)—Williamson developed a considerable reputation as a difficult 'painters' painter'—a reputation he was able to prolong until after the First World War through his friendship with Dr James MacCallum, the Toronto ophthalmologist who was an early supporter of Tom Thomson and the Group of Seven. But he gradually shut himself off and in the years after the war became a cranky, impossible old man whose reputation finally passed into almost total oblivion.

In 1907, however, both Williamson and Morris were deeply disturbed by the tired, old-fashioned look of Canadian art as seen in the various annual exhibitions. They soon discovered that few shared their concern; those who might have been expected to do so had seen no reason to return from foreign studies and in some cases were launched on careers in New York or Paris. Change within existing structures was obviously hopeless: they must somehow lure the real talent back to Canada. Late in 1907, in consultation with some of Morris's collector friends, they formed the Canadian Art Club, a private exhibiting society supported by lay members. Professional membership was by invitation only and only modern 'subjective' work of the highest calibre was to be shown.

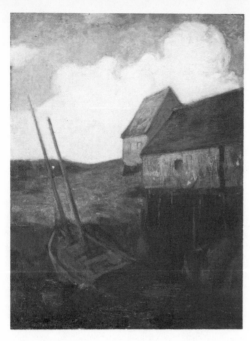

Curtis Williamson. *Fish Sheds,
Newfoundland,* 1908. Canvas,
50 x 38. NGC.

D.R. Wilkie, a Toronto banker, became honorary president, chiefly responsible for soliciting the support of concerned art-lovers. (Sir Edmund Osler took over the post on Wilkie's death in 1915.) It was then necessary to find a mature, successful, yet sympathetic artist as president. The perfect choice was found in Homer Watson, the respected 'sage of Doon', then at the peak of his international career. After a visit from Morris and Williamson, Watson agreed to serve and they began to draw up a membership list. At the top was an old friend of Watson's, Horatio Walker.

Born at Listowel, Ont., HORATIO WALKER (1850-1938) gravitated to Toronto at the age of fifteen and worked at Notman-Fraser's, where he first met Watson. Three years later he left for the United States and settled in New York City in 1878. He continued to visit Canada—in the summer of 1880 even walking from near Montreal to Québec City. The following year he went to Europe where he was obviously much influenced by the famous Barbizon painter Millet. In 1883 he re-established himself in New York and soon acquired a summer home in the Ile d'Orléans looking out on Québec City. Exhibiting principally in New York, he maintained contact with Montreal collectors, and through them (notably Charles Porteous) during the nineties renewed his friendship with Homer Watson. By 1907 he was easily the most famous Canadian-born painter, represented in most major American collections. The Canadian Art Club hoped to bring Walker's work back to Canada.

One of the first major cash purchases of the National Gallery was Walker's *Oxen Drinking* of 1899, which was shown in the Club's 1910 exhibition and was reserved for the Gallery by Sir Edmund Walker. The measure of Walker's reputation at that time can be taken by the price: $10,000! The years of his involvement with the Club in fact coincided with the very peak of his fame. By this time his picturesque Millet-like subjects had become vehicles for virtuoso performances of paint-handling, resulting in brilliant colour feasts like the huge †*Cows* (NGC) of about 1910. Rich and varied in texture, the cows, foliage, and small stream all pitch forward toward the surface of the picture, almost tumbling out of it in their urgent vying for attention.

In 1915 Walker replaced the retiring Watson as president of the Canadian Art Club and that same year received an honorary degree from the University of Toronto. His New York dealer kept him in sales throughout the twenties, but by then he had retired to his private world on the Ile d'Orléans. By the time of his death there in 1938 he was remembered simply as a chronicler of the peasant farming folk of the island. His art seemed as anachronistic as their way of life.

Two other friends of Watson also joined the club at its inception. WILLIAM E. ATKINSON (1862-1926), who was born in Toronto, studied there under John Fraser and Robert Harris, and then with Reid under Eakins in Philadelphia before going to Paris, where he found himself drifting away from the Académie Julian to Brittany and Holland. He worked briefly in Devonshire before returning to Toronto in 1902. His *Willows, Evening* (NGC) of 1908 is a typical 'tonalist' Dutch-influenced work. ARCHIBALD BROWNE (1866-1948) was born in Liverpool of Scottish parents and studied briefly in Scotland and Paris before moving to Toronto in 1888. By the time of the founding of the Club he had developed his own variation on the moody tonal landscapes of Atkinson. Through the Goupil Gallery in London (Watson's dealer and later Morrice's), he had established a small but loyal English clientele. His steady competence, as seen in a work like *Benediction* (NGC) of 1919, maintained his reputation into the twenties. He moved to Montreal in 1923 and shortly after retired to Lancaster, Ont.

The Toronto orientation of the membership worried Morris and Williamson. They wanted the club to be 'Canadian', after all, and so they looked further afield for artists who shared their disaffection with the French academic hegemony. FRANKLIN BROWNELL (1857-1946), a French-trained American artist who had been teaching in Ottawa since 1886, had recently begun to paint in the Caribbean. The light and colour he found there began—as in *The Beach, St Kitts* (NGC) of 1913—to alle-

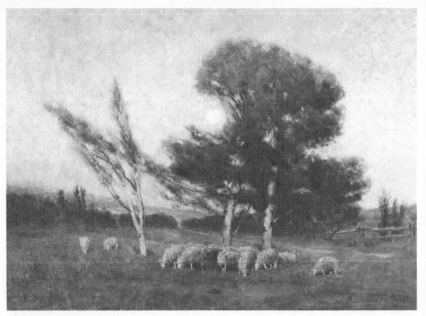

William Brymner. *Early Moonrise in September*, 1899. Canvas, 28½ x 39½. NGC.

viate the academic routine of his earlier work. Although never approaching Impressionism, and always academic in structure, his high-keyed paintings were perfectly acceptable to the membership of the Club. Brownell virtually stopped exhibiting before the end of the First World War, although he kept on teaching in Ottawa until the age of eighty and lived for another nine years!

Montreal, though, was the natural place to turn to for more members, and in WILLIAM BRYMNER the Club found enthusiastic support. He had been gradually evolving towards an atmospheric landscape style quite different from his large figure pieces of earlier years. The atmospheric and moody *Early Moonrise in September* (NGC) of 1899 is typically Barbizon in theme and treatment; the herd of sheep is unified by golden wisps of moonlight refracted through the trees. By 1907 and *Evening* (NGC) he had developed this concern with atmosphere to a point of brooding moodiness, much as Atkinson did.

In 1909 Brymner, with Watson and Williamson, visited the Cape Breton home of the Montreal collector James Ross. Returning there periodically and working on the Ile d'Orléans with Walker, Brymner began to develop his late style of open, light-filled, atmospheric landscapes—particularly marines—like *The Coast of Louisbourg* (NGC) of 1914. During these years Brymner was also president of the RCA and head of the AAM school. He held the latter post until 1921 when he retired to the south of France. Four years later he died in England.

Brymner brought to the Club a number of members from Montreal. The most brilliant was MAURICE CULLEN (1866-1934), as much a pioneer in his early years as Brymner in his, and in the same developing French tradition. Cullen was born in St John's, Nfld, and his family moved to Montreal four years later. Intended for a business career, he convinced his family that he wished to be a sculptor and in 1886 enrolled with the well-known Philippe Hébert (1850-1917). (Philippe and his son Henri (1884-1950) both later showed with the Club as guest exhibitors.) After three years with Hébert he went to Paris and the Ecole where he switched to painting. Established in Paris, by 1894 he was exhibiting in the Salon, was elected an associate the next year, and had a picture purchased by the French government. *The Mill Stream, Moret* (NGC) is typical of his work then. Basically academic landscape, it has the sharp angularities in composition and the relatively intense colour and concern for light of what has been called 'second-generation Impressionism'.

Cullen returned to Canada, painting in the winter of 1895-6 around Beaupré near Québec City with his friend James Morrice. Works completed then were the first in Canada to bring the tenets of Impressionism—albeit in a watered-down form—to the treatment of Canadian landscape. What strikes one immediately in *Logging in Winter, Beaupré* (AGH), and what in fact the picture is all about, is snow—a broad expanse, but infinitely various. Newton MacTavish has explained how 'the paint is not simply swiped on with a brush, but it is built up until it attains a loose, open, vibrant texture. This textural quality in paint makes possible the absorption and radiation of light and suggests the presence of atmosphere. . . .' Already at this date we can see that Cullen will have much in common with the members of the Canadian Art Club.

Cullen returned to Europe that summer and visited Venice with Morrice. In 1897 he was back in Montreal where he began to exhibit, but with little response. In 1900 he was again in Europe, visiting Venice with Brymner and Morrice in 1902. He then settled down in Canada for good. His work at this point is free of impasto, less harsh and more atmospheric.*Winter Evening, Québec* (NGC) of about 1905 is, in fact, a paean to atmosphere. Smoke, steam, and cloudy fog all intermix in thousands of tones of bluish-grey, accented with pin-pricks of light.

During the Club years the future members of the Group of Seven always sought out Cullen's work, and his friend Morrice said that he was *the* man in Canada who 'gets at the guts of things'. Most Canadians were not so enthusiastic, however, and about 1920 Cullen built himself a cabin at Lac Tremblant in the Laurentians and more or less retired

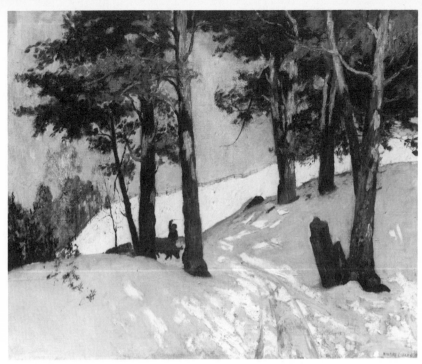

Maurice Cullen. *Logging in Winter, Beaupré*, 1896. Canvas, 25¼ x 33½. AGH.

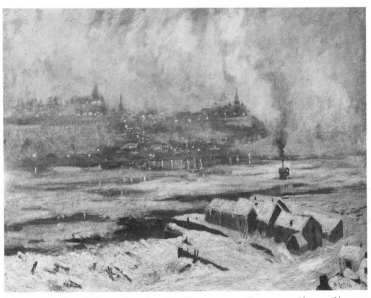

Maurice Cullen. *Winter Evening, Québec*, c.1905. Canvas, 29½ x 39¼. NGC.

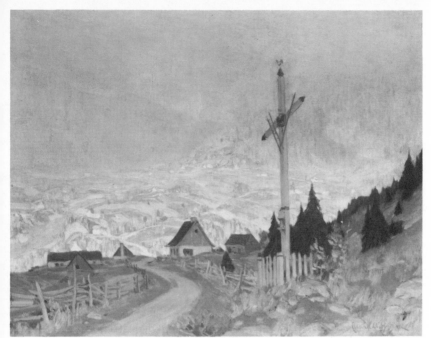

Clarence Gagnon. *La Croix du Chemin, l'automne*, c.1915. Canvas, 20¼ x 28¼. NGC.

there. After this he painted in a more naturalistic landscape style, developing a virtual formula that found success among established collectors.

CLARENCE GAGNON (1881-1942) was born in Montreal, studied under Brymner at the AAM school from 1897 to 1900, and then worked around the area of Baie-Saint-Paul painting scenes of rural life. His *Oxen Ploughing* (MMFA) of 1903 so impressed the wealthy collector James Morgan that he sent the painter to the Académie Julian in Paris. Gagnon followed this with the usual visits to painters' spots around France and Italy. He was strongly attracted to the paintings of James Morrice, although in his *Les deux plages: Paramé et Saint Malo* (BAG) of about 1908 he still felt the need to compound naturalistic detail rather than to simplify his forms as Morrice did. It was as an etcher that he first exhibited with the Canadian Art Club.

In 1909 he returned to Montreal and Baie-Saint-Paul and for a few years painted Québec villages in a misty, atmospheric style similar to Cullen's. *La Croix du chemin, l'automne* (NGC) of about 1915 is one of the more successful of these 'Impressionist' works, the upper two-thirds a study in subtle tonal variations. Gagnon maintained close contact with Paris and after the war moved to the French capital where he lived until 1936, renowned as an illustrator. His post-war paintings, such as

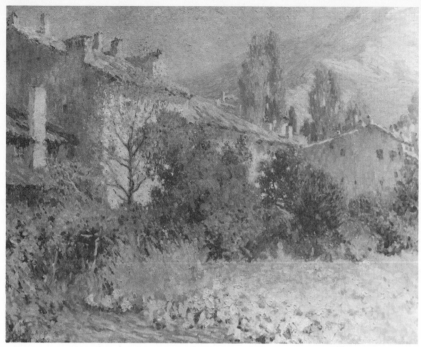

W.H. Clapp. *Morning in Spain*, 1907. Canvas, 29 x 36½. NGC.

the famous *Village dans les Laurentides* (NGC) of about 1926, are like enlarged magazine illustrations. Having lost most of the earlier atmospheric quality, they show a great attention to anecdotal detail, bright clear colours, and striking, easily read forms.

Another student of Brymner's, W. H. CLAPP (1879-1954), also showed with the Club. Born in Montreal of American parents and raised in Oakland, Calif., he returned to Montreal in 1900 to study for four years with Brymner before going to Paris. There he attended the academies but exhibited in the experimental Salon d'Automne and travelled widely in Spain and Belgium. He returned to Montreal in 1908, bringing sun-filled pictures like *Morning in Spain* (NGC) of 1907, painted in a kind of decorative, pointillist style. He persisted with this technique but in 1915, apparently discouraged by hostile reaction to his work, he visited Cuba for two years and then settled again in Oakland. In 1918 he became curator of the Oakland Art Gallery and in 1923 was one of the founders of The Society of Six, a group of painters who introduced broad, bright, post-impressionist painting to the San Francisco Bay area. He never returned to Canada.

Other painters from Québec who studied in France also returned with a superficially Impressionistic style applied to essentially academic com-

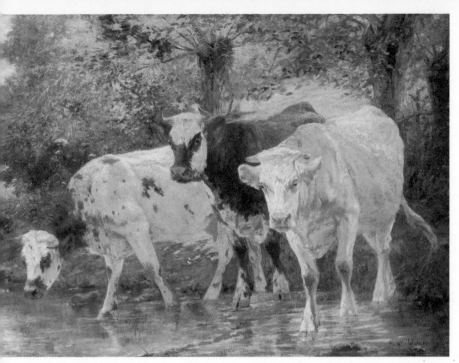

XVIII—Horatio Walker. *Cows*, c.1910. Canvas, 51¼ x 72¼. NGC.

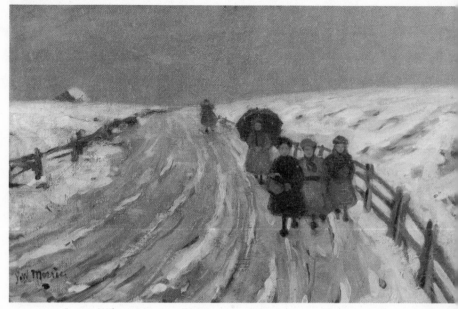

xix—James Wilson Morrice. *Return from School*, c.1900. Canvas, 18¼ x 29. AGO.

positions. Of these, WILLIAM R. HOPE (1863-1931) of Montreal exhibited with the Canadian Art Club from 1912 on; H. IVAN NEILSON (1865-1931) of Québec City showed with the Club in 1914 and 1915; and the famous Marc-Aurèle de Foy Suzor-Coté participated from 1913.

SUZOR-COTÉ was a versatile and eclectic artist of great facility. By the time of his return to Canada in 1908 he had settled on a richly textured, Impressionist-like landscape style that invariably, as in *Le Camp sur la colline* (NGC) of 1909, contrasted an almost pastel, light-filled ground with a darker, often black patterning. His compositions are always solid, though they became somewhat inflexible and even formulary as the years progressed. Never a real innovator, Suzor-Coté nonetheless was able to produce a tasteful amalgam—particularly in his sculpture—that often pleased the Club exhibitors and always pleased the less rigorous collectors.

One of the important contributions of the Canadian Art Club was in presenting sympathetic surroundings in Toronto for the prominent Québec artists of the time. They brought to the Toronto audience a

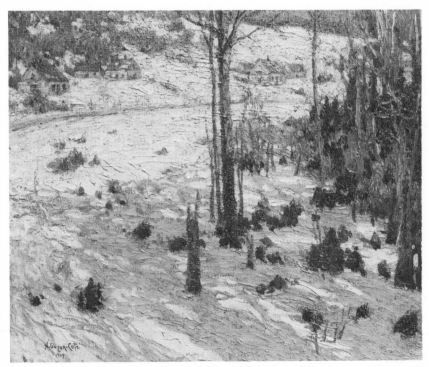

Aurèle de Foy Suzor-Coté. *Le Camp sur la colline*, 1909. Canvas, 23 x 28¾. NGC.

somewhat after-the-fact and often seriously compromised Impressionism that was nevertheless charming to the eye and in colour acted as a relief from the heavy 'Dutch' tones of the Toronto-based artists like Williamson and Morris. But the Club was also intent on bringing to Canadian viewers the work of painters who had left Canada in pursuit of their careers.

Halifax-born Ernest Lawson (1873-1939) would never have exhibited in Canada without Morris's invitation to join the Club, and in later years he even claimed to be a native-born American. A. Phimister Proctor (1862-1950), another Canadian-born American artist, the sculptor of the famous stone lions on the steps of the New York Public Library, was also brought back into the Canadian cultural sphere for a few years by his membership in the Club. But of the expatriate Canadians to whom the Canadian Art Club presented a forum in Canada, the most famous and undoubtedly the most important to other Canadian artists was JAMES WILSON MORRICE (1865-1924). Cullen, Brymner, Williamson, and Morris valued his friendship; Gagnon, A.Y. Jackson, Lawren Harris, and countless other young Canadian painters sought out his work. Along with Walker, he was the Canadian who then had the strongest reputation abroad.

Morrice was born in Montreal where his father was a merchant, and a supporter and later a benefactor of the AAM. So even though James was educated to be a lawyer (in Toronto 1882-9), his interest in painting was accepted by the family, and they even allowed him to go to Paris to study late in 1889. Morrice enrolled at Julian's and there met two painters who became his closest friends during these first years in Paris. One was the American Maurice Prendergast, who was born in St John's, Nfld, seven years before Cullen but was raised in Boston. He arrived at Julian's in 1891, the year after an Australian named Charles Conder had enrolled. The three first visited Saint Malo, the famed painting spot on the Brittany coast from where Cartier had set out for the new world, and over the next three or four years they spent much time together, re-visiting Saint Malo, Dieppe, and other painters' locales. Morrice gave direction to the retiring Prendergast, and the garrulous Conder in turn introduced Morrice to important influences.

The Australian roomed with William Rothenstein, an English painter also enrolled in Julian's. Rothenstein met Whistler in 1892, and was closely associated with him until 1897. Conder then came into contact with the famous American, and it is likely that Prendergast and Morrice did too, although no meeting is documented. In 1898 Morrice actually had a studio just up the street from him, and the influence of Whistler is paramount in most of Morrice's work before the turn of the century. *Prow of a Gondola, Venice* (private collection, Toronto) was painted with Maurice Cullen on a trip to Venice in the summer of 1896. It is an accomplished Whistlerian tonal study, simple and reserved.

It was probably through Curtis Williamson that in October 1895 Morrice met two more Americans, the Philadelphians William Glackens and Robert Henri. (Prendergast had just left for home and so did not meet them then.) Henri, Glackens, Morrice, and sometimes Williamson frequently painted together over the next year in the forest of Fontainebleau, made famous by the Barbizon painters, usually staying at the village of Bois-le-Roi. Perhaps as a consequence of these new relationships, by the turn of the century Morrice's painting had lost the washlike effect of his earlier work and begun to display a more textured 'painterly' quality. †*Return from School* (AGO) of about 1900 is based on sketches made at Beaupré where he often painted with Cullen. How much more elegantly economical a picture this is than Cullen's *Logging*! Morrice's paint is never dry, never arbitrary, yet it is more natural than the somewhat contrived handling of Cullen. And its rich mixture of streaming browns, blacks, and whites could never have been achieved by Cullen, whose effect in comparison is almost confectionary. Morrice's muddy snow is of the earth, of life.

Morrice's contacts continued to change in Paris. Prendergast had left in the winter of 1894-5 and Glackens and Henri returned to the United States in 1897. Also in 1897 Conder moved to London; he continued to visit Paris, however, and saw much of Morrice. It was probably through him that the Canadian became a regular at the *Chat blanc* where, in the upstairs diningroom, he fraternized with a group of Englishmen, including the novelists Arnold Bennett and Somerset Maugham, the critic Clive Bell, the occultist Aleister Crowley, and the Irish painter and disciple of Gauguin, Roderic O'Conor. While regularly enjoying the company of these men, Morrice matured as an artist. As Donald Buchanan has said, he broke 'the tidy bonds of refinement which had held the art of Conder and the other men of the nineties in precious tutelage. From then on he would tend to be influenced more and more by things French.'

Quai des Grands-Augustins (NGC) of about 1903 is still atmospheric, and even painterly in part; but now the paint is thin again. The period between this picture and about 1910 has been called Morrice's 'personal impressionist style'. It culminates in one of the very greatest paintings of Canadian art: *The Ferry, Québec* (NGC). Restrained and balanced, yet lively, even vital in composition, the colour is a harmonious dream of subtle interplay and painterly speculation. The picture is cold with the living cold—the aggressive, stimulating cold of the true north we all know.

Although Morrice found his intellectual and aesthetic life in Paris, he still sought something in Canada and returned virtually every winter until the war. He usually then painted with Cullen or Brymner and Morris around the Ile d'Orléans. He sent paintings regularly to W. Scott & Sons, his Montreal dealer, exhibited frequently with the RCA, and was elected an honorary non-resident member in 1913 (his friend Brymner was president from 1909 to 1918). When the Canadian Art Club was founded in 1907, Morrice was one of the first choices for membership and he sent works loyally every year.

But his home was Paris, and his commitment to French art and his involvement in its developing progress became total. Writing to Edmund Morris about Cézanne in 1910, he said: 'His is the savage work that one would expect to come from America—but it is always France that produces anything emphatic in art.' Morrice had continued to see his American friends on his way back from Canada.* But by 1910 even such periodic contact seems to have stopped.

From 1901 Morrice exhibited with the London-based International Society of Sculptors, Painters and 'Gravers (the only Canadian to do so). It represented everything the Canadian Art Club aspired to be. Although continuing to exhibit with the International Society until 1914, in 1905 he transferred his allegiance to the more radical Salon d'Automne, where that same year the Fauves were first seen.** By 1909 Morrice had come to know Henri Matisse, one of the profound moulders of the twentieth century. He had also begun to travel south instead of north to Brittany and Normandy; in the winter of 1911-12 he followed Matisse to Tangier, and the next winter did so again. On this second trip the two painters spent much time together.

The war forced Morrice out of Paris briefly in 1914 and he made one of his last trips to Montreal on his way to Cuba. After 1916 he no

*Prendergast joined Glackens, Henri, Lawson—who, of course, also showed with the Canadian Art Club—and four others in 1908 to exhibit in New York as 'The Eight'. For what was considered their too-harsh realism, they were dubbed 'The Ash Can School'.

**At this Salon a critic described a room full of paintings by Matisse and others that surrounded a piece of sculpture by Albert Marquet as 'Donatello parmi les fauves' ('Donatello among the beasts'). Fauvism became known as a style of painting in which an aggressive use of colour was all-important. Matisse, Derain, and Dufy were among the important members of the Fauve group.

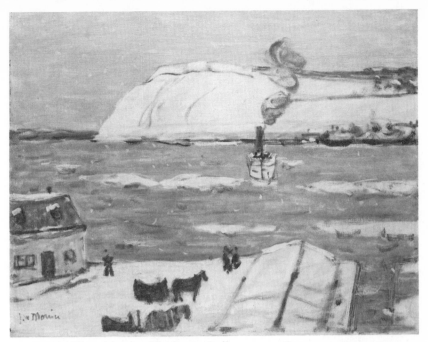

James Wilson Morrice. *The Ferry, Québec*, c.1909. Canvas, 24 x 32. NGC.

longer exhibited in Canada. The Cuban trip was just the beginning of a series of visits to the West Indies that alternated between trips to North Africa and the south of France. He was pursuing a lighter palette and the warm healing rays of the sun. (Throughout his adult life Morrice was a heavy drinker; alcohol began to ravage his body about the time of the war.) His first West Indian pictures of 1915 are not successful. Buchanan determined that 'the influence of Matisse was too directly upon him. He was still labouring to plan, with intellectual effort, a picture.' By 1921, however, and his last visit to the Caribbean, he was painting some of the finest pictures of his life. *Village Street, West Indies* (MMFA) of 1921 is magnificently assured, with a pictorial space that is infinitely deep, ever expanding, yet tautly flat in breathtaking tension. The small, slightly reeling figure on the road, caught in arrested movement, seems almost to be pitched against the earth's turning.

Morrice worked with his friend Albert Marquet, the Fauve painter, in Algiers in 1922, but after that summer he stopped painting. In the fall of 1923, as his health deteriorated alarmingly, it was rumoured in Paris that he was dead and he was listed as deceased in the catalogue of the Salon d'Automne. But Morrice wintered that year in the south of France and was able to call there on his old Montreal friend, William Brymner. Then on to Sicily and finally Tunis, where in January 1924

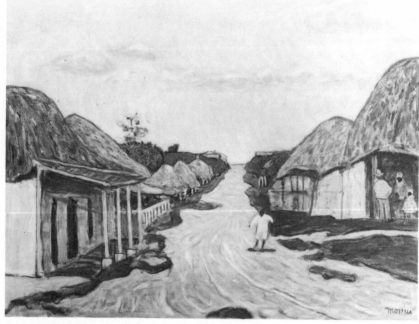

James Wilson Morrice. *Village Street, West Indies*, 1921. Canvas, 24 x 32¼. MMFA.

he died and was buried. The Salon d'Automne held a memorial retrospective that fall.

The Canadian Art Club did not survive the war. In fact the last exhibition was held in 1915. The tragic death of Edmund Morris in 1913 took much of the energy out of the Club. Some have claimed that Morris was essential to its organization and that the two years that were required for it to run down after his death were simply evidence of how well he built. Much of the lay support for the Club—which had assumed very large proportions at its peak about 1913—was siphoned off by the recently reorganized Toronto Art Museum. And there were those, including the artists who superseded these first Canadian 'modernists' in the public eye after the war, who believed that the Canadian Art Club represented a taste and an approach to painting that was unsuitable for Canada. What could Dutch sensibility, even Dutch themes, or on the other hand watered-down French Impressionism, have to do with the Canadian experience?

10

Tom Thomson
and the
Group of Seven
1913-1931

The artists who exhibited together in Toronto as the Group of Seven in May 1920 had by that time developed a doctrine and a style of painting based on the idea that Canadian art could find sufficient sustenance in Canada alone. In 1913, however, at the peak of the public attention surrounding the activities of the Canadian Art Club, even Lawren Harris —in many ways the leader of the Group—found it natural to praise the successes of the internationalists. In showing the work of painters like Morrice, Walker, and Lawson, the Canadian Art Club had after all exhibited Canadian artists who had measured themselves against the standards set in the international centres and could be very good indeed. Slowly, though, first through the assertion of the primacy of Canadian subject matter for Canadians, then through the invention of a distinctive visual language, those who were searching for the 'essence' of Canada arrived at a position of complete opposition to the values, and even the painting technique, of most of the generation who preceded them.

LAWREN HARRIS (1885-1970) was born in Brantford and raised in a family reflecting that usually successful Ontario combination of Protestantism and business. His grandfather and two uncles were ministers, and the Harris family then owned part of the Massey-Harris firm. His upbringing followed the conventions of his social background until he began to have difficulties in his first year at the University of Toronto. His family decided that his inclinations were artistic and he was sent to Berlin to stay with an aunt and uncle who were living there and to study painting. This was early in the fall of 1904.

After studies in Berlin, and a year-and-a-half of travel as a magazine illustrator, Harris settled into a studio in Toronto in the spring of 1909. We know little of his activities over the next two years. Near the end of 1910 he painted the first important work of his to survive: *Houses,*

Wellington Street (Lawren P. Harris, Sackville, N.B.). A striking picture, its bold, assertive brushwork and subject matter reflect his years in Berlin, while its dark moodiness—relieved by intense, almost pure colour in the highlights—suited the taste that was then reflected in Toronto in the exhibitions of the Canadian Art Club.

In November 1911 Harris made a connection that gave new direction to his life and ultimately changed the course of Canadian art. The occasion was an exhibition of sketches held at the Arts & Letters Club. It so impressed Harris that he sought out their author, J. E. H. MACDONALD (1873-1932). The immediate result was to bring Harris into confluence with a group of people and ideas that were fast approaching their moment.

MacDonald was born in Durham, Eng., but was brought to Hamilton at the age of fourteen by his Canadian father. Young MacDonald first took art lessons there, and by the time his family moved to Toronto in 1889 he had decided on a career in commercial art. He was interested in a more personal expression as well and spent a great deal of his free time taking art classes and sketching. Such concerns were relatively common in the commercial studios and a number of clubs sprang up to service the need. The oldest was the Toronto Art Students' League, founded in 1886, which organized life classes and sketching trips and in its annual illustrated calendar (published from 1893 to 1904) encouraged the treatment of Canadian subjects.

One prominent member of the League after the turn of the century when MacDonald became active in it and its various offshoots was C. W. JEFFERYS (1869-1952). He was born in Rochester, Eng., but in 1880 ended up in Toronto, where he began a career in commercial art. In 1892 he moved to New York. He worked as an illustrator on the *Herald* for seven years and familiarized himself with the brilliant magazine and newspaper renderings that were then attracting much attention to Howard Pyle and other illustrators. After returning to Toronto in 1899, Jefferys began to promote ceaselessly the depiction of subjects from Canadian history and the Canadian scene.

Another associate of MacDonald's in the clubs was WILLIAM BEATTY (1869-1941). Born in Toronto, Beatty turned to painting in 1894 and in 1900 went to Paris and Julian's. From 1906 to 1909 he travelled about Europe, particularly in the Low Countries, and when he returned home he was painting rich, dark, moody pictures of Dutch peasant life. In Toronto he frequented the sketching clubs and was soon listening to the argument from Jefferys and others that the expression of personal feelings in art was fine, but that truly meaningful expression was accomplished only when one dealt with subjects that the viewer *shared* with the artist. Canadian history, and even more assuredly the land itself, was the best vehicle for such communication.

League members had been following this course for years in their graphics. As early as 1902 three members had travelled to Algonquin Park in search of Canadian landscape themes. Beatty, with the zeal of the convert, took off for the north the year of his return to Toronto. *The Evening Cloud of the Northland* (NGC), painted in 1910, is essentially a grey monochrome and was thus typical of the kind of work being shown by the Toronto members of the Canadian Art Club. But it was a Canadian subject, and for a group of painters in Toronto at that time, this was of overriding importance. Beatty felt this so strongly that at the time of MacDonald's 1911 exhibition he wrote to the National Gallery and insisted on sending his *Evening Cloud* in exchange for a recently purchased work of his called *A Dutch Peasant* (AGH). 'I am a Canadian,' he wrote, 'I would much rather be represented by a Canadian picture.'

Jefferys, in reviewing MacDonald's exhibition, carefully pointed out that 'in themselves . . . Canadian themes do not make art, Canadian or other, but neither do Canadian themes expressed through European formulas or through European temperaments.' What was so important about MacDonald's pictures for him was that 'so deep and compelling' was the 'native inspiration' that it had 'to a very great extent found through him a method of expression in paint as native and original as itself.' That excited Lawren Harris.

We don't know what sketches MacDonald exhibited at the Arts & Letters Club in November 1911, but from Jefferys' review it is clear that the notable works were at least related to pictures like *By the River, Early Spring* (Hamilton Teachers' College) of 1911. Based on sketches done on the Humber River, near Toronto, it shows the drivers running logs along the ice-filled stream. It is dark and rich, in the Toronto taste of the time, but it is also rough and raw and taut with energy. As a consequence of the reaction to such work, Harris and his friend Dr James MacCallum talked MacDonald into leaving his commercial work (he had been a designer for twenty-two years) and becoming a professional painter. Harris and MacDonald began sketching together almost immediately, and their first large exhibition canvases appeared in the 1912 OSA. Harris's most impressive picture was his own heroic version of log drivers on the Humber called *The Drive* (NGC); and MacDonald's was his famous *Tracks and Traffic* (AGO). Although both pictures are bold and exciting, neither really went beyond the taste

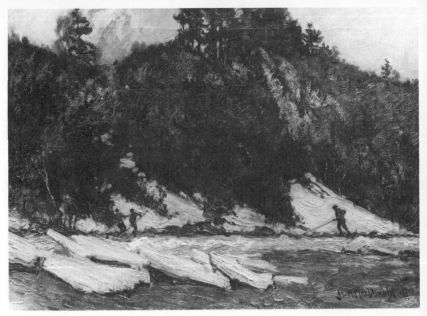

J.E.H. MacDonald. *By the River, Early Spring*, 1911. Canvas, 20 x 28. Hamilton Teachers' College.

established by the Canadian Art Club. However, the subject matter attracted viewers, and critics singled out MacDonald, Harris, and Beatty for praise. 'To a Canadian,' wrote Augustus Bridle, 'scenes in this country are of vastly more interest than all the fishing smacks and brass kettles and sea-weed sonatas of north Europe.'

Harris and MacDonald clearly had their subject. What they still lacked was a meaningful approach, a compatible technique. These were suggested to them the following January when the two travelled to Buffalo to view an exhibition of contemporary Scandinavian art. It was an afternoon they would never forget. There was a shock of recognition in the terrain of northern Europe, so similar to Canada, and there was elation in the direct, clear expression of the exhilarating clarity and expansiveness of the lonely north. The paintings seemed to the two Torontonians, as MacDonald remembered, 'true souvenirs of that mystic north around which we all revolve'.

MacDonald had had his first taste of the north the previous summer when he spent some time sketching in Georgian Bay as the guest of Dr MacCallum, a great northern enthusiast. Returning home from Buffalo, he began to work on a large canvas based on those sketches. *Fine Weather, Georgian Bay* (private collection) is dry in handling and stiff in parts, but it contains a voluminous space that almost echos in a room. The diminutive figures perched on an outcropping of driftwood in the foreground stress the heroic scale and suggest the reverence due such magnificence in nature. In its boldness it is directly the result of the Scandinavian show.

By the spring of 1913 a small group of like-minded commercial artists had assembled around MacDonald and Harris. The eldest of these, and the least likely to have asserted himself as an artist, was TOM THOMSON (1877-1917). Born in Claremont, Ont., and raised in Leith, near Owen Sound, Thomson had in 1901 ended up in a Seattle business school run by a brother. There he studied art and shortly began to work in a commercial studio. By 1905 he was back in Canada—in Toronto—and about 1908 he was working at the same studio as MacDonald: Grip Limited, where he began to develop an interest in painting.

Other designers at Grip also painted in their spare time. In conversations there, and during lunch at the Arts & Letters Club, a number found themselves strongly attracted to the ideas of MacDonald and Harris—Thomson; FRANK CARMICHAEL (1890-1945) from Orillia; FRANK JOHNSTON (1888-1949) of Toronto; and ARTHUR LISMER (1885-1969) and FRED VARLEY (1881-1969), both recently arrived from Sheffield, Eng. They all began to share a common desire. 'We are endeavouring to knock out of us all of the preconceived ideas, emptying ourselves of everything except that nature is here in all its greatness,' Varley wrote in 1914.

The potential for really decisive action was becoming clear. But of the fledgling 'native' group in early 1913, only MacDonald and Harris were professional painters. There was a need for more weight. MacDonald had been corresponding with A. Y. JACKSON (1882-1974) in Montreal from late in 1910, and a number of the Toronto painters had been very impressed with his *The Edge of the Maple Wood* (NGC) when it was exhibited in the 1911 OSA. Late in March 1913 MacDonald wrote to Jackson, informing him that a friend named Lawren Harris wanted to buy *The Edge of the Maple Wood* and that the 'young' group wanted Jackson to move to Toronto. Such news could not have come at a better time.

As mentioned in chapter 7, Jackson was one of those Montreal students of Brymner who, as a matter of course, had to study in Paris. Much like the painters in the Canadian Art Club, he found it difficult to accept the bland indifference of the Montreal art community after the excitement of Europe and in 1913 had just returned from a year-and-a-half abroad. Jackson was not alone in Montreal. He was friendly with Cullen, and of course Brymner, and among his own generation he often saw Gagnon and was particularly close to Albert Robinson (1881-

1956) and Randolph Hewton (1888-1960). All felt that Montreal was moribund. It had no Canadian Art Club to set standards of excellence or to force the acceptance of modernism. Nonetheless Jackson and Hewton were determined to jar Montreal into awareness, and upon their return from Europe they had held an exhibition of their recent work in the AAM galleries. There were no sales and the disappointed Jackson was contemplating the dreary necessity of returning to commercial art when he received MacDonald's letter inviting him to Toronto. There, in May 1913, he met MacDonald, Lismer, and Varley for the first time and shortly afterwards Lawren Harris. Harris described the Toronto artists' plans. He and Dr MacCallum had just decided to construct for them a 'Studio Building of Canadian Art' on the southwest edge of Toronto's Rosedale and he encouraged Jackson to stay. Jackson wanted to think it over and retreated to Georgian Bay for the summer. Harris then asked Dr MacCallum—who had a summer home there—to convince Jackson, and with a year's living guaranteed by the doctor, Jackson agreed to join the Studio Building group.* That winter in Harris's studio he painted the radical *Terre Sauvage* (NGC).

Forceful, almost crude, *Terre Sauvage* demonstrated Jackson's sympathy with the aspirations of the Toronto painters. A stirring northern theme, in its symmetry and symbolic suggestiveness it reflects his response to the enthusiastic reports of the Scandinavian show. It must as well have seemed fresh and original with its touches of pure colour, and in its audacity it became the private touchstone of the new movement. Its gradual creation in Harris's studio fascinated Tom Thomson.

As he watched Jackson paint, Thomson's admiration grew and by January 1914 the two had decided to share a studio in the new building. This pleased MacDonald and Harris, and particularly Dr MacCallum. They had been encouraging Thomson over the preceding two years, convinced of his talent. His first large canvas, *Northern Lake* (Province of Ontario), had only recently been exhibited in the 1913 OSA and had been purchased by the Ontario government. Based on sketches painted in the summer of 1913 in Algonquin Park, it is an ugly picture, but deeply moving. Its colouring derives from the current Toronto taste as exemplified by the work of the Canadian Art Club, but gone is the refined subtlety, the delicate tonal nuances of the 'European' sensibility.

---

*Jackson had a little earlier joined the Arts & Letters Club and he and his friends had been exhibiting their paintings there. He was irrevocably associated with the Toronto painters when the fledgling group was called—half jokingly—'The Hot Mush School' in a newspaper in December 1913.

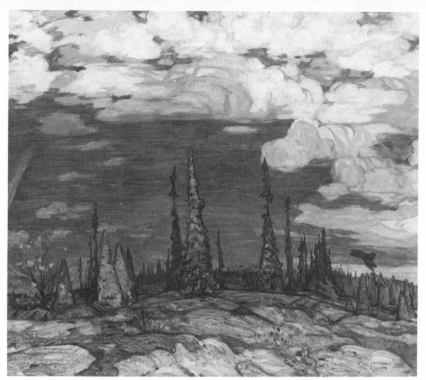

A.Y. Jackson. *Terre Sauvage*, 1913. Canvas, 50 x 60. NGC.

Northern Lake is raw and coarse and was seen by the Studio Building painters as the direct response of untutored genius to the inspiration of the north.

Jackson helped correct the obvious faults in Thomson's style and the latter's *Moonlight, Early Evening* (NGC)—painted directly under Jackson's tutelage that first winter in the new studio—is more unified than the earlier canvas. But at this point Thomson seems to have had even more to teach Jackson, and in his eagerness to learn about the north the Montrealer headed for Thomson's favourite Algonquin Park sketching grounds in the deep of winter. The trip was exhilarating. Now settled in Canada, with Toronto as his new base, Jackson travelled the whole year sketching. Algonquin first, then the Rockies with Bill Beatty, and back to Algonquin for the fall. Three seasons of sketching trips out of four was a pattern Jackson would follow for close to fifty years!

That October of 1914 in Algonquin was also the first 'group' sketching trip. Jackson and Thomson worked together for about six weeks and were joined by Lismer and Varley for the last four. Jackson was in full form. Earlier in the year he had painted the magnificent *†Frozen Lake, Early Spring, Algonquin Park* (NGC), following the basic composition established in Thomson's *Northern Lake* but giving it a brilliance of colour that far surpassed what anyone else in Canada thought to use at that time. From sketches made in October, he painted that November *The Red Maple* (NGC), another landmark picture, amazing in colour and innovative in composition.

Arthur Lismer produced his first ambitious canvas that fall. *The Guide's Home, Algonquin* (NGC) relies heavily on Impressionism, and its high-keyed colour and open, suffusing light are very agreeable. Thomson, however, made the greatest strides. The sketches he produced in 1914 demonstrate a remarkable development of control. On a trip to Algonquin in May 1914 with Lismer, the Englishman taught him to isolate the essentials and to work with a conscious design in mind. A month later, while at Dr MacCallum's Georgian Bay summer home, Thomson produced sketches of admirable simplicity, responses to the sky-filled MacDonalds of two years earlier. Thanks to Lismer and Jackson, he no longer worked up a smooth surface, trying to make the brush-strokes invisible. In a work like *Parry Sound Harbour* (NGC) of late May 1914—certainly one of the first sketches to display the distinctive Thomson genius—the emphatic brushwork supports the natural forms of the scene depicted, but it also leaves the maker's mark all over the surface. It records the union of man and place.

In October Jackson directed Thomson's natural response to the intense colour of the forest to release in him that inspired use of painted colour that has since given us such pleasure. The year was then capped by the production of Thomson's first major canvas, *Northern River* (NGC). Not as good a painting as Jackson's *Frozen Lake* or *Red Maple*, and heavily influenced by reports of the Scandinavian show and by magazine illustrations of Art Nouveau design, it is nonetheless one of the great haunting images of our culture—an unforgettable view of the mysterious yet penetratable mystery of the northern bush.

During the summer of 1914 war had broken out in Europe, and by the fall it was clear that Canada was involved. The 'Algonquin School' was just reaching its moment of assertive public presence; that now had to wait more than five years to be fulfilled. Not that painting stopped; but the group dispersed. Jackson returned to Montreal before Christmas and joined the army in June 1915. In August 1917 he was made an official war artist. In February 1918 Fred Varley was sent overseas, also as a war artist, and in June 1918 Lismer—who had moved to Halifax two years earlier to become principal of the Victoria School of Art & Design—was commissioned. Frank Johnston received his commission in August.

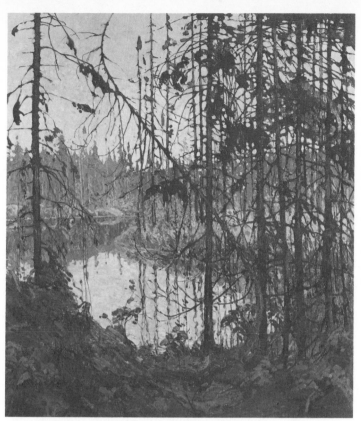

Tom Thomson. *Northern River*, 1914-15. Canvas, 45 x 40. NGC.

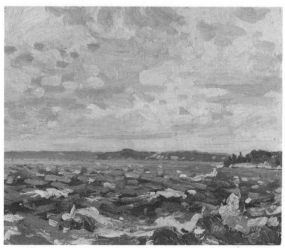

Tom Thomson. *Parry Sound Harbour*, 1914. Board, 8½ x 10½. NGC.

MacDonald and Harris might have been overwhelmed by the accomplishments of Jackson and Thomson during 1914. They worked away, however, principally lightening their palettes. MacDonald's works of 1914-15 are close in colour and paint handling to those of Suzor-Coté, Cullen, and some of the other Montreal 'impressionists' he was still seeing at the annual Toronto showings of the Canadian Art Club. Early in 1916, however, he painted *The Tangled Garden* (NGC). When it was exhibited at the OSA that March the artist was publicly accused of having thrown 'his paint pots in the face of the public'. Hector Charlesworth, the critic who then most strongly attacked MacDonald, and who from that time became a persistent and often vicious enemy of the Group, found the painting a crude affront. MacDonald defended himself ably, determined to persevere in the face of such ignorant attempts at control.

The picture seems disappointing after all the fuss. The colours are more intense than MacDonald had employed before, but the composition, though pleasing, is tight and safe. There is considerably too much anecdotal detail. It had not reached Jackson's level of two years before. Harris's principal picture in the OSA of 1916 is more successful as a painting, more radical in its use of paint and colour. *Snow II* (NGC) proved much more influential over the next three or four years in the flattening and decorative patterning of its image and in the suppression of moody atmosphere. It is also more clearly in the mainstream of the developing ideas of the Studio Building group than *The Tangled Garden*. Still dependent on the Scandinavian show, *Snow II* is very clearly a northern picture—a fresh and stimulating song to the Canadian wilds.

It was probably during the *Tangled Garden* controversy that Harris too decided to enlist in the army. Both Harris and MacDonald saw a great deal of Thomson during the early war years, at least in the winter. Thomson had established a fruitful working pattern. In Algonquin Park by April, he sketched there in the spring, worked at odd jobs for the summer, sketched again in the fall, and returned to Toronto only late in November. The sketches he produced at this time have always been widely admired. A work like †*Autumn Foliage* (NGC) of 1916 is spontaneous yet assuredly controlled. It is emphatically real both as a picture and as a painting. His canvases as well as his sketches had begun to surpass the quality of Jackson and the others. In *Petawawa Gorges* (NGC), probably painted late in 1916, all extraneous compositional devices have been eliminated and colour and texture virtually carry the whole. Magnificently unified, subtle and totally free of any 'showmanship', it is in its depiction of the annual rebirth of the river perhaps the most profound picture painted by any of the Studio Building group

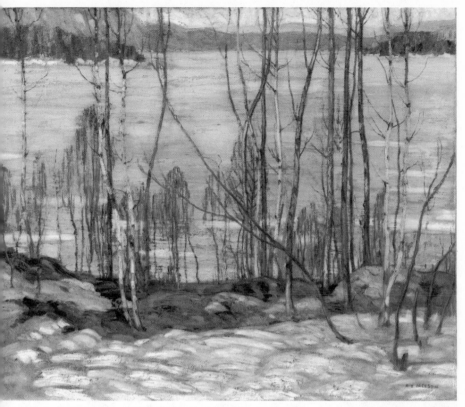

x—A.Y. Jackson. *Frozen Lake, Early Spring, Algonquin Park, 1914.* Canvas, 32 x 39. NGC.

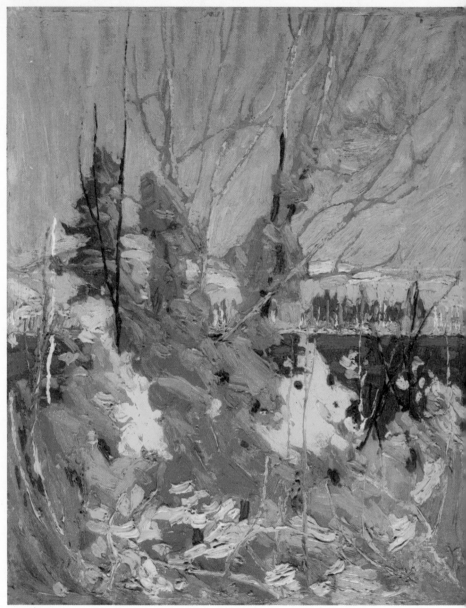

xxi—Tom Thomson. *Autumn Foliage*, 1916. Board, 10½ x 8½. NGC.

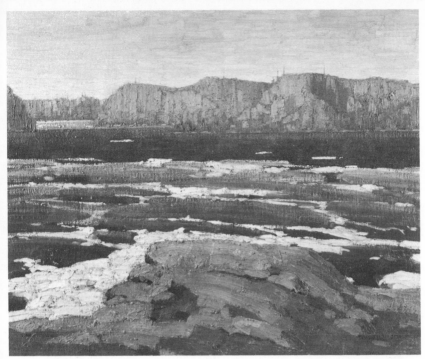

Tom Thomson. *Petawawa Gorges*, 1916. Canvas, 25¼ x 32. NGC.

until after the war. Probably even more than those almost sacred icons, *The West Wind* (AGO) and *The Jack Pine* (NGC), *Petawawa Gorges* is the measure of our loss. For when Thomson drowned in Canoe Lake in July 1917 he was unquestionably approaching the fullness of his powers.

His drowning was a crushing blow to the Studio Building group, even though the tragedy of war had accustomed them to death. MacDonald suffered a breakdown. But with the cessation of the war a series of memorial exhibitions demonstrated that all was not lost, that Thomson had in his life achieved a very great deal, and that his hopes would be fulfilled by his comrades.

Such fulfilment would not be sought in Algonquin Park, though, for after his discharge from the army in May 1918 Harris, accompanied by Dr MacCallum, first visited the Algoma region of Ontario. Excited by what he saw, Harris arranged to return in September with MacDonald and Johnston. This was the first of the famous 'box-car' trips, when they lived out of a caboose that was shunted from siding to siding along the route of the Algoma Central. The following September the same arrangements were made, but this time the recently returned Jackson replaced Dr MacCallum. Then the following May (1920), Toronto saw the first exhibition of the Group of Seven.

The Group now had clear intentions that at this point were largely social. They held 'that an Art must grow and flower in the land before the country will be a real home for its people.' They believed as well that this art, in responding to the particular nature of this country and its people, would be peculiarly Canadian. And they believed that there would be a formidable resistance to such an art. Collectors were seen to be supporters of foreign importations, and the native Canadians who still pleased collectors were seen as 'apes' of European art. From late in 1918 A. Y. Jackson's hearty dislike of Dutch art was proclaimed, and over the next few years he took a number of opportunities to attack 'the Dutchmen'. There were doubtless members of the old Canadian Art Club included in his definition of Dutchmen. Harris has referred a number of times to the years 1918-21 as the 'decorative' period—a reaction against the moody, atmospheric painting current in Toronto before the advent of the Group. The sombre canvases of the 'Dutchmen' were being replaced by the clear, forceful designs of the 'Canadians'. It was Harris's *Shacks* (NGC) of 1919 that was the first emphatic declaration of the 'Group of Seven Style'. There is almost no recession in the picture, although at least two planes of depth are evident. The effect of these is diminished by the hot, aggressive colours that push up onto the surface of the canvas. The picture is almost all surface pattern, and there is certainly no moody 'atmosphere'. It is a painting that could never have been accepted by the Canadian Art Club, even though it clearly surpasses their average level in quality.

Shacks depicts a Toronto subject, but Algoma was the current region of inspiration. It was most sympathetically dealt with by MacDonald and most spectacularly in such works as *Falls, Montreal River* (AGO) of 1920, **The Solemn Land* (NGC) of 1921, and *Autumn in Algoma* (NGC) of 1922. These are MacDonald's best pictures, and among the very finest produced by the Group. All are richly decorative, profound with the blown fullness of the late autumn. And only MacDonald, it seems, had the sensibility to encompass the lush Eden growth of Algoma. Johnston found sweep in burned-over hills, Harris sought the severe monumentality of hidden waterfalls, and Jackson came as close to 'pure' painting as he was ever to come in his breathtaking *First Snow, Algoma* (MCM) of 1919-20. Algoma remained 'MacDonald's country', nonetheless. Lismer found no stimulus to original work there, and Varley never visited it at all.

Lismer and Varley produced their first major canvases in 1920-1 and both resulted from the same sketching trip to Dr MacCallum's island in Georgian Bay. These are, of course, Lismer's *A September Gale*,

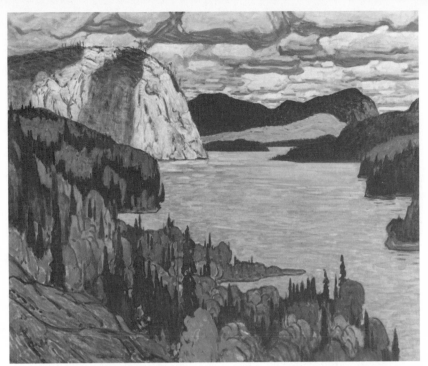

J.E.H. MacDonald. *The Solemn Land*, 1921. Canvas, 48 x 60. NGC.

Georgian Bay (NGC) and Varley's *Stormy Weather, Georgian Bay* (NGC). Both are strong, elemental pictures free of atmospheric concerns. By 1920, Frank Carmichael also had found direction in the decorative, emphatic 'Group' style in such works as *Autumn Hillside* (AGO).

Men change, and as leaders grow, movements find new direction. In February 1921 Jackson returned to Quebec to sketch after an absence of almost eight years. Working in the region of Cacouna on the south shore of the St Lawrence, he later painted his sensitive, delicate sketches of lonely farms and tiny villages into a number of canvases, the most famous being *Winter Road, Quebec* (estate of C.S. Band). Delicate in colour, with forms all soft, blunted, and rounded, this canvas rolls with an easy, deep rhythm that was to become Jackson's trademark in later years. Harris also travelled east in 1921 and his dramatic canvases of the Halifax slums, particularly *Elevator Court, Halifax* (AGO), strike another new chord. The next year MacDonald went to Nova Scotia. *Sea-Shore, Nova Scotia* (NGC) of 1923, based on a 1922 sketch, is almost stark in its simplified, hard-edged forms and its dun, matte colours. A decisive turn had been taken, and the main impetus probably derived from Harris and the North Shore of Lake Superior.

In the fall of 1921, after a trip to Algoma, Harris and Jackson had pushed on north and west looking for more subjects and for the first time travelled as far as the North Shore. This new land was a profound revelation to Harris, and he returned every fall for the next three years. The vast expanse of lake and sky, the harsh yet exhilarating climate, the stark, monumental forms satisfied a developing spiritualism in him. At some point near the end of the war he had come into contact with the theosophical movement and had recently become an ardent member. Theosophy attempted to combine the best elements of the world's religions while stressing the personal development of the spirit to an elevated, highly aware level. The reaching, aspiring forms of *Lake Superior* (AGO) of about 1924—among other North Shore canvases— expressed this desire for spiritual fulfilment through immersion in the vital forces of overpowering landscape.

One can almost trace the course of Harris's spiritual development over the next few years in his canvases. He sought out inspiring land-scape in the Rockies from 1924 on and even in the Arctic in 1930. *Maligne Lake, Jasper Park* (NGC) of 1924 and *Mount Lefroy* (MCM) of 1930 are truly monuments to the breadth and penetration of Harris's spirit. Grave, hushed tributes to the spiritualizing force of the country, they are incentives to the spiritual capacity in us all. *Maligne Lake* is a painting of great force and staying-power. Its wonderful facetted forms, sombre yet rich colour, and imposing composition draw the viewer irresistibly to its centre and then transport him into an almost mystical realm. It was the most influential painting in Toronto prior to 1930.

MacDonald also first visited the Rockies in 1924. He was by then working full time at the Ontario College of Art and was able to sketch only during summer vacations. He returned to the mountains every summer and every winter struggled with canvases that seemed mis-conceived and could never become successful. Taking his lead from Harris, he tried to construct simple, heroic images, coloured in the dry, matte tones of the Nova Scotia pictures of 1923. It was only in 1932, virtually at the end of his life, that he achieved any success with his mountain canvases. *Mountain Snowfall, Lake Oesa* (estate of C.S. Band) of that year finds the solution in moving down into the intimate detail surrounding a small mountain lake. Scale is avoided, and the locked-in force-lines of primeval rock—the simple, massive forms held in balanced tension—evoke a sense of profound equilibrium that rivals that in *Maligne Lake*.

Jackson also visited the Rockies and was the first Group member to visit the Arctic (in 1927), the area around Great Slave Lake (in 1928), and the north Pacific Coast (1926). But he returned to Quebec virtually

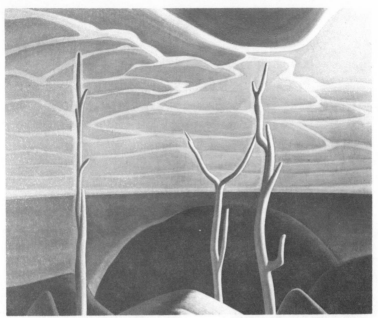

Lawren S. Harris. *Lake Superior*, 1924. Canvas, 40 x 50. AGO.

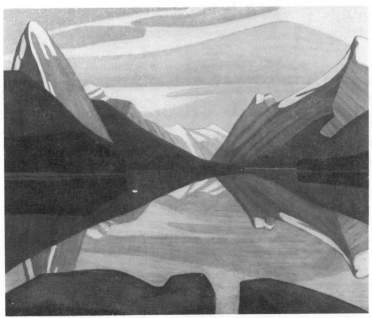

Lawren S. Harris. *Maligne Lake, Jasper Park*, 1924. Canvas, 48 x 60. NGC.

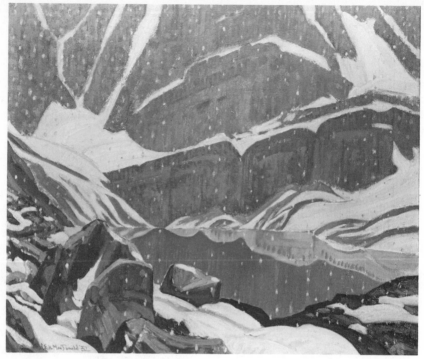

J.E.H. MacDonald. *Mountain Snowfall, Lake Oesa*, 1932. Canvas, 21 x 26. Estate of Charles S. Band, Toronto.

every spring, and it is from those experiences that he produced his most typical and finest canvases. *Early Spring, Quebec* (AGO) of 1926 is one of the best of these. Rich and full in colouring (though limited to tones of brown and grey), it has the easy, rolling rhythms of a mature Jackson. *Laurentian Hills, Early Spring* (AGO) of 1931 is more complex in its rhythmic structure, and even richer in earth colours. Like *Maligne Lake*, it proved to be an influential picture.

Fred Varley also first saw the Rockies in 1924 and fell as passionately in love with them as did Harris and MacDonald. He therefore took the opportunity of a job offer to move to Vancouver in 1926. It was a significant turning-point in his life. First distinguishing himself as a war artist, he had returned to Toronto determined to be a painter and launched on a career as a portraitist. Suited to this work as a painter, he found it difficult as a man, although some of his portraits, notably *Vincent Massey* (HH) of 1920, are deservedly famous. With the Vancouver mountains, however, Varley finally found a piece of landscape that stirred him, just as nature had moved the other Group members for years.

By this time, however, the heroic years of creative struggle were almost over. As it turned out, their work did not meet with the resistance they thought it would. It was on the whole accepted—though with restraint rather than enthusiasm. The Group worked hard to promote it. Between the summer of 1920 and the end of 1922 they organized more than forty small showings throughout the country. The National Gallery had encouraged them in various ways since 1913. In 1922 this support eventually drew the wrath of Hector Charlesworth, the conservative art critic of *Saturday Night,* upon the Gallery. The controversy that resulted lasted for some two years. Then, in 1924, with the announcement that the National Gallery would choose the Canadian representation at the British Empire Exhibition at Wembley, Eng., Charlesworth was joined by the RCA. It resented the Gallery's involvement in the organization of an international exhibition and, more importantly, was convinced that the traditional members of the Academy would be ignored. A jury eventually made a reasonably balanced choice, which included the Group. At the conclusion of the Wembley exhibition the

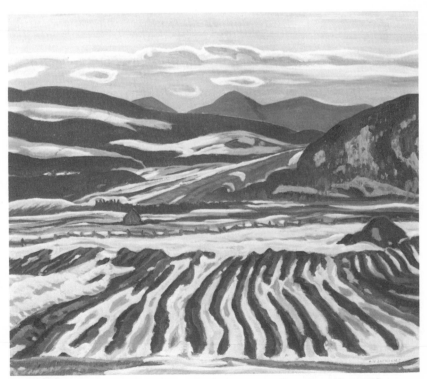

A.Y. Jackson. *Laurentian Hills, Early Spring,* 1931. Canvas, 21¼ x 26¼. AGO.

Tate purchased one Canadian painting: Jackson's *Entrance to Halifax Harbour* of 1919. By 1926 the Group of Seven were the acknowledged centre of serious art activity in Toronto, which in turn was the major centre of activity in the country. Followers and disciples were gathering. And even the broad public began to become aware of the Group of Seven as the 'national' school of art. By 1931, the year of the last exhibition of the Group, their supremacy was acknowledged—both grudgingly and willingly—right across the country. But the group effort had been maintained for too many years. As Bertram Brooker explained to LeMoine FitzGerald after the 1931 show:

J.E.H. has been very ill lately, and in any case, even if he recovers full strength, will probably not do much more painting. Varley was seriously ill this past summer and is very hard up, I hear. . . . He had only one canvas in the show. . . . Casson scarcely counted at all, and Carmichael had only about two things which were very reminiscent of stuff done five years ago. Lismer's Maritime canvases were hurried and rather literal. They did not excite anyone very much. Jackson showed up best of all with a lot of things along his usual line. Lawren has done no painting for six months and very little for a year. . . . The general impression, freely voiced, seems to be that he is repeating himself and has got to the end—of a phase, at least. Holgate has had to concentrate on commercial work and consequently had only two small portraits to show, neither of them very exceptional.

Prestige and power are difficult to set aside, however, and rather than simply dissolve, the Group chose to expand. The reins of direction consequently slipped gradually from their fingers.

II

Emily Carr,
LeMoine FitzGerald,
and
David Milne
1912-1950

By the late twenties the Group of Seven had 'defined' Canadian art in their work. Their national influence was strikingly revealed by the prominence in exhibitions across the country of broadly handled, boldly coloured Canadian landscape subjects. Nevertheless during the early years of their growth a number of other artists—equally Canadian— had been developing other approaches, seeking to satisfy other needs. Largely ignored during the Group years, three of these painters each came into national prominence during the thirties.

The oldest was EMILY CARR (1871-1945). Born in Victoria of English parents, she first studied art in San Francisco at the age of eighteen. In 1894, after five years, she returned to Victoria determined to be an artist and set up a studio in the family barn where she proceeded to paint and offer children's classes. In later years she realized her naivety then. 'As yet I had not considered the inside of myself. I was like a child printing alphabet letters. I had not begun to make words.'

There was nonetheless a desire to grow, to develop. In 1898, aged twenty-seven, she saw her first Indian village on a visit to the mission school at Ucluelet on the Pacific coast of Vancouver Island. And the next year she travelled almost halfway round the world to London to enrol in the Westminster School of Art. Her health soon began to suffer from the London climate, however, so she moved to St Ives for a year, followed by six months at the Herkomer Art School in Hertfordshire. The 'city disease' that was to attack her whenever she settled in a metropolis stayed with her nonetheless, and in 1902 she was admitted to a Suffolk sanatorium, gravely ill with pernicious anaemia. Eighteen months later she was released. Late in 1905, at the age of thirty-four and with almost fifteen years of inconsequential art studies behind her, she decided to establish herself as an artist-teacher in Vancouver.

She had discovered no art scene at all in Victoria. There had been visitors, like William Hind, who worked there from 1863 to 1865, but SOPHIE PEMBERTON (1869-1959) was the first native-born painter to receive even slight attention. She had gone to London to study at the Slade in 1894, and two years later had enrolled at Julian's. Her first exhibition in Victoria was not until 1902, and in 1904, the year of Emily's return, she exhibited at the Vancouver studio of James Blomfield (1872-1951). An uneven and often awkward painter, her best work achieves an academic competence that would have been acceptable in Toronto or Montreal ten years earlier.

The Vancouver scene was not much more lively. The first gallery had opened in 1887, primarily to sell supplies to the many eastern artists who came through by rail after 1886. These painters often made extended visits, even exhibiting in Vancouver as opportunities arose. Many returned frequently, and Mower Martin almost made Vancouver his second home. Their influence held the taste of Vancouver's art public firmly in the nineteenth century. Emily Carr's early Vancouver work was nurtured in this environment. Her watercolours—she then worked exclusively in that medium—followed the taste and even the subjects of Mower Martin and the other easterners, though the native-born painter's compositions are often more dramatic, as in her *War Canoes* (private collection) of about 1908, and show a more sensitive concern for the strengths of Indian designs.

Indian culture, in fact, was becoming her creative inspiration. She frequently visited the reserves at Kitsilano and North Vancouver, and in the summer of 1907 travelled to Alaska with her sister Alice, visiting a number of Indian villages along the coast on her return. Back in Vancouver she resolved—much as Paul Kane had done sixty years before —to paint a programmatic series that would record the villages, and particularly the awesome totem poles, for posterity. Over the next four summers she visited many remote villages, painting hundreds of watercolours, but failed to be satisfied with the results. She realized that she was still not properly equipped to achieve her goal, so she and her sister Alice left in July 1910 for Paris, where Emily hoped to acquire the pictorial language to express herself with force. She was then thirty-nine years old.

An English modernist working in Paris, whom Emily remembered as Henry Gibb (likely Phelan Gibb, 1870-1948), recommended that she study at the Colarossi Academy where the women were not segregated from the male students. After a couple of months in the city, however, her anaemia returned and she was again hospitalized. Three horrible months later she was released and fled with Alice to Sweden for the winter. Returning in the spring of 1911, Emily joined a landscape class conducted by Gibb in a small village two hours out of Paris and then spent the summer with him and his wife in Brittany. She was beginning to achieve good results in her painting and that fall was even accepted in the Salon d'Automne, still the showplace of 'advanced' painting. (Morrice exhibited there regularly, and did that year; Clapp had shown there four years earlier, and John Lyman would after the war.) She crowned her stay with six weeks of study under a woman water-colourist at Concarneau (probably the New Zealander Frances Hodgkins) and returned to Victoria in November.

Early in 1912 she moved back to Vancouver. At the end of March she held an exhibition in her studio of her French work that likely included *Autumn in France* (NGC). A small canvas, it is vigorous in composition and strikingly brilliant in colour. Hot red-browns, oranges, and yellows are kept in lively balance by cool greens, green-blues, and blues. In its use of broad Fauve sweeps of paint and the exploitation of intense colour, it represented the most advanced and most accomplished experimental painting to be seen in Canada in 1912. Strangely enough Vancouver welcomed the exhibition with interest as an example of the exotic contemporary culture of France.

Heartened, Emily spent the summer working in Indian villages in the Queen Charlotte Islands and that fall painted up pictures employing the intense colour and broad, expressive brushwork she had learned in France. These she exhibited in her studio in April 1913. They were, like *Potlatch Figure* (Dr and Mrs Max Stern, Montreal), not as 'radical' in appearance as her French paintings. The colours do not include the hot, dry hues of the Breton countryside but tend largely to lush blues and greens, and the atmosphere is heavy with the warm moisture of the west coast. And the paintings all have a specific figurative concern with depicting Indian carvings. Nonetheless, Vancouver seems to have found these paintings difficult to accept. They were of course exotic without being foreign; they held a threat of change not in the least diminished by distance.* The result for Emily Carr was that no pictures were sold and attendance at the painting classes she depended upon for

*1913 was the year of the Armoury Show in New York and most Canadian papers had picked up examples of the vicious assault the American popular press was mounting against the weird foreign art. The AAM spring show that year had contained a number of radical experiments that were also unequivocally attacked in the press. Lyman's one-man show there had also been ridiculed, and the 'Hot Mush School' of Toronto was christened later that year in a similar assault.

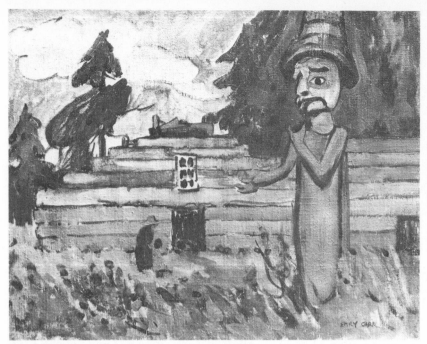

Emily Carr. *Potlatch Figure*, 1912. Canvas, 17½ x 23½. Dr and Mrs Max Stern, Montreal.

her living dropped off. Retreating to Victoria, she built a four-suite apartment in the hope of supporting her art as a landlord. The load was too much. At the age of forty-two she virtually had to accept defeat and ceased all serious painting.

Fortunately during the winter of 1915 Marius Barbeau, world-famous ethnologist from the National Museum in Ottawa, heard of Emily Carr from one of his Indian interpreters and visited her in Victoria. Seeing her paintings as priceless records of lost Indian art, he was also impressed with her talent and bought two of her 1912 works. Visiting again in 1921 he brought her painting to the attention of Eric Brown, director of the National Gallery. Six years later Barbeau and Brown organized an exhibition of Canadian west-coast art that included the work of white painters as well as native art and was virtually built around twenty-six of Emily Carr's 1912 paintings. The importance of this event in her life cannot be overestimated. And most importantly Brown was able to arrange a CNR pass for her to come east for the opening. There she first met and saw the work of Lawren Harris and the other members of the Group of Seven. She wrote in her journal (*Hundreds and Thousands*, Clarke, Irwin & Company Ltd, 1966):

Oh, God, what have I seen? Where have I been? Something has

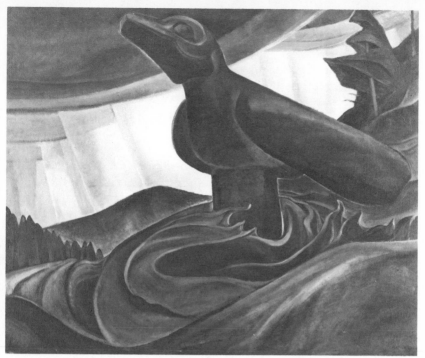

Emily Carr. *Big Raven*, c.1928. Canvas, 34¼ x 45. VAG.

spoken to the very soul of me, wonderful, mighty, not of this world. Chords way down in my being have been touched. Dumb notes have struck chords of wonderful tone. Something has called out of some-where. Something in me is trying to answer. . . . Jackson, Johnston, Varley, Lismer, Harris—up-up-up-up-up! Lismer and Harris stir me most. Lismer is swirling, sweeping on, but Harris is rising into serene, uplifted planes, above the swirl into holy places.

Three days after her return to Victoria she was painting again—after fourteen years. And the next summer she made a heroic journey up the Skeena and Nass Rivers, through the Queen Charlotte Islands, and into the interior. Brown had arranged another CNR pass for the interior trip. He had plans. 'I am looking forward to the time when you and Varley and others will start a West Coast Group,' he wrote.

Her new canvases were a complete departure from the earlier work. As is evident in her *Big Raven* (VAG) of that first year, they were memories of the Harris paintings she had seen in Toronto applied to the lush forest growth and dramatic totems that were her subjects. They are not derivative, however. They throb and sway with the vital energy of conviction. That conviction was reinforced in October 1928 when the American painter Mark Tobey, recently returned to Seattle after two years in Europe, conducted three weeks of classes in her studio. His work was at this time also made up of swirling organic forms; and although more abstract then Emily's, it obviously sought the same life rhythms.

Emily exhibited with the Group of Seven in Toronto in 1930, corresponded with Harris regularly, and met him again in Toronto in 1931, but she did not seek to link herself creatively with Varley and the other painters in Vancouver. In 1930 she held an exhibition of her 'pole' paintings in Victoria, and another at the Seattle Art Museum. After this, Indian themes were no longer her major concern. Encouraged by Harris, and led by her profound understanding of Indian art, she sought deeper into the land itself to express the search for a transcendental state. In paintings like *Forest, British Columbia* (VAG) of about 1932 she portrayed the rain forest itself in the same plastic terms as she earlier had treated the Indian poles. Elaborately interlocking growth is painted sculpturally, as though it were an intricate carving, revealing glimpses of the inner life of the forms.

Emily Carr never used the small oil field-sketch made so popular by the Group of Seven. Instead in 1932 she devised a technique she described to Eric Brown: 'Oil paint used thin with gasoline on paper. I feel I have gained a lot by its use. It is inexpensive, light to carry, and allows great freedom of thought and action. Woods and skies out west are big. You can't squeeze them down.' Woods and skies were her sole concern for the next ten years. In 1933 she bought a house trailer for field sketching, and annual summer trips became the focus of her life. Her vision, her aspirations opened up and out. No longer interested in the heavy infolding sculptural forms of the deep forest, she sought the swirling, airy images of loggers' clearings or of the seashore.

By 1934-5, when she painted †*Forest Landscape II* (NGC), her unique style had become perfectly attuned to every nuance of expressive feeling, her brush responding with a variety of swirls, flutters, streaks, sweeps, and dabs to the least emotive tremble resulting from her highly pitched attentiveness. *Sky* (NGC), dated to that same year, is virtually *all* sky. Radiating a hallucinatory cool white heat, pulsating across the whole field of vision, its transcendental qualities rival even the best of Lawren Harris's images of the North Shore of Lake Superior or the Rockies.

By 1935, aged sixty-four, she was beginning to feel the joy of public recognition of her now fully realized abilities. Although she still felt the art scene in Victoria to be dismal (a 'People's Art Gallery' she started there folded after two months of intense effort over the winter of 1932-3), her eastern successes multiplied. In 1936 she had two solo ex-

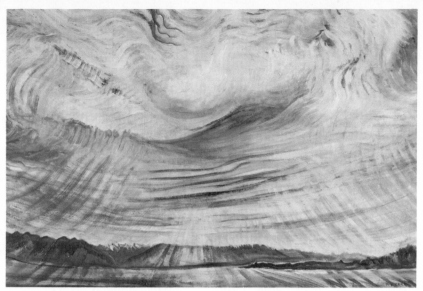

Emily Carr. *Sky*, c.1935. Paper, 22½ x 35. NGC.

hibitions in Toronto and in 1937 the Art Gallery of Toronto gave her a one-woman show. Then in 1938 she held an exhibition at the Vancouver Art Gallery. It was a great success and eleven pictures were sold. 'What made me so pleased about it,' she wrote to Brown, 'was the fact that I had been able to make their own Western places speak to them.'

Emily had had the first of a series of heart attacks in 1937 (she had sold her troublesome boarding house only the year before) and this curtailed travel to some degree. It also turned her with new seriousness to a life-long interest: her writing. She explained to Brown in March 1939 that she was beginning to 'write the story of me, or my work rather'. She was probably referring specifically to her autobiography, published the year after her death as *Growing Pains*, but she could have meant any one of her amazing books, all of which deal with her life, and thus her work. The first to be published was *Klee Wyck* (1941), a classic collection of stories of her life with the Indians that won a Governor General's Award. But she continued to paint and her reputation grew. During the last years of her life she exhibited both on the coast and in the east at least every year; this exposure culminated in her first show in a commercial gallery in 1944. Montreal's Dominion Gallery sold fifty-seven of the sixty works on display. Bedridden by then, she continued to paint and write until her death the following March.

In 1942—the last year of significant painting production—she relived a number of earlier themes of the 1930-2 period. Nostalgic yet strong full works, most depict totem poles, although one, *Cedar* (VAG), returns to the deep interior of the rain-forest. They are not—as Doris Shadbolt has pointed out—closed, heavy, foreboding, but are open, lyrical, light and sure—evidence of the profound resolution achieved by a giant, striving personality.

LE MOINE FITZGERALD (1890-1956) was born in Winnipeg and, like Emily Carr, retained a fierce loyalty and a creative dependence on his home region all his life. Unlike Carr, whose life was one of emotional extremes, buffeted by the vagaries of fortune, FitzGerald's monumental accomplishment was built slowly and steadily, never wavering; it was always internally logical. 'After leaving school,' he wrote, ' I worked in a wholesale drug office, and finding the job not quite satisfying I felt the first real urge to draw, so I got some drawing-paper, a pencil, and eraser and started work.' He was then fourteen years old.

Employed in various ways during the day, he studied nights with a Hungarian painter, A.S. Keszthelyi (b. 1875), and by 1912, aged twenty-two, had decided to become a painter. He exhibited in the RCA the next year—the show was held in Winnipeg to inaugurate the new art gallery—and for the next seven years he worked as a commercial designer and interior decorator, regularly sending work east for exhibit (his *Late Fall, Manitoba*, 1917, was bought by the NGC in 1918). If not then an exciting scene, Winnipeg at least offered mutual support and camaraderie, mainly focused on Brigden's commercial art firm; and the arrival of W.J. Phillips (1884-1963) in 1913 and of Eric Bergman (1893-1958) in 1914 did much to encourage professionalism among the local artists. The foundation of the Winnipeg School of Art and Winnipeg Art Gallery, also in 1913, helped bring art to the attention of the community.

FitzGerald held his first one-man exhibition at the WAG in September 1921. It consisted principally of sketches, but there were some larger canvases, including one called *Summer Afternoon* (WAG) of 1921. Painted in a decorative impressionist style, and almost two-thirds sky, it is elegantly simple in composition and delicate in colour. Though it was likely inspired by magazine reproductions, it demonstrates a fresh inventiveness and the degree to which FitzGerald was this early responding to the basic qualities of the prairies. He later explained that 'the prairie has many aspects, but intense light and the feeling of great space are dominating characteristics and are the major problems of the prairie artist.'

The decorative side of FitzGerald's art found support with the arrival in September 1921 of Frank Johnston of the Group of Seven to become

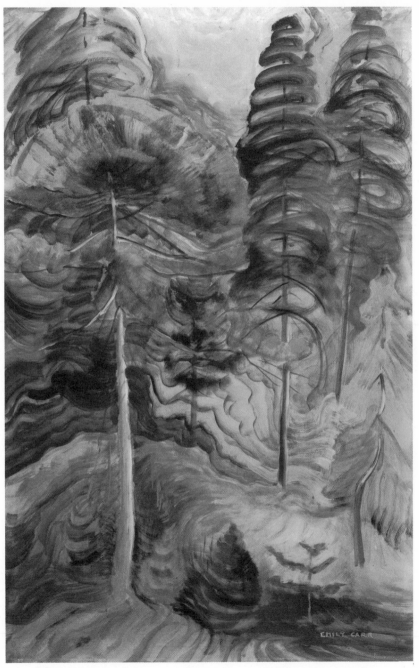

XXII—Emily Carr. *Forest Landscape II*, c.1935. Paper, 36 x 24. NGC.

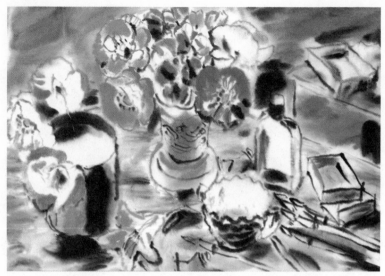

XXIII—David Milne. *White Poppy*, 1946. Watercolour, 14 5/16 x 21⅜. NGC.

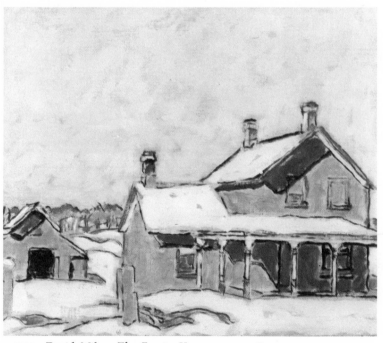

XXIV—David Milne. *The Empty House*, c.1931. Canvas, 20 x 24. NGC.

principal of the Winnipeg School of Art. Johnston would have seen FitzGerald's show, of course, but it was FitzGerald who was impressed. Writing to Johnston from a train passing through Algoma on the way to Ottawa that October, he remarked how 'already I appreciate the truth that you have caught in your things and the big decorative values. . . . To just see your interpretation and then the real thing gives me a more intimate feeling toward the work that you and the others have been doing.' Decorative landscape painting would not much longer be an enthusiasm, however, for even as he wrote the letter FitzGerald was on his way to New York City to enrol in the Art Students League.

He worked there over the winter of 1921-2 under Kenneth Hayes Miller and Boardman Robinson. It was a moment at the League when ideas were first developing that by the end of the decade would emerge as American Scene painting. The smooth sculptural modelling that later became the hallmark of that style was then being advanced. FitzGerald returned to Winnipeg and commercial art probably in the spring of 1922. The summer of 1924 he spent at Banff (Johnston was there in July) and that fall he began teaching at the Winnipeg School of Art.

FitzGerald's work has not yet been studied closely enough to determine its development during these years, but one can imagine that he would have returned home in the spring of 1922 with a changed style and a confirmed approach to his art, both reflecting his New York experience. *Williamson's Garage* (NGC) of 1927 is perhaps typical of his work of the twenties. It is 'regional' in the sense that it has no pretensions as a grand subject but is homely and unaffected in its loving depiction of what would have been a very familiar scene to the artist. Its realism is emphatic, with great concern for 'plastic' qualities: a careful modelling of volumes, a precise description of space and of the placement of forms in that space. It is reverent and still.

In August 1929 FitzGerald became the principal of the school. (Johnston had left in the summer of 1924, before FitzGerald began teaching.) He was also finding his full maturity as an artist, at the age of thirty-nine. *Doc Snider's House* (NGC) of 1931 is one of the important works of this period. It clearly maintains the 'regionalist' and 'plastic' concerns seen in *Williamson's Garage*, but it is more ambitious, larger and more complex, with an exciting play on depth through the variously placed tree-trunks. The rich texture of the earlier painting is gone. As in the work of the Precisionist painters (Charles Sheeler, Charles Demuth, et al.), then popular in the United States, the smooth finish stresses the sensitive interrelationships of the cubic forms of houses

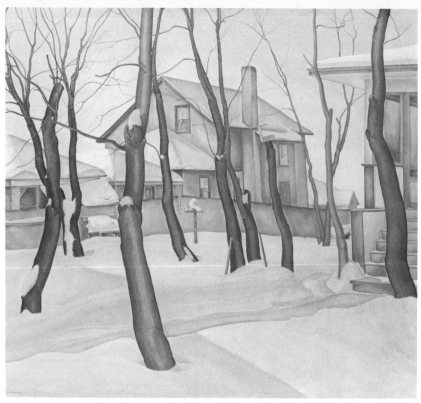

LeMoine FitzGerald. *Doc Snider's House*, 1931. Canvas, 29½ x 33½. NGC.

and outbuildings. The colour—limited to browns, blue, and green—is delicate and moving. It is one of his most accomplished paintings and one of the treasures of Canadian art.

FRITZ BRANDTNER (1896-1969), who arrived in Winnipeg from Danzig in 1928, found in FitzGerald the only sympathetic ear for his theories of art. When in 1934 Winnipeg proved unequal to his eclectic modernism, FitzGerald encouraged him to move to the more cosmopolitan Montreal. In 1929 Brandtner had brought FitzGerald to the attention of another Manitoban then living in Toronto, Bertram Brooker (see p. 181 ff.), who became a lifelong friend and his greatest enthusiast. He showed FitzGerald's work to Lawren Harris, arranged exhibitions in Toronto, and generally kept him linked to that centre of art activity. As a result, FitzGerald was invited to show with the Group of Seven and in 1932 was formally announced a member. The Group was by then no longer exhibiting, but when the Canadian Group of Painters was formed in 1933, FitzGerald was a charter member.

Intensely dedicated, he structured everything towards the accomplishment of his painting goals. In his characteristically measured way he once described how 'it seems impossible for the artist to attain any height without sacrificing at least a little of the ordinary necessities, not to mention the loss of ordinary social contact, that are so essential to others.' He kept his sensibility at a high pitch through constant drawing exercises. Often berated by friends and colleagues for the lack of exhibition canvases, he never made apologies. 'For some reason, I haven't been painting for quite awhile, but drawing. Result—no paintings.' In the same letter he further explained his working pace. '*Doc Snider's House* represents two winters, including two full weeks each Christmas vacation as well as all weekends.'

During the early thirties FitzGerald, in concert with his friend Brooker, became intensely interested in the painting of still-lifes. He achieved amazing results with his painstaking technique, which by the middle of the decade included texture again. *The Jar* (wag) of 1938 is one of the best of these still-lifes—sensual yet austerely controlled. FitzGerald once explained how 'it is necessary to get inside the object and push it out rather than merely building it up from the outer aspect.'

In 1940, feeling the increasing need to paint full time, FitzGerald applied—unsuccessfully—for a Guggenheim grant. Disappointed, but typically matter-of-fact, he explained to a friend that 'I am working along a little different line and have been doing so for the past two years, trying to broaden the previous approach, and I think the work is now showing signs of something interesting. With a year of steady work, I am sure the results would warrant the experiment.' Never accepting setbacks, he systematically continued to explore new areas in his spare time. In 1942 he wrote, 'I am still on the large watercolours with anything as subject matter and finding out quite a lot that I hadn't experimented with before. How successful they are as pictures I have not been worrying about, but the solving of certain problems has been the main issue.' The 'large watercolours' are part of a startling series of works that were first publicly exhibited only in 1963. Mainly female nude studies of great sensitivity and ruthlessly penetrating self-portraits, many, such as *Green Self-portrait* (wag) of about 1942, combine the two subjects in rich overlays that suggest visual puns and play on the relationship of model to artist in a profoundly suggestive way, although the two subjects are ostensibly unconnected on the sheet and might even have resulted from different sessions.

Systematic experimentation continued. In the summer of 1942 he first visited the west coast; he returned the next two summers. Breathtaking large watercolours of rock formations, shoreline, and plants

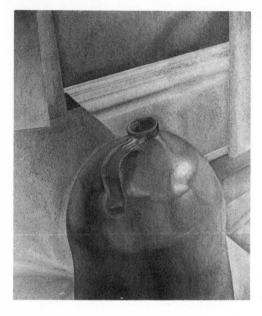

LeMoine FitzGerald. *The Jar*, 1938. Canvas, 24 x 21¼. WAG.

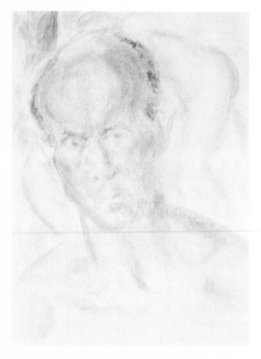

LeMoine FitzGerald. *Green Self-portrait*, c.1942. Watercolour, 23⅞ x 18. WAG.

resulted. Like *Rocks* (private collection) of 1944, all are concerned with complex interlocking forms that manifest a delight in richly modulated surface texture. Throughout the forties almost all the major works were in watercolour, the result of an intense personal need to refine his experiments to an essence. In 1946 a concerted effort by friends to obtain a special government pension so that he could leave the school (he was fifty-six) failed, but it became possible for him to obtain two years' special leave beginning in September 1947. He began gingerly to work seriously in oils again.

His approach was basically the same as in the late thirties, but, as in *The Little Plant* (MCM) of 1947, displayed an even more pronounced surface texture. Each stroke is carefully placed in an effect close to mosaic, resulting in a singing, scintillating surface. The colour radiates like light itself with the clear delicacy of watercolour. That winter (1947-8) FitzGerald and his wife left Winnipeg to live at Saseenos, about twenty miles from Victoria. Painting full time for the first time in his life, he worked and reacted like a student. 'With all this continuous study, I feel a growing power in composing and in the execution, whether a drawing or a painting.' His reserved yet deeply moving reactions were transmitted to friends. 'I am more grateful than ever for this opportunity, realizing how inadequate was the time I had previously.'

The following November (1948) the FitzGeralds returned to the coast again, this time living and working in West Vancouver for six months. They saw quite a bit of Lawren Harris and of B.C. Binning, and were generally impressed with the liveliness of the Vancouver scene. They even considered moving. In September 1949 FitzGerald decided to retire rather than return to the school, and that winter they stayed at home. It was so cold he had to work inside, painting the magnificent *From an Upstairs Window* (NGC). It is a poem to the meaning of form —the distillation of a life of looking and making.

This was not the end of experimentation, however. Probably the following year FitzGerald first responded to the abstractions painted by his friend Brooker almost twenty-five years earlier. Encouraged by Brooker's continuing interest in the underlying forms of all objects, and doubtless egged on by his frequent meetings with Lawren Harris over the last decade, FitzGerald himself began to paint abstractions. They became the major concern of the last five years of his life, and he exhibited one as part of the Canadian representation at the first Bienal do São Paulo in Brazil in the fall of 1951. He exhibited another in the CGP exhibition in November 1952 and completed the best of the series

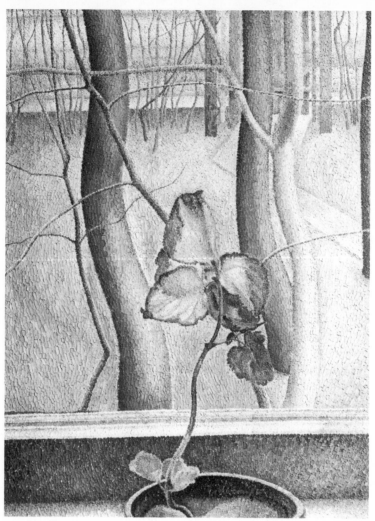

LeMoine FitzGerald. *The Little Plant*, 1947. Canvas, 24 x 18¼. MCM.

in 1954, the beautiful *Green and Gold* (WAG). Displaying the same delicate assuredness of colour and form as his representational works, it was his last major canvas. He continued to work, of course—mainly in chalk, ink, and watercolour—principally on abstractions and still-lifes. He died in Winnipeg of a heart attack in August 1956.

DAVID MILNE (1882-1953) was born near Paisley, Ont., in Bruce County, near the shores of Lake Huron. He was educated there and stayed on as a country teacher. Not so loyal to his region as Carr or FitzGerald, he nevertheless was seldom happy for long in cities and always sought the peace and solitude of the rural life he had known as a boy. A childhood interest in art revived while he was teaching school, and his old high-school teacher suggested he go to New York to study. That was in 1904 and Milne was twenty-two.

The first school he chose closed shortly after he had paid his hard-earned fee, but he immediately enrolled in the Art Students League (seventeen years before FitzGerald attended). The first year he worked nights lettering shopkeepers' window cards to pay his way. This little business expanded and for the next two years he worked days and studied nights. Finally in the fall of 1907, having left the League, he was able to earn enough from commercial work in the mornings to devote the rest of the day to serious painting. He had decided to be a painter (he had gone to New York intending to be an illustrator) and so began to exhibit—mainly watercolours, as the watercolour exhibitions were less rigid and allowed experimental work.

By 1913 Milne was 'known' around New York as an experimental artist and was invited to exhibit in the famous Armoury Show. (The only other Canadian included was Arthur Crisp (1881-1966) from Hamilton.) The experience had little effect on him. He later remarked that 'I already had my feet firmly set on a path of my own.' Nor did inclusion bring fame, as the 'sensational Frenchmen' (Duchamp, Matisse et al.) drew all the attention. The 'path' Milne had chosen can be seen in *Billboard* (NGC) of 1912, possibly exhibited in the Armoury Show as *Columbus Circle*. A striking picture, it is Post-Impressionist, almost Fauve in style, like Emily Carr's work of 1911. Milne's colours, however, are not as aggressive, and he is more concerned with the patterning of his brushstrokes. We are, in fact, primarily impressed by the sense of order this patterning brings to the lively city scene depicted. The effect is very close to watercolours by James Morrice's friend Prendergast, which Milne would have seen in the Eight exhibition in 1908, and could have seen, among other places, at the annual group shows at the Montross Gallery (Horatio Walker's dealer) in which Milne also participated.

By the spring of 1914 the lack of any success in the face of such an extended effort—he had been in New York almost ten years—began to depress Milne and he and his wife retired to the Catskills for the summer. The following May, tired of big-city life, they left for good and by the fall were settled at Boston Corners in the lower Berkshires of New York State. It meant the end of his intensive period of looking and exhibiting, and from then his art developed, like FitzGerald's, in a slow but steady and internally logical way. The roughly rectangular patterning of his city scenes became organic in the Berkshires, more

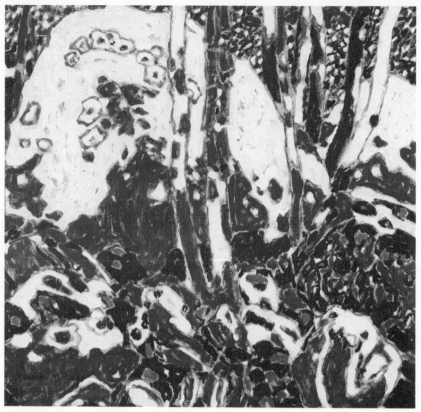

David Milne. *The Boulder*, 1916. Canvas, 24 x 26. WAG.

suited to landscape forms. *The Boulder* (WAG) of 1916 is typical in its
intense overall patterning in white and its harmonious closely valued
hues, suggestive of the work of the Frenchman Edouard Vuillard.

War had broken out in the summer of 1914, but the United States
did not enter until 1917. For reasons unknown, Milne decided then to
enlist in the Canadian army (he had been a resident of the States for
fourteen years!). He entered the First Central Ontario Regiment in
Toronto on March 1, 1918, and was shipped out in September. While
still at arrival camp in England he heard of the War Records program
and was able to arrange for work to be sent to London for consideration.
By May 1919 he was an official war artist with the acting rank of lance-
corporal. He visited Canadian camps in Britain and theatres of action
in France and Belgium (this was after the Armistice), and produced 107
works now in the War Museum in Ottawa. They are the most elegant
paintings in the collection. Mainly dry-brush watercolours, they are
almost oriental in their delicacy. As can be seen most remarkably in
Shell Holes and Wire at the Old German Line of June 1919, the empty

spaces are more important than the lines and forms that define them.

Milne was demobilized in Toronto in October 1919 and by December was back in Boston Corners with his wife. He soon returned to his pre-service routine, which he broke only briefly for a one-man show of his watercolours at Cornell University in Ithaca, N.Y., in 1922. The winter of 1923-4 was spent in Ottawa and the NGC bought six works. He also visited Montreal that winter and was able to arrange an exhibition at the AAM.

He was then painting works like *Carnival Dress, Dominion Square, Montreal* (AEAC). Open and airy, clean in colour yet suggestive of atmospheric space, it is sensitive yet in no way precious. It is totally free of sentimentality yet joyous and buoyant and above all intensely personal. Montreal was not impressed, however. There were no sales, and Milne returned to rural New York for five more years.

Finally late in 1928 he decided to return to Canada to settle—he had been living in the United States for twenty-four years. He first visited

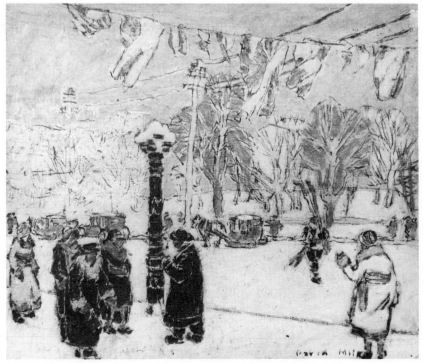

David Milne. *Carnival Dress, Dominion Square, Montreal,* 1924. Canvas, 18 x 22. AEAC.

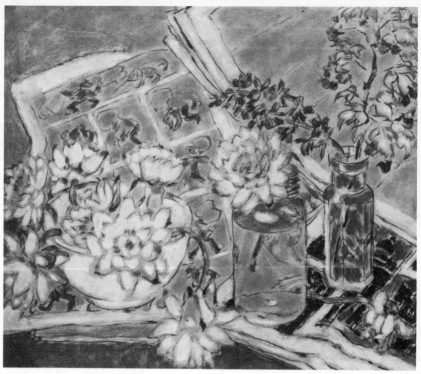

David Milne. *Water Lilies, Temagami*, 1929. Canvas, 20 x 24. HH.

Ottawa and in the spring of 1929 headed north to Temagami for the summer. He had by now established his lifestyle. He sought a solitary existence away from cities, with everything organized to one single end: painting. He had as clearly established his personal painting style. *Water Lilies, Temagami* (HH), painted that summer, demonstrates his remarkable abilities: an incredible delicacy of line within a vigorous composition. The still-life is 'studied' in its arrangement yet spontaneous in treatment. Elegant, it is without pretension. The newspapers spread beneath the bowls and the bottles of water-lilies are taken from the Sunday coloured 'comics'. It is vibrant but harmonious in colour, vital yet tasteful. Milne was a backwoods epicurean; a man wholly sufficient unto himself.

That winter he returned to Toronto (it had been ten years since his last visit) and moved out to Longstaff's Pump Works at Weston, just northwest of the city. Early in 1930 he rented accommodation in Palgrave, also a short drive from Toronto, where he lived until May 1933. There he became an interested but detached observer of the Toronto scene. Writing to friends in Ottawa, he offered capsule evaluations of the current enthusiasms. Jackson he singled out. 'At the moment, I would say, at the top of Canadian Art and something of his own, something great. Harris I would place as your other creative man. . . . Whatever the value of the Group of Seven in art, there is no doubt about their value to Canada. Mr. Bennett could very nicely vote the seven a million dollars each, and the country would still be in their debt.' But most of all he seems to have admired Thomson. 'I rather think it would have been wiser to have taken your ten most prominent Canadians and sunk them in Canoe Lake—and saved Tom Thomson.' Of all the Canadian-wilderness school only Thomson, of course, would ever have attempted a picture like *Water Lilies, Temagami*.

Milne had little interest in the proselytizing efforts of the Group of Seven, and even less in their aggressive nationalism. He was interested in 'pure' painting. Subjects, he claimed, were of minor importance. 'Significant form' made a picture work. As a result of this approach his paintings have never had the wide appeal of the work of the Group of Seven. But he was nonetheless blessed with a few understanding friends. While he was living at Palgrave the NGC arranged to bring his work to the attention of Vincent Massey and his wife, and from this grew a patronage arrangement unique in Canadian art history. The Masseys purchased a large group of pictures from Milne that they then arranged to sell on consignment through the prestigious Mellors Gallery in Toronto, meeting all immediate expenses themselves and depositing all 'profits' in a fund. Milne was never happy with the arrangement. He felt it gave Mellors a guaranteed income through framing and exhibition fees while the Masseys assumed all the risks. The Masseys could afford to, of course, but Milne also doubted Mellors' sympathy for his work. Finally, late in 1938, the arrangement was ended. It had nonetheless given Milne five clear years of full-time painting and at least four annual exhibitions.

In May 1933, the year before the first Massey-Mellors exhibition, Milne had moved into the bush. He built himself a 'painting house in the wilderness' at Six Mile Lake on the Severn River, just north of Orillia, where he could control his contact with cities and people. The drive from Toronto to Severn Falls then took three to four hours but the last seven miles in to Milne's tarpaper cabin added from two to five hours, depending on conditions. Friends nonetheless did visit with news of the outside world, and Milne went to Toronto regularly. He described one trip in 1938. 'The visit to Toronto—exactly a week—was, as usual, interesting and restful, except that I didn't get enough sleep.' In one typical day he met Lismer, Jackson, Barker Fairley (b.1887), Will Ogilvie, and Carl Schaefer, among others.

The years at Six Mile Lake were not completely ideal. (He stayed there until the summer of 1939.) There were long periods in which he was unable to work, notably the winter of 1935-6; and for almost the whole of the last two years he painted only in watercolour. But there are many magnificent pictures. As usual, he was totally uncompromising, and such simplified, almost abstract studies in form as the *Young Poplars among Driftwood* (NGC) of 1937 are certainly among his best pictures. Almost brutal, with a gut thrill of spontaneity, it reveals the absolute precision of his touch in full maturity. Like all of his paintings, it was completed in one sitting.

During the summer of 1939 he moved to Toronto, remaining until the fall of 1940. Douglas Duncan was now his dealer. Duncan had travelled to Six Mile Lake in the summer of 1935, after having been impressed by the first Mellors show the year before. He found himself totally in sympathy with Milne's sensibility. In the fall of 1940 Milne moved to Uxbridge, a small village northeast of Toronto. He spent his autumns in Haliburton, at Coboconk or Gull Lake until 1946, and at Baptiste Lake just outside of Bancroft from 1947. He moved to Baptiste Lake in 1952 and died there the day after Christmas 1953.

Milne's works of the forties seem very different. Mainly wash-painted watercolours, they glow with soft suffusions of colour. Like †*White Poppy* (NGC) of 1946, they usually depict subjects of intense colour. One seldom sees the dry line or aggressive forms of the twenties or thirties, and the pictures often appear, like *White Poppy*, far removed from actuality. It was in fact a period in which Milne indulged himself in numerous 'fantasy' pictures, many of a whimsically religious nature. All are rigorously beautiful, amazingly constructed works of art. They are intensely intimate and modest, with that assurance that arises only from genius.

12

The Canadian
Group of Painters
1933-1945

As early as 1921 A.Y. Jackson had proposed that the Group of Seven expand. 'I would like to see it increased to ten or twelve members,' he wrote to a friend, 'but we do not see any original genius among the young element here. The younger set in Montreal are more promising and eventually we may merge into a Canadian group.' Eventually they did. The first substantial evidence of such a bent came in May 1926 when ten 'guests' were included in the Group of Seven exhibition, all clearly admirers of the Group. That same year the first new member was added in A.J. Casson (b.1898), and in 1930 the role was brought to eight —Casson had replaced Johnston, who had left the Group—with the addition of Edwin Holgate (b. 1892) of Montreal. Fred Varley had moved to Vancouver in 1926, and so Holgate was the second member resident outside of Toronto.

The Group was also beginning to assume 'national' responsibilities in other ways. Jackson's trip with Holgate to the Skeena River region of British Columbia in 1926 was followed by heroic journeys to the high eastern Arctic and the west Arctic. MacDonald and Harris both visited the Rockies at least once a year after 1924, and Harris too saw the Arctic. He was also adventuring into the most advanced art of the day. In 1927 he brought to Toronto an exhibition of the collection of the Société Anonyme.* And that same year Lismer was made Educational Supervisor of the Art Gallery: his educational and propagandizing

*The Société Anonyme was a foundation established by Katherine Dreier—New York patron of Piet Mondrian, Marcel Duchamp, and Wassily Kandinsky, among others—to collect and promote the most advanced modern painting in the world. Lawren Harris was the only Canadian represented in its collection.

efforts were by this time consuming virtually all of his remarkable energy.

But resentment was rising against the Group, much of it simple bitterness at its resounding public success. And in 1928 there was an antimodernist attack from Vancouver against the Group that carried a suggestion of western resentment at eastern presumption. The year before, Clarence Gagnon had chided the 'Seven Wise Men' of Canadian art for keeping others out of their house. And by 1931 there had been a number of reasonable yet fundamental complaints lodged against the Group in the press—not only about their influence but about the exclusiveness of both their vision of Canadian art and their membership. After the opening of the 1931 show Jackson announced: 'The interest in a freer form of art expression in Canada has become so general that we believe the time has arrived when the Group of Seven should expand. . . .' As a result of a series of small meetings in Toronto early in 1933, the Canadian Group of Painters was formed, and the first exhibition of the new group was held that summer in Atlantic City, N.J. The catalogue was explicit in its nationalism. The CGP was an 'outgrowth' of the Group of Seven, it explained, and represented 'the modern movement in Canadian painting'. 'Modernism in Canada has almost no relation to the modernism of Europe', it went on. 'In Canada the main concerns have been with landscape moods and rhythms', and as modernists in Canada roam the country seeking the land, 'their work is strongly redolent of the Canadian soil and has a distinctively national flavour.'

The statement prepared for the first Canadian audience in November was less narrow in its landscape bias, but just as clearly, if somewhat defensively, it took its position from the achievements of the Group of Seven. The CGP, although 'a direct outgrowth of the Group of Seven', had a membership 'drawn from the whole of Canada'. Although recognizing the 'national character' of art in Canada, such an interpretation would allow 'a wide appreciation of the right of Canadian artists to find beauty and character in all things'. The CGP would encompass as well the amateur movement, as promoted by Fred Housser and Lismer, 'to extend the creative faculty beyond the professional meaning of art and to make of it a more common language of expression. . . .' Although painting in Canada was seen as having been until then 'a landscape art', 'figures and portraits have been slowly added to the subject matter, strengthening and occupying the background of landscape. . . . More modern ideas of technique and subject' would also be encouraged. It was a cautious forward step indeed.

Only four years later there were more invited contributors than members exhibiting in the annual November show. The CGP had become a regular exhibiting society like the RCA. It encouraged young painters to exhibit, but, just like the RCA, it failed to discourage derivative work and even in the forties continued to reflect a somewhat old-fashioned landscape style that carried the distinct stamp of the Group of Seven. During the thirties, however, the CGP did focus activities in three cities—Toronto, Montreal, and Vancouver—and encouraged a number of painters of talent who might not otherwise have been seen nationally.

The principal centre of CGP activities remained Toronto, and the principal figures in Toronto during the thirties were undoubtedly ARTHUR LISMER and A.Y. Jackson. Lismer's educational work (rather than his painting) made him even more influential than Jackson. At the Art Gallery of Toronto he was able to establish what was in its time the most successful childrens' art program in North America. This accomplishment was recognized in 1936 when he was invited to South Africa to establish a similar project. After his return he was asked to fill a visiting chair at the Teachers' College, Columbia University, New York, which he accepted for one year, commencing in the fall of 1938. Eric Brown next offered him a job at the National Gallery to initiate a national art educational program. It was a challenge uniquely suited to his abilities and would represent the culmination of his career as an art educator. However, Brown died shortly after Lismer's arrival and the project caved in. Fortunately an offer came from Montreal, and in 1941 Lismer returned to his work with children as Educational Supervisor for the Montreal Museum of Fine Arts, a post he held virtually until his death almost thirty years later!

The greatest painter in Toronto was still A. Y. JACKSON. He clung tenaciously to the old ways, living in the Studio Building until 1955, visiting various parts of the country on field trips every year, and turning out major paintings of such quality that his influence was discernible in the work of most younger painters until the mid-forties. Some have suggested that he failed to develop past 1930, that he rested on his achievement and simply repeated a successful formula. It is true that he did not strike out on any boldly innovative course. But it would be ridiculous to suggest that canvases like *Algoma, November (NGC) of about 1935 or Alberta Foothills (MCM) of 1937 are anything other than vital, stimulating works of art, and among the most important Canadian paintings of the decade. The other members of the Group of Seven to stay in Toronto during the thirties, A. J. CASSON and FRANK CARMICHAEL,

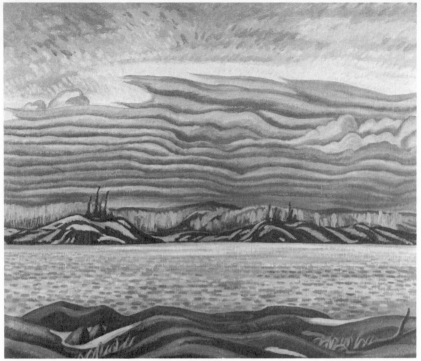

A.Y. Jackson. *Algoma, November,* c.1935. Canvas, 31½ x 39½. NGC.

never approached the position of leadership held by Jackson and Lismer. Both remained modest, if enthusiastic, followers of the Group style as exemplified in the work of Jackson and Harris. Each achieved an individual 'look' within that style, and Casson in particular produced a number of large oils during the thirties—notably *Golden October* (HH) of 1935—that, in spite of their 'Harris' trees and 'Jackson' format, are uniquely his own in colour and mood.

The bulk of the membership of the CGP in Toronto derived from painters roughly contemporary with Casson, most of whom were trained and encouraged by the Group of Seven during the early to mid-twenties, and most of whom, like Casson, carried the Group style into the thirties and beyond. YVONNE MCKAGUE (b.1898) was born in Toronto, studied at the Ontario College of Art during the First World War, and in Paris during the early twenties (1921-2 and again in 1924). Although completing her studies before the advent of the Group of Seven at the College, she began teaching at that institution during its heyday in the mid-twenties, and clearly came under the influence of Lismer's ideas. In 1930 she even travelled to Vienna to study with his mentor in child art, Franz Cižek. In her painting she was drawn to the work of Lawren

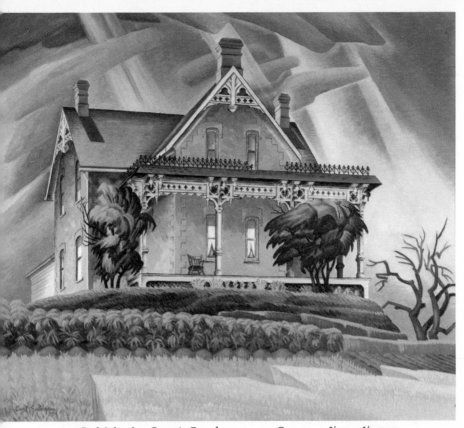

xxv—Carl Schaefer. *Ontario Farmhouse*, 1934. Canvas, 41¾ x 49¼. NGC.

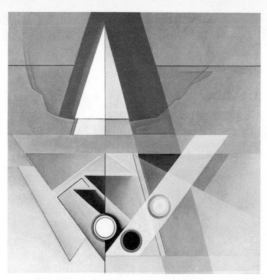

XXVI—Lawren S. Harris. *Composition I*, 1940.
Canvas, 61¼ × 61¼. VAG.

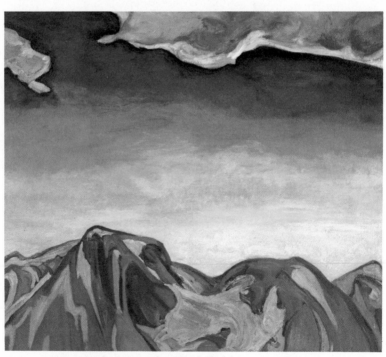

XXVII—Fred Varley. *The Cloud, Red Mountain, B.C.*, 1927-8.
Canvas, 34 × 40. AGO.

Harris—both to the stark simplicity of his North Shore canvases and, as in her well-known *Cobalt* (NGC) of 1931, to his house paintings of some ten or more years before. Her real significance at this time, however, was in her teaching rather than her painting. During the late twenties she was principal adviser to a unique educational experiment in Toronto, the Art Students' League. Inspired by the principles behind the famous New York school of the same name, and aware through J.E.H. MacDonald of the Toronto precedent of the turn-of-the-century, the Art Students' League was founded in the fall of 1926 as a student-administered free school to promote the relationship of art to life: 'the essential idea of Art [is] a quality of human consciousness, rather than professionalism, or commercialism.' The most successful example of Fred Housser's and Lismer's ideal of 'amateurism', the League organized field sketching trips, regular visits to the studios of prominent artists, and contributed art classes to the University Settlement for under-privileged children. By the summer of 1927 the League had rented a house—The Grange Studio—that included accommodation for a number of the members, meeting and studio space for non-residents, a small gallery, and a craft shop. Harris, Jackson, Lismer, and others of similar persuasion often lectured there and, although there were no formal classes, guided students in their work. By 1930 members of the League were publishing a magazine of opinion, poetry, and art that became the voice of Toronto's first bohemian community, then growing in the old 'Greenwich Village' on Gerrard Street.

'Graduates' of the Art Students' League usually maintained an opposition to commercialism and professionalism. Some, inspired by Arthur Lismer, have made great contributions to art education here and abroad. And a few were brought into the ranks of the CGP. GORDON WEBBER (1909-65) was born in Sault Ste Marie, Ont., studied at the Ontario College of Art (1924-7) during its 'Group of Seven' years, and then became active in the League. During the thirties he painted in the modest format suitable to the intentions of a League student, and, in his *Skating in the Park* (AGO) of 1933, in a style expressing the natural unity of life's activities. Not strong painting, it is honest in its presentation of a philosophy of life and art. In 1939 Webber pursued this concern with three years of study under the Bauhaus teachers Laszlo Moholy-Nagy and Gyorgy Kepes at the School of Design in Chicago, followed, upon graduation, by a distinguished career as professor of design at the McGill School of Architecture in Montreal.

Another Art Students' League member involved in the early years of the CGP—she was president in the late thirties—was ISABEL MCLAUGHLIN (b.1903), who was born in Oshawa, Ont. Her father, R.S. McLaughlin—one-time president and chairman of the board of General Motors of Canada—was a prominent collector of the period. Like Gordon Webber, she studied at the Ontario College of Art with Group of Seven members, then, like Yvonne McKague, in Paris before joining the League. Her paintings are intensely decorative and, when she allows her rich fantasy free reign—as in the justly famous *The Tree* (the artist) of 1935—they have the fascination of dream images. Involvement in the Art Students' League thus led some painters to follow their inclinations into areas unexplored by the Group of Seven. Other students of Group members at the college—like George Pepper (1903-62) and his wife, Kathleen Daly (b.1898)—generally accepted the limits of painting as defined by their teachers. Of the many landscape painters who developed in Toronto in the late twenties, only CARL SCHAEFER (b.1903) was able to make a consistently strong and finally unique statement.

Schaefer was born in Hanover, Ont., in an area settled by Germans in the mid-nineteenth century, about twenty miles south-east of Paisley, Milne's home town. Inspired by illustrations in books and boys' magazines, he enrolled in the Ontario College of Art in 1921. There he was instructed by Lismer and MacDonald, among others, and through them came into contact with Jackson and Harris. He graduated in 1924 and celebrated with a small show of oil sketches in the fire-hall at Hanover. For the next three or four years he found employment around Ontario as an itinerant church decorator, as a painter of theatre sets in Toronto, and as J.E.H. MacDonald's assistant on a number of mural commissions. The summer of 1926 he first went north in the Group of Seven fashion and for the next few years painted stylized, decorative reworkings of Group themes, almost indistinguishable from the efforts of other disciples. By the Depression Schaefer was raising a family and able to find employment only as a part-time teacher, and so to save money, every summer and winter holiday break from 1932 through 1939 he and his family lived with his grandparents back in Hanover. It was a period of reaffirmation of traditional values and of assertive creativity, resulting in a long series of stunning canvases.

Working with J.E.H. MacDonald, Schaefer had become friendly with his son, the distinguished black-and-white illustrator, Thoreau MacDonald (b.1901), and had developed his own pen-and-ink work to a high level. In this medium he evolved the stark, simplified realism he was to use in his oils throughout the thirties. It was a style that in watercolour had already been developed to a sensitive degree by the Buffalo painter, Charles Burchfield—whose work Schaefer admired and whom

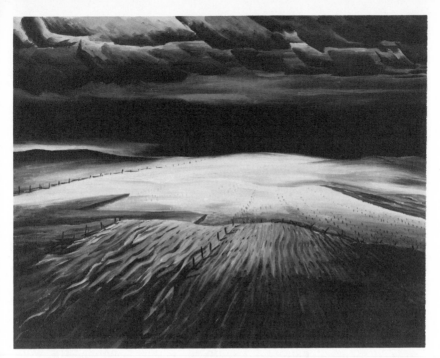

Carl Schaefer. *Storm Over the Fields, Hanover*, 1937. Canvas, 27¼ x 37. AGO.

he met in the later thirties—and that the American Scene painters were just then successfully applying to the depiction of regional themes.

Schaefer's first response to Hanover was nostalgia. But later the country took on a new aspect for him and familiar things began to generate a life of their own. †*Ontario Farmhouse* (NGC), painted on the Voelzling farm in 1934, represents a conjunction of the past and present, a potent image of strength in continuity. With fruitful fields pushing into its porch, the house rises like a ritualistically embellished part of the land itself. 'I felt that I was producing something of permanence,' Schaefer has said. 'I was not painting for posterity, but I painted from morning until night, and even at Christmas when there was snow. I was interested in the cycle of life.' To him the fields revealed the same evidence of man's hand as the house, the same fruitful union of past traditions and present need. The group of spreading 'field' canvases produced at Hanover—some more than four feet wide—is the most moving series of pictures painted in Canada in the thirties. They all display heroic breadth. The long rich furrows and great golden lakes of wheat in *Storm Over the Fields, Hanover* (AGO) of 1937 are as awesome as the clouds so formidably marshalled above; they seem almost to be their man-made counterpart.

Schaefer had had his first one-man exhibition at Douglas Duncan's

Picture Loan Society in Toronto in 1936 (there were to be eleven more there by 1958), and his pictures were a prominent feature of every CGP exhibition. His achievement received formal recognition in 1940 when he became the first Canadian to be awarded a Guggenheim Fellowship. Taking full advantage of a year's free painting, he moved to Norwich, Vt. It was his first long period free of teaching and proved to be one of his most productive years. The Vermont pictures, in oil and water-colour, are distinctive. He responded to the nature of the place while bringing recent tendencies in his work to culmination. *February Thaw, Norwich, Vermont* (NGC) is typical. Dark and moody, almost mono-chromatic, the paint is applied in broad swipes that suggest rather than describe the volume of forms. Objects no longer have massive individual-ity as in the paintings of the mid-thirties but blend into the whole, finding their depth in space through depth of tone. These are his most 'painterly' works, those in which subject is of the least importance and in which sensibility as revealed in handling carries the most meaning.

This great facility of handling found a highly charged subject during the war when Schaefer was attached to the RCAF as a war artist. After-wards he found it difficult to return to 'normal' painting. His work remained dark—he had flown in bombers, always at night—and kept to themes of violence. *Carrion Crow* (the artist) of 1946 is a brutal image of inevitable death. He was also working exclusively in water-colour by then. 'I felt that my painting in oil was restricting and not sufficiently personal,' he has said. 'I became more and more interested in drawing and the calligraphic approach.' Schaefer has continued to find his means of expression in this intimate mode ever since.

Though landscape clearly predominated in the work of CGP painters during the thirties in Toronto, a number of figure painters were also active. None came from Ontario. WILL OGILVIE (b.1901) was from Cape Province, South Africa. He first studied in Johannesburg before immi-grating to Toronto in 1925; two years later he was in New York, work-ing at the Art Students League for three years under Kimon Nicolaides. Ogilvie's principal achievement of the thirties was the wonderfully light mural program in the chapel of Hart House, University of Toronto (1936). Buoyant, decorative, symbolic without being solemn, it is a charming reflection of its time. PARASKEVA CLARK (b.1898) was born in Leningrad. She studied with Ilya Zeidenberg before the revolution, and at the Free Art Studios (formerly the Imperial Academy of Fine Arts) under Kuzma Petrov-Vodkin (1918-21). She lived in Paris from 1923 until she moved to Toronto with her Canadian husband in 1931. Her painting is carefully constructed and coloured. Landscapes, like *The*

Pink Cloud (NGC) of 1937, or portraits, such as the striking *Self-portrait* (NGC) of 1942, are equally rich in intricate formal relationships. (Petrov-Vodkin's paintings are deceptively simple socialist-realist pictures with a similarly complex internal relationship of forms.)

CHARLES COMFORT (b.1900) was born in Edinburgh but immigrated to Winnipeg with his family in 1912. Two years later, at the age of fourteen, he began working for Brigden's, the local commercial art firm. In the late fall of 1919 he moved to Toronto to work in that branch of the Brigden firm, and there in May he saw the first exhibition of the Group of Seven. He determined then to become a painter. Returning frequently to Winnipeg, he received further encouragement after September 1921 when Frank Johnston took over the Winnipeg School of Art and Art Gallery and, the following fall, gave Comfort his first exhibition. That autumn of 1922 Comfort also travelled to New York to study for a year at the Art Students League. Returning to Winnipeg, he was involved in designing sets for the local theatre and became friendly with FitzGerald and W.J. Phillips. The growing art community in Winnipeg still offered too little, however, and in 1925 he and his new wife settled in Toronto.

Comfort soon was known as a young painter of promise. Works like *Prairie Road* (HH) of 1925 had a recognizable kinship with the Group of Seven in boldness of paint handling, but were more arbitrary in colour than Toronto was accustomed to. This brash, startling quality Comfort carried even further in *The Dreamer* (AGH) of 1929, a dramatic portrait study that marshalled all of the talents he had developed as a commercial designer. It launched a series of portraits painted over the next five years that in many ways is his most successful body of work. The best is probably the portrait of Carl Schaefer, **Young Canadian* (HH) of 1932; emphatic and admirably painted, it is notably free of the superficial illustrator's devices seen in *The Dreamer*. Then came a series of landscapes of similar range. The famous *Tadoussac* (NGC) of 1935 is one of the first of these. In its high point of view, delicate atmosphere and colour, and 'cut-out model village' forms, it is the closest to the famous American Scene painter, Grant Wood, of the work of any Canadian in the thirties. Comfort's other landscapes of the period are more aggressive, establishing a clear mood—as in *Lake Superior Village* (AGO) of 1937—or stating a simple theme, as in *Pioneer Survival* (NGC) of 1938.

Another Manitoban was an even more potent catalyst in Toronto in the late twenties and thirties. BERTRAM BROOKER (1888-1955) was born in Croydon, Eng., and immigrated to Canada with his family in 1905, settling in Portage la Prairie. For sixteen years he lived and worked

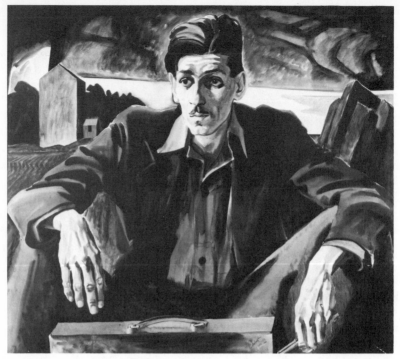

Charles Comfort. *Young Canadian*, 1932. Watercolour, 36 x 42. HH.

around Manitoba and in Regina as labourer, railway clerk, journalist, pioneer movie-house operator, and free-lance advertising artist. Then in 1921 he moved to Toronto to work for an advertising trade journal. About 1926 Brooker began to experiment seriously with painting (he had been drawing and dabbling in paint since about 1913), and suddenly in January 1927 he burst upon the scene with an exhibition of abstract paintings at the Arts & Letters Club. They were the first abstract pictures ever exhibited by a Canadian.* Encouraged by progressive elements in Toronto—Lismer had sponsored the show and Harris lent his support —Brooker continued to work his ideas through, and by early 1928 he had achieved the assured level of *Sounds Assembling* (WAG), which he exhibited that February with the Group of Seven. Perhaps best described as spatial geometric painting, in its use of tubular forms and its complex

*Another early abstract painter was Rolph Scarlett (b.1889), who was born in Guelph, Ont. He moved to the United States in 1918 and first became interested in abstract painting on a visit to Europe in 1923. He applied his enthusiasms as a set designer in Hollywood 1930-4 and then as a member of Design Associates in New York, but apparently began painting non-objective canvases (greatly influenced by Kandinsky) only in the late thirties when he joined the staff of the Museum of Non-Objective Painting (now The Solomon R. Guggenheim Museum).

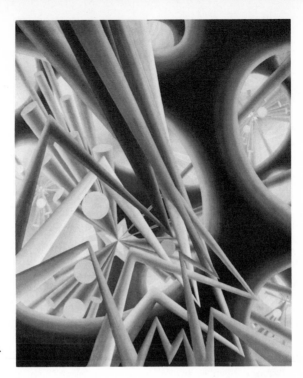

Bertram Brooker.
Sounds Assembling,
1928. Canvas, 44½ x 36.
WAG.

of interconnecting spatial pockets it is similar to the work of the American futurist painter, Joseph Stella, and particularly to his famous *Brooklyn Bridge* of 1918, then owned by the Société Anonyme. Brooker's professed intention—evident in the work's title—was to express in paint the abstract relationships that are so stimulating in the art of music. His guide in this direction was one of the key works of early twentieth-century Western culture, Wassily Kandinsky's *Concerning the Spiritual in Art.*

It was doubtless Lawren Harris who interested Brooker in the writings of Kandinsky. In April 1927 (two months after Brooker's Arts & Letters Club show) Harris succeeded in displaying the collection of the Société Anonyme at the AGT. It must have been an amazing exhibition, including works by Mondrian, Duchamp, Kandinsky, Stella, and vir-

The Guggenheim owns sixty works by him.
    Jay Hambidge (1867-1924) should also be mentioned. Born in Simcoe, Ont., and raised in Ingersoll, Ont., he went to New York as a young man and enrolled in the Art Students League. He later became famous as the discoverer-inventor and chief promulgator of the principles of 'dynamic symmetry', which had a profound influence on painters, both abstract and representational, during the twenties and thirties. He was a life-long friend of C.W. Jefferys.

tually every modernist of distinction. It was, needless to say, the first time these painters had been seen in Canada. The exhibition was a success in terms of public response but it failed to interest any painters other than Brooker in the possibilities presented. The *Canadian Forum*, staunch supporter of the Group of Seven, had observed that 'abstraction is not a natural form of art expression in Canada,' and it would seem that most Torontonians agreed. In March 1931 Brooker held the last exhibition of abstract painting—a retrospective of his early work— Toronto would see for twenty years! He was a man of incredible energy: novelist (winner of the first Governor General's Award for fiction), editor of two yearbooks of Canadian art (1929 and 1936), columnist (his syndicated column on the arts in Canada—the first of its kind—was read across the country), illustrator, and advertising executive and theoretician (he wrote two advertising manuals, 1929-30). Brooker doubtless would have persisted in the face of public apathy had it not been for the convincing example of a new-found friend.

In the summer of 1929 he met LeMoine FitzGerald in Winnipeg and immediately stopped painting abstractions and turned to a 'realistic' idiom. Writing to FitzGerald that fall, he described how the effect of the visit had been to make his work 'perhaps too realistic—in a small way, I mean—but I hope to grow out of that to a bigger appreciation of form —particularly.' The first of his realistic works—*Snow Fugue* (Royal Conservatory of Music, Toronto), exhibited with the Group of Seven in April 1930—follows, as the title suggests, the concerns of the earlier abstractions in its formal patterning of snow-laden branches. By about 1934, however, he had settled on a manner of painting—detailed and somewhat dry—that perfectly suited the detached formal examination of people, places, and objects that had become his concern. The portraits, such as that of his daughter Phyllis, entitled *Piano! Piano!* (estate of M.A. Brooker) of 1934; the still-lifes and landscapes; and the startling *Torso* (NGC) of 1937—are all penetrating in their realism, dynamic in composition, and harmonious in colour and texture. They were certainly among the most original contributions to the CGP exhibitions of the thirties.

Brooker had mentioned to FitzGerald some years before that 'after this apprenticeship to naturalistic painting has been served a little more fully I shall perhaps go back to more abstract things with a greater command of mediums and do something quite different.' Late in 1937 he did something very close to that and exhibited two of the results in the CGP exhibition that November. Neither *Blue Nude* nor *Entombment* (both estate of M.A. Brooker) really is an abstraction like those of the

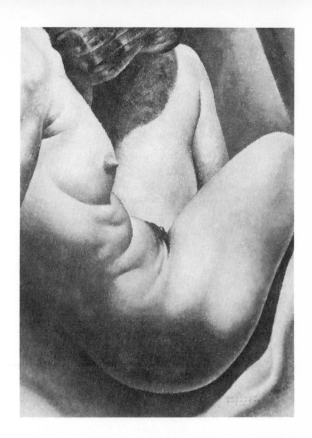

Bertram Brooker.
Torso, 1937. Canvas,
24¼ x 18. NGC.

late twenties. They are rather stylizations; plays on Cubist compositional devices; symbolic figures. Although monumental, ambitious
canvases, they seem, at this remove, to lack the vitality of earlier work.

The same diminished vitality characterized the whole Toronto scene
in general by 1940. After almost seventy years' dominance of painting
activity in Canada, the centre had given way. A.Y. Jackson, really the
only painter in the city by then with the demonstrated excellence to set
standards, was, in his exclusive concern for landscape, out of touch with
the more interesting trends of the day. And Jackson was always a
loner. Harris, the acknowledged leader, had left the city in 1933.
Wyndham Lewis, the English painter and writer, trapped in Toronto
from 1941 to 1943, found life in that 'sanctimonious icebox' unbearable.
Two of the few stimulating personalities he did enjoy during his Canadian years (which extended to August 1945) were a young Canadian
then lecturing at St Louis University, Missouri, named Marshall
McLuhan, who travelled to Windsor to visit Lewis in July 1943, and the
painter A.Y. Jackson. On his return to London, Lewis published an
article in *The Listener*, 'Nature's Place in Canadian Culture', which he

described as having been written 'around the massive and truly typical figure of a celebrated Canadian artist . . . Alec Jackson,' the man who for Lewis represented the '*one* very fine attempt' to creatively engage the Canadian experience.

In Montreal support for the CGP came almost exclusively from a number of artists who, in the early twenties, with the encouragement of Jackson, had formed the Beaver Hall Hill Group. All were English-speaking students of Brymner at the AAM school (as was Jackson), most subsequently trained in Paris, and as a group they were probably the finest figure painters in Canada in the thirties. RANDOLPH HEWTON (1888-1960), the oldest, seems to have set the direction. Born in Megantic in the Eastern Townships, he moved as a boy to Lachine near Montreal. He studied painting with Brymner (1903-7) and then spent five years in Paris. There in 1912 he met A.Y. Jackson and the two agreed to exhibit together at the AAM on their return home early in 1913. His early French pictures, like those of Jackson and Albert Robinson (1881-1956), another Canadian Hewton had met in Paris (and who later settled in Montreal), are fresh, open, 'second-generation' impressionist landscapes of promising ability. By 1920 and the first Group of Seven exhibition (which included both Hewton and Robinson as guest exhibitors), Hewton was painting landscapes not unlike those Quebec scenes Jackson was about to begin. He was also an accomplished and recognized portraitist, working in a loose, sensitive manner. Works like his *Portrait of Audrey Buller* (NGC) of 1921 spread his reputation as a portraitist and figure painter, and it was as such that he largely later exhibited in the CGP. In 1926, however, he accepted the presidency of a family manufacturing business and in 1933 moved to the small company town of Glen Miller, north of Trenton, Ont. He was by then simply a talented amateur, with little real time for painting.

EDWIN HOLGATE was the only one of these Montreal painters to formalize his relationship with the Group of Seven when in 1930 he became their eighth member. Born in Allandale, Ont., he studied with Brymner, and then in Paris, both before and after the war. Despite his connection with the Toronto artists, he remained a figure painter. Like Hewton, he early developed a reputation as a portraitist and during the years of his involvement with the CGP exhibited a number of delightful studies of Quebec types, usually placed in landscape settings. He will be remembered, however, for his lovely series of outdoor-posed female nudes of the thirties. The best of these, *Nude* (AGO) of 1930, is gentle and sensitive in colour, vigorous in composition, and imaginative in its relationship of the figure to the landscape.

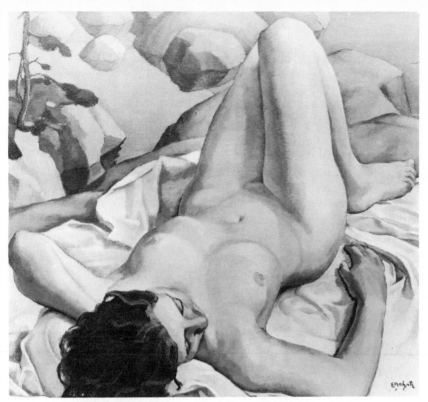

Edwin Holgate. *Nude*, 1930. Canvas, 25½ x 29. AGO.

The Beaver Hall Hill Group is most remarkable, though, for a group of Montreal-born women who dominated its membership during the twenties, and who made up the largest contingent of Montrealers in CGP exhibitions during the thirties. As Norah McCullough has pointed out, these artists were 'by no means careerists, but rather talented gentlefolk, . . . women of superior intelligence and vigorous energy.' A number of these Brymner students were, nonetheless, drawn into extended careers by their talent. LILIAS TORRANCE NEWTON (b.1896) painted portraits in the twenties that are similar to those of Hewton. By the late twenties she had developed a relaxed informal style—perhaps best seen in the *Portrait of Eric Brown* (NGC) of about 1933—that attracted a large following, and by the mid-forties she had painted most of the famous Canadians of the time.

Of those who regularly painted landscape—including Mabel Lockerby (b.1887), Kathleen Morris (b.1893), and the beloved teacher Annie Savage (1896-1971)—the most talented was probably SARAH ROBERTSON (1891-1948). *In the Nun's Garden* (AGO) of 1933 displays many of her qualities: a lyrical charm with a touch of humour, full rounded forms, and sensitive, harmonious colour. But the best of these Montreal women was PRUDENCE HEWARD (1896-1947). She studied with Brymner and had Holgate, Robertson, Savage, Morris, and Newton as classmates. Her training was thoroughly typical of her background, and her work of the twenties reflects the English-speaking Montrealer's world as defined during that decade by the portraits of Hewton and Lilias Newton. *Girl on a Hill* (NGC) of 1928 displays more than a passing acquaintance with the subtle colours and classical compositions so dear to Parisian taste during the early years of the century. It is at the same time permeated with Anglo-Saxon reserve. It won the Willingdon Arts Competition in 1929 and marked Prudence Heward's serious entry on the Montreal scene. Through the thirties she sketched most summers near Brockville on the St Lawrence, often with her friends Sarah Robertson and A.Y. Jackson. But it was as a figure painter, and primarily as a portraitist of deep sensitivity, that she made her mark. *Dark Girl* (HH) of 1935, although ostensibly a conventional thirties Canadian nude study with its simple seated pose and 'outdoor' studio setting, transcends the genre through its gentle revelation of character, its moving sympathetic harmonies, to become one of the most memorable of Canadian portraits. For the next ten years a slow but steady series of female portraits came off her easel, each displaying a more intense union of colour and form,

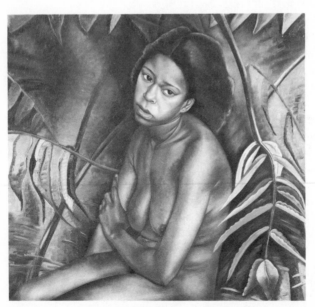

Prudence Heward.
Dark Girl,
1935. Canvas,
36 x 39. HH.

reflecting personalities of vigorous individuality. One of the finest is the aggressively beautiful *Farmer's Daughter* (NGC) of about 1945. Bold, exciting, it is almost shocking in its sugar-acid colours and defiant anonymity. It was also one of Heward's last paintings. Struggling against poor health much of her life, she died suddenly while on a visit to Los Angeles in March 1947.

When FRED VARLEY arrived in Vancouver in September 1926 he found a situation not greatly changed from that Emily Carr had known thirteen years before. Aged forty-five, he had for years been discontentedly managing on a bit of teaching, a bit of design, and some portrait commissions, but his creative work until then showed no central motive, no moving theme. The ten years he was to live in Vancouver provided the necessary focus. While in Toronto he had never been really taken by his friends' enthusiasm for landscape, but once away from them he became one of the most eager exponents of the Group 'method' of intense involvement in the natural environment. Challenged by the prospect of teaching in a new school (he was hired as Head of Drawing, Painting and Composition by the Vancouver School of Decorative and Applied Arts, founded the year before), he was excited by the proximity of the mountains and began weekend sketching jaunts soon after his arrival. During the first summer break, in August 1927, he went camping for about a month and a half in the magnificent Garibaldi Park, situated in the mountains north of Vancouver, and began painting bold, vigorous canvases, like *Mountain Landscape, Garibaldi Park* (Power Corp., Montreal), immediately after returning to Vancouver. Weekend sketching trips and summer camping excursions continued, with colleagues and students invited along, and soon that Vancouver 'group' Eric Brown had hoped to see was beginning to develop in response to Varley's example.

Varley's arrival had happily coincided with the appearance of a small intellectual circle in Vancouver, centred on regular musical evenings at the home of a local gallery owner and accomplished, imaginative photographer, John Vanderpant. He and his friends were interested in mysticism and talked endlessly about the spiritual component in creativity. They even assisted in bringing the famous Indian poet-mystic Rabindranath Tagore to Vancouver to lecture in 1929. Varley had always been interested in such ideas. These discussions coincided with a period of intense motivation in his painting and induced bold experimentation in the use of symbolic colour to express spiritual values in his portraiture, resulting in some of the finest work of his career and early in 1930 that masterpiece of Canadian painting, *Vera* (NGC). As Varley doubtless

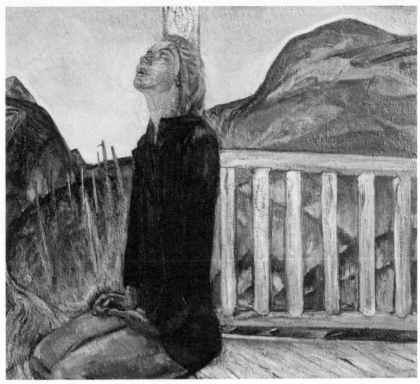

F.H. Varley. *Dhârâna*, 1932. Canvas, 34 x 40. AGO.

recognized, *Vera* marked the peak of his abilities as a painter. It was exhibited no less than six times in the first two years, from Seattle to New York, before being purchased by Vincent Massey.

Varley's elation was somewhat dampened by the Depression, which had forced salary cuts at the school—sixty per cent in Varley's case! In May 1933 he and a colleague, Jock Macdonald, believing that all avenues of redress had been blocked, announced that in September they would found their own school, the British Columbia College of Arts. With the help of concerned friends the College lasted for two years (until June 1935)—during which time it was the effective centre of Vancouver's cultural life—before collapsing under the weight of accumulated debts. Varley's creative painting continued to flower. About 1932 he found a house in Lynn Valley, north of Vancouver. At first he spent weekends there, but during the College period he moved there and this was the time of his closest communion with nature, which he sought to express in the haunting *Dhârâna* (AGO) of 1932. The title refers to the Bhuddist state of spiritual union with nature and the painting boldly asserts that union through the use of greens, blues, and purples—as first seen in

Vera—to describe the features of both the transported girl and the enlivened land. It is a work that strikes an almost shrill pitch of intensity.

With the collapse of the College, forces that had always been in opposition to Varley's aggressive teaching methods and free, indulgent life-style began to gain strength. Coinciding with a marital crisis and something approaching total destitution, the pressure became too much, and Varley left his family in Vancouver and returned to the East.

Varley's influence in Vancouver during those ten heady years had been, nonetheless, unalterably profound. Even mature painters found themselves keying up colour, working with bolder design and broader, more emphatic brush strokes. The man who brought Varley to Vancouver, CHARLES H. SCOTT (1886-1964), director of the Art School, responded eagerly to the Group of Seven type of field-sketching, often accompanying Varley on weekend hikes during the late twenties. English-born W.P. WESTON (1874-1967)—like Scott, a charter member of the CGP—was, when he first arrived in Vancouver in 1909, painting conventional academic landscapes, often even of English scenes. In the early twenties (a Group of Seven exhibition had been shown in Vancouver as early as September 1922) he began to travel into the mountains, and the freer experimentation that Varley's teaching and example later encouraged fitted the direction Weston was finding. By June 1930 a newspaper review was able to remark that he had 'outgrouped the Group of Seven'. Varley's most important contribution in Vancouver, however, was in awakening the painter in JOCK (J.W.G.) MACDONALD (1897-1960), his colleague at the School. Macdonald was born in Thurso, in northern Scotland. Trained in commercial design, he worked or taught in that field until coming to Canada in 1926 as head of design at the new Vancouver School of Decorative and Applied Arts. He had never painted in his life but began to accompany Varley on sketching trips and developed a degree of facility with the small Group-type sketch under Varley's direction. At the age of thirty-three, in 1930, he completed the first canvas Varley had not examined in progress: *Lytton Church, British Columbia* (NGC). It is a promising work of a follower of the Group of Seven and it was purchased by the National Gallery the next year.

The decision to found the British Columbia College of Arts increased Macdonald's involvement with Varley, and the excitement growing from the College's activities stimulated him in experimental directions. *Formative Colour Activity* (NGC), his first abstract or 'automatic' work, was painted early in 1934, the first year of the College's existence, and exhibited that year at the vAG and at the next cGP show in 1936. Unlike Brooker in his abstracts of seven years earlier, Macdonald was not interested in spatial problems but purely in colour. Completing it in one sitting, he followed natural inclinations, automatically, as the first colour led to other colours and forms. The final result suggests fantastic floral images.

Macdonald continued to experiment but did not exhibit abstractions again for seven years. The College collapsed in 1935 and that summer he, his wife, and little daughter moved into a deserted cabin at Friendly Cove, Nootka Sound, an isolated spot on the west coast of Vancouver Island. They remained a year and a half, and Macdonald lost himself in the land. Like Emily Carr he began to understand the profound integration of Indian art with the natural environment and painted brooding canvases of poles and villages. Lack of money and Jock's poor health finally forced them to return to Vancouver in November 1936. He had difficulty finding work, suffered a collapsed lung in April, and finally in January 1938 got a job as a high-school art teacher. Stifled by that work, he continued to seek relief in creative exploration. On his return to Vancouver from Friendly Cove he had tried a new series of abstractions, which he called modalities. All, like *Fall* (private collection) of 1937, are symmetrical geometric designs that bring together suggestive, often representational forms in a pyramidal arrangement. With Varley gone, it was as though Macdonald was reaching deeper into his earlier experiences as a fabric designer in England. About this time he met Emily Carr, whom he considered 'undoubtedly the first artist in the country and a genius without question'. He visited her frequently and they became dear friends. Not the mentor Varley had been, she encouraged a more certain Macdonald to persist in seeking spiritual values in the natural environment. Then in 1940 Lawren Harris moved to Vancouver. He and Macdonald were soon sketching together in the mountains and painting together in Harris's studio. Macdonald was, of course, greatly encouraged in his abstract experiments (Harris had by then been painting abstracts for about four years) and was utterly confirmed in his spiritual aspirations. Harris, the great Canadian proponent of such concerns, introduced Macdonald to Kandinsky's writings, as he had introduced Brooker to them more than fourteen years before.

About this time Macdonald also learned of Surrealism* through

---

*The Surrealists, in response to Freudian psychology and Marxian politics, understood that each man's unconscious harbours vast creative energies that are needlessly suppressed by the complex and vicious machinery of the social order. Their

Herbert Read's *Art Now* and by 1941 had returned to his earliest abstract experiments in exploring again the 'automatic' method he had used in painting *Formative Colour Activity*. This Surrealist approach was reinforced in 1943 when he met two friends of Herbert Read, Dr Grace Pailthorpe, a psychiatrist who was using automatic painting as a therapeutic tool, and Reuben Mednikoff, an ex-patient and enthusiastic proponent of automatic painting. However, Macdonald also still painted landscapes, culminating in the mid-forties in a series of beautiful works done in the Okanagan Valley. Of his landscapes, these last are the most transcendental in intention. In 1946 he accepted a position as director of the art department at the Provincial Institute of Technology and Art in Calgary. At the age of forty-nine he was finally, in his involvement with Surrealism, developing a visual language that would reveal his remarkable creative abilities.

A number of painters who did not live in the three principal art centres in Canada during the thirties also found the CGP exhibitions a valuable national forum. Some—like Henri Masson (b.1907) of Ottawa and André Biéler (b.1896) of Kingston—were, in the late thirties, vigorous and often convincing proponents of a Canadian equivalent to the regionalist concerns that were then so prominent in the United States. One man who might mistakenly have been called a regionalist was JACK HUMPHREY (1901-67), who was born and raised in Saint John, N.B., and lived most of his life there. Studying first at the Museum of Fine Arts School in Boston (1920-3), then at the National Academy, New York (1924-9), with summers at Provincetown, Mass., under Charles Hawthorne, Humphrey received a good academic training. Students at Provincetown who had studied in Munich with Hans Hofmann impressed him with their innovative ideas and in the fall of 1929 he too visited Europe. There for two-and-a-half concentrated months he studied with the world-famous modernist teacher and absorbed his doctrine: that

recognition of the natural creativity of children and of the often profound expressive qualities of the primitive or the insane—each to some degree free of the normal restrictions of society—seemed to confirm their theory. Through rigorous self-examination, often involving the analysis of dreams (those 'windows' into the unconscious), through the bold confrontation of personal and societal taboos, and through intuitive 'automatic' modes of composition that attempted to exclude conscious judgement, they sought to tap that rich creative source and make a new art of total personal freedom, heralding a new era for humanity. Hans Arp, Max Ernst, Salvador Dali, and Joan Miró were among the best-known Surrealist painters around the time the movement began in 1924, when André Breton wrote a manifesto describing Surrealism as 'pure automatism'.

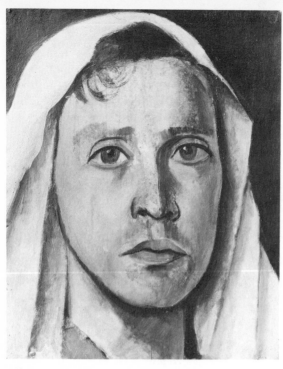

Jack Humphrey.
Draped Head, 1931.
Panel, 16 x 12. hh.

effective composition consists primarily of the judicious placement of dynamic planes of colours. Humphrey applied the lesson well on his return to Saint John. His self-portrait, *Draped Head* (hh) of 1931, is monumental in scale yet infinitely rich in modelling—a living thing.

As Brooker remarked to his friend FitzGerald after the 1931 Group of Seven exhibition, it was generally known that Lawren Harris was going through some kind of crisis: his painting had dried up. He continued to work sporadically—on Arctic canvases, primarily—and of course he exhibited in the 1933 CGP shows. Then in the fall of 1934 the bombshell burst. He and Bess, Fred Housser's wife, had fallen deeply in love! After much deliberation they had decided to spend their lives together. To avoid embarrassing the others affected by their decision, they would leave Toronto. Arrangements were made to move to Hanover, N.H., and later that year Harris was installed at Dartmouth College as artist-in-residence. There was no CGP exhibition that November, nor the following year, but in January 1936 Jackson and the other Toronto people were able to arrange the second local showing of the Group. Harris exhibited Arctic canvases, but at the third show in November 1937 he confirmed news that had already reached the city of a radical turn in his painting: he exhibited four abstract compositions.

Living in partial isolation in Hanover, although periodically visiting New York, Harris had begun to paint abstract pictures probably in 1936. He neither dated nor titled them at the time, and it has so far proved difficult to determine a course of development. A rough outline can be drawn however. *Winter Comes from the Arctic to the Temperate Zone* (estate of the artist) is probably one of the first canvases begun at Hanover, although it was not finished until 1937. Its symbolic super-imposition of snow-covered trees over icebergs—arranged in a sym-metrical, hieratic form—clearly demonstrates how the first ideas for abstraction had developed in the Arctic and later mountain canvases. But even before Harris had completed *Winter,* he had already moved to an area virtually free of associative images. *Equations in Space* (NGC), probably also completed in 1937, employs only clear geometric forms set in an ambiguous, non-representational space. Its elegant severity and precise colour suggest an impressive exactness of expression.

Moving to Santa Fe, N.M., in the summer of 1938, Harris became involved with a newly formed group called the Transcendental Painting Movement. Made up of artists from the Taos and Santa Fe regions—most importantly Raymond Jonson and Emil Bisttram—the movement sought 'to carry painting beyond the appearance of the physical world, through new concepts of space, colour, light and design, to imaginative realms that are idealistic and spiritual.' Harris was the president of the foundation established to promote the movement's aims. His painting seems not to have suddenly changed. There was no Transcendental 'style', although most of the members had been greatly influenced by the writings of Kandinsky. Harris pictures painted in Santa Fe—*Abstract Vertical* (AGH) is one—seem more complex than those completed in Hanover. Interlocking circular forms, folding in together in a complex, almost organic way, suggest the influence of the teachings of Jay Ham-bidge. Bisttram was a Hambidge disciple and gave classes on dynamic symmetry in Taos.

Rather suddenly (he exhibited in the American section at the New York World's Fair in 1939, although also with the CGP) Harris returned to Canada in 1940 and settled in Vancouver. As is evident from the first painting completed in that city, †*Composition I* (VAG), he had by then achieved a level of assured accomplishment in his abstractions, perhaps even surpassing that of his representational works of the Group of Seven years. These canvases of Harris's, along with the paintings brought from Paris early that same year by Alfred Pellan, represent the first solid beginnings of abstract art in Canada.

13

John Lyman
and the
Contemporary Arts Society
1939-1948

The most eloquent critic of the Group of Seven's rugged out-of-doors nationalism was the Montreal painter JOHN LYMAN (1886-1967). Home in the fall of 1931 after almost twenty-four years of self-imposed exile, he experienced the same strong feelings for his country that stirred almost everyone in the decade after the war.* He was nonetheless disturbed by the great clamour surrounding the activities of the Group of Seven. The Group's emphasis on the adventurous exploration of the Canadian landscape—which was almost alone responsible for attracting public approbation—seemed to him to have nothing to do with the art of painting, and he knew that the national aspirations of the Group, whose members were being touted as the only truly 'Canadian' artists, precluded the acceptance of other painters who were as accomplished. 'The real adventure takes place in the sensibility and imagination of the individual,' he wrote early in 1932. 'The real trail must be blazed towards a perception of the universal relations that are present in every parcel of creation, not towards the Arctic circle.' Easily the most underrated figure in Canadian art history, Lyman addressed himself to the identification of the quintessence of Canadian culture as vigorously as did the Group of Seven. He once remarked that 'if an association of the spirit of the two races that dominate in Canada can offer any indication of what a Canadian art might theoretically become, Morrice is automatically indicated as its father.' He looked upon Morrice as *his* cultural father and dedicated the last thirty-five years of his life to seeking that special 'association' that he believed would lead to the achievement of a living Canadian art of unprecedented accomplishment.

*In 1927 he had written in his diary after a brief visit: 'even before the flattest Quebec landscape I feel that I have more to say than before the magnificent sites of Europe.'

Lyman's parents were Americans of old New England stock who had settled in Vancouver and there become Canadian citizens. The summer of 1886 they moved to Montreal, but their new house was not ready and Mrs Lyman withdrew to her parents' home in Biddeford, Maine, where John was born that September. Raised in Montreal, at fifteen he was sent to a Connecticut prep school (his mother died when he was three) and later spent two years at McGill. At the age of twenty, perhaps encouraged by his uncle James Morgan, well-known Montreal collector of Barbizon and Hague School pictures, Lyman decided to study art, and the spring of 1907 found him in Paris. He worked briefly under Marcel Béronneau, once a pupil of Gustave Moreau, then spent the summer sketching in Brittany. His father had persuaded him to study architectural design at the Royal College of Art, South Kensington, so he enrolled there in the fall. But by January 1908 he was in the French capital again, working under Laurens at Julian's.

At the Salon that year he was drawn to a small canvas that glowed with a soft, suffusing light. To his amazement its title was *Ice Bridge over the St Lawrence* (MMFA), the work of a Canadian, James Wilson Morrice. Lyman called on him and they soon became friends, Morrice encouraging the student and instilling in him a love for French culture that he never lost. The summer of 1909 Lyman sketched at Etaples and there met an agreeable young Englishman named Matthew Smith. Back in Paris in the fall, both decided to enrol in the school that had recently been opened by the great Fauve painter, Henri Matisse.

A severe case of measles forced Lyman's withdrawal from the Académie Matisse after only six months, but the work of the master always remained his chief inspiration. In the summer of 1910 he and Smith painted in Pont Aven, and after visiting the Englishman's home in Manchester, Lyman returned to Montreal. He was back in Europe the next April with his bride and the two travelled until the winter, which was again spent in Montreal. After another year in Paris, the winter of 1912-13 was passed in Bermuda. Some time in March 1913 the Lymans returned home once again. He had been painting now for five years and felt it time to assert himself in his home town. Four works were hung in the AAM Spring Show and were roundly attacked in the press.

Lyman was probably surprised. He had been exhibiting in Montreal since 1910 with little critical reaction. The Armoury Show had opened in New York only six weeks before, however, and Randolph Hewton and A.Y. Jackson had been criticized for their French efforts exhibited at the AAM in February. In the Spring Show there was enough experimental work to suggest a trend, and the conservative critics panicked. One

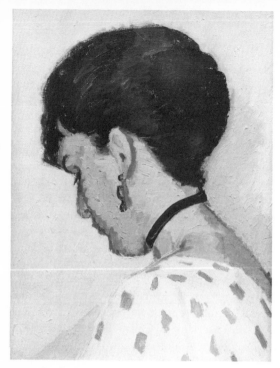

John Lyman. *Profile of Corinne*, 1913. Board, 14 x 10½. Maurice and Andrée Corbeil, Montreal.

remarked that Lyman's *A Brunette* (perhaps the *Profile of Corinne*, collection of Maurice and Andrée Corbeil, Montreal) reminded him 'of the crude attempt of an amateur to depict a beauty in a signboard advertisement for cigars'. But it was Morgan-Powell of *The Star* who recognized the real source of the threat. 'Post Impressionism is a fad,' he announced. 'London is laughing today at the latest freak of Matisse, the Post-Impressionist leader in Paris. . . . If Montreal joins hands with London and laughs, the craze will soon pass.' Lyman nonetheless proceeded with a one-man show that opened on May 21 in those same AAM galleries that had been occupied by Jackson and Hewton three months earlier. It was an intelligent, assertive exhibition, with forty-two oils divided into five groups by year of production. Montrealers probably found the titles pretentious, but *Adventure in Ochre, Floral Caprice, No. 2, Nude Girl, Scherzo,* or *Wild Nature Impromptu, 1st State* were so identified to clarify the artist's principal concern. Matisse taught that painting was an art of sensation, of feeling response to the stimulus of colour and form, and that such sensation could be ordered to produce a rich, profound effect not unlike that of music. One strengthened the sensation by suppressing everything extraneous to it. Forms were to be simplified, made more massive, more significant; colour was to be chosen for aesthetic, not imitative reasons; and the composition was to achieve an intelligently economical fusion of these elements. The simple, unpretentious force of *Profile of Corinne*, with the bold black choker effectively relating the rising shoulder to the beautifully modelled head of hair, demonstrates that Lyman learned his lesson well.

The critics did not learn theirs. Morgan-Powell again led the pack with a letter-to-the-editor in *The Star* entitled 'Extraordinary Display of Crudities and Offensive Things at the Art Gallery', in which he made it clear that he would resist any repetition of the exercise. Lyman's wife, Corinne St Pierre, nonetheless had, if not the last at least the most effective word. Her 'Avant-propos' (doubtless the first French text to appear in an AAM catalogue) ended with an almost Baudelairian impact. 'Ceux qui ne veulent trouver dans l'art qu'un narcotique pour leur procurer une douce et vague somnolence, ou qu'une friandise pour délecter leur vacuité d'esprit, ne doivent pas s'arrêter ici: ils n'y trouveront qu'un breuvage âcre des sucs corrosifs de la vie.'*

The Lymans left for France before the end of the exhibition and, with infrequent visits to Montreal, lived abroad—chiefly in France, Spain, and North Africa, but also in Bermuda and even Los Angeles during the winter of 1918-19—for the next eighteen years. In 1922 Lyman bought a villa in Cagnes-sur-mer in the south of France and re-established contact with Matisse. He also kept in touch with Matthew Smith, who had attracted some fame in introducing Fauvism to England and later would be knighted for his contribution to British art. And he continued to see Morrice and to collect his paintings. Lyman now had much in common with the older man. Both freely indulged their love for Paris, knowing their painting was unappreciated in Montreal; both travelled constantly to sunny climates; both greatly admired the painting of Matisse; and both had an independent income that allowed them to follow their inclinations.

It was probably the Depression, with the consequent loss of this income, that caused Lyman to return to Montreal in 1931. Like Morrice, he had kept up some contact with Canada (although there was a gap of eight years after 1920 when he didn't even exhibit at the Spring Show), and in October 1927 he had held his second one-man show, at the Johnston Art Galleries on St Catherine Street. It had been more politely received than that of fourteen years earlier. The critics had become more familiar with experimental art in the interim, and the wonderfully calm, classical pictures Lyman was painting by the mid-twenties appealed to

*Those who wish to find in art only a narcotic to induce a mild and vague drowsiness, or a choice tidbit to delight their empty spirits, should not stop here: they will find only a draught pungent with the corrosive juices of life.'

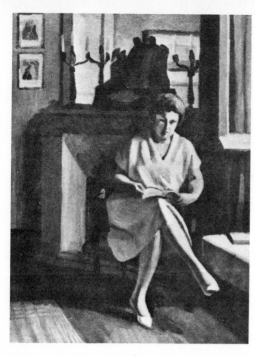

John Lyman. *Reading*,
1925. Canvas, 25 x 18.
Anatoly Ciacka, Montreal.

them more than the discordant Fauve works of before the war. *Reading
(Anatoly Ciacka, Montreal) of 1925 is typical of his work of the twenties. There is little distortion of colour or form, a smoother application
of paint, and a greater emphasis on plastic qualities, on the full modelling of forms in space.

Lyman's third exhibition was held just before his return to Montreal,
in February 1931. Made up chiefly of pictures painted at Saint-Jean-
de-Luz in the south of France and in Almeria, a remote Andalusian
town, it was his first show with Morrice's old dealer, W. Scott & Sons.
Finally settling in the city in the fall, he wasted no time in making artist-
friends and in devising a means to make a living. With André Biéler
and two others he established a school, called the Atelier, in the old
studio of the Montreal Repertory Company. Modelled on a Parisian
academy, the school offered models, space, and the criticism of a master.
Lyman ran the study classes. The Atelier intended to foster painting in
the new vein, however. A brochure outlining their specific goals stated
that'. . . the essential qualities of a work of art lie in the relationships
of form to form, and colour to colour. From these the eye, and especially
the trained eye, derives its pleasure and all artistic emotion.' The Atelier
group attempted to foster its views through exhibitions as well as by its
teaching. In the first of these exhibitions, at the Henry Morgan Galleries
in April 1932, Lyman was joined by André Biéler; the bright, decorative

painter, Marc-Aurèle Fortin (1888-1970); Edwin Holgate; and two others. The Atelier proved uneconomical, however, and was closed after only one year. The second and final exhibition was held in May 1933, again at Morgan's. This time a young painter from Ottawa was included: GOODRIDGE ROBERTS (b.1904).

Roberts had been born in Barbados while his parents were on holiday. His father was Theodore Goodridge Roberts, the poet and novelist; his uncle and cousin were also well-known writers, Sir Charles G.D. Roberts and Bliss Carman. Goodridge lived mainly in Fredericton, N.B., as a child, but also in England, France, and for about two years after the war in Ottawa. Although surrounded by writers, by the age of twelve he had decided to be a painter, and after graduation from high school in 1923 he entered the new Ecole des Beaux-Arts in Montreal. He studied there for two years and saw the Morrice memorial retrospective held at the AAM in January 1925. 'The pictures made a vivid impression on me,' he later remembered. 'It was my first visit to a good exhibition.'

The next year he went to New York and the Art Students League where he studied under one of Morrice's old friends, John Sloan (who had earlier described Morrice in his diary as 'one of the greatest landscape painters of the time'), and with Boardman Robinson (1876-1952), who was born in Somerset, N.S., and the American cubist pioneer, Max Weber. Weber encouraged Roberts to examine the French modernists, and it was in New York that he first saw the work of Cézanne, Picasso, and Matisse. After leaving the League he worked for a year as a draftsman in Fredericton, and then in the fall of 1930 he moved to Ottawa, where he worked first as a Fuller Brush salesman and then as a teacher for the local art association. The summer of 1931 he and two friends opened an art school in a farmhouse near Wakefield, Que., on the Gatineau River, and the following year he found even cheaper accommodation in a tent on a piece of Gatineau property near Kingsmere that was owned by H. O. McCurry, director of the National Gallery. In November he held his first one-man exhibition at the Arts Club, Montreal; it was organized by Ernst Neumann (1907-55), an old friend from the Ecole des Beaux-Arts days. His tentative, Cézanne-influenced landscape watercolours there caught the eye of Cleveland Morgan, art patron and president of Morgan's department store, and he drew them to the attention of his cousin, John Lyman. Both agreed that Roberts should be encouraged, so Lyman wrote him, and the following year he was included in the second exhibition of the Atelier at Morgan's.

Lyman's encouragement did not help Roberts' financial situation, however, and the summer of 1933 was spent once again in a tent—this

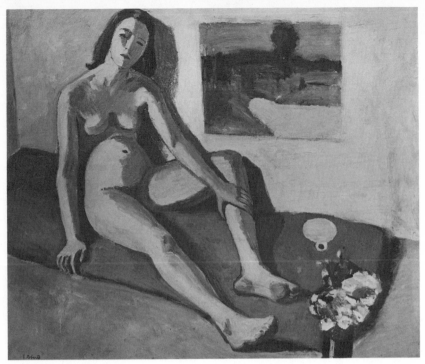

Goodridge Roberts. *Nude on Red Cloth*, 1939. Board, 27 x 32. Miss Mary Filer, Aldington, Eng.

time on the Montreal Road just outside of Ottawa. An offer to become the first resident artist at Queen's University in Kingston was eagerly accepted in September, and although the teaching was burdensome and his painting production fell off, he found the steady salary reason enough to stay for three years. In September 1936 he finally moved to Montreal where he shared a studio with Neumann, with whom he opened a school later in the fall. He was then thirty-two and responded enthusiastically to the growing Montreal scene. With his first commercial one-man show in Montreal at Scott's in January 1938 he was recognized as a strong, individual talent. The inspiration not only of Lyman but of Matisse was in his work, particularly in a series of nudes (1938-9). *Nude on Red Cloth* (Miss Mary Filer, Aldington, Eng.) of 1939 draws on Matisse for its theme (an informal pose in what appears to be the painter's quarters) and its shallow space. But the great concern for full modelling seems more like the recent Lyman. Intense and unified in composition, it is painted within a tight range of harmonious colours and evokes admirably Roberts' unique sensibility—what Donald Buchanan has called his 'silent, solitary stubborness'.

Roberts still had to struggle for a living, and in the fall of 1939 he joined with Will Ogilvie (who had arrived from Toronto the year before) to teach at the AAM school. Summers were free and were usually spent at St Jovite in the Laurentians north-west of Montreal as a guest of the Lymans. *Nude on Red Cloth* was painted there, but Roberts was mainly drawn to the landscape. By 1940—the date of *Hills and River, Laurentians* (AGO)—he had developed a landscape style that, like his figure painting, had a family resemblance to the work of the Montreal painters who were gathering about Lyman but that nonetheless displayed a unique sensibility. These landscapes were featured in a one-man show at the AAM in April 1942 (he was still teaching there) and were largely responsible for the success of the retrospective exhibition the critic Maurice Gagnon organized for him at the new Dominion Gallery in the spring of 1943. (Emily Carr's equally successful show would be held there the next year.) Forty-two paintings were sold and Roberts was given a salary contract against future sales that finally allowed him to quit teaching. During the early forties the chaste delicacy of his painting, as seen most notably in figure pictures like *Nude* (NGC) of 1943, inspired the respect and emulation of a number of young Montrealers, principally Jacques de Tonnancour (b.1917).

The enthusiasm with which Montreal received Roberts in the late thirties was in large part stimulated by John Lyman. The failure of the Atelier must have represented a certain setback, but three years later, in March 1936, Lyman began an art column in *The Montrealer* that over the next four years would even more effectively promote the values of pure painting as typified by the School of Paris. Lucid, intelligent, entertaining, he established a level of art criticism previously unknown in Canada. The great Morrice retrospective at the AAM in February 1938 (to which Lyman lent two works) and the remarkable group of exhibitions of modern French painting at W. Scott & Sons during this same period gave Lyman ample opportunity to demonstrate the excellence against which he measured the accomplishments of the younger Montreal painters who were more and more frequently finding opportunities to exhibit.

Lyman himself was experiencing a surge of creative painting that was reflected in three one-man exhibitions: in New York at Valentines in May 1936, at Scott's in February 1937, and at the McGill Faculty Club in April 1939. In his middle age (he turned fifty in 1936), a small devoted following had developed and his work was generally admired by those who bothered to bring a seriousness of observation to their viewing. His portrait of Mrs Leonard Marsh of 1936, exhibited as †*Lady With a White Collar* (NGC) in the Scott's show, for instance, was praised by one young critic (Graham McInnes) for its 'austerity, its restraint which barely conceals—rather underlines—the most passionate sincerity of its conception and execution.'

Convinced that talent was developing in Montreal, Lyman was equally sure that the Toronto-based Canadian Group of Painters had failed to strike a vital direction that would stimulate these young painters. 'The talk of the Canadian scene has gone sour,' he wrote in February 1938, just after the Canadian Group exhibition at the AAM. 'The real Canadian scene is in the consciousness of Canadian painters, whatever the object of their thought.'* A few months later he brought together a number of painters who shared his view. There was, of course, Goodridge Roberts; and also Jack Humphrey of St John, N.B.; and Jori Smith, Eric Goldberg, and Aleksandre Bercovitch, all of Montreal—none of them members of the CGP. They first exhibited in December 1938 as the Eastern Group, and their common point-of-view was immediately recognized: a marked affiliation with the School of Paris. Yet each painter was found to be 'extremely individualistic'. 'They are not busy about being of their own time or following any line—self-conscious regionalism, formalized pattern or social comment,' one critic wrote. 'They are not racing after the band-wagon of the Canadian scene. That was once good ballyhoo to get people away from foreign stereotypes, but today it is just sentimental rhetoric.' The Eastern Group was devoted to beautiful painting for its own sake. A second exhibition was held in January 1940, but by then Lyman had devised a more effective forum—the Contemporary Art Society—and although three more Eastern Group shows were held (May 1942, April 1945, and January 1950), by January 1940 the CAS had clearly become the focus of modern painting in Montreal.

The CAS was Lyman's most inspired creation. Suggested by the British organization of the same name, it quickly evolved into a unique body, responsive to the particular needs and trends of the most advanced painters in Montreal. Born from a meeting organized by Lyman in

---

*The CGP was never effectively to answer such complaints by Lyman. A.Y. Jackson, its acknowledged spokesman, never came up with anything stronger than that 'the chief difference between the two groups [the CGP and the Montreal painters] is that we have roots in the soil and they have not; they think being Canadian is parochial.' He repeated such sentiments frequently in private—this particular time in a 1942 letter to McCurry. The NGC, also unable to forget its intimate involvement with the Group of Seven, never fully supported Lyman and his friends and almost came into direct conflict with him in 1942 over an exhibition of contemporary Canadian art chosen by an American for showing in Andover, Mass., and a subsequent tour. It stressed the vital new Montreal scene and deliberately played down Group landscape ideals.

January 1939, its purpose was simply to promote living modern art. (The only condition for artist membership was that one *not* be a member of the RCA.) Its first public effort was an exhibition that May of contemporary foreign art from Montreal collections entitled 'Art of Our Day', which was described as 'the first adequate presentation in Canada of modern work by leading foreign artists'. (News of the Société Anonyme showing in Toronto eleven years earlier apparently failed to reach Montreal.) The only artist included who could be considered essential to an understanding of modern art was Kandinsky (three works of 1909-13). The general level could best be described as contemporary School of Paris—without Picasso or Matisse. Derain, Dufy, Laurencin, Modigliani, Pascin, Utrillo, and Zadkine were the high points. This first exhibition, in fact, established one of the inherent weaknesses of the CAS: the belief that an external ultimate standard of excellence existed. The Society's other major weakness was brought to its attention in a review of its March 1941 show by Marcel Parizeau: there were too few French Canadians involved.

At the first members' exhibition in December 1939, however, such issues were not raised at all. Consisting of the twenty-one key professional members, it was rigorously selected to demonstrate the degree of local accomplishment. Various segments of Montreal's artistic community were included. Prudence Heward, Ethel Seath, and Mabel Lockerby were the only CGP members. There were two painters with developed interests in abstraction. MARIAN SCOTT (b.1906) was born and raised in Montreal, studied at the AAM school and, shortly after it opened in 1922, at the Ecole des Beaux-Arts. She then completed her formal training with Henry Tonks at the Slade in London. Her great work of the CAS period is the mural called *Endocrinology*, completed in 1940 for the McGill University medical building. Themes suggested by that commission led to a series of fine abstract paintings—*Atom, Bone and Embryo* (AGO) of 1943 is probably the best—playing on a complex interrelationship of different life forms. Scott's work is much more coherent in theme and consistent in quality than that of her friend Fritz Brandtner. Arriving in Montreal from Winnipeg in 1934 (see p. 162), Brandtner was soon established as a commercial designer and experimental painter. An ardent socialist, his first Montreal one-man exhibition was held at Morgan's in February 1936 to benefit the Canadian League Against War and Fascism. Unlike many of the early members of the CAS, Brandtner saw his art as an exhibition of his various human concerns. This led to his co-operating with Dr Norman Bethune (the Canadian surgeon shortly to achieve heroic distinction in Spain and

China) in the establishment in 1936 of a Children's Art Centre for the underprivileged. When Bethune left Montreal, the burden of the centre rested on Brandtner, but with the help of Marian Scott he made it a great success and maintained its program until 1950.

The first CAS show included as well the work of three Jewish artists. ALEKSANDRE BERCOVITCH (1893-1951)—who was born near Odessa, trained in Russia, and later worked there and in Palestine—immigrated to Montreal in 1926. ERIC GOLDBERG (b.1890) was born in Berlin, studied at the Ecole des Beaux-Arts and Julian's in Paris (1906-10), and then taught in Berlin and Palestine and painted in the south of France, Italy, and Spain before immigrating to Chicago in 1921. He moved to Montreal in 1928. Bercovitch's work now seems quite ordinary. Goldberg's, though often over-pretty, is distinctively personal in style. *Figures* (NGC) of about 1941 shows his delicate colours, soft lights and wistful forms partially picked out with scratch-like lines. Bercovitch and Goldberg had participated in the first Eastern Group show, but LOUIS MUHLSTOCK (b.1904) was first associated with Lyman only in the 1939 CAS exhibition. Born in Narajow, Poland, he was brought to Montreal as a young boy of seven. He first studied art in Montreal, at the Conseil des Arts et Métiers, then at the AAM school, and finally at the Ecole des Beaux-Arts. In Paris (1929-31) he worked under Louis Biloul. An intensely personal artist, he was best known during the CAS years for quiet, sombre scenes of forest glades—*Sous Bois* (MMFA) of about 1941 is a good example— that evoke a sense of primeval nature, even though they were usually painted in the park on Mount Royal. His most personal work during the forties, and since, has been executed in charcoal and coloured chalk. Mainly portraits and monumental female nude studies, they have attracted a devoted following over the years.

The main identifiable 'group' within the CAS during the first years, though, was that composed of painters, like Goodridge Roberts, who demonstrated a particularly close relationship to the School of Paris style favoured by Lyman. (It should be pointed out that, especially in the first show, the 'Parisian' qualities of painters like Heward, Muhlstock, or Goldberg were particularly stressed as a result of the rigorous selection procedure.) JORI SMITH (b.1907) was born in Montreal, studied under Hewton at the AAM school, then, like Muhlstock, at the Conseil des Arts et Métiers, before going abroad to complete her training in England and France. Her brusque, forceful portrait studies reveal the simplifications of a 'modernist', but as in *La Petite Communiante* (Maurice and Andrée Corbeil, Montreal) of about 1940, their raw emotional directness suggests the work of an untrained naive. PHILIP SURREY (b.1910) has also had his work likened to that of a naive. Born near Calgary, he was raised by his foot-loose parents on a long and erratic round-the-world tour. At the age of ten he returned to Canada with his mother (she had separated from his father) and they settled in northern Manitoba. Philip was sent to high school in Winnipeg and three years later took an apprenticeship at Brigden's. He also studied nights at the Winnipeg School of Art (1926-7), where he must have come into contact with LeMoine FitzGerald. In October 1929 he moved to Vancouver where he lived and worked for seven years. During this time he took lessons from Fred Varley and began to exhibit his drawings and paintings. In October 1936 he left Vancouver for three months at the Art Students League in New York before settling in Montreal early in 1937. He met Lyman that first year, and when Jack Humphrey decided after the first Eastern Group exhibition that he could not afford to ship his works west so often, Surrey replaced him in the second show. (He had already become an exhibiting member of the CAS.) Surrey's earlier Montreal paintings certainly have the charming naivety of the primitive at first look, but closer examination of a typical canvas of the period—*The Crocodile* (AGO) of 1940 is one of the better known—reveals a well-constructed, elaborate structure. Surrey has since continued in this vein, producing delightful images of the unique urban flavour of his adopted city.

STANLEY COSGROVE (b.1911) was born in Montreal and studied at the Ecole des Beaux-Arts (1927-31) and later (1935) under Edwin Holgate at the AAM school. By 1939 and the first CAS exhibition he had absorbed many characteristics of recent Parisian painting without leaving the city of his birth. *Madeleine (Jules Bazin, Montreal), painted that year, shows that Cosgrove was far from being a derivative painter, however. It is gravely serious, and in the simple shallow curves of cheek, jaw, collar, and hair swings with the subtle rhythm of life. That same year his abilities were recognized when he was awarded a Province of Quebec prize, enabling him to study in France. War made such a trip impossible, so he chose New York, but soon moved to Mexico City. There he approached the great Mexican muralist Orozco, with whom he then spent four years studying fresco technique. Returning to Montreal in 1944, he must have felt out of touch. He exhibited with the CAS only once again (February 1946 at the AAM), although he was still on the membership roles in January 1948.

LOUISE GADBOIS (b.1896) was also born in Montreal and also studied under Holgate at the AAM school (1932-4), but subsequently took lessons from Lyman. Her most accomplished works of the CAS years are her

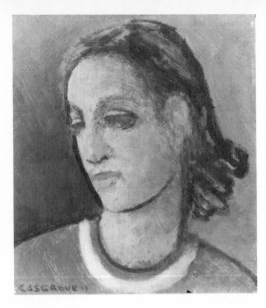

Stanley Cosgrove.
Madeleine, 1939. Board,
10 x 9. Jules Bazin,
Montreal.

portraits. *Le Père Alain Couturier* (the artist) of about 1941—subtly complex in modelling and rich in character—is among the best of the work produced by the Lyman-influenced members of the CAS. In the simple directness of its pose, however, and in the blurring of the boundaries of its forms, suggesting a soft, suffusing atmosphere, it probably borrows as well from the earlier work of another charter member of the CAS, PAUL-ÉMILE BORDUAS (1905-60).

Borduas worked as a church decorator until he was almost thirty. Born in Ozias Leduc's home town of Saint-Hilaire, east of Montreal, he apprenticed with the master at the age of sixteen and first worked on Leduc's most successful commission: the decoration of the Bishop's Chapel in Sherbrooke, east of Saint-Hilaire. With a characteristic display of intense energy Borduas occupied his evenings in further art studies at the Sherbrooke Ecole des Arts et Métiers. In 1923 he enrolled in the new Ecole des Beaux-Arts in Montreal (both day and evening courses) and after the first year continued as well to assist Leduc with large commissions: in Halifax in 1924 (chapel of the Sacred Heart Convent), in Saint-Hilaire in 1926 (chapel of the Couvent des Saints Noms de Jésus et de Marie), and in Montreal in 1927 (the baptistery of Notre-Dame). Upon graduation from the Ecole in 1927 he was hired by the Montreal Catholic School Board to teach art in the high schools, and after a year of teaching was able to afford a short sightseeing trip to New York and Boston. Teaching again in September, he quit after only two weeks when his duties, and salary, were summarily cut in half. Leduc and the sympathetic curé of Notre-Dame, Olivier Maurault, saw this as an opportunity

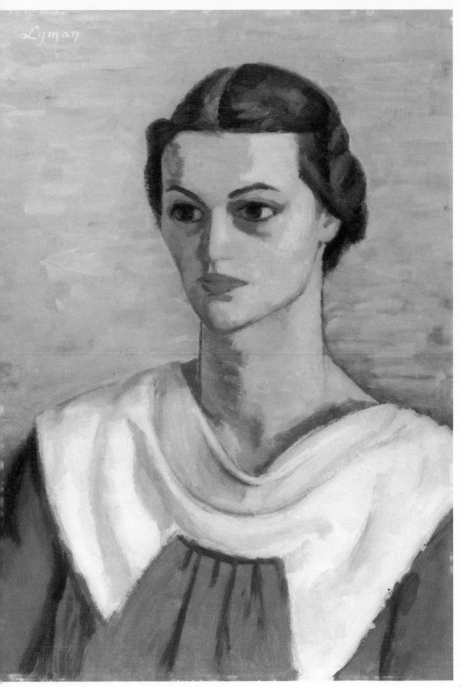

XXVIII—John Lyman. *Lady With a White Collar*, 1936. Canvas, 24 x 17½. NGC.

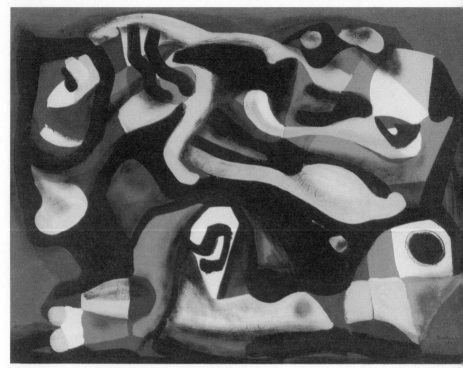

xxix—Paul-Emile Borduas. *Composition*, 1942. Gouache, 17 x 23½. Maurice and André Corbeil, Montreal.

for Borduas to complete his education—he was almost twenty-three—
and sent him to the Ateliers d'Art Sacré run by Maurice Denis and
Georges Desvallières in Paris. Denis, the Nabis painter who had founded
the Ateliers in 1919 to promote a vital contemporary church decoration
by the practice of his theories of the symbolist use of colour and form,
had for some years been an inspiration to Leduc. The French artist had
also praised one of Leduc's church paintings to Maurault on a visit to
Montreal only the year before.

Borduas arrived in France on November 11 and studied at the Ateliers
from January until April. (Denis left on a trip to Egypt and the Holy
Land in March.) He had found work in a stained-glass window shop
while still in school, and so remained in Paris until at least June, when
he moved to Rambucourt in the Meuse to work on some churches with
a French friend, Pierre Dubois. There he helped an artist-priest from the
Ateliers d'Art Sacré, Alain Couturier, who was installing windows in a
nearby church. In August Borduas travelled in Brittany, but by September he was again working in Rambucourt, and the day before Christmas
he was back in Paris. His money ran out in June; a ticket sent by Leduc
got him home to Saint-Hilaire. By the end of September he was working
again with Leduc, in the Eglise des Saints-Anges in Lachine.

Borduas continued to work with Leduc into 1931, picking up whatever
other small decorative or mural commissions he could. Then in
September he once again took a part-time teaching job, at the Collège
Saint-Sulpice. The following year he received a commission for a stations
of the cross for a new church at Rougemont, near Saint-Hilaire, and in
July he opened a studio and advertised for more commissions. After a
number of proposals were rejected by various parishes as being too
'modern', he finally in September 1933 returned to teaching for the
Montreal Catholic School Board. The next summer he spent at Knowlton
in the Eastern Townships, where he produced some landscape sketches,
and over the next two years he completed a few small religious pictures,
portraits, and lyrical, almost sentimental studies of young people. All
are clearly influenced by the religious work of Denis that he had seen
in Paris, but the few that have survived—particularly a tiny, stunning
Autoportrait (NGC)—are subtle, hauntingly intimate colour-poems. A
larger portrait, *Maurice Gagnon (NGC), was painted in 1937. At first
look it appears tentative in conception and execution, but there is
assurance in the way the subtle modulation in the tones of the background and the suit reacts with those of the flesh to set up a richly
harmonious, delicately coloured atmosphere. This effect is accentuated by
the gently blurred edges of the forms which, with the puffing of the

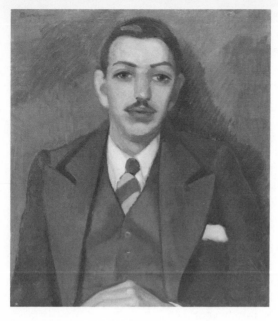

Paul-Emile Borduas.
Maurice Gagnon, 1937.
Canvas, 19½ x 17½.
NGC.

vest and the comfortable breadth of the lapels, have a convincing plasticity.

In September 1937 Borduas took yet another teaching job, at the Ecole du Meuble, retaining his posts at the Collège Saint-Sulpice and with the Catholic School Board. It was an important step. His colleagues at the Ecole—principally Maurice Gagnon, librarian and professor of art history, and Marcel Parizeau, professor of architecture—encouraged his involvement in the larger art world of Montreal (he had been working as a decorator-muralist or teacher for seventeen years) and in 1938 he exhibited his first work in the AAM spring show. One of his small lyric figure pieces, *Adolescente* (Jean-Marie Gauvreau, Montreal), caught the eye of John Lyman. 'It showed the influence of Maurice Denis,' he later remembered. 'It was not very strong . . . but the fact that is was expressed in true painter's language made it stand out.' Jean Palardy, Jori Smith's husband, introduced Lyman to the painter, and the next January when the CAS was formed Borduas was elected vice-president.

The choice of Borduas as vice-president of the CAS doubtless reflected Lyman's concern to encourage the assertion of a French-Canadian cultural entity. How poorly it was even then represented is difficult now to believe. Of the twenty-six artist members in May 1939, only five were French speaking. Of the twenty-one exhibitors in the December show, Lyman and Jori Smith were married to French-speaking Quebeckers; Cosgrove's mother was French Canadian; but only Louise Gadbois and Borduas really represented the stirring French cultural community. Having suffered commercial domination by English-speaking Montrealers since far back in the nineteenth century, and subject as well to the control of the institutional Roman Catholic Church—which had convinced Quebeckers that their cultural survival in an English-speaking continent lay in unquestioning obedience to the faith—French Canadians had been virtually isolated in their own country. This isolation from the larger world was very pronounced in cultural areas, where the conservative and inevitably restrictive influence of the Church was pervasive. But a significant change took place in Quebec society in the 1940s. By January 1948, of the forty-six artist-members of the CAS, some twenty-five were French, and of the seventy-one lay members listed, as many as forty-eight were of French ancestry! John Lyman's efforts helped prepare the way for the increased involvement of these artists, but the first major stimulus came from France.

Or perhaps one should say from Québec via France, although ALFRED PELLAN (b.1906) found many reasons to continue the expatriate tradition that had begun with Morrice. Pellan was a remarkable prodigy. Born in Québec, he entered the Ecole des Beaux-Arts there at the age of fourteen, had his first work bought by the NGC at the age of seventeen, and shortly after graduation in 1925 was the first painter to win a Province of Quebec bursary, enabling him to leave for Paris in August 1926, two years before Borduas. In Paris the young Quebecker enrolled in the Ecole des Beaux-Arts under the rather traditional portraitist Lucien Simon, but he soon began making the rounds of the academies and before long was deeply involved in the frenetic, stimulating world of the Parisian art student. Such a different experience from that of Borduas! He first had a work accepted for the Salon d'Automne in 1934 (eight years after his arrival), and in 1935 won first prize in a mural exhibition, participated in a number of other group exhibitions, and held his first one-man show, at the Académie Ranson where he had recently been a student. The following year he again participated in a number of group shows, then decided to return home. His father, who had been supporting him since his bursary ran out in 1930, believed his son could find employment in the school from which he had graduated with such distinction some eleven years earlier. Pellan arrived in Québec, presented himself at the Ecole, was rejected as too 'modern', and immediately returned to France. In Paris again, he associated himself with a group called the Surindépendants, contributed to numerous group shows, and in 1939 held his second one-man show, this time in the commercial Galerie Jeanne Bucher. He had become enough a part of the scene that the same year he was even included in an American

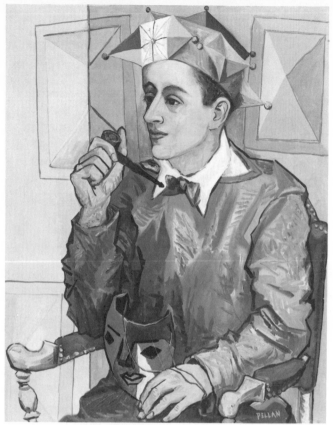

Alfred Pellan. *Jeune Comédien*, c.1935. Canvas, 39½ x 31¾. NGC.

exhibition entitled 'Paris Painters of Today'. Then the German invasion forced another return to Canada, early in 1940.

The climate in Québec was changing so rapidly that this time he was received as a returning hero, the very embodiment of modern art. 'Fauve, cubist, surrealist, Pellan is much more than that,' wrote a local critic, 'he is the synthesis and the moving image of the modern era.' Almost immediately, in June 1940, he was given a large retrospective at the Musée du Québec that was then shown at the AAM in October. Its impact was tremendous. The critic Parizeau described Pellan as the first Canadian to have 'taken on international significance'. A less temperate reviewer in Québec went even further. Pellan was a 'European painter . . . born in Québec'. He was 'in the very first rank of those innovators who often determine the orientation of an epoch'. Of course such a description would have seemed absurd in France. Pellan was never, in his years in France, an innovator. Quite to the contrary, he was vigorously eclectic, soaking up elements of style from most of the modern masters.

Pellan has such a happy facility of hand and such an eager, untiring mind that there is nonetheless much to enjoy in his work. And for Montreal late in 1940 there was also—simply in terms of sheer quantity of new ideas—much to learn from it. Many of his best French pictures —*Jeune Comédien* (NGC) of about 1935 comes to mind—are quite successful amalgams of cubist forms, 'classical' modelling, and ambiguous, surrealist-like space, all held together by bold, cutting brushwork and passionate colour. Pellan's colour, in fact, is uniquely his own, and one suspects it will be the later abstractions, free of modelling and relying almost completely on his native colour sense, that will prove to be his lasting works of the French years. *La Fenêtre ouverte* (HH) of 1936— with its shallow, segmented space, vaguely anthropomorphic calligraphic shapes, brilliant colour, and emphatic spontaneity—is certainly one of the works to be singled out as having pointed the direction of the future in Montreal.

Pellan settled in Montreal early in 1941 in a studio shared with Philip Surrey and began to exhibit with the CAS people, first at the Indépendants exhibition organized by the refugee French priest Alain Couturier— whom Borduas had met in France in the summer of 1929 and who arrived in Montreal in March 1940—which was shown in Quebec in April and at Morgan's in Montreal in May 1941. Pellan then took a long summer holiday in the Charlevoix region and returned to Montreal in

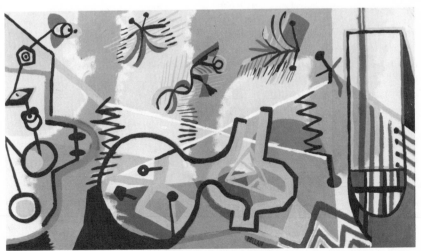

Alfred Pellan. *La Fenêtre ouverte*, 1936. Canvas, 17½ x 32. HH.

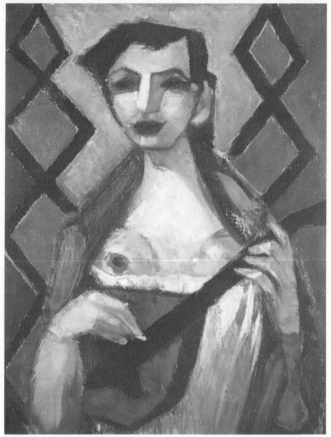

Paul-Emile Borduas. *La Femme à la mandoline*, 1941. Canvas, 32 x 26. MAC.

the fall with a group of forcefully executed portraits of young children and startlingly realistic scenes of the villages he had visited. They would not have been out of place in a CAS exhibition, but they must have disappointed those painters who saw in Pellan the beginnings of a radically innovative art in Montreal. By 1942 he had returned to a flat image abstracted from real objects—as in *Le Couteau à pain* (private collection)—made up in large part of cleverly interlocking ovoid forms. By then, however, Borduas had taken the bold step that would set him on the path of true creative innovation and, in the course of a few years, allow him to outstrip Pellan and all other Canadian artists.

During 1939-40 Borduas appears not to have painted a great deal; in 1940 Maurice Gagnon could still describe him solely as a religious painter. He spent the summer of 1939 working with Gagnon for Gérard Morisset on the inventory of Quebec art, searching out old material in the Montreal region. And he was eagerly reading, thinking, and talking with friends from the Ecole and the CAS. Then in 1941, as though in response to the Pellan retrospective of October 1940, his production resumed. The most ambitious work of this period is *La Femme à la mandoline* (MAC), a lusciously beautiful painting, free of compromise to sentiment or 'taste'. Borduas employs a geometric pattern in the background, as Pellan did in *Jeune Comédian*, but whereas the latter then used heavy outlines and a deliberate modelling of the figure to set the pattern back in space, Borduas accomplishes the same end with colour alone. Boldly aggressive yet subtle, even delicate in passages, it is homogeneous in conception and execution. Beside it the Pellan seems a pastiche. About six inches shorter and narrower than *Jeune Comédien*, it is easily twice the picture.

Borduas was painting with an awareness of the relationship of act to image that few artists ever understand. He had been reading the Surrealists (see pp. 192-3) for some years, and his experiences with teaching children, beginning in 1939, had doubtless corroborated the Surrealist view that the source of creation lies in the unconscious, where it has been slowly obscured by the process of 'maturation'. The strength of *La Femme à la mandoline* lay not in its subject, he knew, but in the naked emotion of its expression. Its beauty resulted from the successful penetration, and then projection, of the artist's self. It was a simple yet monumental step to decide to touch even deeper, and then to flow with the full springs thus released. With a rigorous discipline few could muster, Borduas accomplished such 'automatic' compositions may times over the winter of 1941-2, painting in gouache. (He had decided to experiment with the inexpensive and flexible water-based medium.) Forty-five of the paintings that resulted—which range from clearly identifiable images situated in a dream-like surrealist space, through to great looping, slightly modelled ovoids of colour—were exhibited under the title 'Peintures surréalistes' at the Hermitage Theatre late in April 1942. The occasion was immediately recognized as historic by a number of critics. Charles Doyon was ecstatic. Borduas's exhibition was 'une preuve indubitable de son talent vigoreux, et un autre instant mémorable dans l'histoire de notre peinture'. The young painter, Jacques de Tonnancour, wrote: 'Dans l'histoire de la pensée picturale au Canada, elles constituent un apport de tout premier ordre.' Thirty-seven of the paintings were sold. Borduas's first one-man show represented a resounding confirmation of the path he had chosen to follow. He was thirty-six years old.

The gouaches were not the first abstracts Borduas exhibited. Four months earlier, in January, he had taken part in a group show in Joliette, forty miles north of Montreal, and exhibited three abstract oils that he later destroyed. *Harpe brune* is well known from photographs. It is surprisingly close in certain respects to Pellan's *La Fenêtre ouverte*. Borduas used the same angular black line, darting nervously over coloured compartments of space, and even included barred, ladder-like forms that are similar to the kind of patterning one sees in Pellan. Borduas's paint appears heavier and rougher, however, and *Harpe brune* is more of a vigorous whole, with no consistent distinction between background and drawn forms. Pellan's *Fenêtre* is more like a sheet of separate drawings; it lacks the tight completeness of the Borduas. Some of Borduas's gouaches are also related to the French abstractions of Pellan in the use of heavy lines to string together forms and warp the shallow space. But the best do not resort to such an obvious solution to the structuring of a homogeneous image. †*Composition* (Maurice and Andrée Corbeil, Montreal) is one of a number of gouaches in which the full swelling forms intertwine effortlessly in a solemn, endless dance of becoming. There is really no discrete image. There is just the grave, rolling breadth of the painting itself.

In April 1943 Borduas visited New York for the second time (his first visit had been in the summer of 1928) and is certain to have seen as much as he could of the work of the great Surrealist painters, most of whom were refugees by then, living in New York or its environs. He would also have seen and purchased the Surrealist magazine *VVV*, which first appeared in New York the summer before. The second issue, with a striking cover by Duchamp, had just appeared in March.

As Borduas's own work and expanding interests led him through new growth, his relationships with his students at the Ecole du Meuble were becoming more meaningful. By 1943 he had attracted a number of disciples and in early May eleven of these, and four other young friends who frequented Borduas's studio, appeared in an exhibition of twenty-three painters under thirty organized by Maurice Gagnon for the Dominion Gallery. 'Les Sagittaires', as the exhibition named them, were the first real evidence of a new generation.

In June Pellan was appointed to a professorship at the Ecole des Beaux-Arts (which produced a falling-out with Borduas, to whom the appointment was a seriously compromising decision) and during the fall he too collected a group of adherents.

Pellan may have been responding to Borduas's great gouaches in his *Le Couteau à pain*, with its flat colours and interlocking ovoid shapes, but he soon found a major new direction that led him completely away from Borduas's experiments. Late in May 1943 the great French painter Fernand Léger, a friend of Père Couturier, travelled to Montreal from New York, where he was then living, to lecture and screen a Surrealist film he had made some years before in Paris. Pellan had met Léger in Paris, and perhaps in New York in 1942 when the Quebecker held a one-man show at the Bignon Gallery. Léger was then painting large canvases filled with a solid mass of entwined human figures. They impressed Pellan greatly and he employed the same approach in a large canvas commissioned by the shoe manufacturer Maurice Corbeil in 1945 (*La Magie de la chaussure*). He soon then turned this new idea into something uniquely his own, as in *Quatre Femmes* (MAC) of 1945, principally by overlaying the interlocked figures with intense, frenetic design patterns. Such patterning—joyous, and often compelling in the manner of folk decoration—became his distinctive feature over the following years.

After the success of his gouaches, Borduas attempted the same spontaneous approach in oils. Oil is less tractable than gouache, however, and although—as we can see in *La Danseuse jaune et la Bête* (Luc Choquette, Montreal)—these experiments are often very moving, they are also awkward and are not so thoroughly homogeneous as the gouaches. An exhibition at the Dominion Gallery in October 1943 was a commercial failure. He hardly painted at all the next year. His involvement with his students now took up most of his time and he was building himself a home in Saint-Hilaire, which he moved into in 1945.

That year Borduas was re-elected vice-president of the CAS. Some of the Sagittaires had at first been grudgingly accepted into the ranks as non-voting junior members in 1943 (there were ten so listed by 1945—all French-speaking). By 1948 they had been given a voice in the administration of the Society. As most were sympathetic to the direction being pursued by Borduas, they effected his election as president, replacing Lyman. Pellan and *his* young followers, seeing this as a partisan narrowing of the objectives of the CAS, refused to co-operate and soon withdrew. Borduas, as the new president, sought the support of Lyman. He refused to take sides in what he later called a 'sectarian contention'. Borduas then felt that he had no alternative but to resign, and Lyman, with only the older members remaining, recommended to the council of the CAS that it be dissolved. At a meeting on November 18, 1948, dissolution was accomplished. Some were sad, but all realized that the CAS had reached the extent of its flexibility. It could never have hoped to contain the vigorous force that already had given a new shape to Canadian art.

14

Paul-Emile Borduas
and
Les Automatistes
1946-1960

'Enfin! La peinture canadienne existe!' exclaimed the critic Claude Gauvreau in the course of reviewing the December 1946 exhibition of the CAS, his excitement aroused by the paintings of seven Montreal artists. Marcel Barbeau, Roger Fauteux, Jean-Paul Riopelle, Pierre Gauvreau, Paul-Emile Borduas, Fernand Leduc, and Jean-Paul Mousseau were then in the midst of accomplishing a pictorial revolution, part of a widespread reaction among painters throughout the western world following the Second World War against figurative painting—even against, as the historian Bernard Teyssèdre has remarked, the great French tradition as rejuvenated by Matisse, Picasso, and Léger. Though in part nurtured by the CAS, the Montreal painters soon found it necessary to turn their backs on Lyman and the others, and even on Pellan— not so much because they felt contempt for 'l'académisme fauviste' or 'l'académisme des nouveaux Beaux-Arts' but because, like that other group of seven painters who professed to 'begin' Canadian art in Toronto a quarter of a century before, Borduas and his followers were moved by a new vision of their society to initiate a Canadian painting that would respond for the first time to the deepest needs of Canadians. The story is mainly Borduas's. Eleven years older than his eldest associate in the Automatiste group and with twenty years on the youngest, he was literally the teacher of them all.

All six were born in Montreal and were students there when Borduas first brought them together. PIERRE GAUVREAU (b.1922) was encountered as an exhibitor in a show of student work Borduas judged in the fall of 1941, and he soon introduced the older man to fellow-students at the Ecole des Beaux-Arts, including FERNAND LEDUC (b.1916) and FRANÇOISE SULLIVAN (b. 1925). That same fall Borduas had been impressed by the work of a fourteen-year-old student of his friend Frère Jérôme at the

Collège Notre-Dame, JEAN-PAUL MOUSSEAU (b.1927). Pierre Gauvreau's brother Claude, a poet, first met Borduas at the time of his famous exhibition of gouaches in April 1942, and the rest of the group—MARCEL BARBEAU (b.1925), then only sixteen, and JEAN-PAUL RIOPELLE (b.1923)——was drawn from Borduas's own class at the Ecole du Meuble in the fall of 1942. The group met regularly in Borduas's studio, where they discussed those things in which most shared an interest: idealistic social theories, psychoanalysis, and, most enthusiastically, Surrealism (see pp. 192-3)—all three subjects denounced by the Church. An intense involvement in leading these explorations into new areas would absorb much of Borduas's creative drive for the next three years.

Guy Viau (1920-71), another Borduas student at the Ecole du Meuble, and his brother Jacques organized a series of small exhibitions and seminars in collèges around Montreal, beginning in the spring of 1943 and continuing into early 1945. These showings reflected the developing ideas of the Borduas group and to them must be given much of the credit for a growing student interest. Student activities, in fact, were almost solely responsible for the broadening of the radical cultural movement in the Montreal area during these years. In the fall Viau took charge of the art pages in the Université de Montréal student newspaper *Le Quartier Latin,* beginning a tradition of support of the activities of the Borduas group that continued for years. (The Gauvreau review quoted above appeared there.) The following summer Leduc, young Mousseau, and three other students from the Beaux-Arts—the Renaud sisters—rented a house in Saint-Hilaire in order to be closer to Borduas. (Leduc and Guy Viau frequently visited him there the summer before.) That fall one of the sisters, Louise, took a job in New York as a governess to the children of the art dealer Pierre Matisse. Matisse's gallery was then a centre of activity for the refugee Surrealists who had fled to New York in large numbers because of the war, and Louise sent back to Montreal all the latest news of their activities. The next April, Fernand Leduc also visited New York and, on Good Friday, actually met the famous leader of the Surrealist movement, André Breton.*

Back in Montreal the French artist Fernand Léger, who had visited the city in the spring of 1943, returned to deliver a public address on May 10 and in the course of his lecture encouraged the audience to oppose actively the restraining influences of every conservative element in the

*Breton had been in Quebec from August 20 to October 20, 1944, at Percé in the Gaspé and at Saint-Agathe, north of Montreal, but had made no effort to contact Leduc or Borduas, both of whom had corresponded with him.

art world. The art students of Montreal soon found an opportunity to confront the forces of entrenched academicism when Pellan and Charles Maillard, the French-Algerian director of the Ecole des Beaux-Arts, disagreed over the inclusion of certain controversial exhibits in the annual student show. The students quickly and effectively rallied to Pellan and in a series of demonstrations forced Maillard's resignation. The victory has always been seen as Pellan's, but Pierre Gauvreau was one of the student leaders, and the young 'surrealists' certainly considered the accomplishment their own.

Also in May 1945 Borduas moved into his new house in Saint-Hilaire. As they had done the summer before, a number of his young friends and students rented a house there too. By then it had become clear that the student activity—which involved poets, dramatists, and dancers as well as painters—represented a cultural movement in the widest sense. Their inspiration was generally the thought and activity of the great Surrealists. And their one common concern was becoming more and more clearly social—the struggle against personal repression and social oppression, the liberation of the creative force.

The first concrete manifestation of the Montreal 'surrealist' group was held in New York, a city that early in 1946 could still just barely lay claim to being the world centre of the Surrealist movement. Françoise Sullivan had studied dance there with Franciska Boas after graduating from the Ecole des Beaux-Arts, and it was in the Boas studio in January 1946 that Borduas, Leduc, Gauvreau, Riopelle, and Mousseau first exhibited as a group.

The first Montreal exhibition was three months later (April 20-9), in an office on Amherst Street lent by the Gauvreaus' mother. Organized by Leduc, it included, as well as the five who had shown in New York, Barbeau and Roger Fauteux (b.1920?). It was the first exhibition by a group of abstract painters ever held in Canada, and in its evidence of experimentation was as bold as any then to be seen anywhere. Borduas in 1946 was clearly the most accomplished of the seven. Although the intense intellectual activity of the preceding three years had left little time for painting, a work of 1946 like *L'Eternelle Amérique* (estate of the artist) presents an intelligent solution to the awkwardness of the 1943 oils; a solution derived principally from the work of the then most-acclaimed of the New York Surrealists—the Chilean, Matta. It consisted in releasing the intertwined forms seen in his earlier paintings and letting them float individually in an infinite dream-like space. Borduas brought to the final result his rough but brilliant paint handling, his sure sense of colour and love of radiant light. The method of composition—as is

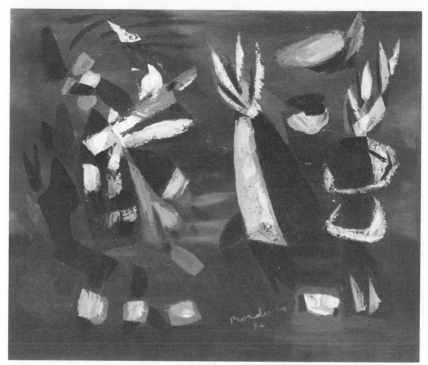

Paul-Emile Borduas. *L'Eternelle Amérique*, 1946. Canvas, 38 x 47. Borduas Estate.

obvious from the natural, flowing interrelationship of the elements—
was that 'automatic' process he had perfected over the winter of 1941-2.

The younger members of the Montreal surrealist group (some of whom were still in school) showed work more radically 'advanced' than Borduas's 'abstract figuration'. A few had no figurative tradition of their own to overcome, having painted from the first with the automatic technique of the Surrealists. Leduc achieved the most resolved image. His 1946 *Dernière Campagne de Napoléon* (the artist), although overly busy, even arbitrary in parts, is still an exciting, violent picture in its exploitation of free gesture, yet it is rigorous in its pursuit of a tight, integrated composition. In 1946 Jean-Paul Riopelle was working in inks and watercolour and he too soon commanded the easy flow of automatic composition. His admirable feeling for texture and tone and his natural sense of drama are revealed in the many untitled works of that year. Marcel Barbeau followed youthful enthusiasm even beyond the limits then comprehended by Borduas himself. *Le Tumulte à la mâchoire crispée* (MAC) is his only canvas of 1946 now extant—a frozen explosion in which every part of the surface has been vigorously assaulted. It is a dynamically spontaneous, if undisciplined, work. Barbeau was thrilled with it and with others done at the time, remarking 'It is the first time

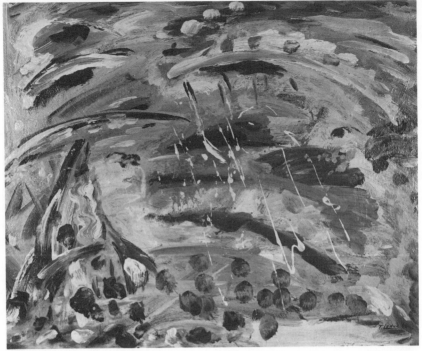

Fernand Leduc. *Dernière Campagne de Napoléon*, 1946. Board, 20 x 26. The artist.

I have painted with perfect joy.'* His young friends were delighted, but Borduas was severely critical. 'There must be an object on an infinitely deep ground,'** he had stated dogmatically. Barbeau dutifully destroyed the results of his excess! The other three participants were more faithful to the limits as then defined by Borduas.

The following year another group show was held (February 15 to March 1, 1947), this time in the Gauvreau apartment at 75 Sherbrooke Street West. The furniture was removed and the walls covered with neutral jute as a background for the pictures. There were six participants (Riopelle was missing) and it was, according to Claude Gauvreau, the most homogeneous and generally impressive of the Automatiste exhibitions. They were first called by that name in a review of the show in *Le Quartier Latin*—Tancrède Marsil coined the term from a Borduas canvas in the exhibition, *Automatisme 1.47*. It was a name they accepted gladly, for surrealist automatic painting was then central to their whole creative stance.

Riopelle was absent from the exhibition because early in December 1946 he had left for Paris, which was once more, after the war and the

*'C'est la première fois que je peins avec une joie parfaite.'
**'Il faut que ce soit un objet sur un fond allant jusqu'à l'infini.'

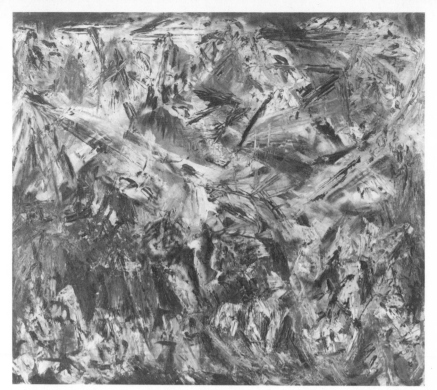

Marcel Barbeau. *Le Tumulte à la mâchoire crispée*, 1946. Canvas, 30 x 35. MAC.

return of Breton, the centre of the Surrealist movement. Leduc joined him on March 7, and by June the two had organized for the little Galerie du Luxembourg an exhibition of the work of six of the Montrealers (Gauvreau did not participate) entitled 'Automatisme'. It was a valiant statement of independence within the Surrealist milieu. Then on June 21 (the exhibition had opened only the day before), Riopelle signed the *Ruptures inaugurales,* the manifesto of the renewed world Surrealist movement. In July he was one of eighty-seven artists from twenty-four countries included in the vast Exposition Internationale du Surréalisme organized by André Breton and Marcel Duchamp at the Galerie Maeght in Paris, the last major group show of the Surrealist movement.

Borduas had been invited by Breton to participate but had refused. He also that year refused to co-operate with Père Couturier, who wished to organize an exhibition of contemporary Canadian art for the Musée d'Art moderne de Paris. He clearly feared the absorption of the Automatistes in Breton's ambitions for a rejuvenated world movement of Surrealism, and probably mistrusted French cultural advances in general. The full trappings of Surrealism were brought to Montreal that

December, nonetheless, when a Mousseau-Riopelle exhibition was installed in the Gauvreau apartment against walls covered with a dark padded material; the pictures were strikingly suspended from web-like nets strung about the rooms. Riopelle and Leduc were by then settled in Paris, however, and although they continued to support the Automatistes, they also began to associate with those painters in Paris who, like the Abstract Expressionists in New York, had developed a free abstract style from the theories of Surrealism. (Their approach to painting has been called 'lyrical abstraction'.) Riopelle has never returned to Canada, save for brief visits; and except for occasional group shows he didn't exhibit in this country again for ten years. Leduc returned only in 1953—by which time Borduas had left Montreal—then moved back to Paris in 1959.

The principal inspiration of the Montreal movement remained Surrealism. Borduas's *Sous le vent de l'île* (NGC) of 1947 is a classic Surrealist picture, with its featherlike forms floating in an infinite, atmospheric space. Pierre Gauvreau was also painting 'dream images', as he had been virtually since his first involvement with Borduas. His *Sans Titre* (MAC) of 1947 is like a monstrous opening flower. Mousseau's first significantly independent works were his beautiful gouaches of 1948 that are jammed with densely packed forms, as in *Bataille moyenâgeuse* (the artist). In the diminishment in size of the elements towards the top of the sheet, they also suggest an infinite space. And MARCELLE FERRON (b.1924), a new adherent from Louiseville recently graduated from the Québec Ecole des Beaux-Arts, also conceived of her paintings as depicting atmospheric if indeterminate space, as in her *Yba* (the artist) of 1947. Riopelle, having moved physically closer to the French Surrealists, was going beyond them. His **Abstraction* (Maurice and Andrée Corbeil, Montreal), painted in 1947, already shows the first perception of a new kind of space, the result not of perspectival recession but of the simple juxtaposition of colour, the forms seeming to play within a shallow rectangular box. Barbeau was still the most experimental of the painters in Montreal. His *Forêt vierge* (Madeleine Arbour, Montreal) of 1948 shows that he too was aware of the possibilities of a shallow arena of space—articulated, though, with slashing string-like lines (strongly reminiscent of the string installation by Duchamp in the 'First Papers of Surrealism' exhibition held in New York late in 1942, which the Montrealers would have known from magazine illustrations).

Though hindsight now leads us to consider the younger painters more 'advanced' in their experiments with depicted space than Borduas prior to 1950, the centre still rested solidly on him. During these months of

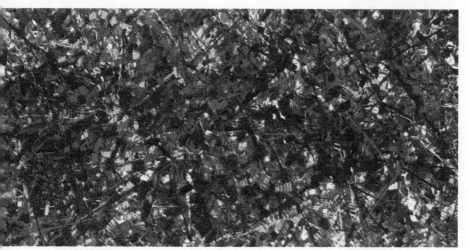

xxx—Jean-Paul Riopelle. *Knight Watch*, 1953. Canvas, 38 x 76¾. NGC.

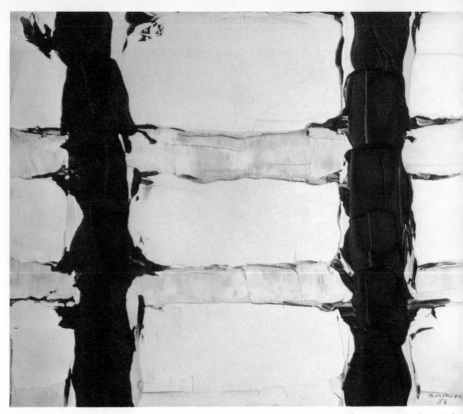

xxxi—Paul-Emile Borduas. *Fence and Defence*, 1958. Canvas, 19½ x 24. Martha Jacks
Gallery, New York.

Jean-Paul Riopelle. *Abstraction*, 1947. Canvas, 30 x 36. Maurice and Andrée Corbeil, Montreal.

late 1947 and early 1948 he determined that his commitment to the realization of a fully free and creative life must be total. This determination resulted in what is perhaps the single most important social document in Quebec history and the most important aesthetic statement a Canadian has ever made, the *Refus global*. A hand-assembled mimeographed book, it was simply illustrated with a few halftones and was wrapped around with a reproduction of a Riopelle ink drawing. The title essay was by Borduas and there were a number of shorter pieces by Borduas, Claude Gauvreau, Françoise Sullivan, Bruno Cormier, and Fernand Leduc. It seems impossible to overstress its importance. Because of the *Refus global*, one commentator has stated flatly, 'modern French Canada began' with Borduas! Four hundred copies were placed on sale on August 9, 1948.* They exploded like so many bombs.

Through the personal experience of one man, or at least of an amalgam of those honest intellectuals around Borduas, he records the awakening of a culture. He first describes the country that formed him—'since 1760, a colony trapped within the slippery walls of fear, the usual

*Since its initial appearance it has been reprinted in full or substantial part at least six times.

refuge of the vanquished.'[1] A colony where the Church is central, its priests the guardians of the faith, of knowledge, truth, and the national wealth. This Church extorts from society so much more than it returns in good works, however, and in fear fosters ignorance and welcomes the worst of outmoded conservative Catholicism from Europe. Nonetheless, cracks have appeared. Revolutions, foreign wars, travel, and education have stirred thoughts. Borduas describes the exhilaration of first reading 'forbidden' authors and discovering that, rather than 'des monstres', they are the ones who 'dare to express loud and clear what the most unfortunate among us have suppressed in self-hatred and terror of being buried alive'.[2]

The only hope for change lies in the ideal of personal liberation, and from that realization a course of action is derived.

Break permanently with the customs of society, disassociate yourself from its utilitarian values. Refuse to live knowingly beneath the level of our psychic potential. Refuse to close your eyes to the vices, the frauds perpetrated under the guise of knowledge, of services rendered, of favours repaid. Refuse to live in the isolation of the artistic ghetto, a place fortified but too easily shunted aside. Refuse to be silent—make of us what you please, but you must understand us—refuse glory, honours (the first compromise): those stigmata of the 'nuisance', the unconcerned, the servile. Refuse to serve, to be made use of for such ends. Refuse every INTENTION, *pernicious weapon of* REASON. *Down with both of them; put them behind us.*

MAKE WAY FOR MAGIC! MAKE WAY FOR OBJECTIVE MYSTERIES!
MAKE WAY FOR LOVE!
MAKE WAY FOR THE REAL NECESSITIES!

Balancing this utter refusal to co-operate with the controlling forces, however, must be the realization of total personal responsibility for

[1]'Colonie précipitée dès 1760 dans les murs lisses de la peur, refuge habituel des vaincus.'

[2]'Osent exprimer haut en net ce que les plus malheureux d'entre nous étouffent tout bas dans la honte de soi et la terreur d'être engloutis vivants.'

[3]'Rompre définitivement avec toutes les habitudes de la société, se désolidariser de son esprit ultilitaire. Refus d'être sciemment au-dessous de nos possibilités psychiques. Refus de fermer les yeux sur les vices, les duperies perpétrées sous le couvert du savoir, du service rendu, de la reconnaissance due. Refus d'un cantonnement dans la seule bourgade plastique, place fortifiée mais trop facile d'évitement. Refus de se taire—faites de nous ce qu'il vous plaira mais vous devez nous entendre—refus de la gloire, des honneurs (le premier consenti): stigmates de la nuisance, de l'inconscience, de la servilité. Refus de servir, d'être utilisables pour de telles fins.

one's actions. 'The self-seeking action remains with its author—it is still-born. Passionate acts take wing by their own energy. We cheerfully take the entire responsibility for tomorrow. . . . In the meantime, without rest or cessation, in a community of feeling with those who thirst for a better existence, without fear of a long deferment, in the face of encouragement or persecution, we will pursue in joy our desperate need for liberation.'[4]

Some think the *Refus global* has nothing to do with aesthetics. But for Borduas and his followers the creative act could be realized to its fullest potential only in a liberated individual; therefore politics, personal security, and joyful fulfilment were essential concerns of the artist.

A few months before the actual appearance of the *Refus global*, just about the time Borduas was elected president of the CAS in February 1948, Pellan rallied 'the anti-Automatiste' faction among Montreal painters with a manifesto (prepared with the help of Jacques de Tonnancour) establishing the 'Prisme d'yeux' group. 'We seek a painting freed from all contingencies of time and place, of restrictive ideology, conceived without any literary, political, philosophical or other meddling which could dilute its expression or compromise its purity,' it was reported to read in *Canadian Art* magazine. The group attracted fourteen participants in its first exhibition that year, held in space provided by the Montreal Museum of Fine Arts. They included young disciples of Pellan like Léon Bellefleur (b.1910) and Albert Dumouchel (1916-71), and more conservative members of the CAS like Jacques de Tonnancour, Goodridge Roberts, and Gordon Webber. It lasted as a group for less than a year and a half. The real opposition to the *Refus global* came not from the artistic community, however—the critic Charles Doyon explained it merely as 'a cry of distress stirred up by the nausea of the young before a generation that is established, fawning'[5]—but from

Refus de toute INTENTION, arme néfaste de la RAISON. A bas toutes deux, au second rang!

  PLACE À LA MAGIE! PLACE AUX MYSTÈRES OBJECTIFS!
  PLACE À L'AMOUR!
  PLACE AUX NÉCESSITÉS!

[4]'L'action intéressée reste attachée à son auteur, elle est mort-née. Les actes passionnels nous fuient en raison de leur propre dynamisme. Nous prenons allègrement l'entière responsabilité de demain. . . . D'ici là, sans repos ni halte, en communauté de sentiment avec les assoiffés d'un mieux être, sans crainte des longues échéances, dans l'encouragement ou la persécution, nous poursuivrons dans la joie notre sauvage besoin de libération.'
[5]'Un cri de détresse suscité par l'écoeurement des jeunes devant une génération d'assis et d'encenseurs.'

those who at least partially felt the correctness of Borduas's statements and sensed his threat to their position: the politicians and the clergy.

Borduas received a letter on September 2, 1948, less than a month after the first appearance of the *Refus global*, informing him that the minister of social welfare and youth of the province, Paul Sauvé, had ordered that he be dismissed immediately from his post at the Ecole du Meuble, 'because the writings and manifestos he has published, as well as his general attitude, are not of a kind to favour the teaching we wish to provide for our students.'[6] Borduas of course informed the newspapers, and some people reacted with shock. But most remained silent. It was the directness of Borduas's attack on the Church, it seems, that had paralysed them with fear.* Only twelve of his former students condemned the government and upheld Borduas's views in a letter in *Le Clairon* (October 15). Then, at the end of October in *Le Clairon*, Pierre Gauvreau, Riopelle, and Maurice Perron, another Automatiste, tried unsuccessfully to shame the intellectual community into supporting Borduas.

In an editorial in the prestigious *Le Devoir* (November 13), Gérard Pelletier, doubtless expressing the point of view of the liberal Catholic intellectual, openly rejected Borduas's position. He was opposed to Surrealism. 'We do not accept the rule of instinct because we believe in sin,' he explained. He was equally unable to accept the *Refus global* because 'we have faith in God, whose name does not once appear and whose Presence is nowhere alluded to in your manifesto . . .'.[7] Borduas had described how 'beyond Christianity we touch the fervent human brotherhood to whom it has become a closed door.'[8]

Such strong feelings did not soon subside. As late as February 1950 two young students of the Jesuit Collège Sainte-Marie were expelled for attending the opening of a Mousseau-Ferron exhibition. And even in the later fifties there were disconcerting reminders of 1948. Marcelle Ferron,

---

[6] 'Parce que les écrits et les manifestes qu'il publie, ainsi que son état d'esprit ne sont pas de nature à favoriser l'enseignement que nous voulons donner à nos élèves.'

*As early as 1946 a book by René Bergeron, *Art et Bolchevisme*, condemned the recent modern trends in Quebec. The 'surrealists' were there presented as demons, followers of Marx and Freud (both anathema to good Catholics), and violently anti-Christian.

[7] 'Nous n'acceptons pas la règle de l'instinct parce que nous croyons au péché' . . . nous avons foi en Dieu, dont le nom n'apparaît pas une seule fois et dont la Présence n'est pas évoquée dans votre manifeste . . .'

[8] 'Par delà le christianisme nous touchons la brûlante fraternité humaine dont il est devenu la porte fermée.'

then living in France, was questioned by the police for Algerian sympathies and was greatly surprised to discover that her interrogators had been supplied with a personal dossier that, unknown to her, had been assembled by the RCMP at the time of the appearance of the *Refus global*!

The fall of 1948 was excruciating for Borduas: little money for his family (he had three children), no possibility of employment as a teacher, few painting sales, and society turned against him as at the least emotionally unstable and at the worst a dangerous, violent criminal. (One Jesuit had claimed in print that Borduas was insane.) There were, fortunately, a few friends who stood by him and, most important, Borduas retained his courage. His probing self-explorations had resulted in more brilliant accomplishments in his painting over the last five years than in the whole twelve years of his career as a church painter. At the age of forty-three he knew he would be able to continue to find strength in his creativity, and so he pressed on. His entry in the MMFA spring show won first prize in April 1949, and his supporters took strength in interpreting this as a criticism of Sauvé's action. In the second half of May he held a one-man exhibition in the studio of the Viau brothers, and that summer he taught painting to children in Saint-Hilaire. He also led the Automatistes in a demonstration to protest police violence during the famous Asbestos strike.

Then in July, almost one year after the appearance of the *Refus global*, he published his *Projections libérantes*. In it he confirmed the reading of Quebec society as set out in the *Refus global* with a simple description of his own development as a painter and teacher up to the point of his dismissal. Intensely personal and nobly impassioned, it tells how his brutal treatment at the hands of the established order moved him just that much closer to the freedom to seek his own destiny: 'Enfin libre de peindre.'

Borduas was hospitalized during August and September 1949 for an appendectomy and an ulcer operation; he spent the fall again teaching children in his home. He exhibited at every opportunity and was rewarded with a few sales. Two canvases were bought by the Musée du Québec that fall. The winter found him working hard on watercolours. 'Ma peinture est en pleine transformation ou mutation,' he wrote to Leduc at the end of January. But then his painting had always developed through evolutionary change—through 'mutation'. The fluid ease of the watercolour medium was leading him toward a single integrated image. His intention was still ambiguous, however. In *Au paradis des châteaux en ruines* (Louise and Jean McEwen, Montreal), for instance, he floats castle-like forms in an indefinite space. Those few examples that do almost obliterate deep space, like *Bleu* (MQ), are tense and taut, rippling with strength across the whole surface. Subsequent oils, nonetheless—*Floraison massive* (AGO) of 1951 is one of the most gloriously beautiful—returned to an object-like shape centred in atmospheric space. His watercolours often thus led him on excursions that could predate a definite 'advance' by as much as two years.

Although Borduas continued to exhibit frequently, there were few sales and his financial situation remained desperate. He held an exhibition of the new watercolours in his house in late November 1950 (it had been specially designed for such a purpose), and the following February his friend Robert Elie hung a showing in his home and encouraged friends and associates to buy, with some success. Then in April 1951 he had his first serious exposure in Toronto when he was rather insensitively linked with the Prisme d'yeux supporter, Jacques de Tonnancour, in a two-man exhibition at the Art Gallery of Toronto. Early in June he held another exhibition in his house that included some remarkable wood sculpture he had recently completed, and then in mid-October he travelled to Toronto for his first one-man show there—an exhibition of 'Colour Ink Paintings' at Douglas Duncan's Picture Loan Society. Returning to Saint-Hilaire, he was distressed to find his family gone. He had pridefully refused to allow his wife to work even in the face of poverty, and she had finally been driven to leave Borduas to support their children herself.

The MMFA asked him for an exhibition in January and he showed ten of his own paintings (a mini-retrospective of the last nine years) with the work of ten followers, only three of whom had been among the original Automatistes. The Automatistes themselves had arranged a group exhibition in May 1951—the first in four years—called 'Les Etapes du Vivant' that included the work of thirteen artists, but not Borduas. The older 'youngsters' were clearly going their own way. At the end of April 1952 Borduas exhibited recent works in his home once again—for the last time. He was forced to sell the house he had built himself and went to live temporarily with his brother. He had decided to move to New York. Long delays with his visa caused worry (McCarthyism was then rampant; 'godless communists' were as feared there as in Canada), but finally on March 31, 1953 he set off for New York City. The National Gallery bought *Sous le vent de l'île* just before he left.

Why New York instead of Paris? He was possibly still concerned to keep out of the Breton sphere of influence, and although New York was much more foreign than Paris in that he didn't speak English, Borduas did have some familiarity with the American metropolis. He had visited it in 1943 and his friends had associations with it. Françoise Sullivan had lived there for two years and Barbeau had had a small exhibition at Wittenborn and Shultz the year before. But Borduas was probably most influenced by the knowledge that the French Surrealists, before their return to Paris, had stimulated a group of young American painters. In January 1950 an exhibition of contemporary art from Great Britain, France, and the United States, organized by the AGT, was shown in Montreal. The works included by the Americans de Kooning, Gorky, Motherwell, Rothko, and Tomlin—with their abstract object-shapes variously related to ambiguous Surrealist space—were then very close to Borduas's own concerns. And Jackson Pollock, whose breathtaking *Cathedral* was one of the largest pictures in the show, must have impressed him greatly. Pollock had achieved the most profound statement of all the Americans with an automatic 'drip' technique that was seemingly even more abandoned than that used by the younger Montreal painters.

Arriving in New York, Borduas soon discovered that little could be accomplished before the fall, so in May he left for Provincetown, Mass., a resort town well known to painters as the location of Hans Hofmann's summer school. 'I have passed a magnificent and unique summer,' he wrote to a friend, '40 new canvases. That is greater than my production during five years in Canada.'⁹ In September he returned to New York and settled into a studio at 119 East 17th Street. In January 1954 he had his first one-man exhibition there at the Passedoit Gallery, showing works painted during the fall and, we can assume, some of the Province-town canvases. Two basic types of pictures are identifiable; both tend toward an active engagement at so many points that the whole surface of the canvas seems enlivened. As in his late Montreal works, the distinction between object and ground is diminished. In *Les Signes s'envolent* (MMFA) 'object' forms cover about one third of the surface, but the 'ground' itself, worked up in texture with a palette knife, presses forward on the objects, as though seeking to integrate with them. The other approach in these 1953 canvases can be seen in *Figure aux oiseaux* (AEAC). Here a neutral-coloured background is clearly visible, but the 'objects' explode all over in a burst of brown, white, red, and gold; the colour is slashed on with a palette knife, but with innate precision. Though neither type of picture presented a radical change—they showed

⁹'J'ai passé un été magnifique et unique . . . 40 tableaux nouveaux. C'est plus que ma production de cinq ans au Canada.'

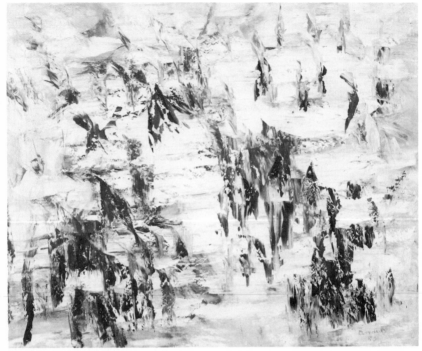

Paul-Emile Borduas. *Les Signes s'envolent*, 1953. Canvas, 45 x 58. MMFA.

rather a logical development out of earlier work—as the first examples of a consistent concern for the 'all-over' integrated image, they mark an important turning point.

Borduas would have seen such expanded all-over images soon after his arrival in New York in late March and early April 1953 when Willem de Kooning held the first exhibition devoted to his violent, slashing *Woman* canvases at the Sidney Janis Gallery. There was also the magnificent example of Jackson Pollock, and the memory of works by Barbeau, Leduc, and Riopelle. All would have been brought into sharp focus at the time of his Passedoit showing by a glittering and highly successful Riopelle exhibition then on view at the famous Pierre Matisse Gallery. The NGC, responding to the prestige of the event, bought two paintings. The larger, †*Knight Watch*, is brilliantly decorative. Swatches of colour are laid on with a palette knife to a thickness of almost half an inch, built up to a dense but facetted surface that completely covers the canvas. At first appearance it is similar to Pollock's work, its shallow but dynamic space articulated with darting lines, suggesting a grid ordering the multiform accidental effects of facture.

Borduas's opening at the Passedoit Gallery was attended by Robert Motherwell, one of the leading American painters to evolve out of the Surrealist milieu in wartime New York. And the Montrealer later came into contact with some others of the American Abstract Expressionist persuasion. But Borduas did not speak English well and so found communication difficult. Besides, he was primarily concerned to digest the great resources of information about him, and so during the spring of 1954 he turned again to watercolours, a medium that allowed him to work out new ideas rapidly. The resulting series was as fine as that of early 1950. Some of these watercolours, like *Forces étrangères* (NGC), are in fact similar to those earlier ones in their structuring of shallow space. Others, like *Baguette joyeuse* (MQ), are much closer to Pollock, even to the extent that the paint is splashed, perhaps even dripped in a controlled 'accident' to produce an open but full image. In these 1954 watercolours Borduas for the first time seems thoroughly free of his old concern with the infinite space of Surrealism. He is no longer making dream-images but has learned from the American Abstract Expressionists how to produce an image of 'actuality'—an image that is not of anything but itself—in which the 'making' and the 'being' have become one, and everything.

The degree of Borduas's involvement with Abstract Expressionism could subsequently have been seen in Montreal at the end of June 1954 when he held an exhibition of his recent watercolours at the Lycée Pierre Corneille.* The next January he exhibited them again in New York at Passedoit. 'The American response was warm, more eager,'[10] he wrote to a friend. The Museum of Modern Art and the Carnegie Institute each purchased one. He was by then working hard on canvases and was pleased with the results. 'My painting becomes more and more "transparent", perhaps. More crystalline, in any case. May it tell us more about that which none of us can comprehend by ourselves.'[11] These were the first canvases in which he sought to refine the new 'all-over' compositional format. The whole surface is worked over in thick paint, often methodically applied with a palette knife as in the paintings of

*He had earlier revealed this new interest in a prepared statement circulated while he was jurying the exhibition 'La Matière Chante', which Claude Gauvreau had arranged at Antoine's Art Gallery in April. The relationship of Surrealism to Abstract Expressionism would then have been a topic of animated discussion.
[10]'La réponse américaine se fait plus chaud, plus pressante.'
[11]'Ma peinture devient de plus en plus 'transparente', peut-être?, plus cristaline, en tout cas. Puisse-t-elle nous renseigner davantage sur ce que nous ignorons tous de nous-mêmes.'

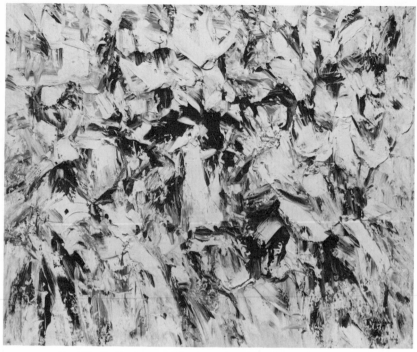

Paul-Emile Borduas. *Pulsation*, 1955. Canvas, 38 x 48. NGC.

Riopelle. Some works, like *Pulsation* (NGC), emphatically reveal the 'gesture' of application, as though the paint had been 'whipped up'. The transparent or crystalline quality Borduas mentioned is due to the illusion of seeing through small broken planes: a jumble of facets trapped within a shallow space. An effect of dynamism is achieved without disruption of the homogenous texture of the surface.

Borduas had always intended to move to Paris after New York, and then to Japan. (His dream was to settle in Tahiti!) He passed August 1955 in Montreal preparing for this next stage of his journeys, and on the twenty-first he left for the French capital. He was in the highest spirits. That spring three Montreal collectors had together purchased eighteen pictures to help him finance the trip, and in July the well-known Martha Jackson Gallery became his New York dealer, agreeing to purchase a regular portion of his production. Montreal's Dominion Gallery made a similar arrangement. He arrived in France on September 27 and soon found a studio in Paris at 11 rue Rousselet. By December he was terribly homesick. 'I would give at this moment Paris and everything good in the world for a comfortable little corner, if it was in

Canada,' he wrote home to a friend. By the end of May 1956 he was beginning to despair. 'Never have I felt such loneliness . . .'[12] While in New York he had been able to return to Montreal every two or three months. Hoping that travel would break his despair he bought a car, and from September through to November 1956 he visited Italy. Then in November he received a further boost when Martha Jackson bought everything he had painted since July.

Although homesick, he had painted feverishly during the spring and summer of 1956, anxious to work through new developments. He was mainly concerned to order and substantiate the shallow space he had developed in the works of 1954-5. He appears to have begun, as in the accomplished *Fond blanc* (NGC), by smoothing out large contiguous areas of white with a long palette knife loaded with pure colour, leaving streaks of whitened colour across their surfaces as well as curled-over acretions of coloured paint along their borders. The coloured 'objects' of his earlier work have here become the residue of process, an actual part of the ground. The overall appearance is of a crude grid of rectangles. Borduas was certainly aware of Mondrian in New York, and the first major monograph on that artist who had himself so successfully ordered shallow space with a rectangular grid was published that year.

In *Sea Gull*—painted before the beginning of August 1956—the solution is even more effectively economical. Virtually all colour has been suppressed except for delicate tints left by the sweep of the knife; then, embedded in the 'ground', are large areas of solid black, like rocks in a Japanese sand-garden. These 'black-and-whites' continued into 1957, culminating in *L'Etoile noire* (MMFA). Here the surface has been caressed with the long blade to a pearly, slightly flushed hue, leaving delicate ridges where the knife has stopped. The rectangles thus formed into a loose pattern glow with a soft light, reflected through the translucent surface as through fine marble. Imbedded in this sensitive 'flesh' are five roughly rectangular shapes of black and dark brown, like malignant growths frozen in perfect, living balance with the sustaining host. Ominous, sombre, it is more majestic than horrible.

In March and April 1957 Borduas was given his first one-man show at the Martha Jackson Gallery; there was another, also that April, at the Gallery of Contemporary Art in Toronto. That spring his painting activity declined—he was by then close to collapse from fatigue and rapidly deteriorating health. In July he left for Spain and Portugal,

[12]'Je donnerais en ce moment Paris et tous les biens de la terre, pour un petit coin douillet, fut-il au Canada . . . Jamais je n'ai eu le sentiment d'une telle solitude.'

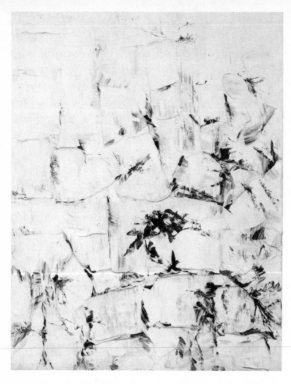

Paul-Emile Borduas.
Fond blanc, 1956.
Canvas, 58 x 45.
NGC.

returning in October. The next two years he followed much the same pattern. There were important shows at Lefort in Montreal (May 1958), Schmela in Dusseldorf (July), Tooth in London (Oct.), Martha Jackson (April 1959), and he had his first one-man show in Paris at the Galerie Saint-Germain (May). He continued to travel as relief from his feverish working schedule: to Switzerland and Italy (March 1958), Brussels (June), Dusseldorf (July), and Greece (June-Oct. 1959). Nevertheless he still thought of home. That April in a letter to a childhood friend he described plans to build a studio on the Richelieu River near Saint-Hilaire.

A European reputation was developing. In November 1959 he described how 'growing friendships in the European critical world are bringing me moral and intellectual consolation. They are interested above all here in the last canvases, in comparison with which 'L'Etoile noire' seems "charming".'[13] It is in the promise of these 'last' canvases that the measure of his genius can be taken. Refining and eliminating everything except the simplest elements of form and struc-

[13]'. . . des amitiés naissantes, dans le monde de la critique Européenne, apportent réconfort moral et intellectuel. On s'intéresse surtout, ici, aux dernières toiles en comparaison desquelles "L'Etoile noire" semble gracieuse.'

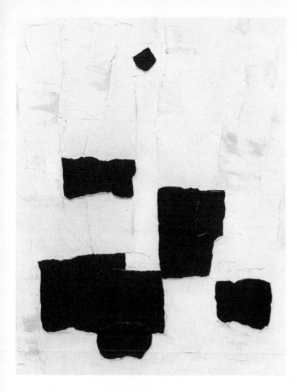

Paul-Emile Borduas.
L'Etoile noire, 1957.
Canvas, 63¾ x 51¼.
MMFA.

ture, he applied himself during his last two years with punishing rigour, seeking a severe statement, free of sentiment or prettiness. Much less 'pleasing' even than the sombre majesty of *L'Etoile noire*, †*Fence and Defence* (Martha Jackson Gallery, New York) of 1958 certainly avoids even the slight 'charm' of the earlier canvas. The conceptual simplicity of the composition—much as in the paintings of Mondrian—allows infinitely exact attention to the sensitive placement of each element to create an image of total unity. It is so full of interrelationships that close examination produces a feeling of profound fulfilment. It is a complex, living thing.

The rich fecundity of these last two years found release in a large number of small canvases equally as rigorous in their economical state-ment of the profound force of simply related forms. Any one could, and did, trigger numerous exploratory variations in which Borduas tested the extent of his potence. His spirit spumed fruit even as his body was failing. 'La vie devient dure,' he wrote Gérard Lortie in Montreal late in January 1960. Less than a month later he was dead of a heart attack. In December of the same year Amsterdam's Stedelijk Museum presented a projected 'mid-career' retrospective as the first tribute to one of the great courageous spirits of the mid-twentieth century.

15

Painters Eleven

1953-1960

In comparison with the brilliant activity in Montreal, the painting scene in Toronto during the forties was moribund. The war weighed more heavily there than in Montreal—Borduas's followers had been almost all under military age—and many of the local artists were involved overseas in the war art program. There was also in Toronto no informed interest in the European modernist tradition, as had developed around Lyman in Montreal during the later thirties. In fact, after the departure of Lawren Harris, the only sophisticated stimulation derived from Douglas Duncan's Picture Loan Society, and even there the lines ran largely to the past during the forties rather than to the future. Remarkably, A. Y. Jackson still represented the heart and soul of vital painting in the city—in fact in most of English-speaking Canada.* And memories of the Group of Seven, which his presence so readily called up, were even intensified after 1945 with the return to Toronto that year of Fred Varley.**

There were some few promising new faces. JACK NICHOLS (b. 1921) first arrived from Montreal in 1939, and his beautiful oil-in-turpentine washes soon attracted the attention of Douglas Duncan. Most of his work of the forties—*Sick Boy With Glass* (AGO) of 1942 is particularly

---

*Jackson's opinions were kept very clearly before the public in a weekly column he wrote for the *Toronto News* from 1942 through into 1946.

**Varley had left Vancouver for Ottawa in 1936, where he taught at the local art association and completed some portrait commissions arranged by the NGC. In 1938 the Gallery also arranged for him to accompany a government ship, the *Nascopie*, to the eastern Arctic. The sketches he brought back are among the most beautiful works of art ever produced by a visitor to that region. In 1940 he moved to Montreal, where he lived for four years, probably the most desperate years of his life. Alone and virtually penniless, he drank heavily and painted little. He was welcomed generously on his return to Toronto, however, and soon was reinvigorated.

fine—is in its full modelling and stark simplicity reminiscent of Louis Muhlstock (with whom Nichols studied in Montreal), and in its soulful humanity not unlike Varley's portrait sketches (Nichols had close contact with that painter too). Nichols joined the navy as an official war artist in 1944. The year after his discharge in 1946 he was awarded a Guggenheim Fellowship that enabled him to study in California until 1948. So at the time when he should have been making an impact in Toronto, he was occupied abroad.

The influence of another Duncan 'discovery' was also lost on Toronto during the forties. ROBERT 'SCOTTIE' WILSON (1890-1972) was born in Glasgow. After a stint in the army, he worked throughout Britain as a junk dealer. He first came to Canada during the twenties, staying only briefly; but he returned about 1931. Finally in 1938 he set up a junk shop on Yonge Street in Toronto. In between sorting scrap metal he began to draw pictures of particularly vivid dreams. He left Toronto in 1942, settling briefly in Vancouver, but was back within the year. He then met Douglas Duncan, who was immediately taken with his madly intense ink drawings of dream-creatures. Carefully composed of simple forms, each element is painstakingly cross-hatched with straight, evenly spaced lines, and brightly coloured in with crayons. The staring-eyed monster of *The Bird Head-Dress* (NGC) of about 1943 wears a radiating halo made up of bird-shapes, exquisitely spaced with that exact sense of placement one usually associates only with the Orient.

Duncan gave Scottie Wilson a show at the Picture Loan Society in April 1943, and in June and July the artist himself staged another in a Vancouver store-front to which he charged admission. There was a second Duncan show in February 1944, and Scottie arranged another one himself in St Catharines, Ont., in June. Later that year he returned to Britain and settled in London. Exhibiting there at the Arcade Gallery in 1945, he was presented as a proto-Surrealist painter of hallucinations and was subsequently included in the same 1947 Parisian Surrealist exhibition in which Riopelle participated. Two years later Scottie's drawings were shown at the Passedoit Gallery where, in 1954, Borduas was to have his first New York show.

Although Duncan was the first to show Scottie Wilson's drawings, he exhibited them as those of a primitive or naive. The connections London and Paris later made between his work and Surrealism would not then have been possible in Toronto.* During the forties, in fact,

*Unlike Montreal, which had its own 'Baie Saint-Paul' primitives. However, Yvonne Bolduc (b. about 1915), Mary Bouchard (1912-45), and Robert Cauchon (1914-69) were of the 'Grandma Moses' rather than the 'psychedelic' variety.

Toronto painters were seemingly detached from most currents of international thought and were no longer really motivated by the nationalist-landscape movement. When at the end of the decade the famous Massey Commission (the Royal Commission on National Development in the Arts, Letters and Sciences) convened, Charles Comfort, representing the English-speaking painters of the country, delivered a paper on the contemporary international scene and its impact on Canadian art. 'By far the most stable expression in the visual arts today is emanating from the United Kingdom,' he observed, 'the most eclectic and experimental from the United States . . . It would be of great value to Canadian painters and sculptors if a closer relationship were maintained with the United Kingdom and with France. Such a policy would be in line with those sympathies and loyalties which are part of our cultural heritage.' But when new forces finally gathered in Toronto, it was in order to seek experimental new directions, not stability.

As in Montreal some ten years before, those forces were engendered in the union of a mature teacher with the largely undisciplined energies of ambitious youth. In Toronto the teacher was JOCK MACDONALD; youth, however, was represented principally by one man: William Ronald.

Although he painted his first abstract in 1934, Macdonald began serious experiments with automatic painting in watercolour and inks in Vancouver in 1941 (see pp. 191-3), roughly the same time as Borduas. He continued to experiment with his 'automatics' in watercolour throughout the forties—in Vancouver and then in Calgary, first exhibiting them in a one-man show at the VAG in September 1946. The following August, at the end of his year in Calgary, he exhibited thirty-six of them at the San Francisco Museum of Art. All, like *Russian Fantasy* (AGO) of 1946, are similar to Borduas's 1942 gouaches in that fortuitous shapes are sometimes allowed to develop into recognizable forms (fish, birds, etc.) and at other times are simply left as non-objective elements. For both artists, an expanding, rich field of imagery was the desired result. Macdonald, however, tends to 'doodle' (he used a pen as well as washes). He had developed more of an interest in the 'fantasy' aspect of Surrealism than had Borduas and his followers in Montreal, and it was this vein he would explore, still principally in watercolours, during his first years in Toronto.

In September 1947 Macdonald settled in Toronto, where he had taken a position teaching drawing and painting at the Ontario College of Art. He found the size of the city stimulating and was excited by the relatively large number of painters. The first year or so he was absorbed in organizing his heavy class load: he taught four full days a week through-

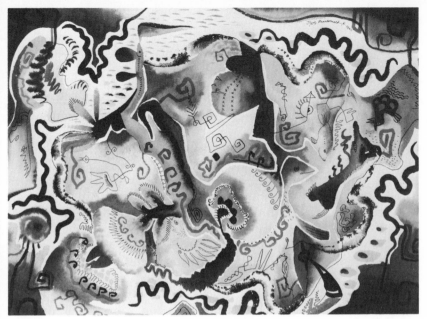

Jock Macdonald. *Russian Fantasy*, 1946. Watercolour and ink, 9½ x 13½. AGO.

out his career at the College. But the next year he became interested in a third-year drawing and painting student, WILLIAM RONALD (b. 1926). Born William Ronald Smith in Stratford, Ont., he was raised at Fergus, some fifty miles due west of Toronto, where his father was a market gardener. After raising some money working in an airplane assembly plant at the end of the war, he enrolled in the Ontario College of Art. An aggressive, independent young man, Ronald was frustrated by the conservative nature of the college, became rebellious, and was failed. Macdonald encouraged him to return. Coaching him almost as if he were an athlete, he saw him graduate in the spring of 1951 with honours and a scholarship. Ronald then took a job as a display artist with the Robert Simpson Co., the Toronto department store.

The next year, Macdonald—who had by then developed an engrossing personal involvement in Ronald's career—persuaded him to take six weeks off and visit New York City to attend Hans Hofmann's painting school. Macdonald himself had spent two brief periods with Hofmann at Provincetown in the summers of 1948 and 1949 and greatly admired the spiritual basis of the theories of the great teacher. Ronald's sojourn was the opportunity for his first extended contact with the work of the New York Abstract Expressionist painters.

Back in Toronto, Ronald left Simpsons, now convinced that commercial art represented a serious drain on his creativity. Supported by sporadic teaching, free-lance designing, and some tour lecturing at the Art Gallery of Toronto, he painted with a driving ambition, inspired by his lessons from Hofmann and by gallery-viewing in New York. *In Dawn the Heart (AGO) of 1954 is one of the best of these pictures, reflecting Ronald's intense interest in Abstract Expressionism. It is also reminiscent of Borduas's canvases of the last four years in Montreal (1949-52), although in its vigorous handling it is an 'action' painting of the sort that Borduas would approach only the next year.

Even by the time of his short visit to New York in 1952, Ronald was hardly alone in Toronto in having such interests. Every society exhibition was beginning to include one or two works revealing some awareness of current abstract painting in New York or Montreal.* None of these painters was known other than by isolated works, however, except for two or three who had shows at the Picture Loan Society or at Hart House. Nonetheless Ronald must have been noting such sporadic appearances.

Early in the fall of 1953—frustrated by the lack of any attention, commercial or critical—Ronald approached his old employers at Simpsons and to his delight they agreed to feature local abstract pictures in a display of contemporary furniture interiors. Publicized as 'Abstracts at Home', this unusual exhibition was mounted that October with a full-page promotion in the newspapers. Of the seven painters assembled by Ronald, only two other than himself were not then full-time advertising artists. One was KAZUO NAKAMURA (b. 1926), who was the same age as Ronald. Born in Vancouver, he was moved east with his Japanese parents during the war and settled with them in Hamilton, Ont., in 1947. He began studying art at the Hamilton Technical School in the evenings and the next year enrolled full-time at Central Tech in Toronto, graduating in 1951. Like Ronald, he took what commercial work he had to in order to live but spent most of his time making delicate drawings, watercolours, and small oils—mainly stylized landscapes. He had his first one-man show at the Picture Loan Society in 1952 and another at Hart House in 1953.

ALEXANDRA LUKE (1901-67) was twenty-five years older than Ronald and Nakamura and had married into the wealthy McLaughlin family of Oshawa, so she did not need to waste painting time with commercial

*An exhibition of contemporary art from Great Britain, France, and the United States at the Art Gallery of Toronto in November-December 1949 included work by Pollock, de Kooning, Tomlin, Rothko, and Motherwell, among those who had developed out of the Surrealist years in New York during the war and were by then beginning to attract considerable attention. The work of Borduas was certainly

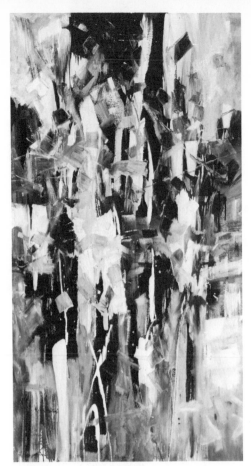

William Ronald. *In Dawn the Heart*, 1954.
Canvas, 72 x 40. AGO.

work. Born in Montreal, she moved to Oshawa (thirty miles east of Toronto on the lakeshore) at thirteen. She studied with Jock Macdonald at Banff the summer of 1946, and from 1947 through 1954 spent her summers at Hofmann's Provincetown school. She had her first one-woman show at the Picture Loan Society in late March 1952, but her bold Hofmann-influenced canvases were received with almost total bewilderment. Realizing that her audience had probably never before experienced abstractions, she sought to educate it and organized the Canadian Abstract Exhibition, which opened in the Oshawa YWCA in

known in Toronto. He first showed there in a five-man show at the AGT in 1942, and virtually every year thereafter in CGP or other group shows. In April 1951 he was seen in a two-man show with de Tonnancour at the AGT, and in his first one-man show in October 1951 at the Picture Loan Society.

October 1952 and then toured the southern-Ontario gallery circuit. It was shown at Hart House in Toronto. Including most artists who had experimented with abstracts in Canada, she rather surprisingly left out the bulk of the Quebeckers; only Léon Bellefleur, Louis Muhlstock, and Marian Scott from that province were shown. Luke did include all of the participants in the later Abstracts at Home exhibition (except Naka-mura), including two commercial artists who had only recently settled in Toronto: Ray Mead and Oscar Cahén.

RAY MEAD (b. 1921) was born in Watford, Eng., and had studied at the Slade. An RAF pilot during the war, he was stationed in Hamilton in 1946 and chose to stay in Canada. He moved to Toronto to become art director of an important advertising firm in the late forties. OSCAR CAHEN (1916-56) was also brought to Canada by the war. Born in Copenhagen, he studied art at the Dresden Academy and in other schools around Europe. A teacher of illustration and design in Prague when war broke out, he made his way to England in 1938 and was taken into custody as an enemy alien the next year. In 1940 he was sent to an internment camp in Canada. Released after the war and settling in Montreal, he became a citizen in 1946. Cahén soon moved to the Toronto area and quickly developed a reputation as an illustrator. Always interested in personal expression, his earlier paintings in Toronto —such as *Ascend* (RMCL) of 1951—were mainly of formal, abstracted still-life themes, painted in a highly finished style developed out of Cubism.

The last two of the painters Ronald assembled in October 1953 were Toronto born. JACK BUSH (b. 1909) was raised in Montreal, though, and first studied there in 1926-8 with the longtime secretary of the RCA, the Frenchman Edmond Dyonnet (1859-1954) and the Scottish muralist Adam Sherriff Scott (b. 1887). Sent back to Toronto at nineteen to work in the main office of the commercial art firm for which his father ran a Montreal branch, Bush continued his studies evenings at the College of Art, notably with Charles Comfort. He later married and settled in Toronto to pursue a career as a commercial designer. In his spare time Bush sketched and painted with his designer friends (a longstanding tradition in Toronto), and first exhibited publicly in a two-man show with R. York Wilson (b. 1907) at the Women's Art Association in 1944. The next year he began exhibiting with the CGP and also held his second two-man show. This 1945 exhibition was at Hart House with his partner in a small advertising firm, William Winter (b. 1909). Bush was then working in the Group of Seven landscape tradition, with strong elements of that 'regionalist' style that had been popular in the United

States and with some Canadians during the thirties. The deeply felt and emphatically presented sentiment of paintings like *Village Procession* (AGO) of 1946 began to attract some attention, and in 1949 he was given his first one-man show, at the Gavin Henderson Galleries in Toronto. Three years later he was taken on contract by the Roberts Gallery. By then he was stressing simple shapes in his painting. *The Old Tree* (AGO), exhibited in a one-man exhibition at the Roberts Gallery in 1952, is made up of stylized, angular forms derived from Cubism, clearly modelled in space.

At the same time Bush was discovering an interest in the kind of abstract art that had developed out of Surrealism—some of his gallery work even suggested dream imagery. The first time he met Jock Macdonald (soon after Macdonald's arrival in Toronto, Bush remembers), he had been impressed with the westerner's ideas. 'He believed strongly in intuition; painting how you feel,' is how Bush later put it. He himself had recently been inspired by the example of Borduas, and had privately begun to experiment with automatic composition. In 1952 (the same year as Ronald) Bush paid his first visit to New York.

The other Toronto-born exhibitor in Abstracts at Home was raised on Toronto Island. TOM HODGSON (b. 1924) first attended Central Technical School and then the Ontario College of Art. He first exhibited with the OSA the year of his graduation in 1946 but then took a job as an advertising designer and stopped painting. He resumed about 1951, dividing his spare time between his art and paddling. A serious athlete since high-school days, he was a member of Canada's Olympic paddling team in 1952 and again in 1956. He took his painting just as seriously and had his first two one-man shows in 1953, at those unique showplaces of experimental art of the day, the Picture Loan Society and Hart House. Decorative stylizations of recognizable objects, his work was related most closely to Cubism, like that of his friend Cahén.

If Abstracts at Home had simply *assembled* these beginners at abstraction, it would long ago have been forgotten. But the seven participants were called together one night for publicity shots (they were not really friends, except Hodgson and Cahén, and some had never even met before), and afterwards all but Bush—who had another engagement—ended up at Ronald's Bloor and Spadina studio. Out of conversation there grew the idea of a 'real' group exhibition, co-operatively financed, and the agreement to meet later at Alexandra Luke's cottage-studio in Oshawa to discuss the possibilities further. To this now-historic meeting Ronald brought Jock Macdonald (he was to have been included in Abstracts at Home but had no work ready). Ray Mead brought HORTENSE GORDON (1887-1961), a Hamilton-born-and-raised painter he had met while posted there with the RAF. Gordon, who taught design at the Hamilton Technical School, had, like Alexandra Luke, spent the summer of 1947 with Hans Hofmann. She had had a one-woman exhibition in New York at the tiny Creative Gallery in January 1952, and at sixty-six was the oldest of the painters at the meeting. And Oscar Cahén brought two more advertising artists: Walter Yarwood (b. 1917), born in Toronto and a graduate of Western Technical School, and HAROLD TOWN (b. 1924), also of Toronto and a graduate of Western Tech and (in 1944) of the Ontario College of Art. During the latter half of the forties, Town worked at painting in his spare time, developing an angular, spiky style of abstracting figuration that, like the work of Cahén and Hodgson, grew out of an interest in Cubism. Town first exhibited, with the OSA, in 1949.

That first meeting was stormy (as each of the subsequent meetings were to be), but out of the clash of personalities grew the decision to finance an exhibition jointly. The group soon also determined on a name —Painters Eleven—which avoided committing the membership to any one position. Bush, the only one with a dealer, approached the Roberts Gallery, which agreed that if all expenses were met, space could be made available. The exhibition was set for February 1954 with plans to send it later to Ottawa and Montreal.

The huge crowd at the opening was unlike any the staid Roberts Gallery had ever seen. There was a charge of excitement, the sense of an event. But Toronto generally ignored the paintings and there were only one or two sales. Reviewers were at a loss to evaluate the art and basically limited themselves to remarking on the aggressive nature of the work and on the variety of approaches to abstraction it revealed. Pearl McCarthy of the *Globe and Mail* agreed, though, that it reflected a positive desire to 'disagree harmoniously'. Shown at Ottawa's Robertson Gallery in March, the planned Montreal exposure fell through.

The painters themselves were delighted to see their work hung together and believed that there was indeed strength in numbers—particularly in the struggle against indifference. So they returned to the Roberts Gallery in February of the following year. By this time they apparently had been considered in relation to the Montreal movement of some eight years before; a statement presented at the exhibition suggests one eye half-cocked on the Refus Global and the other on Pearl McCarthy's head-line of the year before. 'There is no manifesto here for the time,' it read. 'There is no jury but time. By now there is little harmony in the noticeable disagreement. But there is a profound regard

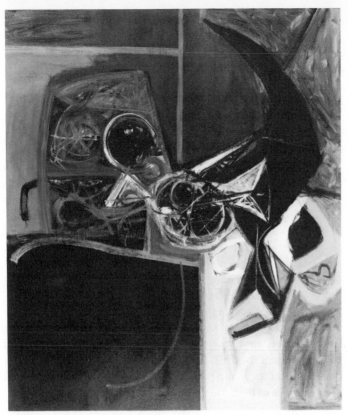

Oscar Cahén. *Painting on Olive Ground*, 1956. Canvas, 60 x 52.
John and Mable Ringling Museum of Art, Sarasota, Fla.

for the consequences of our complete freedom.' The exhibition was then
again sent to a smaller Ontario centre—Oshawa this time.

The following year the Roberts Gallery—concerned by the lack of
sales, and unconvinced that any appreciable public was developing—
showed only 'Small Pictures by Painters 11'. But Painters Eleven had
indeed begun to attract interest, if not support, and that year from late
in February 1956 through to December an exhibition toured the western-
Ontario circuit. The real turning-point was reached not in western
Ontario, however, but in New York. From April 8 to May 20 Painters
Eleven were guest exhibitors with the American Abstract Artists* at
the Riverside Museum. The Canadians were generously received by the
American critics and of course back home the exhibition drew more attention than had any of their previous activities. It really marked the
acceptance among the informed public of the existence in Toronto of

*An association founded in 1936 in New York to exhibit abstract painting.

contemporary 'modern' artists. Painters Eleven had to that degree achieved their aim. What, though, of their individual progress during these two years? There was certainly no Painters Eleven style in the way that one can say there was an Automatiste style.

Oscar Cahén—who was tragically killed in an automobile crash late in November 1956—had in his work established a greater distance from the illustration that brought him his livelihood until his death and in his last two years accomplished a series of compelling pictures. *Painting on Olive Ground* (John and Mable Ringling Museum of Art, Sarasota, Fla) of 1956, with its threatening, jaggedly angular forms and dense concentrations of frenetic scribblings, hung on a simple grid partitioning the olive background, is a provoking image of arrested violence. During the last three years of his life, Cahén drew some of the younger painters away from their stylized figuration with his intense, concentrated brush drawing and his method of composing in cell-like, often individually coloured, compartments.

Harold Town held his first one-man show in February 1954, at the Picture Loan Society. ('Any real interest in my work begins precisely with the moment I first met Douglas Duncan,' he once said.) He did not exhibit paintings but his unique 'single autographic prints'—which he had begun producing the year before—and drawings. The next year, in October, he showed 'colour print collages' at another gallery, and in November 1956 he held another exhibition of his prints at the Picture Loan Society. (He exhibited paintings only in group shows during these years.) In his drawings, and particularly in his prints and collages, he developed a great formal facility, a highly refined sense of design, and this growing ability began to appear in his paintings. By 1956 he was capable of an assured painting like *Dead Boat Pond* (NGC), which he exhibited with the American Abstract Artists that year. It reveals a familiarity with Abstract Expressionism (Town had stayed in New York for some months in 1948) in the boldly blocked-in black forms and slashing 'gestural' brushwork. And it also reflects his earlier interest in Cubism and the work of Cahén. It is nonetheless clearly Town's own in its commanding unification of a large, complex image.

Late in 1956 or early in 1957 Town resigned from the executive of the Toronto Art Directors' Club. Tom Hodgson had already quit his job as a commercial artist in 1955, although he freelanced until 1957 when he once again took a position as an art director. He had continued to paint quasi-geometric figurative pictures until 1955—*Red Lanterns* (NGC) was made that year. Then, drawing heavily on Cahén and to a lesser degree on Town, he turned to full abstractions like *This*

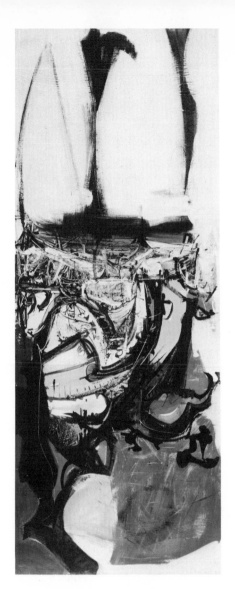

Harold Town.
Dead Boat Pond,
1956. Canvas,
95½ x 38. NGC.

is a Forest (Owens Art Museum, Mount Allison University, Sackville, N.B.).

Both Alexandra Luke and Hortense Gordon continued to find inspiration in the theories and painting of Hans Hofmann. Although they experimented continuously and thrilled their colleagues with their bold enthusiasms, even their most successful work carries a strong mark of derivation.

WALTER YARWOOD continued to work as an advertising artist and had

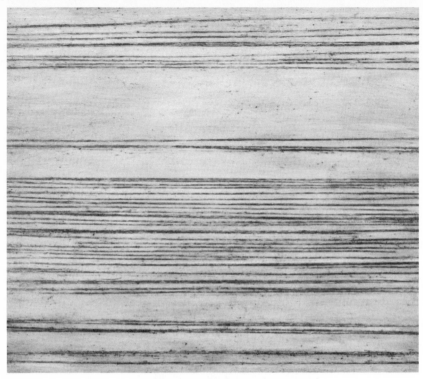

Kazuo Nakamura. *Waves*, 1957. Masonite, 27 x 33½ NMAG.

his first exhibition—with Ray Mead—only in 1957. His work of this period shows the same spiky, angular quality as that of Cahén and Town, but contains more massive forms, clearly set in space. As in *The Lost Place* (AGO) of 1956, it is usually very sculptural. Yarwood in fact totally abandoned his painting in 1960 and turned to sculpture. Ray Mead also continued as a successful advertising artist, painting very reserved, almost geometric pictures in his spare time. Mead moved to Montreal the year of his show with Yarwood.

Kazuo Nakamura, working in his quiet, very personal way, organized his painting ideas into a number of overlapping 'series'. He continued with his stylized landscapes, dwelling particularly on the phenomenon of water reflections. There is also a well-known series of strange, brooding pictures depicting monolythic structures set in otherwise empty landscapes. But the most beautifully profound are his 'string' paintings. Among the most radically simple works being produced in Canada at the time, all—like *Waves* (NMAG) of 1957—are expansive, infinitely subtle pictures. Without scale, they are equally without limit to their meaning.

Jack Bush was exhibiting Surrealist-like figurative pieces as late as

1956, but he was also displaying abstractions with Painters Eleven, of course, and even in some CGP and OSA exhibitions. These early non-objective paintings—like *Holiday* (the artist) of 1954—had developed out of his earlier interest in Borduas and subsequent experiments with automatic painting. They already reveal some of the simple forms and distinctive, luminous colour that Bush was later to exploit so profoundly. By the middle of the decade, however, he had settled on a New York type of Abstract Expressionism (he had returned to that city a number of times since 1952). *Reflection* (RMCL) of 1955—which was exhibited with the American Abstract Artists in 1956—seeks, in its strong tonal contrast, to achieve a deep moodiness. The sooty-grey 'swipes' in the upper portion of the picture—strange objects flying in close formation from dark into an area of most intense light—are suggestive of elements in Borduas's paintings of some two or three years before. They also are a common mannerism of developed Abstract Expressionism. Dramatically striking, they function as a successful device rather than as an inspired creation.

During these earlier Painters Eleven years Jock Macdonald was having even more difficulty than Bush in finding a moving expression of his ideas about form and about the 'natural forces' that supported form. His initial enthusiasm for the Ontario College of Art had soon subsided and by 1951 he found himself in a constant struggle to advance his ideas. While Macdonald coaxed and encouraged his students to find personal freedom in their decisions, most of the faculty resented both his spontaneous enthusiasms and the questioning spirit he brought out in the students. Early in 1954 he even considered leaving the College to teach on his own, like Hans Hofmann, but the decision was postponed when he received a government fellowship for one year of study in Europe. He was ecstatic. 'It will give me the chance to find out at last what I am capable of doing in art,' he wrote.

The Macdonalds left in the fall of 1954, and after a visit to Scotland and a brief stopover in London (Jock was unimpressed with what he saw of current British art), they installed themselves on November 19 in the ground floor of a furnished villa in Vence in the south of France. They stayed there until April 1955. The most important event of the sojourn was meeting the French painter Jean Dubuffet, who moved to Vence with his wife at the end of January. Macdonald was deeply impressed with Dubuffet, whom he described as a 'sensitive and delicate looking fellow with a friendly disposition and a deep awareness of spiritual values in art.' They visited many times and Dubuffet encouraged the Canadian. Most impressed with Macdonald's watercolours,

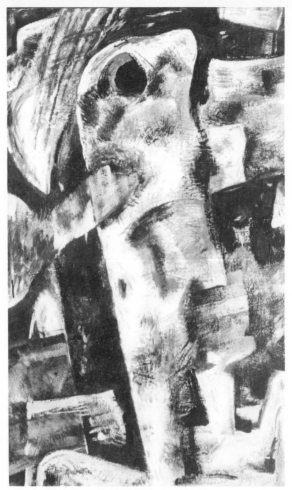

Jock Macdonald. *Obelisk*, 1956. Canvas, 40 x 24¼.
Mrs Barbara E. Macdonald, Toronto.

he suggested that he thin his oil paints to more closely approximate
the fluidity of watercolour. 'Start experiments of technique immediately,'
he advised; 'it is only a technique discovery you have to find, everything
else you have already.'

Back in Toronto Macdonald had a sense of imminent breakthrough
and applied himself determinedly to its success. 'I just feel I want to
work, to experiment, to find my next pathway. I believe in myself that
my work is saying things and will say more ere long—so my direction
seems to be to continue striving and forget about exhibiting for the immediate future.' Consequently the works of 1955-6 are experimental,
revealing a great variation in style, format, and medium. *Obelisk* (Mrs

Barbara E. Macdonald, Toronto) of 1956 has sand imbedded in its plastic enamel. In its raw texture, and in the suggestion of a primitive human form, it is the closest of all of Macdonald's work to that of Dubuffet. And in the shallow modelling of its forms, one sliding ambiguously either over or into another, it sets the direction he will pursue. But early in 1956 he was still unsure of his new work and so exhibited two pre-Vence paintings of 1954 with the American Abstract Artists in New York. Both were painted in a studio he had then in the same building in which Bill Ronald worked, and one, *White Bark* (Mrs Barbara E. Macdonald, Toronto), was painted in the summer of 1954 partly in consultation with Ronald. He encouraged Macdonald in a developing interest in a larger, more prominent single image, away from the elaborate and somewhat diffused results of his earlier automatic style.

That summer of 1954 Ronald was more aggressively self-assured than ever. Out of school only three years, he had been painting almost full-time for two, producing pictures like *In Dawn the Heart* and the Pollock-inspired *A Nearness and a Clearness* (NGC), also of 1954, that were, as individual works of art, then unmatched in Toronto in their coherent, direct impact. Ronald knew what he was after and was singleminded in its pursuit. 'Nothing saps your creativity and your energy the way commercial work does,' he has said, and he would occasionally forego eating rather than put aside his painting for a paying job. At this time all of the other members of Painters Eleven except for Nakamura, Luke, Gordon, and Macdonald were employed as advertising artists, and the latter two were full-time teachers. (Macdonald even had to add some evenings to his four full days at the college in order to afford to rent a studio.)

Ronald held his first one-man show in January 1955, at Hart House. Later that year he moved to New York City. He was convinced that if he was to make his mark as an Abstract-Expressionist painter—and that style in 1955 certainly seemed to be the only viable language of visual expression—it would have to be in the birthplace, and still the spiritual home, of the movement. Most of the members of Painters Eleven watched Ronald's departure with excited anticipation. He did not disappoint them.

Shortly after his arrival in New York, Ronald began to meet painters associated with the American Abstract Artists group. Primarily through Henry Botkin he learned that they sometimes invited foreign groups as guest exhibitors. Ronald told them about Painters Eleven and to his delight—and not a little amazement—the Toronto group was invited to participate in the twentieth annual exhibition the next April. The show

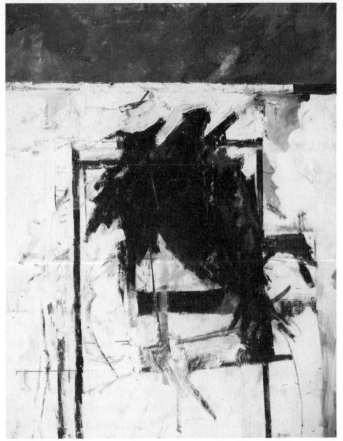

William Ronald. Central Black, 1955-6. Canvas, 84 x 65½. RMCL.

opened on April 8, 1956, and Macdonald, Luke, and Bush flew down to join Ronald for the opening.

It was a most important recognition of Painters Eleven, and Macdonald was particularly pleased by the generous welcome they received. 'The Americans were superb to us. We have the best room, more space per painting . . . and they used a large canvas by Ronald to place over the main stairway entrance to the Exhibition rooms.' This was Ronald's *Central Black* (RMCL), painted that first winter in New York. It is the first landmark Painters Eleven picture. Boldly aggressive, and very much a 'New York' painting in scale and slashing brush work —its central black image on a whitish ground suggests Franz Kline, though it is more organic in shape and less calligraphic than the work of the American—it is still deeply personal in expression. It impressed American viewers with its control. The crudely emphatic centering of the almost chaotic black form presents a satisfying image of dominant will.

As a painting it clearly marks a divergence from the free, almost abandoned approach to abstraction earlier espoused by the Montrealers and the first generation of American Abstract Expressionists. Interestingly enough, it coincides almost exactly with Borduas's turn to a new interest in structure in his art.

The American Abstract Artists exhibition was Ronald's first public display in New York. It brought him some attention, and one collector—the Countess Ingeborg de Beausac—introduced him to Samuel Kootz, an important dealer who handled some of the major Abstract Expressionists. Ronald was given his first show (his first commercial exhibition ever) at the Kootz Gallery in April 1957. Parker Tyler, a well-known New York critic, wrote in the introduction to the catalogue of his amazement at how, after only two years in New York, Ronald had been able to 'clairvoyantly appropriate its milieu of paint'. Like a conqueror, Tyler observed, the Canadian 'bows to take over'. It was doubtless this ability to command the New York idiom with such seeming effortlessness that led to Ronald's amazingly rapid rise. This first show was a great success, and it was followed by another in 1958, and four more by 1963. Already by 1959 Ronald had become such a 'star' in the Kootz stable that it was his one-man show that opened a new Madison Avenue location that October.

Ronald's first New York success in 1957 also had immediate and far-reaching consequences for Painters Eleven back in Toronto. Realizing the importance of the occasion for Macdonald ('It was everything Jock and I had talked about coming true,' said Ronald), a Toronto university professor and his wife—collectors and supporters of Painters Eleven—paid Macdonald's air passage to the opening. It was a brilliant New York affair. Macdonald was 'as proud and happy as if it was his own show'. Hofmann, Franz Kline, and Mark Rothko were all there, and Clement Greenberg, an influential critic, talked with Macdonald about Painters Eleven. He was impressed by Ronald and curious about the kind of scene that produced him. The upshot was that Greenberg said he would be pleased to be invited to Toronto to see these painters. Jock later related the incident to Ronald, who believed that it represented a wonderful opportunity for Painters Eleven—perhaps a crucial break. Later, back in Toronto, a meeting was held to discuss the proposal. Ronald was so convinced of its worth that he flew up from New York to encourage an affirmative decision. The meeting, however, resulted in the first serious division in Painters Eleven when Town and Yarwood strongly opposed paying the way of an American critic to view their work. The others were so enthusiastic, however, and Ronald pressed so firmly, that the dissenters finally decided to opt out rather than block the project. Greenberg came up in June 1957 and spent a half day in the studio of each co-operating painter. None ever later discussed with others in the group these strangely intimate communions with one of the principal theoreticians of modern American painting. Jock, however, wrote to a friend in Calgary: 'At long last I am really on the road—so says Clement Greenberg. He arrived here after I had two of the new things done so he told me that my new work was a tremendous step forward, in the right direction, completely my own and could stand up with anything in New York. The step forward is through my being able to completely free myself from the canvas limitations—or what he calls "the box".'

Which were these first two new canvases—done after viewing Ronald's New York show—we don't know. But they were followed by a summer of intense production. Writing to his friend in Calgary again early in August, Macdonald reported: 'I have twenty-two new things done since the college closed in the middle of May and I am still at it with increased enthusiasm.' These would have included a number that were very clearly painted in response to Ronald's exhibition. *Airy Journey* (HH), in fact, is limited to the black, white, and red-yellow of *Central Black*, although its centred black shape is closer to Franz Kline's calligraphy than is Ronald's. Others, like *North Wind* (Mrs and Mrs Avrom Isaacs, Toronto), grew directly out of *Obelisk*. The modelled form has now completely broken down, though, and the shimmering planes float effortlessly over or through one another.* 'They are altogether different from anything I have ever done and in our opinion far superior. I am really surprised . . . Greenberg gave me such a boost in confidence that I cannot remember ever knowing such a sudden development taking place before. The only parallel was when I concentrated for five months producing automatic watercolours every day. This work is also automatic.' That November 1957 at Hart House he had his first one-man exhibition after ten years in Toronto.

Jack Bush is the other member of Painters Eleven who was demonstrably affected by Greenberg's visit. Looking at paintings like *Reflection*, he was apparently much more critical of Bush's accomplishment than of Macdonald's. Greenberg immediately questioned the Abstract-Expressionist mannerisms; he called the facile brush effects

---

*Town had introduced Macdonald to Lucite 44 in the summer of 1956. Fluid and quick drying, it has many of the characteristics of watercolour in handling, while finishing like oil. It assisted Macdonald in achieving this easy interpenetration of transluscent forms.

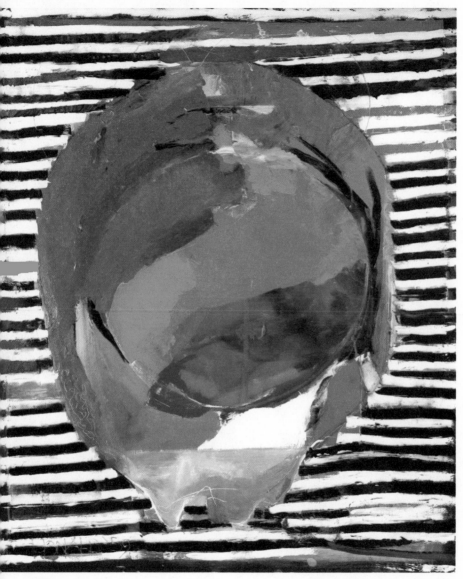

XXII—William Ronald. *Gypsy*, 1959. Canvas, 70 x 60. Dr and Mrs Sydney Wax, Toronto.

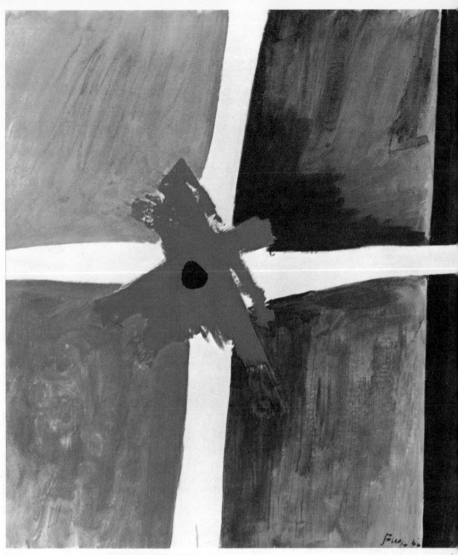

XXXIII—Jack Bush. *The White Cross*, 1960. Canvas, 80 x 70. AEAC.

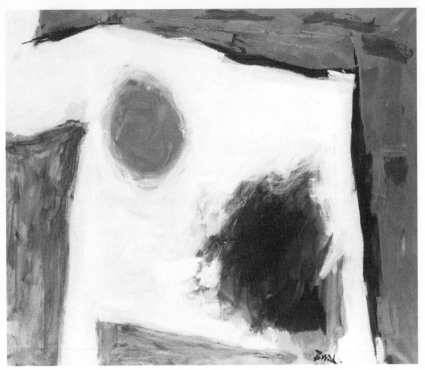

Jack Bush. *Painting with Red*, 1957. Canvas, 48 x 60. RMCL.

'hot licks'. Bush considered the use of such hard-learned devices an accomplishment, and this criticism totally destroyed the confidence he had built in his work over the past years. Greenberg did have suggestions, though. He believed Bush to possess real promise, and in some watercolours in particular—likely similar to the beautifully constructed and sensitively coloured *Theme Variation No. 2* (AGO) of 1955—he found a simplicity that allowed the most essential characteristics of Bush's sensibility to shine through. Greenberg suggested that Bush strive to achieve a similar quality in his oils. He also invited Bush to call on him when he next visited New York.

Bush decided to try a couple of canvases that were simple in composition and straightforward in handling. They turned out so simple and unimbellished that he was hesitant to consider them complete. He turned them to the wall and went back to his Abstract-Expressionist style. But he kept turning them around, beginning to feel that they were indeed more 'full' as paintings, and they began to influence his exhibited work. By January 1958, when he held a one-man show at the new Park Gallery—his first since that initial visit to New York six years before— a very distinct change was evident. *Painting with Red* (RMCL) of 1957 was in that show. Its simple structure is largely responsible for the picture's compelling interest. The forms have a moving awkwardness where they used to be almost facile, and the colour—limited to mustard-brown, brown, red, grey, and white—is unaffectedly direct. Bush had achieved a profoundly human statement with simple, uncontrived means.

The Park Gallery, which opened at the end of the summer of 1957 across from the Park Plaza on Avenue Road, was run by two men connected with one of Toronto's leading advertising firms who were friends of most of the commercial artists in Painters Eleven and a local critic, Paul Duval. The Roberts Gallery had failed to follow up their 'Small Picture' show—which had proven no more successful commercially than had the previous two—so when plans were announced for the Park Gallery, it seemed natural that Painters Eleven should find a new Toronto showplace there. Ronald expected this commercial gallery to pay for shipment of his works (owned by his New York dealer) from New York. Other members, and particularly Town, felt that Ronald should, like the others, bear the expense of transporting his own work. Ronald also disliked the idea of associating publicly with the critic-dealer Duval. In the argument that ensued, Town and Ronald squared off (Town felt Ronald had become 'inflated' by his New York success), and Ronald resigned from Painters Eleven on August 27, 1957. The Park Gallery show, with a sixteen-page illustrated catalogue, went on without him that November and received the most enthusiastic local reaction to date. In spite of Ronald's absence, the international ambitions of the group were stressed in the catalogue statement. 'What might seem novel here in Ontario is an accepted fact everywhere else. Painting is now a universal language; what in us is provincial will provide the colour and accent; the grammar, however, is a part of the world.'

In May 1958 the Park Gallery show was shown at the Ecole des Beaux-Arts in Montreal, owing to the efforts of Jacques de Tonnancour. And from that showing Richard Simmins of the National Gallery selected thirty works to circulate across Canada. Also in 1958 Painters Eleven prepared a statement for a 'confrontation' show organized by the London Art Museum that placed their work opposite that of the conservative Ontario Institute of Painters. This statement claimed that Painters Eleven had received 'more individual honours and collective acclaim than any other group in Canada. In so doing, we have secured recognition for the vital, creative painting being done in this province. In this sense, our work will soon be accomplished, and no doubt we will return to the singular ways that are best for painters, anywhere, anytime.' The last

Toronto exhibition was held shortly thereafter, at the Park Gallery in November 1958, with ten of the Montreal hosts of May as guests. The group accepted invitations to show later—in April 1960 at the MMFA and in December 1960 at the Kitchener-Waterloo Art Gallery—but these exhibitions were a belated recognition of a phenomenon that was already over. In October 1960, in fact, they met at Tom Hodgson's studio and formally disbanded. All present agreed that the adventure begun some seven years before had ended in success.

'Painting contemporary with its time' had been brought to Toronto, and by the late fifties a vital scene had once again developed in that city, a scene that went far beyond the activities of Painters Eleven. But probably even more important as an accomplishment than this general enlivening—for surely something would have forced the issue during the decade if Painters Eleven had not existed—was the individual achievement of virtually every member of the group.

Ronald's New York success had become legendary in Toronto by the end of the fifties, and he was probably then the single most influential painter in the city, even though he continued to live in New York. He had exhibited at Av Isaacs' Greenwich Gallery in November after his first Kootz show in 1957. And his New York exhibitions were even reviewed in the Toronto papers. In October 1959 Robert Fulford covered the Kootz show of that year, noting Ronald's increasing concern for 'structure' in his still basically Abstract-Expressionist canvases. All presented large, roughly circular images against patterned backgrounds (since *Central Black*, he had made the centred image his own particular concern). Fulford singled out *The Visitor* as 'the most striking and memorable work', interpreting it as 'a huge head which explodes off the canvas in a dozen directions, filling the room with its presence'.

In April 1960 Ronald had an exhibition at Toronto's Laing Galleries. It was to many of the local artists the 'return of the conquering hero'. This show, displaying his most recent refinements on the 'central image' works, included †*Gypsy* (Dr and Mrs Sydney Wax, Toronto), which had developed directly out of *The Visitor*. It is rather an *implosion*, though; the pinkish red and almost electric blue are in direct juxtaposition, building to an intense level of inward-concentrating energy. The central form in *Gypsy* is almost spherical, floating freely against rough dark and white stripes—free of the pattern where *The Visitor* had been held by it. It is a consummate work, almost magical in its effortless levitation; a featureless Veronica veil.

The Toronto buyer of *Gypsy* waited until it was shown at Kootz in November before purchasing it, however, and Ronald realized that his great success in New York—his work was owned by over twenty American museums and was part of every important collection in that country—tied him to that scene. Comfortably settled in Kingston, N.J., just two hours from New York, he took out American citizenship in September 1963.

At the new Gallery of Contemporary Art in Toronto, Harold Town held his first one-man show to include paintings in 1957, the year he gave up full-time commercial art, though this exhibition also included examples of his famous 'single autographic prints' (it was only in 1962 that he exhibited canvases alone). His prints and collages are obviously central to his art. Both the collages and Town's unique method of print-making encourage judicious deliberation in the placement of each of the discrete elements—his is an art of carefully interrelated components. The problem is to achieve a sense of natural wholeness with such an 'additive' technique. Like most of the other members of Painters Eleven, and as is evident in *Dead Boat Pond*, Town usually found unity in the broad sweeping gestures of Abstract Expressionism.

His most ambitious essay in 'action painting', and probably his most successful, is a huge (10 x 37 feet) mural he painted between early May and late July 1958 for the Robert H. Saunders Generating Station on the St Lawrence Seaway. The paintings he exhibited later that October—in a two-man show with Borduas at Arthur Tooth & Sons in London, Eng. —are closer to his delicate large collages (of which two-thirds of this showing was made) than the bolder approach seen in the mural; but an aggressive, broad paint handling began slowly to dominate in his canvases during the next year. He continued to show mainly his collages and graphics, however, and to great acclaim. Alan Jarvis, then Director of the National Gallery, referred to his drawing as 'Picasso-esque in its fluency, its authority and its range' in his introduction to the catalogue of the Tooth show. And Robert Fulford in January 1959 contributed a note to the catalogue of a Town collage exhibition at the Jordan Gallery in Toronto, and an introduction to a catalogue for a drawing show at Laing Galleries the following September. 'As a draughtsman,' he said then, Town 'is unequalled by any member of the present generation in Toronto or anywhere else in Canada.'

In March 1961 the Laing Galleries exhibited collages, prints and—for only the second time in Toronto in a one-man show—paintings. Robert Fulford, again, was particularly moved. 'Town's search is not necessarily for beauty—though he achieves that, even formal beauty, in some of his best work; nor for power, though that too is a vital characteristic of his larger canvases. His real search, though, is for the heroic gesture.'

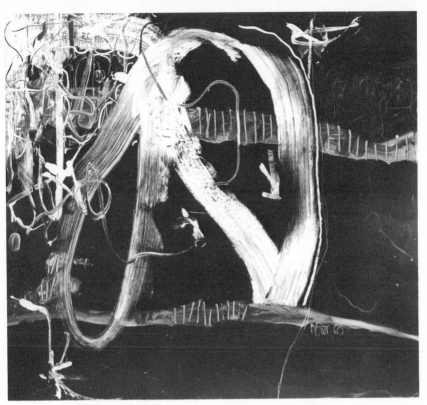

Harold Town. *Side Light*, 1960. Canvas, 68 x 77. AEAC.

Among the canvases in this show, like *Side Light* (AEAC) of 1960, were some of the most freely 'gestural' Toronto had ever seen. They are consistent with earlier paintings in their intricately busy detail and in displaying Town's usual assured design sense, but they still represent a vivid new departure in their dashing, almost calligraphic images. Even though they show a fascination with the central-image format— which is pronounced in *Landscape* (AEAC), bought from Laing before the show—they are fresh and inventive variations on Abstract Expressionism and are in no essential way dependent on Ronald. (Many Toronto painters had been moved to deal with that format after Ronald's April 1960 exhibition in those same Laing Galleries.)

Jack Bush has never really looked back since his first Park Gallery show in 1958, although he asserts that he was not thoroughly used to his new direction until 1960. He showed at the Park Gallery in 1959 and again in 1961, and continued to visit New York on a more-or-less regular basis. He became a good friend of Clement Greenberg's and through him met a number of American artists who were concerned in the same way as he was to emphasize colour and basic structure through ruthless simplification. These contacts gave Bush that last bit of assurance he needed. †*The White Cross* (AEAC) of 1960—which Bush calls *Spot on Red*—is certainly assured. The harmonious conjoining of its quarters—each coloured in a different, difficult, shaded hue—with the black-spotted mark of intense red is, in spite of its effortless appearance, a brilliant achievement.

Jock Macdonald too moved from strength to strength after Greenberg's visit. He believed that he was very close to the culmination of his life's search and struggled almost desperately to find time to paint. In 1958 he sent works to exhibit everywhere he could, but the expenses only increased the financial difficulties that plagued him. In the summer he took on yet another teaching load when he accepted a position at the Doon School of Fine Arts. It meant the loss of at least three weeks of his valuable summer-vacation period, and probably more, because such breaks from the intense concentration of his painting routine threw him off stride. Nonetheless he moved into a new phase that year, emphasizing large slabs of radiant colour sliding one into the other, which culminated early in 1959 in the monumental *Heroic Mould* (AGO). The largest canvas he would ever paint (six feet tall), it is still breathtakingly delicate in its colouring and complex and involving in spite of its boldly simple form.

In April 1959, after more than ten years, Macdonald was able to give up his evening classes—sales were gradually appearing. He was painting literally every free minute. During this year and into the next he seems to have worked through a number of series of paintings, each a variation on a different colour combination or image. The pictures that culminated each series are of astounding quality. All—like *Fleeting Breath* (AGO) and *Earth Awakening* (Mr and Mrs John David Eaton, Toronto) of 1959 or *Nature Evolving* (AGO) of 1960—are complex yet emphatically unified descriptions of a profound world-view. They move with the stately grace of natural inevitability. By early 1960 Macdonald was working full-out, racing with the pounding excitement of a man freely lucid after a lifetime of struggle to speak.

Dorothy Cameron gave Macdonald a one-man show in January 1960 at her Here and Now Gallery, and at about the same time the Art Gallery of Toronto approached him for a retrospective exhibition. He was very pleased. Everyone knew he would be the first living Canadian, other than members of the Group of Seven, to have been afforded such an honour. Then in the midst of the preparations he heard that the Ontario College of Art had changed their policy and would insist on

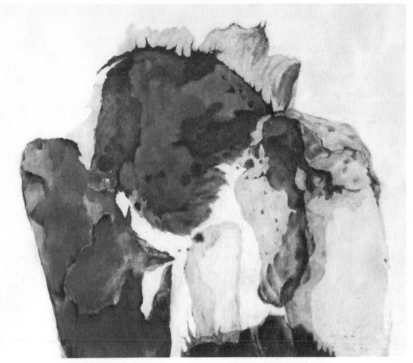

Jock Macdonald. *Nature Evolving*, 1960. Canvas, 44 x 54. AGO.

retirement at sixty-five. Macdonald was crushed by the news. It meant that he would have to retire after the following year on a monthly pension of only $100 and he had no savings. The work on the retrospective rushed him along, however, and it opened on April 29 to an enthusiastic reception. Sales increased markedly and the Roberts Gallery signed him on. That summer his pace slackened and his painting became softer, even more spiritual. As is evident in *All Things Prevail* (NGC), he was blending his colours, building up rich moving combinations of green, blue, red, and white, at times rubbing the lucite into his canvas to produce an intense stain. *All Things Prevail* was his last completed canvas. He died of a heart attack on December 3, 1960, less than two months after Painters Eleven had been formally dissolved. The magnificent creative flowering of his last three years is its greatest testament.

16

A Continuing Tradition
1955-1965

The continuing Canadian tradition in painting has naturally flourished most vigorously on its two principal stalks: those nurtured in Toronto for some hundred and thirty years and in Montreal for almost two hundred and sixty-five years. By the mid-sixties of the twentieth century, however, it was clear that painting had found a sympathetic and sustaining response in other parts of the country as well. Vancouver has seen at least four consecutive generations of creative artists. London, Ont., is now one of the places in Canada where it is possible to see art of consequence. And in numerous other communities across the nation there are serious, committed painters contributing principally to their region but often rising to national, and at times even international, significance.

Outside of the metropolitan centres the incentive for excellence has derived mainly from university art departments. The oldest such department in Canada is at Mount Allison University in Sackville, a small town in New Brunswick near the Nova Scotia border. Since 1893 its art school has been centred on the Owens Art Gallery, a charming late-nineteenth-century structure housing a small but interesting permanent collection.*

The first director to pull the Mount Allison school fully into the twentieth century arrived only in 1946. LAWREN P. HARRIS (b.1910), the son of Lawren Harris of the Group of Seven, was born and raised in Toronto. He received his formal training at the school of the Boston Museum of Fine Arts (1931-2) but learned much more from the intense

---

*John Owen, a ship-builder and merchant of Saint John, left a sum of money on his death to be spent on the religious and artistic education of the youth of his city. The Owens Art Institution was consequently founded in 1885 in Saint John with a local painter of some national prominence, John Hammond (1843-1939), as its principal. Hammond, in between extensive travels, ran the school in Saint John

artistic activity surrounding his father in Toronto in the late twenties. Harris began teaching at Northern Vocational School in Toronto in 1936, then in 1939 switched to Trinity College School in Port Hope, Ont. He joined the army in 1940—first serving as a lieutenant in a tank regiment—and in 1943 was made an official war artist. With an eye for a striking image, he produced a number of canvases for the war art program depicting the strange nightmare world of mechanized warfare. *Tank Advance, Italy* (Canadian War Museum, Ottawa) of 1944 shows a pack of heavily camouflaged tanks speeding across a plain like so many armoured hillocks churning up great obscuring clouds of dust. Such highly finished paintings, in a style we would today call 'magic realism', were the works by which he was known when he assumed the directorship of the Mount Allison University School of Art in September 1946. Harris soon moved on to geometric abstraction, inspired— as is evident in the beautifully serene *Project* (the artist) of 1947—principally by Kandinsky and the work of his own father. Such explorations in fundamental colour and form have occupied him since.

Harris was joined in Sackville in September 1946 by a young local man also just returned from service as a war artist. ALEX COLVILLE (b. 1920) was born in Toronto. When he was seven his family moved to St Catharines, Ont., and two years later to Amherst, N.S., near the head of Chignecto Bay, the northeastern arm of the Bay of Fundy. In 1938 Colville enrolled in the Fine Art Department at Mount Allison University in Sackville, a few miles northwest of Amherst. He graduated in 1942 and joined the army; two years later he was commissioned as an official war artist. Upon his discharge in 1946 he took a position teaching art at Mount Allison. Colville's war paintings are realistic, like those of Harris, but his forms are not so smoothly modelled nor are the subjects chosen so strikingly horrific. He often, in fact, seeks out the most ordinary of moments, as in *Infantry* (Canadian War Museum, Ottawa) of 1946, where a long line of tired soldiers tramps toward us through muddy snow, away from battle, each man lost in his own thoughts.

In Sackville, Colville became involved in his teaching duties and painted little before 1950, the year of his haunting *Nude and Dummy* (New Brunswick Museum, Saint John, N.B.). In it a nude woman stands

until local interest fell off in the early nineties. Both he and the school were moved to Mount Allison Ladies College in Sackville in 1893 and the gallery was that same year built to house the collection Hammond had helped to assemble on his travels. He continued to travel widely in America, Europe, and the Orient until 1901 when he decided he would be content to settle in Sackville. He ran the school until 1919 when he retired, and continued to live in Sackville until his death in 1939.

at the window of a bare attic room, looking back over her shoulder towards us at her dressmaker's dummy in the foreground. The picture is precisely organized, with the architectural lines of the room dividing it exactly down the middle, the woman small in her space, the dummy looming large in its. The colour is gentle, almost pastel, and the paint is applied in small separate strokes. Shading is accomplished by cross-hatching.

All of Colville's subsequent paintings reflect a similar interest in the precise, geometric articulation of space. And most show figures—usually in juxtaposition with inanimate objects, animals, or other human beings—carefully placed at the most *concentrated* point in that space, drawing substance from the charged atmosphere. This precision suggests arrested action, the 'magic' moment. The way the invariably passive subjects often contemplate their co-inhabitants—the woman her dressmaker's dummy, or a child a Black Labrador in *Child and Dog* (NGC) of 1952—suggests as well self-reflection. Such an interpretation leads *us* to reflect on their self-contemplation (their bodies are often nude or only partially clothed), and gives rise—as much as Colville's precise rendition of texture does—to an acute tactile sensation. It is the unfulfilled desire to touch and become involved in the painting, half realized in anticipation but discouraged by the 'distant' quality of his pictures, that gives his work its poignant ambiguity. This is unusual in painting; one more often senses it in films. Colville's images are in fact much closer to those of the best film-makers of the British-American popular tradition—particularly Alfred Hitchcock—than to those of other painters. There is the same concern for precise composition and the arrested moment, the same understanding of the body as being somehow the focus of the space through which it moves. And like Hitchcock, Colville is often unashamedly contriving, fully aware that the exact configuration of his scenes can—as in *Woman, Man and Boat* (NGC) of 1952—make of his usual sensuality an overt yet far from explicit sexuality, or, as in *Couple on Beach* (NGC) of 1957, an ambiguous primal image of the conjoining of two seemingly detached beings.

Colville's painting is collected avidly both in Canada and abroad and in 1963 he was able to quit teaching, though he continued to live in Sackville for another ten years. He now lives near Wolfville, N.S. Before leaving Mount Allison, however, he had a great influence on a number of his students who, like him, have chosen to stay in the Atlantic region. CHRISTOPHER PRATT (b.1935) of St John's, Nfld, graduated from Mount Allison in 1961 and has since worked in his native province. His painting is more generalized in form, more austere than Colville's, but his

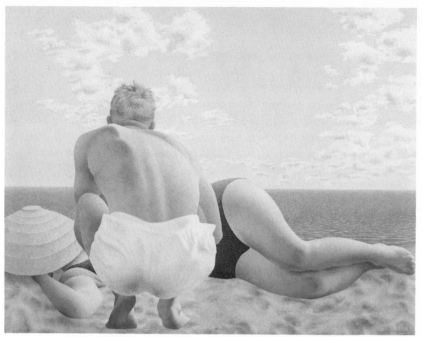

Alex Colville. *Couple on Beach*, 1957. Board, 27 x 36. NGC.

interest in evocative images of isolation—always in a Newfoundland setting—is clearly derived from his teacher. Another student of Colville's, TOM FORRESTALL (b.1936), was born in Middleton, N.S., and studied at Mount Allison from 1954 to 1958. He too has stayed close to home, working in Fredericton, N.B., although his realistic pictures diverge from Colville in theme more clearly than do those of Pratt.

If a continuing tradition does develop in the Atlantic provinces it will perhaps grow around the work of these 'magic realist' painters. The only other promising beginning was in Saint John, N.B., where Jack Humphrey (see pp. 193-4) and MILLER BRITTAIN (1912-68) both worked for some thirty-five years. But that start seems to have ended with their deaths. Brittain, like Humphrey, was born and raised in Saint John. He then studied drawing in New York at the Art Students League (1930-2). Back in Saint John, he worked as an artist for the rest of his life—except for four years in the Air Force (one as an official war artist)—responding to an increasingly more personal vision. *Boy and Torsos* (estate of the artist) of 1954 is typical of his mature, visionary art. Awkward, strident, but with serenely beautiful passages, it and many other of his paintings will doubtless find a secure place in the history of Canadian painting. Unfortunately they have until recently been little known outside of the Maritimes.

The prairie West—a region, like the Atlantic Provinces, of rigorous climate, relatively sparse population, and limited economic development (mainly of resources)—is in artistic matters similar to the Maritimes area in that the most important sustained activity has centred on art educational institutions. In the West there have been primarily two of significance: at Banff, Alberta, and, most importantly, at the University of Saskatchewan in Regina. The Banff School of Fine Arts—primarily a summer school for hobbyists—has served mainly as a place of meeting and a source of income for the more serious artists in the West. An outgrowth of an art camp first held in 1935 by the English mountain-painter A.C. Leighton (1901-65), it has subsequently employed most of the artists of local importance and has annually attracted one or two painters from elsewhere in the country. A.Y. Jackson, who has relatives in southern Alberta, taught for six summers beginning in 1943, and Jock Macdonald also taught there in the summer of 1946. Macdonald then stayed on in Alberta as director of the art department at the Provincial Institute of Technology and Art in Calgary. The Provincial Institute first began to give classes in art in 1926, conducted by a Norwegian 'impressionist', Lars Haukaness (1864-1929). Upon his death, classes were run by that same Leighton who was later to start the summer school at Banff, and he in turn was replaced in 1935 by the Englishman H.G. Glyde (b.1906), who also, from 1937, headed the painting department at Banff. When Jock Macdonald taught in Calgary for one year in 1946-7, he was most impressed with two painters: a teacher at the institute, Marion Nicoll (b.1909), and a local architect-painter, MAXWELL BATES (b.1906).

Bates was the first Albertan artist to achieve national prominence. Born in Calgary, he began to work in the office of his architect father at the age of eighteen. Two years later he enrolled in the new painting class in the Provincial Institute under Lars Haukaness and was soon drawing and painting in an expressionist figurative style derived from art books and magazines; in 1928 he even tried his hand at an abstraction. Bates's efforts were met with bewilderment, even hostility, and in 1931 he decided to move to England. In London he worked in an architectural office and continued to paint until 1939 when he joined the British army. Captured by the Germans in 1941, he spent the rest of the war in a POW camp, returning to Calgary in January 1946. He had been abroad for fifteen years.

Jock Macdonald arrived in September, and, with Marion Nicoll and one or two others who were also interested in personal expression, formed a loose-knit 'Calgary group' around Maxwell Bates. Macdonald left the following summer, but for the next fifteen years (with a year out in 1949-50 to study with the German Expressionist painter Max Beckmann at the Brooklyn Museum Art School) Bates continued to make his living in Calgary—primarily as an architect—and acted as the centre of a group of painters made up mainly of teachers in the Provincial Institute. Each pursued personal experiments in expressionist figuration, and by the later fifties in abstraction, but no one in the group focused its activities. In 1961 a partial stroke caused Bates to give up his architectural practice and the next year he moved to Victoria, B.C., where he has continued to paint cynical but brightly coloured, highly expressive comments on the human condition.

The most important concentration of creative activity in the West has developed in Regina. Interest in art first appeared there just before the First World War with the arrival of two British artists, Inglis Sheldon-Williams (1870-1940), who taught at Regina College from 1913 to 1917, and James Henderson (1871-1951), who worked in the city from 1911 to 1916. It was only in 1936, however, that the potential for the growth of an active climate for the arts was first recognized. That year Augustus Kenderdine (1870-1947)—another British-born-and-trained painter who had been teaching at the University of Saskatchewan in Saskatoon since the early twenties—moved to the provincial capital to start an art department at Regina College and arranged for the university to take over and develop some property he owned on Emma Lake, in the wilderness north of Prince Albert, as a summer school for the arts. Established at about the same time as Banff, it grew into an annual six-week summer course, administered by the School of Art at Regina College. Nineteen years later, in 1955, two young painters connected with the School of Art—Kenneth Lochhead and Arthur McKay—persuaded the university to extend this summer camp two weeks so that a workshop could be held for professional artists.

KENNETH LOCHHEAD (b.1926) of Ottawa, who had been named the director of the Regina College School of Art in 1950 at the age of twenty-four, had studied at the Pennsylvania Academy at Philadelphia and at the Barnes Foundation, Merion, Pa (1945-9). ARTHUR MCKAY (b. 1926) from Nipawin, Sask., east of Prince Albert, who had joined the art school as an instructor in 1952, had studied at the Provincial Institute of Technology and Art in Calgary (1946-8), where he came into contact with Jock Macdonald, and then in Paris (1949-50). The first artist they invited to lead the workshop at Emma Lake was Jack Shadbolt from Vancouver; then, in the summer of 1956, they invited Joe Plaskett (b. 1918), also from Vancouver though resident in Paris (as he is now). The following year they had their first American guest: Will Barnett from the Art Students League in New York. The most far-reaching impact, however, resulted from the visit in the summer of 1959 of Barnett Newman. Now seen to be one of the giants of the post-war generation of American painters (he died in 1970), Newman was then almost unknown outside the New York painters' world, although an exhibition that March at the new French & Co. galleries (his first in New York since 1951) had been recognized in some reviews as a landmark. Newman had developed out of that same wartime milieu that produced Abstract Expressionism, but he rejected many of the elements of that style. His usually very large paintings seem radically simple, with vast, unmodulated areas of colour articulated by one or more vertical stripes. They are radiant, and in their monumental presence unique. By 1959 it was clear that Newman's work was pointing in a new direction, away from Abstract Expressionism. Indeed, the 'action' painters would be replaced by more reflective, contemplative spirits.

Newman was invited to Emma Lake by McKay and two others then connected with the art school, Roy Kiyooka and Ronald Bloore. Each found himself ready to consider the direction the American proposed. A Canada Council grant had allowed McKay to take a year off (1956-7) to study at Columbia University and at the Barnes Foundation (where Lochhead had studied ten years before). He has described his work then as 'an abstract version of English landscape painting'. In New York he saw the memorial retrospective of the work of Jackson Pollock, who had died in an automobile crash in August 1956. McKay, prior to his New York trip, had been introduced to the hallucinogenic drugs LSD and mescaline through the pioneering controlled experiments then being conducted at the University of Saskatchewan.* His drug experiences intensified an interest in contemplative art and would have opened for him the expanding yet effortlessly contained 'all-over' cosmic images of Jackson Pollock.

ROY KIYOOKA (b.1926)—born in Moose Jaw, about fifty miles west of Regina, although raised in Calgary (where, because of his Japanese ancestry, he was registered as an 'enemy alien' during the war)—first studied art at the Provincial Institute in Calgary (1946-9), with McKay, and like him came into contact there with Jock Macdonald. He then worked in Calgary as a display artist, teaching an evening class at the Institute and associating with the small Calgary group around Maxwell Bates. In 1954 he worked on a display job in Nelson, B.C., but the next

*It was Dr H. Osmond, then superintendent of the Saskatchewan Hospital, who in 1957 suggested the term 'psychedelic' to describe LSD and related drugs.

year a scholarship allowed him to study for a year at the Institute Allende in Mexico. There he too was introduced to hallucinogens and, as he has recorded, 'did my first real paintings'. In September 1956 he took a position as an instructor at Regina College. His paintings of that period—'controlled' Abstract-Expressionist works, with an expanding, often centred image—reveal interests not unlike McKay's.

The third painter involved in inviting Barnett Newman was not a westerner and had moved to Regina only the summer before. RONALD BLOORE (b.1925) was born in Brampton, west of Toronto. He studied art history at the University of Toronto, graduating in 1949, and then spent two years at the Institute of Fine Arts at New York University and a year at Washington University, St Louis, Mo., where he received an M.A. After two years of lecturing at Washington U., he studied two more years at the Courtauld Institute of the University of London (1955-7) and then lectured for a year back at the University of Toronto. The summer of 1958 he became the director of the Norman Mackenzie Art Gallery at Regina College.* With a thorough academic training in art history and a developed, broad interest in aesthetic theory, Bloore brought an intellectual rigour and assertive purposefulness to the Regina group.

For there was a definite 'group' forming around the college for whom Barnett Newman would act as an amazing catalyst. Newman did no painting at Emma Lake in the summer of 1959, but his intense commitment and his unquestionable seriousness in the exploration of new areas of human experience moved the Regina painters deeply. McKay seems to have responded directly to Newman's own painting practices. He stopped making oil paintings and proceeded to experiment with flat black paint on paper. (Newman had the year before painted the first two of his famous *Stations of the Cross*, using only black paint, and there is a well-known series of black ink-on-paper works of 1960.) The results do not resemble the work of Newman, however, being, as Terry Fenton has pointed out, much closer to Pollock in their 'all-over' interlocking forms. None of the other painters began producing 'Newmans' either, although many were inspired to seek to make solemn paintings of vast scale, simplified in form and colour. Four of the people involved in the workshop, and Kenneth Lochhead—in Italy on a year's leave during Newman's visit—were by the next year painting distinctively new work, and beginning late in 1961 an exhibition of this 'Regina Five' was given a cross-country tour by the National Gallery. McKay and Bloore were

*Opened in 1953, the Norman Mackenzie Art Gallery houses the collection (since extensively augmented) left in 1936 by the Regina lawyer after whom it is named.

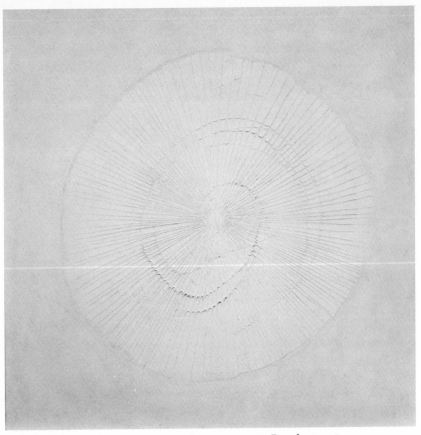

Ronald Bloore. *Painting, June 1960*, 1960. Board, 48 x 48. NGC.

among the 'Five'—Kiyooka had left Regina to take up a position at the Vancouver School of Art in 1959. The two other members were Douglas Morton (b.1926) from Winnipeg, who had moved to Regina in 1954, and Ted Godwin (b.1933) from Calgary, the youngest of the group (all the rest were born within a year of one another), who had arrived in Regina in 1958.

Of the 'Five', Bloore and McKay were in the early 1960s the most accomplished, the most resolved, and they have since continued to develop the basic approach they were able to establish then. Two pictures by Bloore of 1959, *Painting No. 1* (NMAG) and *The Establishment* (Mr and Mrs A.W. Johnson, Regina), are without pictorial 'image'. Both are four-feet-square masonite panels covered with a homogeneous coat of paint—freely impastoed in the latter; carefully laid on in even, broken stripes in the former, giving the appearance of the stratification of a bed of slate. Then, early in 1960, Bloore painted a number of centred circu-

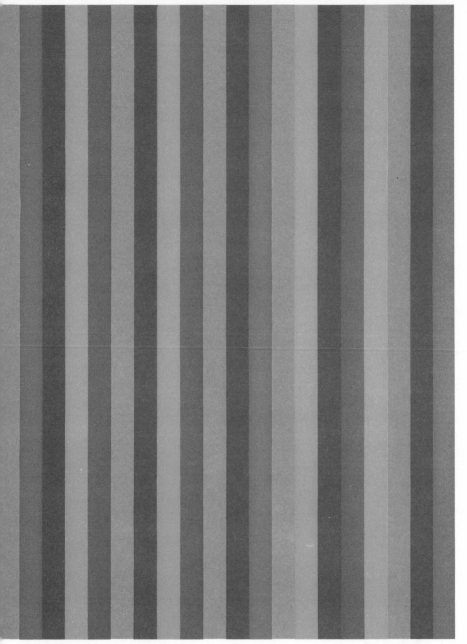

xxxiv—Guido Molinari. *Mutation rythmique,* 1965. Canvas, 79 x 60. The artist.

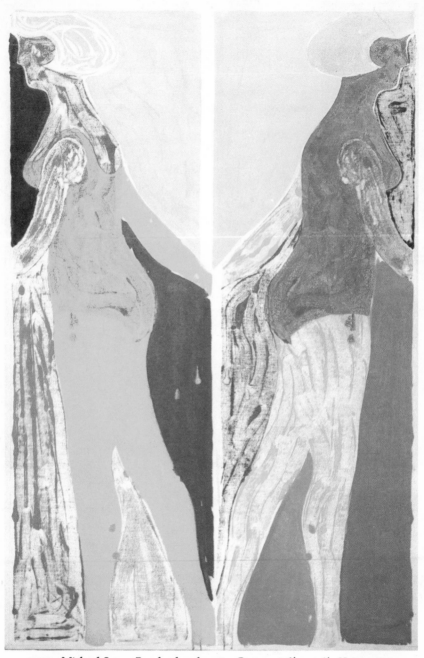

xxxv—Michael Snow. *Beach—hcaeb*, 1963. Canvas, 63½ x 41½. University of Western Ontario, London, Alumni Collection.

lar image paintings on similar 4′ x 4′ masonite. The most impressive is *Painting, June 1960* (NGC). Made with slightly tinted paint on a white ground, the circular image is worked up in a delicate relief of radiating lines, broken in a whorl that extends out to about halfway along the radius. Resembling the underside of a mushroom, the minimal differentiation between the radiating image and the ground induces a concentrated examination that draws the eyes inexorably to the centre. The fine lines then stand out like taut wires, running in and out at invisible speed. The effect is almost hypnotic.

Bloore, unlike many of his colleagues in Regina, never became involved in creative experimentation with hallucinogens, although an interest in oriental thought and expression gave him common ground with the others. And his mandala-like, contemplation-inducing pictures of 1960 certainly helped point a direction for McKay. The westerner had attempted to translate his paper works of 1959 into a larger format by employing—at the suggestion of Bloore—enamel on masonite. Experimenting late in 1960, he devised a method of 'skimming' freshly applied enamel that left a heightened negative pattern of the irregularities in the surface of the masonite as the enamel darkened in the depressions where it was thickest and was left thin and transparent on the ridges. By preparing the masonite surface a range of effects is possible, all of them ambiguous because the enamelled surface appears textured when it is in fact as smooth as glass. In 1961 McKay began to paint circular shapes on 4′ x 4′ sheets of masonite employing this technique. *Effulgent Image* (Mr and Mrs Clifford Wiens, Regina) is one of the best of these first mandala pieces. It is radiant, and with extended contemplation it begins to 'breathe', to become an organic, ever-changing enlivened space. Magically complex, it nonetheless has a simple, bell-like clarity. It reflects a view of the world immediately and profoundly real to those who have exercised the discipline of meditation or have experienced a union with their environment through the medium of hallucinogens.

Bloore turned to more 'painterly' concerns in 1961, completing a group of pictures of crosses, spoked wheels, and other 'centred' devices, all of them painted with warm colours freely brushed. Then in 1962 he received a Canada Council grant that allowed him to spend a year on the Greek island of Lesbos. When he returned to Regina he destroyed most of his earlier pictures and proceeded to work exclusively in white-on-white relief on masonite. He discovered that many of his colleagues had also gone through a change over the last year, induced primarily by the visit of another influential American to Emma Lake in 1962. The workshop that summer had been conducted by Clement Greenberg, the New

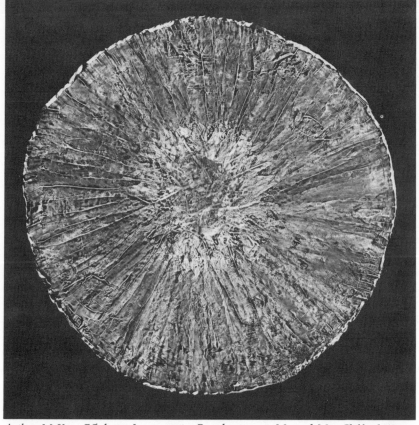

Arthur McKay. *Effulgent Image*, 1961. Board, 48 x 48. Mr and Mrs Clifford Wiens, Regina.

York critic who had been involved with Painters Eleven in Toronto five years before. Surprised to discover painters of the calibre of the Regina Five on the Canadian prairies, he encouraged them—as he had the Toronto painters in 1957—to abandon even those last vestiges of Abstract-Expressionist mannerisms that were evident in their work in order to seek a more direct expression through the configuration of simple forms of colour. Lochhead responded most readily, abandoning the calligraphic, black-grey-and-white 'action' paintings he had been making in favour of large, simple 'colour' paintings like *Dark Green Centre* (AGO) of 1963. When Greenberg in 1964 organized his 'Post Painterly Abstraction' exhibition for the Los Angeles County Museum of Art in order to define the new generation of 'colour' painters he believed had supplanted Abstract Expressionism, Lochhead, McKay, and Jack Bush were each included.

Lochhead left Regina to take a teaching post in Winnipeg in 1964;*
Bloore took one in Toronto in 1965; and with their departure the intense
interactions in Regina diminished, although it has remained an interesting painting centre since. It is no longer the only one in the province,
though. Greenberg had discovered on his visit a group of landscape
painters working out of Saskatoon that he considered to be as accomplished in its own way as the Regina Five. DOROTHY KNOWLES (b.1929)
was particularly moved by Greenberg's encouragement. Born in Unity,
Sask., she first studied biology and then gradually came to art through
summers at Banff and Emma Lake. It was only during Greenberg's
session in the summer of 1962, however, that she felt confirmed in the
naturalistic landscapes she had been inclined to pursue. Subsequent
workshops led by Kenneth Noland, Jules Olitski, and other American
colour painters have led her to concentrate on her colour and paint
handling, and since about 1964 she has been painting highly individual,
beautiful landscapes, full of the light and air of northern Saskatchewan.
They are certainly among the best landscape work presently being done
in Canada and are probably surpassed only in the recent work of
ERNST LINDNER (b. 1897).

Lindner—who was born in Vienna—immigrated to Saskatchewan in
1926 and by 1931 was teaching night classes at Saskatoon's Technical
Collegiate Institute. By 1936 he was head of the art department and
teaching full time; he retired only in 1962. Throughout these years of
teaching Lindner was an essential force in the artistic life of Saskatoon,
and even of the province. He and his wife (from Prince Albert) established a summer home at Emma Lake the year before the summer school
began, and although his involvement with the painters and students
there has usually been informal, it has been constant. The bush around
Emma Lake has been his chief inspiration and it was the naturalness of
his response to this environment that drew Clement Greenberg's attention. His encouragement, and that of the colour painter Jules Olitski—
who led the workshop in 1964—has doubtless had some effect on the
wonderful flowering of Lindner's art during the decade since his retirement. But there has been no essential change, just an intensification. He
no longer has to think about anything else but his painting, and his
beautiful watercolour studies of tree stumps—*Decay and Growth*
(NMAG) of 1964 is very fine—and more recently his profoundly moving

*He arrived in Winnipeg at just the right moment to contribute to a growing scene
there. However, the important work of Don Reichert (b.1932), Ivan Eyre (b.1935),
and Esther Warkov (b.1941) appears after 1965, my cut-off point.

acrylics reveal a lifetime of experience focused sharply on the phenomenon of generation.

The painting of abstractions has an even longer history in Vancouver than in Montreal, although the number of years of continuous production is about the same, beginning in 1940 with the arrival of LAWREN HARRIS and the painting of *Composition No. 1* (see p. 195). Nature is always present in Vancouver—spilling lush growth into every empty space, looming over the city in the form of mountains, pushing long inlets of the ocean right into its heart—and it inevitably creeps into painting. By 1945, in smaller works like *Mountain Spirit* (University of British Columbia, Vancouver), Lawren Harris was again considering landscape forms, atmospheric space, and looser, more 'subjective' brush work. By 1950 landscape was supplying the vocabulary for his abstractions. *Nature Rhythm* (NGC) of that year is a powerful evocation of the force-forms of ocean and mountains.*

That is not to say that all artists working in Vancouver have succumbed to the encroaching landscape. B. C. BINNING (b.1909) has consistently proclaimed the virtues of formal abstraction. Born in Medicine Hat, Alta, Binning was brought to Vancouver at the age of four, and has lived there ever since. Studying art first at the Vancouver School of Art under Varley and Macdonald (1927-32), he became an instructor there in 1934. In 1938 he visited London, studying at various schools, including the Ozenfant Academy under the French abstract painter Amédée Ozenfant and the British sculptor Henry Moore. The next year was passed at New York's Art Students League. Returning to Vancouver, he remained teaching at the School of Art for nine years, attracting a reputation with witty, beautifully full line drawings. Then in 1948, during a year's leave of absence, Binning painted his first oils. *Ships in Classical Calm* (NGC) of that year is a tightly constructed yet impressively light and open abstraction made of simple geometric shapes—all based on the forms of ships' hulls—overlapped, interlaced, but always inter-related in a flat, dynamic pattern. It is clearly derived from the work of Ozenfant, his teacher of ten years before. The next year Binning took a teaching post at the University of British Columbia where

---

*Harris continued to pursue 'nature' forms (suggestive of landscape, flowers, insects, etc.) in his work throughout the fifties in paintings he called 'abstract-expressionist'. Only in his last great mystical paintings of 1967-8—*Abstraction, The Rising Sun,* and *Two Hemispheres* (all estate of the artist)—did he once again return to geometric forms, although these are painted with unusual 'feathered' strokes, and glow with the white light of pure spirit.

he has continued to work. His lucid formal abstractions have now been an essential part of the Vancouver scene for more than twenty years.

The dominant concern among Vancouver's painters during the fifties, however, was pervasive nature, which found its principal spokesman in JACK SHADBOLT (b.1909). The same age as Binning, he too was forty years old before he began to find his way as a painter. Born in Shoeburyness, Eng., Shadbolt was brought to Victoria at the age of three and was raised there. Studying to be a teacher, he moved in local cultural circles and knew Emily Carr before taking a job as a high-school teacher in Vancouver in 1931. On a trip east in 1933, Shadbolt resolved to become an artist, and the next year he began night classes with Varley at the Vancouver School of Art. After graduation in 1936 he studied for a year in London and Paris, and on his return in 1938 became an instructor at the Vancouver school. Joining the army in 1942, he was appointed a war artist in 1944. He returned to the school once again the next year as head of the drawing and painting section. Then in the fall of 1947 he followed Binning's lead of some seven years earlier and spent a term at the Art Students League. It is at this point that his strong work begins to appear. The first notable pictures are surrealistic images based on northwest-coast Indian themes, followed—while he was building himself a house on a wooded suburban lot (1948-51)—by a lengthy series of surreal landscapes peopled with strange plant forms. Shadbolt moved into his new house in 1952 and continued to explore the cycles of nature—painting, as he had before, in casein, gouache, watercolour and ink, always on paper. Some of these works—like *Presences after Fire* (NGC) of 1953—are surreal abstractions from seed and leaf forms, but many are free representations of bouquets of flowers, birds, and such.

Shadbolt began painting canvases in 1957 while on a trip to the Mediterranean, an experience that revealed to him a new world of colour. (Most of his earlier works on paper are in dark earthy hues.) His subjects hardly changed, though, and the works of the late fifties and early sixties are usually based on landscape experiences. Some are quite literal, but many—and the best—are ambiguous in scale and point-of-view. *Winter Theme No. 7 (NGC) of 1961 grew initially from the memory of boats clustered around a jetty; but passing through numerous configurations, it has emerged a rich, many-levelled painting representing for the artist 'the evocation of growing nature—of insect-larvae-boat-root-cutbank. All these welded into a dark poetry of sleeping cocoons harbouring in the shelter of roots during the winter, waiting like boats behind a winter-bound pier.'

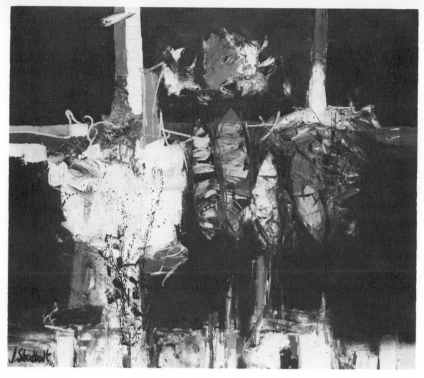

Jack Shadbolt. *Winter Theme No. 7*, 1961. Canvas, 42½ x 50¾. NGC.

A surprisingly large number of painters with a similar persuasion appeared in Vancouver during the fifties. GORDON SMITH (b.1919) was born in England. He arrived in Winnipeg at the age of fifteen and first studied art there with LeMoine FitzGerald. He later moved to Vancouver and graduated from the Vancouver School of Art at the end of the war. He joined the staff in 1946 and in 1957 moved to the Fine Art Department of the University of British Columbia. In his work of the fifties he is concerned to recreate an actual experience or mood rather than, like Shadbolt, to create a new multi-levelled reality. But, as is clear in *Orchard* (AGO) of 1954, he employs stylized natural forms within an abstract structure much as Shadbolt did. Most other painters in Vancouver at the time, like Takao Tanabe (b.1926) and Donald Jarvis (b.1923), were even more lyrical than Shadbolt or Smith in their interpretation of the landscape and were often more freely abstract. (Tanabe and Jarvis both studied with Hofmann in New York.) Seven of these lyric-abstract landscape painters (including the four mentioned here) were grouped in an exhibition by Ian McNairn that was shown across the country in 1959. The seven painters 'are not interested in the visual recording of nature alone,' McNairn pointed out in his introduction to the catalogue. 'They don't escape into the hills for inspiration. Each in

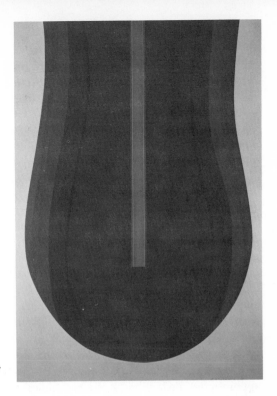

Roy Kiyooka. *Barometer No. 2*,
1964. Canvas, 97 x 69. AGO.

his own way expresses the environment of nature, of society and the
excitement of growth. This is not an art form of direct observation but
is the result of contemplation, self-analysis. It is a reflective art form.'

These painters, exploring their subjective reactions to nature, dominated the art scene in Vancouver until well into the sixties, and (partly
as a result of the McNairn show) were then seen nationally as the most
coherent 'group' working outside of Montreal. This local movement was
bolstered in 1959 by the arrival in Vancouver of Toni Onley (b.1938)
from the Isle of Man. But a powerful stimulus for change also appeared
that year in the person of ROY KIYOOKA.

Kiyooka brought from Regina pictures with broad areas of freely
brushed colour that in their contemplative, reflective nature were not
entirely foreign to the Vancouver painters, but in scale, and in their
quality of brooding presence, introduced a new factor. Vancouver related
these paintings to current New York art and, as Doris Shadbolt has
remarked, they soon 'brought bigger issues into local focus'. Over the
next years Kiyooka developed a lyrical 'hard-edge' style of large-scale
colour painting of wonderful economy and beauty. *Barometer No. 2*
(AGO) of 1964 is awesome, primal, seemingly not man-made. It is compelling yet 'cool', and it and his earlier Vancouver paintings set the sensi-

bility for a phenomenal 'rush' of painting in Vancouver in the mid-sixties. Most of the young artists who later effected that flowering had come into contact with Kiyooka as a teacher at the Vancouver School of Art and virtually all would have known him as a key figure in the thriving cultural sub-community that began to grow on the lush western edge of the country during the early sixties. To many people, in fact, Kiyooka personifies the most convincing strengths of that peculiarly distinctive 'coast' mentality, even though he lived in Vancouver for only five years.*

The continued dominance of Montreal over the artistic activity of Québec has been offset only slightly by the presence in the capital city of a few painters who have been concerned to reflect their unique heritage. The most important of these is JEAN-PAUL LEMIEUX (b.1904). Born in Québec, he was taken to California by his family at the age of twelve and the following year was brought back to Canada to settle in Montreal. Graduating from the Ecole des Beaux-Arts in 1934, he became a professor at the new Ecole du Meuble the next year. In 1937 he left for Québec (Borduas replaced him at the Ecole du Meuble) to become a professor at the Ecole des Beaux-Arts there. (This was presumably the appointment Pellan had been too 'modern' to be given a few months earlier.) He remained there until 1965, when he retired to the Ile-aux-Coudres on the St Lawrence River. The stylized portraits of French-Canadian types for which Lemieux is so well known today first began to appear after a Royal Society grant allowed a trip to Europe in 1954. Moody, simplified studies of strong sentiment, they confront the solitude the Quebecker has traditionally felt in his struggle with a harsh climate and an isolating social environment. By implication they celebrate 'la survivance' of the basic values of the true Quebec.

Such an interpretation of 'folk' values in a stylized figurative idiom has found other adherents. JEAN DALLAIRE (1916-65), who was born in Hull, taught with Lemieux in Québec from 1946 to 1952. There he developed his personal vision, drawing on modernist techniques as transmitted by Pellan and on the folk imagery of his province. From 1952 to 1957 he worked for the National Film Board in Ottawa and Montreal illustrating educational films on local history and folklore.

These painters mean much to Quebeckers who were born before the Second World War. ALFRED PELLAN also derives his present following primarily from this group, and most commentators have seen indigenous 'folk' values in his brightly coloured, exuberantly decorative paintings

*He left for Montreal in 1965 but has recently returned to Vancouver.

of the fifties and sixties. Pellan continued to teach at the Ecole des Beaux-Arts in Montreal until 1952. Then a research bursary from the Royal Society of Canada allowed him to spend three years in Paris, a sojourn that culminated in a full retrospective at the prestigious Musée National d'art moderne in February-March 1955. He returned to Montreal a few months before Borduas set out for the French capital.

While Pellan was in Paris, though, a new moving spirit stirred to life in Montreal. This was first announced by four young painters in an exhibition staged in February 1955 at the Echourie coffee-bar: LOUIS BELZILE (b.1929) from Rimouski (he studied at the Ontario College of Art in Toronto from 1948 to 1952); RODOLPHE DE REPENTIGNY (1926-59), a mathematician and philosopher from Montreal (Université de Montréal and the Sorbonne) who was art critic for *La Presse* and who painted as 'Jauran'; and the two Montrealers JEAN-PAUL JÉRÔME (b.1928) and FERNAND TOUPIN (b.1930), both of whom had studied in the studio of Stanley Cosgrove (1949-53). These painters first began to work out their ideas during the summer of 1954 in a series of exhibitions at the Librairie Tranquille.* By the time of their February show they had developed a clear position, proclaimed—as had by then become traditional in Montreal—in a manifesto that they signed simply *Les Plasticiens*.

'The Plasticiens', it read, 'are drawn, above all else in their work, to the "plastic" facts: tone, texture, form, line, the ultimate unity of these in the painting, and the relationships between these elements . . . The significance of the work of the Plasticiens lies with the purifying of the plastic elements and of their order; their destiny lies typically in the revelation of perfect forms in a perfect order. . . . The Plasticiens are totally indifferent, at least consciously so, to any possible meanings in their paintings.'** Diametrically opposed to the spontaneous expression of the unconscious—replete with associative meaning—as was earlier sought by the Automatistes, the Plasticiens hoped to achieve a precise, uncomplicated response to the painted object. To create such a refined vehicle of pure aesthetic pleasure, they restricted themselves to composing coloured geometric forms, much like the De Stijl group that had

*A Montreal bookstore that had acted as distributor of the *Refus global*.

**Les Plasticiens s'attachent avant tout, dans leur travail, aux faits plastiques: ton, texture, formes, lignes, unité finale qu'est le tableau, et les rapports entre ces éléments. . . La portée du travail des Plasticiens est dans l'épurement incessant des éléments plastiques et de leur ordre; leur destin est typiquement la révélation de formes parfaites dans un ordre parfait. . . . Les Plasticiens ne se préoccupent en rien, du moins consciemment, des significations possibles de leurs peintures.

grown around Mondrian and Theo Van Doesburg in Holland after the First World War.

The Plasticiens were just the leading edge of a new sensibility, however, and by February 1955 even some of the Automatistes were revealed to be seeking a more ordered form of expression in an exhibition entitled 'Espace 55' that was shown that month at the MMFA. Both FERNAND LEDUC (who had returned from Paris in 1953) and Mousseau showed pictures composed of roughly rectangular forms of juxtaposed colour.* Leduc in fact formally joined the Plasticiens the following year, by which time he was painting hard-edged geometric compositions. Works like *Nœud papillon* (NGC) of that year—with its gently arcing forms producing a delicate internal rhythm—quickly set the measure within the group.

The Plasticiens, however, failed to generate any systematic exploration of the formal problems they presented. They diminished their impact as well through involvement in a larger group of abstract painters, the Non-figurative Artists' Association of Montreal, founded in February 1956 with Leduc as president and de Repentigny as secretary. Its membership was made up of the Plasticiens and most of the people who had shown in the 'Espace 55' exhibition, including those who were still working in the Automatiste tradition: Léon Bellefleur (earlier associated with Pellan in the Prisme d'yeux group, he became interested in Borduas's Automatisme in the early fifties); Rita Letendre (b.1929) from Drummondville, Que.; and the Montrealers Jean McEwen (b.1923) and Paterson Ewen (b.1925). A non-juried exhibition association, it presumed to be no more than a free forum for serious abstract painters in Montreal.**All the members had in common, other than their general interest in abstraction, was that they frequented the Galerie l'Actuelle, a small avant-garde showplace dedicated exclusively to the exhibition of non-figurative art. Opened in June 1955, it was energetically directed by GUIDO MOLINARI (b.1933), a twenty-two-year-old painter who was even then wholeheartedly committed to aesthetic exploration with the rigorous seriousness introduced to Montreal by Borduas some dozen years earlier.

Molinari was born in Montreal, and while still in high school at the

---

*Borduas came up from New York to see this exhibition and publicly expressed his disappointment at the evidence of both a new group of late arrivals to Automatisme and the revival of an 'archaic' form of geometric painting (thinking of the Dutch of the twenties) in the work of Leduc and Mousseau. In the argument that ensued, Leduc broke with Borduas.

**It was much like Painters Eleven of Toronto in that respect. Ray Mead in fact became a member after he moved to Montreal in 1957.

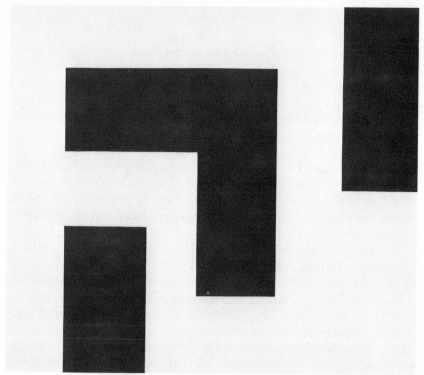

Guido Molinari. *Angle noir*, 1956. Canvas, 60 x 72. NGC.

age of fifteen he enrolled in night classes at the Ecole des Beaux-Arts. He followed the course for three years; then in the spring of 1951 he studied under Marian Scott at the MMFA school and that fall returned for a term in the second-year course under Marian Scott and Gordon Webber. Both his teachers were abstract painters committed to formal statement rather than to the Automatiste type of intuitive expression. Molinari began exhibiting about two years later—mainly drawings in which he explored the formal possibilities of the automatic technique. He also began to paint, notably a group of small pictures—*Emergence* (the artist) of 1955 survives—in which the paint is generously applied with a palette knife in long, crude rectangles of intense, harmonizing colour. Though similar in configuration to the canvases of Mousseau and Leduc of that year, there is no evidence at all of the concern for 'atmosphere' they revealed.

During 1955 Molinari's energies were absorbed in running the Galerie l'Actuelle, but in May 1956 he held his first one-man exhibition of paintings. All displayed simple arrangements of black straight-edged forms on white. All—like *Angle noir* (NGC)—are so composed that after a moment the white assumes form, the black becoming the intervening space; finally an exquisite resolution is achieved in which neither black nor white is form and yet neither is space or ground. As paintings they are limited to the plastic 'facts' but are much more economical and finally more emotionally satisfying than anything the Plasticiens were ever able to achieve.

The following month (June 1956) an even more radical exhibition was staged at L'Actuelle. Devoted to the work of another young Montrealer, CLAUDE TOUSIGNANT (b.1932), it consisted of a series of nine rigorously simplified colour 'panels' painted with shiny automobile paint. One, covered completely with unvarying orange, presented a pure colour experience. Tousignant studied at the MMFA school (1948-51) under Jacques de Tonnancour and—like Molinari—Gordon Webber, so he was also introduced to formal abstract painting almost from the outset. In October 1952 he went to Paris to further his studies but was unimpressed with current French painting and returned to Montreal the following May. There he was soon swept up in the group of young painters who met at L'Echourie. He held his first one-man show there in March 1955, a month after the Plasticiens. (Molinari had shown drawings there in December 1954.) Employing intense, clear colours—which also appealed to Molinari at the same time—Tousignant, in works like *Les Asperges* (the artist), applied the paint in long, asparagus-like forms, densely packed but never crossing. The result is an excited 'all-over' effect of dynamic colour. Tousignant had by this time met Molinari, and in fact joined with the architect-painter Robert Blair (b.1928) early in 1955 to assist in the launching of the Galerie l'Actuelle.

In January 1959 Tousignant and Molinari took part in an exhibition entitled 'Art abstrait' at the Ecole des Beaux-Arts that brought together the two tendencies of geometric painting developing in Montreal.* Leduc, Belzile, and Toupin of the Plasticiens were revealed as basically European-oriented painters of small-scale pictures. Diffused in intention, they seemed involved simply in the manipulation of decorative forms. Tousignant, Molinari, Jean Goguen (b.1928), and Denis Juneau (b. 1925) formed the by-then clearly identifiable 'nouveaux plasticiens'— exponents of large-scale, American-oriented colour paintings. The Plas-

---

*After their 1956 shows at L'Actuelle—which met with little understanding even from the Plasticiens—Molinari and Tousignant had continued their experiments, but in more modest format. Tousignant worked mainly in watercolour for two years; Molinari drew with pencil or pen and painted with gouache. Then in 1958 the two began again to make large canvases with colours. L'Actuelle had folded in 1957.

ticiens would soon disappear from the scene.* The Nouveaux Plasticiens would be recognized as the leading painters in Montreal, and Molinari and Tousignant as among the greatest artists in the country.

Tousignant's representation in the 'Art abstrait' exhibition included *Verticales jaunes* (the artist) of 1958, a tall (8 feet), narrow painting made up of six sloping or trapezoid vertical planes of red, yellow, and green. In the catalogue the painter wrote: 'What I wish to do is to make painting objective, to bring it back to its source—where only painting remains, emptied of all extraneous matter—to the point at which painting is pure sensation.' Molinari that year was making paintings just slightly wider than tall, composed of a series of vertical bands of uniform width, some of which, however, were divided horizontally into two colours or widened by the juxtaposition of a band or bands of identical colour. *Equivalence* (the artist) of 1959 is yellow, red, black, and white. Not so 'sensational' as Tousignant's paintings, there is a deeper, more 'classical' rhythmic interrelationship of the coloured forms as the eye runs over the surface, unable to find a static point of rest. Both artists were clearly establishing a dynamic integration of colour with structure.

Over the next two years Tousignant also turned to the almost-square format, but employed distinct rectangles and horizontal bars to structure his colour. Then in 1962, on a trip to New York, he first saw the work of Barnett Newman. It recalled the pure colour experience of his own 1956 works, and the desire then 'to say as much as possible with as few elements as possible'. He soon began to re-examine this concern in a series of simple compositions involving the placement of large, austere rectangular and circular shapes. This led finally in 1963 to the isolation of the circle as the most satisfying motif, and the following year, in *Œil de bœuf* (NGC), to the use of a 'target' form of concentric circles, breaking the rectangular format in its inexorable radiation. In 1965 Tousignant logically moved on to a circular canvas, and in the *Transformateur chromatique* group of that year, to working in thematic series. He had successfully achieved a profound, rhythmically pulsating surface of colour. Free of any associative image (no longer even resembling a target), and without compositional 'tension', his pictures had finally arrived at the desired 'pure sensation'.

Molinari first came close to abandoning the composition of various-sized elements in 1961 in *Hommage à Jauran* (VAG), a canvas made up only of vertical bars of colour. But it was not until 1963 that he con-

* Rodolphe de Repentigny died tragically in a mountain-climbing accident in the Rockies later that year, aged only 33, and Leduc returned to Paris soon after the 'Art abstrait' exhibition. He lives there still.

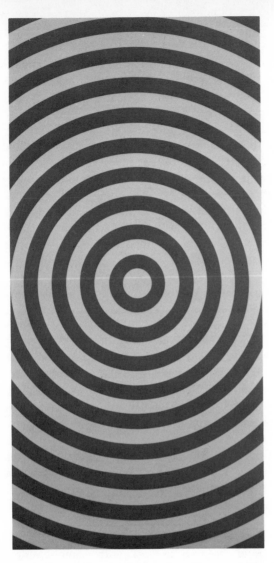

Claude Tousignant. *Œil de boeuf*, 1964. Canvas, 71¼ x 35. NGC.

sistently made the bars of uniform width. This was found to be as ideally suited to his intention as the circular format was later to Tousignant's. It removes completely any need to devise an 'image' from variable forms. The emphasis is solely on colour structure. In works like †*Mutation rythmique* (the artist) of 1965, Molinari is able to present a complex experience with the most simple means. Although there are only four colours (green, red, blue, and orange), each appears different every time it is repeated because it is surrounded by different colours. The longer one looks at it, the more incredible are the changes the painting accomplishes. The peculiar property of colour—that it derives its nature in part from its relationship to other colours, and is consequently never stable—makes possible what Molinari calls 'the continuous perceptive restructuring of the painting'. In their full response to our examination, his paintings ultimately arrive at a point in which colour is the sole reality—a substantial space of pure joy.

Although Molinari and Tousignant made colour painting the most important concern among serious artists in Montreal during the first half of the sixties, there were at the same time at least three other painters of strong individuality who should be cited. Young JACQUES HURTUBISE (b.1939), who held his first one-man show at the MMFA in 1961, soon became a prominent figure on the Montreal scene. If he attracted attention nationally only with his scintillating 'optical' works produced after 1965, his earlier canvases—in which the controlled 'accident' of splashed paint is formalized, isolating the immediate impact of colour on our senses—nonetheless represented an important variation on the dynamic colour-space experiments of the Nouveaux Plasticiens.

Two other painters of commanding presence in Montreal during the early sixties worked largely outside of such pure colour concerns, however. JEAN MCEWEN (b.1923) first studied to be a pharmacist at the Université de Montréal, but just before he graduated in 1949 he met some of the Automatistes and decided to become a painter. Two years in Paris (1951-3) in contact with some of the lyrical abstractionists around Riopelle encouraged him, once back in Montreal, to work through surrealist-derived abstract expression. By 1956 and the foundation of the Non-figurative Artists' Association (McEwen later replaced Leduc as its president), he had arrived at a statement of unique force. Amorphous, floating forms, virtually filling the whole canvas (often resulting in images reminiscent of the American Mark Rothko), later came to display a surface burnished to the texture of old leather. By the early sixties his distinctive, ominously brooding canvases, such as the *Meurtrière traversant le bleu* (MMFA) of 1962, were widely admired by those with a developed taste for refined experience.

CHARLES GAGNON (b.1934), born and raised in Montreal like Hurtubise and McEwen, studied graphic art and interior design at the Parsons School of Design in New York from 1956 to 1959. He returned to Montreal in 1960. During his four years in New York he became familiar with the brilliant activity and ideas concerning randomness and chance arising from the composer John Cage and his associates, the dancer Merce Cunningham and the painter Robert Rauschenberg. Gagnon took his lead from these important figures and by the early sixties had developed a cool but seemingly spontaneous style of painting. The primal lushness of his *Hommage à John Cage* (Department of External Affairs, Ottawa) of 1963 derives from the imaginative exploration of various ways of applying paint. A natural order arises from the methodical execution of a precisely defined though ostensibly 'free' activity.

It is certain that art activity in Canada will never again be so centralized as it was in Toronto between the wars. It seems equally sure that that city has nevertheless once again become the main focus of artistic activity for the nation. And although this is due largely to the fact that Toronto is the principal art market-place (virtually every artist in the country of more than local interest exhibits there regularly), that status could not have been attained without the large number of painters of quality who assembled there during the late fifties and early sixties.

At least three members of Painters Eleven remained prominent within this expanded scene: WILLIAM RONALD in a tragically reversed role. Although he was at first the inspiring example of local success at the centre of world art, he came to be as moving an example of the cruel vagaries of the 'international league'. Only three months after he had finally decided that he would make his home in the New York area, he was given his last exhibition at the Kootz Gallery (December 1963). By this time Abstract Expressionism had been superseded by more rationally 'cool', un-'expressive' forms, and the so-called second generation of Abstract-Expressionist painters was, in a body, *out*! Ronald struggled to accommodate the new sensibility, but with work that was at the time generally rejected. A 1965 show at the new David Mirvish Gallery in Toronto was interpreted as an attention-seeking gimmick (movable painted panels allowed the viewer to re-compose the picture). Ronald stopped painting shortly after.*

HAROLD TOWN held his first one-man show in New York just about a year before Ronald staged his last there. At the Andrew Morris Gallery from November 2, 1962, Town displayed works from his 'Tyranny of the Corner' series. Most of the pictures—like *Tyranny of the Corner–Glass of Fashion Set* (the artist)—reveal a concern for surface: they are covered with a uniformly textured paint that suggests an industrial

*I have generally adhered strictly to 1965 as the cut-off date but believe this to be inordinately unfair in Ronald's case. He went on in 1966 to host a TV show on the arts in Toronto, and has remained in that city since as a notable TV and radio performer. He returned to painting periodically, once to execute an excitingly imaginative mural in a condemned Toronto Island chapel. Then in June 1968 he began a commission for the National Arts Centre in Ottawa that resulted in a brilliantly bold mural. Since then painting has become again a major activity in his life.

product. Limited in colour to black, silver, and white, the consequent 'high-contrast' effect causes an optical vibration that stresses the silhouette of the forms. But the main concern in these pictures has been explained by Town himself. 'Painting is still to a great extent dominated by a central image; corners in most paintings are like uninvited guests at a party, uneasy and unattended. In my series I have invited the corners to come early to the party and tried, if anything, to make all the elements of the painting that arrived later a trifle uncomfortable.' Town, like everyone in Toronto, was acutely aware of Ronald.

The early sixties was the period of Town's real prominence in Toronto as a painter, culminating in a pair of large exhibitions of paintings held simultaneously at the Jerrold Morris and Mazelow galleries in February 1966. The well-known *Great Divide* (AGO), in the Morris portion of that show, has since generally been held to be his finest picture. The critic Harry Malcolmson saw in it evidence of Town's 'deep affection for Canada'. In his introduction to the show's catalogue he described how 'The entire canvas is suffused with the unshadowed golden light that floods the Northern landscape prior to sunset.'

Many would now argue that the *Great Divide* in fact presaged the 'setting' of Town's brief sun-like presence on the Toronto scene. Like Ronald, he has since largely existed in the eyes of younger artists as a controversial 'personality' rather than as a painter. JACK BUSH, to the contrary, has over the same period assumed more and more relevance for the younger painters in the city. This local importance has derived, at least in part, from Bush's rise to a position of international eminence seldom achieved by a Canadian.

Bush had his first New York show the same year as Town: 1962. Robert Elkon had consulted with Clement Greenberg before opening a new gallery, and the critic recommended Bush. The 1962 show was reasonably successful, and was followed by two more in 1963-4 and a steadily growing reputation. Bush then signed a contract with the prestigious André Emmerich Gallery, the New York showplace for a number of the so-called 'post-painterly' abstractionists. These painters proposed a 'cool', rational abstraction that, like the work of the Montreal colour painters, sought to integrate colour with structure. They differed from the Montrealers in that their substantial colour images were typically achieved by staining paint into raw canvas. Of this group—which includes Kenneth Noland and Frank Stella—Bush is the most openly lyrical, the most 'emotional', the least cerebral. In his great works of the sixties—*Dazzle Red* (AGO) of 1965 is one of the most monumentally beautiful paintings of the decade—there is a boldness that is in no way brash. It is a huge great living banner of colour in which Bush has even managed to infuse naturally cool blue and green with vital human warmth. It reflects the open joy of personal fulfilment.

The succession in Toronto was very different from that in Montreal, where there was a distinct group who broke clearly with the position of the Automatistes. In Toronto it was rather individuals finding their way out from the example set by Painters Eleven. In fact to some of the older members of the second 'generation', Painters Eleven must have seemed a parallel, rather than a preceding development. Michael Snow and Graham Coughtry held their first exhibition less than a year after the inaugural Painters Eleven show.

GRAHAM COUGHTRY (b.1931) was born and raised in St Lambert, east of Montreal across the river, where his father was a commercial sculptor. He first studied art at the MMFA school (1948-9) under de Tonnancour and Webber, and then moved on to the drawing and painting course at the Ontario College of Art in Toronto. Through a common interest in jazz he there met MICHAEL SNOW (b.1929), a design-course student a year ahead of Coughtry. Snow was born in Toronto, but was raised in a number of cities—particularly Montreal and Chicoutimi, the home of his French-Canadian mother—as his engineer father followed his work. He entered the Ontario College of Art in 1948 with an already highly developed interest in jazz, fed in his second year—with a forthrightness that was to become typical—by trips to Chicago, where he played in the home of the great boogie-woogie pianist Jimmy Yancey. Snow soon became an accomplished jazz musician himself.

Coughtry, upon graduation, won a scholarship that allowed him to travel to Europe, and he and a school friend, Richard Williams (b. 1933), left in the fall of 1953. First visiting Barcelona, they soon ended up on the island of Ibiza, where they stayed for about six months. In the spring they spent a few months in Paris where they ran into Snow, who had over the past year been working his way as a musician around holiday resorts in Italy and France. Back in Toronto, all three found work in a small film-animation company recently launched by George Dunning. Graphic Associates, as it was called, supported a concentration of nascent talent then unmatched in Canada outside of the National Film Board, and virtually all of the staff went on to do impressive work in film after the business folded in 1956.*

*Dunning then went to England where he later directed the landmark animation success, *The Yellow Submarine*. Richard Williams also moved to England where he has followed a successful career inventing animated film credits, most remarkably in *What's New Pussycat?* and *The Charge of the Light Brigade*. At Graphic also

At Graphic, Snow met the woman he would later marry. JOYCE WIELAND (b.1931), a Torontonian who had joined the company—like Snow, Coughtry, and Williams—after returning from European travels, studied commercial art at Central Technical School but in Europe had decided to become a painter. Snow and Coughtry of course were also then determined to be painters, and they held their first exhibition—a joint venture—at Hart House in January 1955. The works they exhibited reflect interests fostered in school and on their European trips. Coughtry's *Figure on a Bed* (AGO) of 1954 shows the influence of the American social-realist Ben Shahn in its severe line, though it is virtually overwhelmed by Bonnard-like vibrating colour. (He had seen the sensual paintings of that French artist in Paris.) Snow's *A Man with a Line* (Mr and Mrs O.D. Vaughan, Toronto) of 1954 also combines a clean line with rich surface. His witty, ambiguous play on the nature of the 'line' the man holds suggests an interest in the work of the great Swiss artist, Paul Klee. Sensuous, expressive colour became the dominant characteristic of Coughtry's later work, while rigorously intelligent 'play' is at the heart of everything Snow does. These nearly antipodal sensibilities mark the poles between which painting developed in Toronto over the next decade. That first exhibition also inadvertently revealed the relationship their generation would hold to the local establishment when some gentle nude drawings curiously outraged the mayor of Toronto, Nathan Phillips. And these two artists as well soon found the base from which the new Toronto painters would most effectively operate. In the spring of 1956, they joined with three others—William Ronald and two figurative painters of some strength, Gerald Scott (b. 1926) and Robert Varvarande (b.1922)—in the inaugural exhibition of Av Isaacs' new Greenwich Gallery. Coughtry held his first one-man show there soon after, and Snow his first that October.

The Greenwich Gallery was located in the old 'Greenwich Village' area around Bay and Gerrard, since the twenties the centre of Toronto's small contribution to Bohemia. During the second half of the fifties it blossomed. A number of galleries joined the Greenwich, specialty shops and coffee houses opened, and the House of Hambourg began to attract devotees of avant-garde jazz, poetry, and drama. DENNIS BURTON (b. 1933), a young painter just out of art school, ran a small gallery in the House of Hambourg over the winter of 1956-7.

was Sidney J. Furie, who subsequently made two feature films in Toronto (1957 and 1958) before he too went to England. He is now best known as director of *The Ipcress File*. Graham Coughtry moved over to the CBC to establish its animation section. His award-winning work there set the standard for years.

Born in Lethbridge, Alberta, Burton came east to complete high school and enrolled in the Ontario College of Art in 1952. At the time of his graduation in 1956 he was living in a rooming house with a number of friends, including GORDON RAYNER (b.1935). Rayner was born in Toronto, where both his father and uncle were commercial artists. When the time came to work, with no school training in art at all, Rayner was sent out by his father to find an apprenticeship in commercial art and was hired in 1953 by a small firm that included Jack Bush among its partners. Rayner observed some of the early Painters Eleven meetings but was then unimpressed with 'fine' art. He left Bush late in 1954 for a trip to Europe. Back in Toronto the next year, an interest in jazz brought him into contact with Burton, who soon involved him in painting. The two travelled to Buffalo to see a de Kooning that had been recently purchased by the Albright-Knox Gallery. Rayner soon began to appreciate Painters Eleven.

Because of Painters Eleven, Abstract Expressionism had, by 1958, become the current local idiom in Toronto—almost as much as in New York itself. Dennis Burton remembers that 'the knowledge that in the forefront of American Abstract-Expressionist painting there was a Toronto artist, William Ronald, assured us that there was a direct line of communication to the source.' The major Ronald shows in Toronto—at Av Isaacs' Greenwich Gallery in 1957, at Laing in 1960, and at the Isaacs Gallery in 1961—kept that line wide open. Jock Macdonald's teaching at the Ontario College of Art also assured an interest in New York painting among many of the graduating students. (Burton had studied with him.) And less than one hundred miles away, across the American border, Buffalo's Albright-Knox Gallery began to acquire important examples of Abstract Expressionism. Many artists who matured in Toronto at this time could even today describe de Kooning's brilliant *Gotham News* of 1955 almost stroke by stroke. Dennis Burton, of all the younger painters, then most enthusiastically embraced the example of de Kooning. His *Intimately Close-in* (NGC) of 1958-9 is an audacious, vigorous variation on the passionate work of the American.

Coughtry had received his first significant attention with a sensitive series of interior studies. The carefully worked paint surface of *Interior Twilight* (WAG) of 1957 results in shimmering colour effects that dissolve the depicted chair and table in atmosphere. The intense local interest in post-war New York painting encouraged him to follow a more freely expressive bent in subsequent paintings. In a group of 'imaginary' portraits, delicately modelled heads grow out of paint thickly congealed at the centre of the canvas.

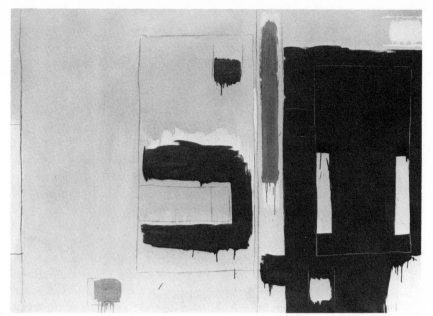

Michael Snow. *Secret Shout*, 1960. Canvas, 52 x 75. Graham Coughtry, Toronto.

The rapid evolution of Michael Snow, however, is the most amazing of all of the Toronto artists. In 1955 he made a group of full yet wonderfully controlled collages, gently tinted with photo dyes. During the next two years he, like Coughtry, followed an obsessive interest in .crowded interiors, splayed tables and chairs—the furniture of the mind. Then about 1958 he addressed himself to some of the problems raised by New York painting, working through pictures—like *Secret Shout (Graham Coughtry, Toronto) of 1959—which, with their carefully positioned but roughly blocked-in forms, resulted in a clear but open structure, much like that of jazz. (Snow had been supporting himself working as a jazz musician since Graphic folded in 1956.) Improvisational options were then reduced in a series of works over 1960. *Lac Clair* (NGC), the most lusciously beautiful of these, is a large square canvas, completely and evenly covered with generous blue strokes. Brown paper tape is pasted a bit less than halfway along the edge of each side starting in the lower right corner, placing the canvas in a tension anticipating spinning. Suggesting pervasive order underlying the variation of stroking, the whole painting swells out imperceptively and serenely, with the great placid force of a northern lake.

By 1961 there was unmistakably a 'new' Toronto scene and the Isaacs Gallery was at its centre. (The Greenwich had taken the name of its proprietor early in 1959.) Joyce Wieland had first exhibited there in February 1959 with Gord Rayner (their first commercial exposure) but had then shown briefly at Dorothy Cameron's Here and Now Gallery before settling with Isaacs in 1961. Her husband, Michael Snow, had been with Av Isaacs from the beginning, as had Graham Coughtry. Dennis Burton's work had been noticed at the House of Hambourg by Barry Kernerman, and he gave the young painter a show at his new Gallery of Contemporary Art in May 1957.* There he met Robert Hedrick (b.1930), a young artist from Windsor, Ont., who was then beginning to attract appreciative reviews of his painting. Kernerman's gallery survived only about two years, and Burton then had a show at the Park Gallery early in 1959. But in 1960 both he and Hedrick moved to the Isaacs Gallery, and Rayner too held his first one-man show there that year.

Although the scene was no longer geographically situated in the Gerrard Street 'village' (the Isaacs Gallery moved to Yonge Street above Bloor in the fall of 1959), it soon found a spiritual centre in a new quarterly magazine, *Evidence*, which first appeared in 1960. With photo-stories on Rayner and Snow, and with written or drawn contributions from—among others—Leonard Cohen, Snow, Gwendolyn MacEwen, William Ronald, Wieland, Burton, and Austin C. Clarke, it helped to define that Toronto scene. Jazz continued to be the most important uni-fying force, and by the time of the appearance of *Evidence*, marihuana and other mood-altering drugs traditionally associated with jazz had also become a regular part of the lives of most of the painters. Spontaneous, free creativity was celebrated in regular 'jam-sessions' held on off-nights at the First Floor Club, then the local outlet for live jazz. As many as fifteen or twenty would gather to play, and out of this grew the Artists' Jazz Band, an institution that has continued to this day around a hard-core made up of Coughtry, Rayner, Robert Markle (b.1936) from Hamilton—who graduated from the Ontario College of Art in 1959 and soon became involved with the Isaacs group—and Nobuo Kubota (b. 1932), a Vancouver-born architect-sculptor.

In retrospect Joyce Wieland appears, in a series of vast paintings shown at the Isaacs Gallery in February 1962, to have exploited most successfully the liberating energies of this moment. One of the largest and most beautiful of these is *Time Machine Series* (AGO) of 1961, in which a great round shape—suggestive of an open vagina as well as of a fleshy clock—floats in a sea of ethereal blue. She pursued the theme

---

*The month after Borduas's one-man show there. Burton and a number of the younger Toronto painters greatly admired the work he exhibited.

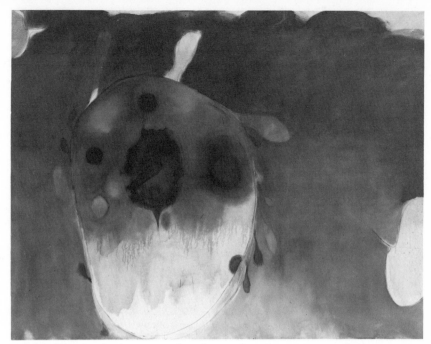

Joyce Wieland. *Time Machine Series*, 1961. Canvas, 80 x 106¼. AGO.

of female sexuality in a number of subsequent works of equally vast scale and consuming, timeless space. *Heart-on* (NGC) of 1962 is a large piece of draped linen with cut-out and drawn hearts scattered across its surface and red ink poured and splashed on it: blood on the sheet.

The fall 1961 issue of *Evidence* carried a photo of Marcel Duchamp on the cover and a short interview with the great living master of the Dada movement inside.* The extent of local interest in Dada ideas was then revealed that winter in a 'Neo-Dada' show at the Isaacs Gallery (from December 20, 1961 through to January 9, 1962), to which most of the Isaacs artists contributed works assembled from various objects they had found. The show was humorous, imaginative, and unpretentious, working beyond 'taste' and 'style' and encouraging personal expression with the means immediately at hand. A number of the artists continued to employ 'assemblage' techniques—Gord Rayner with the most consistent success. His *Homage to the French Revolution* (AGO) of

*Dada was a nihilistic movement that initially developed in Zurich during the First World War. Deliberately anti-'high' art, Dada artists revealed aesthetic significance in chaotic, random, or fortuitous acts. Duchamp's 'ready-mades'—everyday objects that he 'chose' to be art—are the most famous artifacts of the movement. Dada thought and activity were currently enjoying a resurgence in New York in the light of Robert Rauschenberg's painting and the informal theatre-pieces called 'happenings'. Pop Art would soon grow out of this interest.

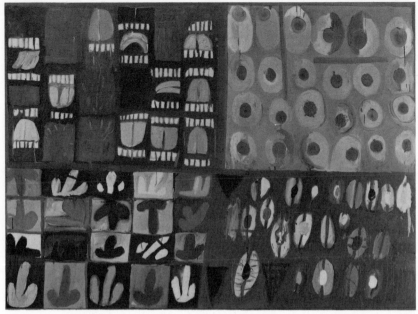

Dennis Burton. *The Game of Life*, 1960. Canvas, 54 x 78. NGC.

1963 is a witty, suggestive work of art made from an old extended table top.

The very *direct* attitude revealed by such assemblage work is also a characteristic of much of the painting that was done in Toronto in the early sixties. As early as 1960 Dennis Burton, in his *The Game of Life* (NGC), painted a huge game board with each square containing a mouth or a breast or male or female genitals—the 'pieces' in the game. Burton, with Snow, was one of the first to discard as well the essentially Abstract-Expressionist notion that a statement requires the support of a personal 'style' in order to achieve credibility. Burton feels that the weight of a work must lie in its essential content, and he has placed most of his emphasis on the meaningful ordering of the information he has been able to gather on the subjects that interest him. His most famous extended exercise of this sort has been his examination of the idea of contemporary woman as revealed by her underclothing in his 'Garterbeltmania' series.

Lyrical abstraction remained popular as well, though always of a 'post'-Abstract-Expressionist sort and very personal. Robert Hedrick's work has been notable. And Gordon Rayner has explored a lyric 'northern landscape' theme on summer trips to the Magnetawan River west of Algonquin park. *Magnetawan No. 2* (NGC) of 1965 is a charged, expanding evocation of the north. Spontaneously new and fresh, it is still lodged securely in a rich Canadian tradition.

RICHARD GORMAN (b.1935) of Ottawa, who studied with Macdonald and graduated from the Ontario College of Art in 1958, had his first exhibition at Isaacs in 1959. A year later he was exhibiting original work that already had gone beyond Abstract Expressionism. Like others in Toronto, he had derived from that style a sense of scale and presence, seeking evocative, primal abstract images that touched the fundamental human concerns of creation, life, and death. Gorman achieved his greatest success in large canvases he exhibited in 1964. *Kiss Good-Bye* (AGO) of 1963, with its great opening red and orange striped form on a yellow field, is ominous in spite of the bright colours. Like much of the painting of the period in Toronto, it seems to be dealing with perception at the outer edges of consciousness.

Travel has been important to the painters of Toronto, and Spain, particularly Ibiza, has exercised a continuing fascination for many. Graham Coughtry has made a second home there. After he left the CBC graphics department in 1959 he returned to Europe; he married in Paris

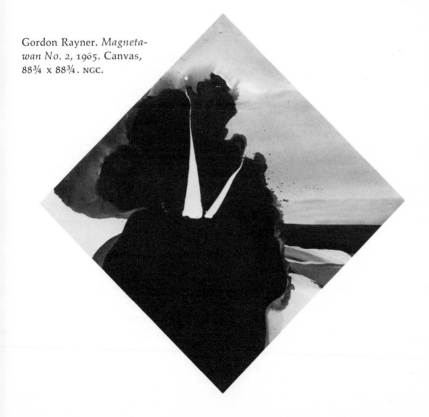

Gordon Rayner. *Magneta-wan No. 2*, 1965. Canvas, 88¾ x 88¾. NGC.

and he and his wife moved to Ibiza. He returned to Toronto for an exhibition in 1961. One of the amazing canvases he brought with him is *Corner Figure* (Larisa Pavlychenko Coughtry) of 1960. Dependent to a degree on the tortured figuration of the Englishman Francis Bacon and on the attenuated sculptural masses of the Swiss Alberto Giacometti, it is nonetheless profoundly personal and moving. Coughtry returned to Ibiza and continued to create figures emerging from thick muscle-like concentrations of paint. He sought a quality of presence, to establish a 'living' space between the figure and the viewer.

In 1962 he was back in Toronto again to execute the commission of a mural for the Toronto airport and took a studio at the corner of York-ville and Yonge.* Coughtry had just separated from his wife; he was hurt and confused and couldn't get the mural started. He began painting pictures of two figures in sexual confrontation, working off his own frustrated energies in explosive, expressionistic paint handling. Gradually, as he worked through one canvas after another, he released his anxieties and frustrations and the figures seemed no longer so specifically locked in sexual struggle but became rather the vehicle for more gentle feelings concerning the nature of sexual union. With the completion of the mural early in 1964 he returned to Ibiza again, and alone there continued to paint the two-figure series. Changes accelerated over the nine months he spent there, with the paint becoming thinner and the images more balanced, more resolved. As is evident in *Two Figure Series XIX* (Mr and Mrs Avrom Isaacs, Toronto), he became concerned principally with the harmony of the shapes and the pleasure in the colours. The upper portion of *XIX* is a hot red-orange, the bottom a warm yellow-green. The figures are a dripping magenta-purple fusion of the two. The series was exhibited in October 1964 at the Isaacs Gallery and was immediately recognized as one of the most beautiful shows ever mounted there. We will finally see it as one of the triumphs of Canadian art.

The giant figure of painting in Toronto, however, is Michael Snow. He and Joyce Wieland moved to New York City during 1962 (to stay for ten years and become an important part of the New York scene **), but they still continued to exhibit and visit regularly in Toronto. In October 1960 Snow had invented 'The Walking Woman', a simple cut-

---

*According to Coughtry and friends it was haunted by Curtis Williamson, who had occupied it during his final years as a total recluse and had died there.

** Particularly in their film work. Both began making personal films in 1963. Wieland's *La Raison avant la passion* and Snow's *La Région centrale* will doubtless

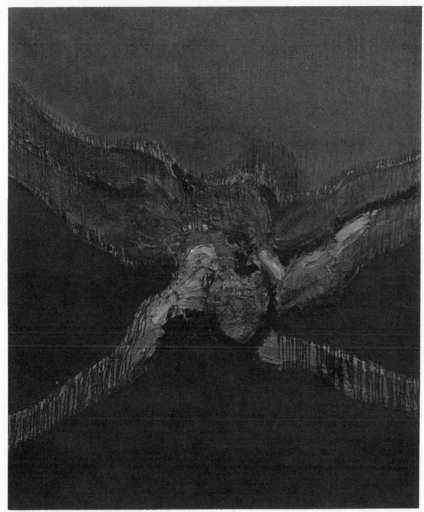

Graham Coughtry. *Two Figure Series XIX*, 1964. Canvas, 72 x 65. Mr and Mrs Avrom Isaacs, Toronto.

out silhouette of a typical young woman of the sixties. For the next seven years she became the 'subject' of every one of his paintings. Such fidelity freed him to try anything. Because the 'subject' never varied, everything else could, and any one painting would still remain a coherent part of the whole. For in a sense the Walking Woman Works

be seen as among the finest films made anywhere in the world during the decade, and a number of informed observers look upon Snow as one of the greatest innovative geniuses film has ever attracted. Their accomplishment can hardly be overstressed.

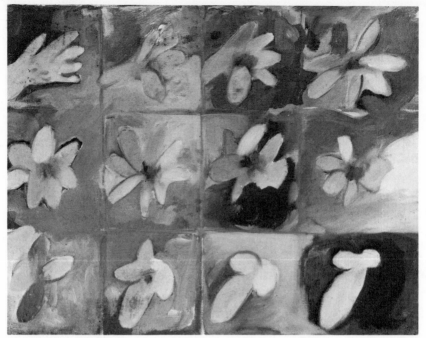

Joyce Wieland. *Nature Mixes*, 1963. Canvas, 12 x 16. Mr Udo Kasemets, Toronto.

are one: a massive dispersed monument that explores in imaginative re-creation virtually the whole of western man's aesthetic possibilities. They are usually separately perceived, though, and each piece does stand on its own, creating a specific experience and raising specific questions about creating and about viewing art; about how we make and how we perceive.

†*Beach-hcaeb* (University of Western Ontario, London, Alumni Collection) of 1963 is spontaneously radiant. The paint was applied half to one side, half to the other; the lower space behind the right-hand figure, for instance, was left blank, and on the other side it was painted in. While the paint was still wet, the canvas was folded down the middle and the two halves were pressed firmly face-to-face. Pulled apart, they reveal an 'accidental' image of subtly perfect symmetry.

Joyce Wieland's work is also richly allusive. Where Snow meets you at mid-point in some incredible structure out of his mind, Wieland draws you in with the wonder of her woman's work. She leads you to see in feeling, as Snow leads you to feel in seeing. The poetry of *Nature Mixes* (Udo Kasemets, Toronto)—in which in a story-board series of frames a hand turns gradually into a flower and then into a penis—surpasses logic and beggars description. It is the colour of wild-strawberry plants in the grass.

Two painters who began exhibiting in Toronto in the late fifties began to make an impact on the scene only near the end of this period, an impact that subsequently revealed the merit of their earlier work as well. GERSHON ISKOWITZ (b.1921), who was born at Kielce, Poland, was an art student when he was imprisoned by the Germans. He miraculously survived six years in Buchenwald and Auschwitz and continued his studies after the war at the Munich Academy and privately with Oscar Kokoschka. He arrived in Canada in 1949. Always a landscape painter, his magnificent colour-field paintings of the mid-sixties—*Summer Sound* (AGO) of 1965 is gloriously expansive—evoke the sky, trees, earth, and water in a great amalgam of joy.

JOHN MEREDITH (b.1933), the brother of William Ronald, was born in Fergus, Ont., but raised in Brampton. He commuted to the Ontario College of Art (1950-3) and maintained a studio in his parents' basement until 1964. Although he began exhibiting in 1958 with a one-man show at the Gallery of Contemporary Art, his residence in Brampton made him an elusive figure in Toronto. His strange, highly personal paintings, with their suggestions of Eastern magical forms, simply added to his mystery. When the huge triptych *Seeker* (AGO) was exhibited in 1966 a steadily growing reputation leaped suddenly to bring him to the forefront in Toronto. Eccentricly intense in colour, it is a weighty but joyful object of veneration, dedicated to the celebration of a religion whose dogma will forever be hidden in the cryptic symbols the painting so triumphantly displays.

Although only a bit more than one hundred miles south-west of Toronto, London, Ont., a city with a population of about a quarter of a million, has now been able to support one of the more active groups of artists in the country for more than ten years. London had produced artists before—notably Paul Peel in the nineteenth century—but had never been able to keep them. That in the early seventies there is already a relatively large and active second group who have responded to the efforts of the recent pioneers suggests that London will continue to be one of the major places in Canada to see art. That promise is almost entirely due to the activities during the first half of the sixties of three painters: Jack Chambers, Tony Urquhart, and Greg Curnoe.

JACK CHAMBERS (b.1931) is the oldest. Born in London, he studied art there at Beal Technical School and then worked sporadically at painting. In the fall of 1953 he left for Europe, travelling in Italy and Austria and then, in January 1954, visiting Spain, settling in Madrid in February. There he enrolled in the Royal Academy of Fine Arts where he stayed—

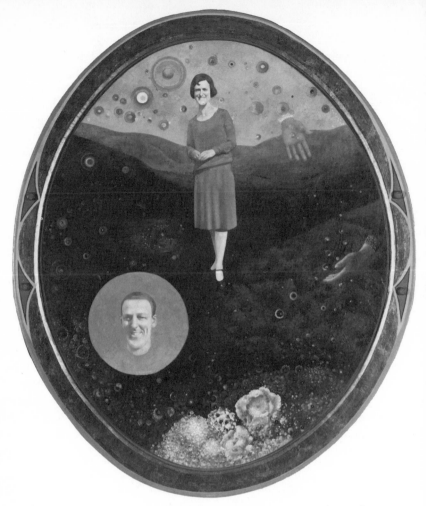

Jack Chambers. *Messengers Juggling Seed*, 1962. Board, 54½ x 45½. NGC.

distinguishing himself in rigorous academic exercises—until 1959. He then moved to the small village of Chinchon near Madrid, where he painted and taught until 1961. Returning to London after eight years' absence, he was soon struck by the degree to which the local environment seemed to take hold of his life.

In Spain he had painted stylized figurative pictures that were not unlike American regionalist art of the thirties. But in London he set such an approach aside in a desire to explore memories, to bring together those associations that moved him so much. In paintings like *Messengers Juggling Seed* (NGC) of 1962 he assembled images of smiling faces, each presumably recalling an occasion of importance. These dis-

parate and disembodied presences he floated in a hilly landscape, pop-
ping with mad seeds—flowers exploding like brightly coloured mould
sperm.

Chambers continued to explore his familiar environment, creating
many-layered images of precious moments. Such evocative nostalgia
reached an exquisite level with his *Olga and Mary Visiting* (London
Public Library and Art Museum) of 1964-5. An accumulation of sensory
associations, it shows how every new moment, in adding to the remembered experience, thus alters it. With its muted colours and fragmented
forms it reveals the gentle pain of time.

TONY URQUHART (b.1934), who was born in Niagara Falls, Ont.,
studied at the Albright School of Art in Buffalo, graduating in 1956. He
then enrolled in the University of Buffalo and graduated with a BFA in
1958. Already, though, he had had a successful one-man show at the
Greenwich Gallery in 1957. In 1960 he became artist-in-residence at
the University of Western Ontario in London and settled in for a five-
year stretch—with a one-year break—in that community. He is an artist
of many parts, but at the time he was probably most admired for his
'allegorical' landscapes. *In Hiding* (NGC) of 1961 is a particularly strong
example. Beautiful in its rich and subtle brush-work, there is a strong
sense of the earth in it: germination, growth, and decay. Its ominous
swellings and gill-like infoldings evoke the ambiguity of the natural
order. Nature gone wrong is still right. Urquhart too is concerned to
reach deep, to touch some common stream, to bring us into closer contact with the forces that make life.

GREG CURNOE (b.1936) was, like Chambers, born in London and also
studied art first at Beal Tech. During his year there (1954-5) under Herb
Ariss (b.1918), he was introduced to an intelligent sampling of virtually the whole development of modern aesthetic thought: Cubism, Dada,
Surrealism, and Jackson Pollock. He remembers seeing the work of Borduas in a four-man show with that of Bush, Cahén, and de Tonnancour
at the London Art Museum in the spring of 1955.* The summer of 1956
Curnoe attended the Doon School of Fine Arts in Kitchener, and then in
the fall he enrolled in the Ontario College of Art in Toronto. This was,
in spite of Jock Macdonald's presence there, an unsatisfying experience,
and he came away thoroughly disillusioned with 'fine' art. It seemed to
him to have no relevance to his life. In 1960 he returned to London and
the next year rented studio space. He and some friends began to explore

*The London Public Library and Art Museum began collecting in 1940, but it was
only from 1953 that the addition of suitable galleries allowed a full exhibition
program.

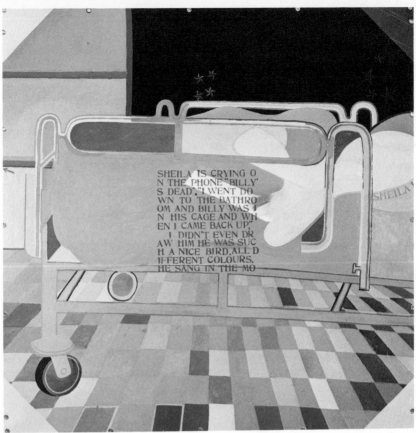

Greg Curnoe. *Family Painting No. 1—In Labour*, 1966. Board, 48 x 48. Mr M. Winberg, Toronto.

their own cultural roots, and out of a consideration of the meaning that popular heroes, music, and art (comic books, etc.) held for them, they affirmed a sense of place and of their location in that place. *Region* magazine was founded in 1961 as a forum for their investigations. Their questioning and finally their massive rejection of much of established 'culture' led to the foundation of the Nihilist Party in 1962, followed shortly by the appearance of the Nihilist Spasm Band, a kazoo free-music group.

Curnoe realized the degree to which his position found historical precedent in the Dada movement of the earlier twentieth century, and in fact he participated in the 'Neo-Dada' exhibition at the Isaacs Gallery in the winter of 1961-2. He was spending time in Toronto visiting with Graham Coughtry and Mike Snow and had met there as well Michel Sanouillet—prominent authority on the history of the Dada movement—

who was then teaching French literature at the University of Toronto. In February 1962 Curnoe arranged a 'happening' at the London Art Museum, a vigorous audience-participation piece called *The Celebration*. Wieland, Snow, and Sanouillet were among those from Toronto who went to London for the event.

The Celebration in a way sets the tone for all of Curnoe's work, which is, before anything else, a celebration. For him the 'ordinary' hardly exists. The world can open out from a single observation or reflection made in his home or studio. In his painting, Curnoe usually focuses on an event of deep personal significance, as in *Family Painting No. 1—In Labour* (Mr M. Winberg, Toronto) of 1966. Depicting his wife in labour, it is a direct, powerful image. As we try to see her un-painted face, we constantly focus on the hard line of the chrome bed-side. The floor is a rushing hallucination of rainbow tiles. The low point-of-view puts us on our knees, and although we are incessantly drawn to feel the tender anxiousness in his wife's arms, our eyes are snapped to the block of letters in the centre which, in a fragment of matter-of-fact prose, describes not birth but a death. It is a work of intense concentration.

I have not chosen 1965 as the cut-off for this historical study because it is intended—as is the closing date of each of the preceding chapters—to mark the end of yet another generation's dominance. In most in-stances the painters discussed in this final chapter are in fact just now (1973) enjoying their full maturity. It is rather that, after 1965, and particularly as a result of the centennial celebrations of 1967 (which coincided with a period of general admiration for the qualities of youth), a large number of young artists of promise were rushed into the spot-light. This telescoping of the generations has made it impossibly difficult —for me at least—to attempt at this time to write a 'history' of the last ten years. I keenly anticipate a later opportunity, however, for it has been the most dynamic decade of all. At this point in the 1970s we are blessed with artists—including Michael Snow, Guido Molinari, Joyce Wieland, Jack Bush, and Greg Curnoe—who are among the finest creative spirits working in the world today. They deserve our closest attention.

Index

Paintings given italicized page numbers are illustrated.
Colour reproductions are indicated by Roman numerals.